Military Deterrence in History

MILITARY DETERRENCE IN HISTORY

A PILOT CROSS-HISTORICAL SURVEY

RAOUL NAROLL
VERN L. BULLOUGH
FRADA NAROLL

STATE UNIVERSITY OF NEW YORK PRESS

Published by State University of New York Press
99 Washington Avenue, Albany, New York 12210

© 1974 by The Research Foundation
of State University of New York
All rights reserved

Printed in the United States of America

Library of Congress Cataloging in Publication Data

Naroll, Raoul.
    Military deterrence in history.

    Bibliography: p.
    1. Deterrence (Strategy)   2. Military history.
I. Bullough, Vern L., joint author.   II. Naroll, Frada, joint author.
III. Title.
Ul 62.6.N37 1974   355.03'35'09   69-14647
ISBN 0-87395-047-X

To Thomas W. Milburn

CONTENTS

* * *

List of Maps

* * *

★ ★ ★

PREFACE

THIS BOOK is a study of military deterrence as it has been used at various times and places throughout twenty-five hundred years of history. We first hope to shed some light on the powers and limits of military deterrence as a strategy in international politics; but, more important, we offer this book as a working model of the cross-historical survey. The cross-historical survey is a method of comparative historical research, a sample survey whose unit of study is a particular historical period of a particular society. Our idea is to study comparatively dozens or even hundreds of such units and to draw statistical correlations from them. The cross-historical method we propose is simply an application of the well-known cross-cultural survey method of anthropological research to the comparative study of history.

We beg every reader, and especially every trained historian, to bear in mind the crucial distinction between our goal and that of the historiographer. A historiographer constructs a theory that will interpret events in a particular historical period at a particular time and place. We here are trying to find patterns common to many different times and places. Our data are not the primary sources of the historiographer but rather the patterns governing each particular historical period. By noting how and under what conditions these patterns vary from one period to another, we, as comparative historians, hope to arrive at a statement of "laws" governing these separate sets of patterns. This principle is known to anthropologists as *Goodenough's Rule* (see Goodenough 1956:37).

We hope that this working model may interest those who want to study written historical records in search of general regularities which tend to repeat themselves. In other words, this method is offered as a means of testing the value of supposed "laws" of history.

In this preface, we review the accomplishments, techniques, and problems of the cross-cultural survey method of anthropology. Then we suggest how we see these problems manifesting themselves in historical source materials. We suggest specifically how these methods might be applied to historical materials. And we call attention to the possible comparative advantages and limitations of cross-historical surveys as compared to cross-cultural surveys.

Historians and Laws of History

One of the deepest and most persistent philosophical questions which faces professional historians is the possibility of discovering laws of history. This is not the place to review the extensive literature by historians and philosophers of history discussing this question. On one hand, Jacques Bossuet, Giambattista Vico, Henry Buckle, Brooks Adams, Oswald Spengler, Arnold Toynbee, Pitirim Sorokin, Carroll Quigley, Julian Steward, Karl Marx, Friedrich Engels, S. N. Eisenstadt, Karl Wittfogel, and Rushton Coulborn are only a few of what we call *nomothetic* historians: those who have made serious attempts to discover and state fundamental regularities in the overall pattern of history. On the other hand, Eduard Meyer, Ernst Bernheim, Benedetto Croce, Charles A. Beard, and R. G. Collingwood are only a few of those whom we may call *idiographic* historians: scholars who doubt that any such laws exist, or that their discovery or scientific validation is possible (see Meyerhoff 1959). It is interesting that of the presidential addresses delivered before sixty-two annual meetings of the American Historical Association, which were studied by Ausubel (1950), as many expressed hope that such laws might be found and demonstrated as were doubtful that any such laws exist or could be demonstrated. We can roughly classify the methods of study of the nomothetic historians according to universe studied and method of selecting data. The older tradition is to concentrate on the history of the Western world from its beginnings in the Middle East, through classical Roman and Greek antiquity, to the medieval and modern European worlds. Such studies commonly omit the histories of the Islamic world, India, and the Far East, as well as what is known of the histories of the higher pre-Columbian civilizations of the New World. Examples include the works of Bossuet, Vico, Sorokin, and (in large measure) Quigley. However, many twentieth-century nomothetic historians give considerable attention to Oriental and Amerindian cultures outside the main line of the Western historical tradition.

Most nomothetic historians have traditionally selected those events from the vast body of available material which support and illustrate their concepts and theories. Sometimes particular incidents are mentioned only in brief allusions, sometimes rather detailed case studies are presented; but nearly all of these writers, including certainly both Toynbee and Spengler, are vulnerable to the criticism that they have selected supporting data as an attorney prepares a brief. However, in contrast to the forensic system, nomothetic historians are not regularly coupled with adversaries who study precisely the same problems to maintain the contrary view. Abiding by the judgment of a Toynbee or a Spengler on the basis of his evidence is much the same as supporting a verdict on the case for the plaintiff without hearing the case for the defendant.

Idiographic historians have pursued two lines of critical argument in their opposition to the nomothetic theory. First, they have always maintained the skeptical position. It has been easy for them to discredit the writing of nearly all nomothetic historians, because they, the critics, have had no trouble selecting cases inconsistent with the nomothetic conclusions. These idiographic historians have been able to get the better of the argument since neither adversary has *counted* supporting or discrediting evidence, and both adversaries usually had *invariable* and *precise* laws in mind. Second, these critics have argued that every historical event is a unique experience dominated by unique individuals. The importance of change in human events, the influence of a dominant individual such as Alexander the Great or Napoleon Bonaparte, and the constant interplay of free will in human affairs combine to make the existence of regular natural laws impossible.

They have also argued that the vast mass of historical records makes it impossible for any student of human affairs to master all the relevant data they contain even if he could read the dozens of languages in which these data are recorded. The fact that the authors of original historical sources arbitrarily selected the events they recorded from a much wider mass of events implies that any historical study lacks pertinent information which might have been recorded but was not. Naturally, the idiographic historians also call attention to the distortions, biases, and downright false-hoods which basic historical source records so often contain; and in criticizing the writings of nomothetic historians, these writers are sometimes also able to point out distortions and biases of a serious sort on the part of the nomothetic historians themselves.

There is no point in further speculative discussion about how laws of history *might* be found. The professional journals are full of such talk.

There have already been a few cross-historical surveys of an imperfect sort—including this one. Their results are encouraging to us nomothetic historians but not overwhelming. We look forward to cross-historical surveys of a better sort—surveys which support some laws of history so persuasively as to compel a presumption in their favor from any open mind.

Needless to say, by a law of history we do not mean an invariable relationship but only a strong tendency. Whether hard and fast invariable laws exist anywhere in nature is open to dispute. The laws of physics and chemistry, once thought rigid and immutable, are now regarded by many scientists merely as high probabilities. However that may be, we for our part expect no such rigid invariable relationship; we seek only probabilities.

For this reason we advocate here the cross-cultural survey method, now highly developed by anthropologists. This is a mathematical method; it seeks measures of degrees of relationships through coefficients of correlation or association, and it seeks to measure probabilities through tests of statistical significance. It offers a solution to many classic dilemmas of historical method. Let us turn to a review of its accomplishments and problems.

THE CROSS-CULTURAL SURVEY METHOD

Most American anthropologists today suppose that general sociological laws of culture change (i.e., laws of history) exist and can be discovered. Anthropological interest in such laws has revived since World War II, manifesting itself in a lively renewal of interest in the study of cultural evolution. However, one still finds, especially in Great Britain, prominent anthropologists who maintain the idiographic viewpoint about the comparative study of culture. This viewpoint is particularly associated with Oxford (Evans-Pritchard 1963).

Yet the case for validating nomothetic generalizations in comparative anthropology is quite different from that in comparative history. Nomothetic anthropology in general and the cross-cultural survey method in particular are clearly much further along, have much wider recognition, much higher academic standing, and have earned this status by far more sophisticated methodological techniques than those practiced by nomothetic historians.

I have recently completed a review of the accomplishments of 154 cross-cultural surveys (Naroll 1970). While weaknesses of method led me to reserve judgment about most of these, I accepted several important results as scientific presumptions. By this I do not mean to say that they have been demonstrated beyond any possibility of doubt; I do not think that anything may ever be that clearly shown. Rather, by a *scientific presumption* I mean a result so strongly supported that a formal study of equal rigor with contradictory results would be needed to discredit it.

ACCOMPLISHMENTS OF THE CROSS-CULTURAL SURVEY METHOD

What anthropological results then have been scientifically established to such an extent by cross-cultural surveys? To begin with, a general theory of kinship. As it happens, all modern Western societies have substantially similar systems of kinship. (Anthropologists technically classify them all as belonging to the Eskimo type. The definition of this concept is too technical to give here; see Murdock 1949:226–228.) Therefore, historians are likely to be unfamiliar with this topic unless they work outside modern Western history. Those studying classical antiquity, the Middle East, India, or the Far East will be much more at home with the subject matter of kinship theory. Still, only an acquaintance with the wide variety of kinship systems found among primitive tribes can suffice to understand the full implications of that theory.

The prime conundrum of kinship theory has been the theory

of kinship terminology. A kin term is a word that designates a class of relative, for example: *mother, father, son, daughter, uncle, aunt, husband, wife.* Comparison of such terms in English and Spanish shows that Spanish has different words for these terms than English. But for nearly every English term, there is a Spanish term which exactly corresponds to it. What an Englishman understands by *mother*, a Spaniard understands by *madre*—no more, no less. Similarly, *uncle* as a kin term in English is exactly translated by *tio* in Spanish. The only major failure of correspondence is the English word *cousin.* That word has no exact Spanish equivalent; for in Spanish, as in most other European languages, that class of relative is distinguished by sex, and so we have *primo* for a male cousin and *prima* for a female one.

But if we look over the range of kinship terminology systems among all known human societies, we see that the meaning of these kin terms varies tremendously. For example, in classical Latin, the term *pater* includes both *father* and *father's brother*; there is no exact equivalent to the English term *father.* In Hawaiian, there is one and only one term for all male relatives of the father's generation. Among the Crow Indians of Montana, *basbaxia* designates a certain class of female relative, namely: father's sister, and father's sister's daughter, granddaughter, and great granddaughter. These wide variations in kinship terms are not random, but patterned into systems (see Murdock 1949). All known systems of kin terms can be classed into some eight or ten general types. Now what is the source of the variation among these types? Cross-cultural surveys have created a strong presumption that this variation arises from variations in *rules of descent.* A rule of descent is one designating membership in kin groups. Our own rule is called *bilateral descent*, meaning we belong to the families of our fathers and our mothers alike. The two other major rules of descent are patrilineal and matrilineal; under patrilineal descent, as in ancient Rome, a child belonged to the lineage and clan of his father and was not a member of his mother's lineage or clan. Under matrilineal descent, which prevails today among many North American Indian people, a child belongs to his mother's lineage and clan, not to his father's. What is the source of the variation among these rules?

Cross-cultural surveys have created a strong presumption that differences of descent arise partially from variations in *rules of residence* which govern the customary location of the household of a newly-married couple. If they usually set up a new household of their own, they are following the rule of *neolocal residence*. If they live with or very near the bride's parents, that rule is called *matrilocal residence*; if they reside with or very near the groom's parents, as today in India for example, that rule is called *patrilocal residence*. There are still other variations, which we need not go into here. It is enough to say that cross-cultural surveys have shown that neolocal residence usually leads to bilateral descent, which in turn leads to an Eskimo type of kin term; patrilocal residence usually leads to patrilineal descent, which in turn leads to Iroquois or Omaha types of kin terms; and matrilocal residence usually leads to matrilineal descent, and that in turn leads to Iroquois or Crow types of kin terms. There is not space here to define these kin terms accurately; see Murdock (1949:223–224). The six types vary in the way they classify a man's female cross-cousins (his mother's brother's daughters and his father's sister's daughters). These girls may or may not be distinguished from each other, from other kinds of female cousins, from sisters, from certain kinds of aunts (like father's sister or mother's sister) or from certain kinds of nieces (like sister's daughters or brother's daughters). For example, our word *cousin* includes daughters of either brothers or sisters of either father or mother, but does not include sisters, aunts, or nieces. Iroquois-type kinship terminologies have a special word for female cross-cousin; other female cousins often are lumped with sisters. Crow lumps father's sister's daughter (a cousin to us) with father's sister (an aunt to us).

Whence comes the variation in rules of residence? Cross-cultural surveys strongly suggest that this variation in rules of residence tends to arise from variation in the importance of the respective roles of wife and husband. Originally, it was thought that this variation was exclusively an ecological one, but now it is known that political or military factors may likewise be influential.

In addition to these findings on kinship, cross-cultural surveys have created strong presumptions for seven main characteristics of *cultural evolution*. From the comparative study of modern societies,

both primitive and civilized, they have presumably thus reconstructed seven main currents of human prehistory in the past
twenty-five thousand years. This linkage between level of development of modern societies and prehistoric ones depends upon two
working hypotheses. But both working hypotheses are unchallenged
today. The first is that, by and large, the human mind has functioned
much the same for at least the past twenty-five thousand years.
Whatever innate differences have occurred during that space of
time among human populations survive today. The second is that
twenty-five thousand years ago few if any human communities
were more populous than two or three hundred people per camp
or village; in other words, no such thing as a city or even a large
town or a large camp (over twenty thousand people) was then
known. The first of these working hypotheses derives, of course,
from human paleontology; the second derives from archeology.
If both of them hold true, then the comparative results of cross-
cultural surveys do enable us to reconstruct the main currents of
human prehistory. For from them it follows that those characteristics of contemporary societies, primitive and civilized, still
functionally associated with settlement size must have been so associated in the past at least throughout the last twenty-five thousand
years.

The main currents of cultural evolution during the past twenty-
five thousand years thus presumably established are these:
(1) Human societies have tended to become increasingly *stronger*,
more numerous, and in greater command of energy and the natural
resources of the environment. (2) Human societies have tended
to develop an ever-increasing variety of *occupational specialties*, and
associated with this development is a general tendency for human
societies to command an ever-increasing fund of information.
(3) Human societies have tended to develop ever more complex
team organizations: kinship teams, territorial (or political) teams,
military teams, teams of free associates. (4) Human societies have
tended to develop an ever-increasing degree of *urbanization*, and
this fact is not only the key link with archeology, but also the key
link among many of the other characteristics of cultural evolution:
there is a regular mathematical (loglog linear) correlation between
the number of people in the largest settlement of a human society

and (a) the number of its occupational specialties; (b) the degree
of complexity of its organized teams; and (c) the total inventory of
its cultural traits. (5) Human societies have tended to develop
economies which promote *concentration* rather than distribution of
wealth. (6) They have tended to develop more and more *authoritative
leadership*, rather than the consensual type of leadership characteristic of the most primitive present-day human societies; and
(7) Human societies have increased the reasons for *warfare*; once
waged exclusively for vengeance or territorial maintenance,
warfare has tended to embrace acquisition of wealth, prestige and
political control.

Finally, to garnish these findings about the fundamental character
of human prehistory, cross-cultural surveys have established strong
presumptions that several sorts of trait styles are associated with
varying levels of cultural evolution: art styles, game styles, and
song-and-dance styles are the best documented of these; but
several other styles of life have also been investigated with correlations whose validity is more or less in doubt.

At this writing most of the work here reported is so recent that
it has not become generally known as a whole to anthropologists,
much less to other social scientists. The interested reader needs to
look over these reports himself (see Naroll 1970 and compare
Marsh 1967).

PROBLEMS OF THE CROSS-CULTURAL SURVEY METHOD

Since the first cross-cultural survey was published by Sir Edward
Tylor in 1889, a considerable body of critiques of these surveys has
been written. Until the last decade, these surveys have been crude
and defective in many ways; and only now are these earlier weaknesses being overcome. If historians had to reinvent this comparative
statistical method, they conceivably might take twenty-five to
fifty years to solve its methodological problems. For this reason I
believe that the nomothetic historian would be wise to consider
carefully what have been the difficulties and weaknesses of the
cross-cultural survey method and what has been done to overcome
them. Eleven main problems of comparative statistical method are
listed in Naroll (1970), and with this list goes a body of citations
to the methodological literature. Most of the problems, though

not all, are discussed in great detail in Naroll and Cohen (1970). They fall into two classes: (1) the problems of basic epistemology, and (2) problems of spurious correlation.

The cross-cultural method itself is one that samples all known human societies and seeks causal inferences from mathematical correlations resulting in the following problems of basic epistemology.

Problems of Basic Epistemology

1. *Statistical significance.* What is the likelihood of an association of the sort observed occurring through mere chance? The measurement of this likelihood in random samples is the main business of mathematical statistics. As an introduction to this topic for comparative historians, see Freeman (1965), Blalock (1960), Siegel (1956), and Kendall (1962)—all four books to be studied in the order listed.

2. *The "combing," "dredging" or "mudsticking" problem.* If as in the present study of deterrence, a large number of correlations are computed, how many of these would be expected to attain a value commonly termed "statistically significant" even if they were compiled from entirely meaningless data, such as a table of random numbers?

3. *The causal analysis of correlations.* Is a causal relationship established? The existence of a correlation between a supposed cause and its supposed effect is usually very far from enough to establish a presumtion in favor of the cause-effect hypothesis. The validity of such a presumption would depend upon the plausibility of rival hypotheses to explain such a correlation. Commonly, plausible rival hypotheses are not difficult to think up. But where three or more variables are intercorrelated, newly developed methods of causal analysis often serve to rule out by mathematics many otherwise plausible rival hypotheses.

4. *Conceptualization, classification, and coding.* Are the conceptualization, classification, and coding of the concepts used in the study valid in the light of varying cultural (or historical) contexts?

5. *Paucity of relevant data.* How can we investigate suicide frequency, for example, if accurate data on suicide rates are not to be had?

6. *Units of study*. Exactly what is meant by a society or a tribe? How are its boundaries to be fixed in time and space?

7. *Deviant case analysis*. How can deviant cases be explained, societies which depart considerably from the general tendency observed? For example, what about the absence of writing among the Incas or of metal tools among the Aztecs?

Four final problems of comparative method are problems of spurious correlation. This point is quite important and not widely appreciated. In other words, none of these four problems is any problem at all *unless* it leads to a spurious correlation. However, any of these four problems *can indeed* lead to spurious correlations, make no mistake about it. Each of them has done so in at least one cross-cultural survey.

8. *Sampling bias*. Statistical tests of significance assume random sampling. If samples depart from randomness in such a way as to tend to raise the absolute value of a correlation being studied, this departure could cause a spurious correlation. (Consequently, samples should depart from randomness as little as possible and all such departures must be measured.)

9. *Galton's problem*. To what extent do observed correlations reflect mere coincidences of joint cultural diffusion? Traits spread through borrowing or migration, and such patterns are well known sometimes to produce very high correlations simply by coincidence of diffusion patterns without any functional linkage at all.

10. *Data inaccuracy*. To what extent do reported correlations merely reflect systematic reporting or coding errors? Such errors can be introduced by native informants, ethnological field workers, or comparativists. But the key thought to bear firmly in mind is that many such errors are purely random and random errors tend to lower correlations, not to raise them. Consequently, it is only systematic errors which we need to guard against. But systematic errors are not unusual.

11. *Regional peculiarities*. To what extent do the observed correlations merely reflect the special circumstances of a particular region or continent rather than the general tendencies of all human society?

"Generations" of Cross-Cultural Surveys

It is useful to distinguish by design three successive "generations" of cross-cultural surveys. The first generation consists of all those studies published before 1934, together with Wright (1942). These studies do not use any method of sampling, but instead seek to treat all known primitive societies. They use no coefficients of correlation or tests of significance, and they are extremely careless about tribal unit definition. Indeed, they pay little attention to any of the eleven problems listed above.

The second generation comprises nearly all studies published since 1934. The model for most of these has been Murdock (1949). Sampling is usually judgmental, although since Swanson (1960) the use of the probability sample has become more frequent; there is no precision of ethnic unit definition, nor any control of systematic data bias, for Galton's problem, for the mudsticking problem. On the other hand, ethnic units are carefully chosen, representative sampling is an explicit ideal, and mathematical statistical measures of relationship and significance are systematically used. Concept definition is usually elaborate and sophisticated.

At this writing, we seem to be in a transition period moving into a third generation of cross-cultural survey design. No study yet published has all the following characteristics, but each characteristic is to be found in one or another recent study in print or in press. Samples are to be in third generation studies, as I envision them, probability samples from a universe comprising substantially all adequately described tribes. Societal units are to be pinpointed in time and space on particular communities, and the societal unit to be measured for ethnic distinctiveness. Formal reliability tests are to check for random factual error, and formal data quality control tests are to check for systematic error. All concepts, classifications, and coding rules are to be explicit and highly reliable. Formal tests of clustering or neighbor resemblances are to establish that correlations are functional (semidiffusional) rather than mere artifacts of migration or borrowing (hyperdiffusional). Formal significance tests are to consider not only the significance levels of individual associations but also those of the entire group. Separate regional correlations are to show that the association concerned is a worldwide one, not found merely in one or two regions alone. Deviant case analyses should seek to explain exceptions systematically. Finally, and most important of all, formal causal analysis of correlational matrices are to establish the direction of causality, at least among all the variables considered in the study; and these are to include all those considered relevant by any professional social scientist.

THE CROSS-HISTORICAL SURVEY METHOD

THE BASIC PLAN

The purpose of the cross-historical survey method as we see it is to test proposed laws of history. Our hope, I repeat, is not that such laws will hold good invariably, but only that they will display a clear tendency. Laws thus validated would enable predictions about the future, like weather forecasts, to be statements of probability, now and then mistaken but usually fairly dependable.

I again remind my readers of the crucial distinction between what we are trying to do here and what a historiographer tries to do. We as comparative historians are looking for principles common to many times and places. We seek to note how these principles vary and under what conditions. The historiographer in contrast is trying to discern the patterns present in a single, unique event.

A representative sample of historical periods from all the major Old World civilizations is selected. Such samples may, at the investigator's option, involve a time-lag to permit cause-effect sequence analysis (more on that below). The test of the theory consists in seeing whether correlations turn out in the manner predicted.

To illustrate the idea consider one of Sorokin's proposed laws of history. A basic design for a future cross-historical survey is sketched to test his theory.

Hypothesis: The change of basic value systems tends to make for more frequent and intense civil wars (Sorokin 1937–1941).

Sample Design: Higher civilizations may be precisely defined as *paideias* according to the criterion of their higher educational script, as set forth in this preface, further below. Every second or every third century is randomly chosen from each such paideia. Every sampled century is studied during its first and sixth decades; if there are less than two examples of the necessary indicators of a value system available for each decade, the century is rejected from the sample and the following century substituted.

Coding Variables : Remember that each sampled century is to have two decades, fifty years apart, as periods for study. In each of these decades the frequency of civil war and the stability of value are measured. The frequency of civil war is measured from the attention given to it in standard encyclopedic sources like Langer (1948), Steiger (1944), and Michaelis (1964). Note well that if more than one of these is used, one or two hundred randomly chosen pages from each will need to be compared to see if any of these authors tends to pay more attention to civil wars than either of the others; if so, ratings will have to be adjusted accordingly. Apart from that, the measure of an encyclopedia's attention to civil wars would be a simple fraction, A/B. A would represent the total number of words devoted to reporting any civil wars during the decade; B would represent the total number of words given to the decade in all. Using this fraction avoids any bias arising from the fact that encyclopedic historians tend to devote more attention to more recent centuries and to Western civilization than to earlier centuries and non-Western civilizations. Obviously, the relative attention paid to civil wars by encyclopedists is a far from perfect measure of civil war frequency. But the rival hypothesis is not merely that discrepancies between variable (civil war frequency) and indicator (encyclopedist's attention) occur, it is also that these discrepancies are systematically related to indicators of value like codings of art styles. This point is extremely important.

Stability of value is measured by assembling up to half a dozen examples of each of several indicators of values such as art styles and philosophical treatises. This assembly must be performed by "naive" coders who do not know the purpose of the study and whose instructions are as clear and explicit as possible. The sets of assemblages for each indicator are then ranked for internal consistency or inconsistency by other "naive" coders. At least two such coders independently perform each ranking, and their work is compared and their agreement measured. None of this work is done by the people who measure frequency of civil war.

The Hypothesis Test:

Indexes measuring the frequency of civil war for the first decade of each century are called W_1: for the sixth decade they are called W_2. Indicators of consistencies of values for the first decade of each century are called V_1, for the sixth V_2. For each century, W_1 is correlated with V_2, and W_2 with V_1 (Rozelle and Campbell 1969). Sorokin's hypothesis predicts not only that both those pairs will be correlated from century to century, but that the W_2V_1 correlations will be significantly higher than the W_1V_2 correlations. (Technical note: The test statistic might well be a test for the significance of difference between gamma coefficients, since these are non parametric and their sampling distribution is known—see Goodman and Kruskal [1963].)

Discussion:

The foregoing research design improves upon causal analysis of historical tendencies as done by conventional historiographical studies is two important ways:

(1) Selection bias of the historian is avoided. By drawing up selection instructions which describe the type of material wanted without revealing its theoretical relevance, selection by "naive" coders is uninfluenced by the historian's theories.

(2) Causation is inferred not only from objectively established associations (correlations) but from sequence, through the device of cross-lagged correlations just described.

But a properly designed cross-historical survey would offer many further advantages in addition. By considering and guarding against the problems of cross-cultural method already listed, as applied to historical rather than to ethnographic materials, many other rival hypotheses which might explain away the results can be disposed of. Let us review these problems in a historical context to consider in more detail how this might be done.

PROBLEMS OF CROSS-HISTORICAL SURVEY METHOD APPLIED TO LAWS OF HISTORY

Units of Study

The general nature of historical units of study is given considerable attention in Toynbee (1934), Spengler (1926), and Kroeber

(1944). We must consider the problem not only in space but also in time.

The nation-state. To take as a unit of study a nation state—particular political organization, or linguistic group, or a combination of the two—is the most common practice among historiographers. For some purposes such an approach is valuable, but in a large-scale comparative study, the number of such units to be considered is extremely great and most of these units are likely to be but slightly documented.

The higher civilization. The *higher civilization* has tended to be the unit of comparison for large-scale comparative studies of "all history" for two reasons. The numbers of such units are relatively few (about one to two dozen, depending upon how they are classifi d); and for elements other than political history, all the states within any such civilizations tend to share their major cultural characteristics at any given point in time. This community of culture is less evident to insiders looking at their own civilization than to outsiders. From our vantage point on earth, the Milky Way does not look like a spiral nebula, but when we look at other spiral nebulas, their form is at once apparent.

The measurement of levels of civilization in cross-cultural surveys has advanced so far in the past decade that the distinction between higher civilizations and primitive societies is easy to make through the use of any of half a dozen different indexes; those all give similar results (see Naroll and Cohen 1970). The simplest measurement is the presence of cities. Call a city any collection of fixed dwellings housing at least twenty-five thousand people within six kilometers of one central point. Any state or language group which has at least one such city is called a higher civilization. All cities contain a wide variety of complex team organizations, support several dozen occupational specialties, and many full-time specialists. Nearly all cities contain professional recorders of records which are usually, though not always, written records. Moreover, most cities are found in large nation-states, and most have massive stone or brick architecture. Their cultures are far richer in total trait inventories than those of societies without cities.

Cities, then, distinguish higher civilizations from lower ones.

What distinguishes one higher civilization from another? Toynbee (1934) suggests we look at their religions; Spengler (1926) suggests that we look at their underlying ethos or life styles; and Kroeber (1944) suggests that we look at their art styles. None of these writers however, gives a clear and unambiguous set of criteria by which we can in practice apply their suggestions. The lists each produces resemble each other closely, but no two are exactly alike. I here propose another set of criteria, that of higher educational script. The unit thus defined is called a paideia.

The Paideia. By a *paideia* I mean an intellectually influential higher civilization. I wish to distinguish intellectually influential from intellectually unifluential higher civilizations. I define an intellectually influential civilization as one with a written literature which has been extensively translated into another script and whose moral or scientific ideas have been advocated by writers in another script (i.e., belonging to another civilization). I would furthermore classify particular states or cities as belonging to that paideia whose literature (whether in the original tongue or in translation) is widely taught by its professors.

A *script* is a set of visual symbols intended to make possible the reproduction more or less faithfully of actual speech, word by word, and is thus to be distinguished from conventional symbols which merely communicate *ideas* without specifying the particular words in which they are expressed. For example, the highway signs on the continent of Europe today specify such ideas as 'railroad crossing', 'one way street', 'dangerous curve', and the like. They constitute a system of conventional signs independent of particular words. For the idea 'railroad crossing' can also be conveyed by the phrase *train tracks in the road*; the idea of dangerous curves by the phrase *winding road* and so on. While several important scripts have symbols containing clear ideas, they all make extensive use of phonetic as well as ideational principles in order to specify not merely an idea but a particular spoken word which stands for it (Gelb 1963:60–61; Voegelin and Voegelin 1961:68–86). For our present purposes, it is irrelevant whether such a script represents many entire words by single symbols or logograms (as in Egyptian, Babylonian, Chinese), whether it instead characteristically and usually represents a spoken word by a group of symbols standing for individual syllables (as in Japanese *kana*, Minoan Linear B), or whether it more or less tries to represent the individual phonemes of speech (as in the Greek, Latin, and Cyrillic alphabets).

I consider as a single body of literature all that which originally has been written in a single script, including all its allographs. (An allograph is an alternate form of a given sign. Thus we who use the Latin alphabet understand that *A*, a, and *a*, however different in form, stand for exactly the same item in our set of symbols.) Since minor variations in script symbol inventory are to be ignored, we can for our present purposes consider as a single script any two sets of symbols at least 75% of the shorter of which contains at least one allograph sharing a common referent with a recognizably similar counterpart in the longer set.

As an operational measure of the influence of a body of literature upon a foreign civilization, I impose two requirements. I consider a body of literature widely influential if at least one million words have been translated into another script by A.D. 1900; and if some moral, theological or scientific (including pseudoscientific) idea originating in one body of literature was advocated by a writer in another body of literature in that same year, I think we may recognize nine or ten such bodies of literature, and I then propose to treat these paideian literatures from their beginnings.

In classifying particular states or independent cities as members of particular paideias, I ignore literature originally written in an uninfluential script, such as Japanese *kana*, Ethiopian, or Tamil script. So I consider only literature which is taught by professors and which was originally written in an influential script. If, as so commonly happens, more than one such script is represented in the curriculum, I then assign the society and period to the paideia whose literature is most used. Thus in Caesar's time Roman professors (many of whom were Greek slaves) may well have made chief use of Latin language-materials; but it seems likely that they mostly taught materials originally written in Greek, whether they taught them in the Greek original or in Latin translation. Hence I would not classify the Roman state or its Latin-speaking regions as part of the Western paideia until its professors came to teach predominantly materials originally written in Latin script.

A. Paideia Classification

1. *Mesopotamian.* This paideia is defined by its body of literature written in *cuneiform* script. The extent of translation is undocumented, since all have been lost; but considering the known extent of the original literature, as preserved on clay tablets in the library of Nineveh and elsewhere, as well as the known high intellectual prestige of that literature during the second millenium B.C., extensive translation into such script as Hittite and Egyptian, not to speak of possible later translations into Phoenician and Greek, seems probable. Historians of science (Maury 1860:62–65; Cumont 1912:36–100) ascribe to this literature the origin of such widely influential studies as astrology (whose validity is beside the point) and astronomy, as well as the division of angular measure into 360 degrees. There were, presumably, professors among the temple priests who dominated the intellectual life of this civilization from its beginnings.

2. *Egyptian.* This paideia is defined by its body of literature written in *hieroglyphic* script, with many allographic forms, including hieratic and demotic (see Gelb 1963:76). Manetho's history is known to have been translated from Egyptian into Greek and it seems hard to doubt that dozens if not hundreds of other works were likewise translated at the Alexandria library in Hellenistic times. Herodotus (*Histories.* 2.4) praised the Egyptian calendar as superior to the Greek one; and Julius Caesar later adopted it for Roman use. There were temple priest professors, evidently.

3. *Hebrew.* This paideia is defined by its body of literature written in the *Hebrew* alphabet. The Hebrew script differs from the closely related Phoenician, Palestinian, Aramaic, and Syriac scripts rather more than Latin and Cyrillic differ from Greek (see Gelb 1963:137). The only translations of consequence have been the Old Testament and the Talmud; but the influence of the former has of course been immense. There were temple priest professors in ancient times (Luke 2:6) and Talmudic schools later.

4. *Islamic.* This paideia is defined by its body of literature written in the *Arabic* alphabet. Writers in this alphabet include Arabic peoples proper, Osmanli, and Seljuk Turks, Persians (since the seventh century), Afghans, and Moslems of India. Medieval Islamic

scientists like Averroes and Avicenna were of course widely translated and influential in medieval Europe (*Encyclopaedia Britannica*,
11th ed., s.v. "Arabian Philosophy"); one could doubtless also
document the influence upon Europeans of the Koran, and the
poems of Omar Khayyam, not to speak of the *Arabian Nights*.
Islamic learning has been taught from the beginning by the professors of its famous universities.

5. *Greco-Roman*. This paideia is defined by its body of literature
written in the Greek alphabet. It seems likely that until the third
or fourth century after Christ, the professors of the western as well
as of the eastern regions of the Roman Empire taught predominantly
Greek literature, whether in the original or in Latin translations;
hence the Latin-writing world is not at first a distinct paideia, since
not until literature originally written in a Latin script dominates
the teaching of professors in the West do we begin the Western
paideia.

6. *Western*. This paideia, our own, is defined by its body of literature
in the *Latin* alphabet, including a wide variety of allographs. There
were translations and influence in Russia from the seventeenth
century, in India from the eighteenth century, and in the Far
East from the nineteenth century. Early medieval professors were
priests.

7. *Russian*. This paideia is defined by its body of literature written
in the *Cyrillic* alphabet. Although that alphabet is also used to
write other Slavic languages like Serbian, Bulgarian, and Ukrainian,
it is the Great Russian literature which constitutes the body of
learned work. Nineteenth-century Russian literature was extensively
translated into Western languages; perhaps Tolstoy was the most
influential nineteenth-century Russian thinker. As in the West,
professors were originally priests; but secular academies and
universities were later developed.

8. *Hindu*. This paideia is defined by its body of literature written
in the *Devanagari* script, including a wide variety of allographs.
There were influential translations of Buddhist classics into Chinese
during the Han dynasty; ancient Hindu classics were admired in
Western translation in the nineteenth century. Hindu professors
commonly were unattached to any permanent institution, but

gathered around them groups of disciples, a pattern that is well documented for Buddha's time and continues along with British-model universities to the present day.

9. *Chinese.* This paideia is defined by its body of literature written in the Chinese *logographic* script. This script has been widely used also in Korea, Vietnam, and Japan, alongside of other locally used scripts (Vietnamese *quoc-ngu*, Korean alphabet, Japanese *kana* syllabaries). Beginning in the seventeenth century, Chinese history and classics began to be extensively translated into European languages and to be widely read by European philosophers. Chinese moral, philosophical, and scientific thinking predominated intellectual life in Japan, Korea, and Vietnam until the latter half of the nineteenth century; furthermore, Chinese political theory and practice provided the original model for the English civil service examination system.

Classification Problems:

The foregoing was a preliminary attempt to use single *fundamentum divisionis* to classify the world's intellectually influential higher civilizations. The list omits the Central American and Andean civilizations of the New World before Columbus. Although their material culture has been widely influential (maize, chocolate, potato, turkey fowl, tobacco), and their intellectual culture included a calendar more accurate than any in use in the Old World, the Andeans had no script and only a few fragments of the Central American literature escaped the bonfires of the Spaniards. New World civilizations then in fact have not produced an influential literature, although they may have produced one deserving of influence.

Further research is needed on the relationship between Tibet and Mongolia before it can be clear whether or not Lamaistic Tibet is also qualified as a paideia by virtue of extensive translations of Tibetan and Buddhist literature into a distinctive Mongol alphabet derived from the Tibetan.

It is clear that the modern Chinese script descends in unbroken tradition from Shang dynasty times (about 1300 B.C.) and that the present form of the characters was more or less settled by about the time of Christ; furthermore, antique forms of the most widely used characters survive today as seal characters for specialized use. But whether the characters in use in Confucian times (about 500 B.C.) were sufficiently similar from region to region throughout the China of that day to constitute a single script, and whether that script is to be classified as an allographic version of the present one, needs to be checked. If not, then like Toynbee and Quigley (1961), we would have to recognize an earlier Sinic paideia, preceding and ancestral to the later Chinese paideia,

Similarly, the Devanagari alphabet used everywhere in India today to write Sanskrit and in most of North India to write the languages spoken there is a direct lineal descendant of the script preserved in several inscriptions of the Maurya period (about 250 B.C., see Gelb 1963:185–87). Whether the ancient forms correspond closely enough to the modern ones and are still sufficiently well recognized by educated users of Devanagari to constitute in effect allographs of modern Devanagari still needs to be checked. If not, then we would have to recognize an earlier Indic paideia, preceding and ancestral to the later Hindu paideia, again, as Toynbee and Quigley do. However, it does not seem that the various South Indian alphabets used to write such Dravidian languages as Tamil and Telugu constitute a serious classification problem. Although Devanagari is almost never used in daily affairs in South India, it seems most doubtful if any of these Dravidian scripts have an extensively translated or influential literature; indeed, it seems likely that Dravidian professors have chiefly taught literature in the Sanskritic tradition—and Sanskrit is always written in Devanagari.

In classifying India, however, one may well have to consider region by region and period by period the relative extent of the use of Islamic or Western literature by professors there.

The intellectual culture of Iran before Islam provides another classification problem. Coulborn (1959) and Turner (1941) each recognize a distinctive Iranian civilization during this period, and Toynbee likewise speaks of an Iranic civilization later coalescing with an Arabic one to form Toynbee's Islamic civilization. Before Islam the Iranians made wide use of a Palestinian alphabet, and their religious thinking had considerable influence in the Near East and Europe. Whether this influence was manifested in the form of translated literature is however not so clear; the question needs further study.

Toynbee, Coulborn, and Quigley all distinguish Byzantine from classical Graeco-Roman civilizations. My classification would not. The Greek literary tradition, religious and secular, would be treated as a continuous single paideia from its origins until a few centuries ago.

Toynbee, Kroeber, and Quigley treat Japan as a separate civilization distinct from China despite the huge role played by Chinese literature in Japanese thinking. It does not seem that much Japanese *kana* literature was translated into another script before A.D. 1900, nor that the little which was translated had much influence. But it would be well to study this matter further to verify or correct this tentative conclusion. If, to my surprise, a minimally influential body of translations of Japanese *kana* literature were to be discovered, it would then have to be investigated if Japanese professors, whether priests or not, predominantly taught *kana* materials before the Meiji restoration (1858). Before Meiji times, *kana* was a low-prestige script considered suitable for amusing tales like that of Genji, but not for serious learning.

Further research is also required to establish when, if indeed ever, literature originally written in Cyrillic became the predominant basis of study in Russia, whether in medieval church centers of learning or in modern universities.

Finally, in establishing the beginning of our own Western paideia, we need to establish when the professors of the Latin-writing area began to teach predominately literature that had been written originally in Latin script. It seems perfectly clear on one hand that until the very last year of the Roman Republic, Latin literature was but a small portion of the course of study of the educated Roman, with Greek literature constituting the bulk of his course. It seems rather doubtful that the Roman writers of the classical period supplanted the Greeks in bulk; more likely it was not until the triumph of Christianity and the extinction of pagan schools that literature of Latin origin became predominant among the professors of the West. But more study of this question is needed.

TIME PERIODS

The basic unit of historical study is a given culture (nation, society, community, region) during a given period of time. Each civilization and each nation with a written history is of course divided by its historians into named periods. Political events or art styles are most commonly used to designate such periods.

It would be useful to have some objective criterion, some single *fundamentum divisionis*, by which all civilizations could be divided into successive time periods for cross-historical survey purposes. There need be no requirement that such periods be of approximately equal length. After all there is no requirement that societies, classified in space, are of approximately equal area or population. What is to be made as nearly equal as possible is cultural distinctiveness.

Another approach might be simply to take the commonly accepted or received periodizations—those used by Langer, perhaps—by whatever criteria they may be made, however inconsistently. Each period as thus delimited could be contrasted with its predecessor and follower for distinctiveness according to whether it differs in each of these five respects: (1) regime (through disruption of normal mechanism of succession to power); (2) constitutional structure; (3) religion; (4) architectural style of public buildings (as measure of underlying ethos); (5) character of body of literature accepted as authoritative. For example, Cromwell's regime differed from its predecessor and follower in seventeenth-century England with respect to regime, constitutional structure, and religion; but not with respect to public building style or authoritative body of literature. Lenin's regime differed from Kerensky's in twentieth-century Russia with respect not only to regime and constitutional structure but also with respect to religion and authoritative body of literature. The degree of difference in each of these criteria would need to be measured according to some sort of objective standard.

From such measures as these five, an index of temporal distinctiveness can be compiled. Using this, the degree of difference between successive periods can be established in either of two ways: as a criterion for evaluating any scheme of periodization, or as a test of the hypothesis that the sharpness or indistinctness of period boundaries has anything to do with the results of a cross-historical survey and its correlations. In my judgment such sharpness would almost always be irrelevant. By measuring that sharpness and correlating it with the variables in the study, this irrelevance could be established; critics concerned about alleged lack of comparability because of inconsistent periodization could thus be reassured.

In the meantime, it is perfectly simple to do as we do in this study: stratify time periods by centuries and within each century sample randomly by some specified shorter period—we take a decade here.

SAMPLING

Theoretically, in a cross-historical study, one could take for the sampling universe all those states whose histories are recorded in some specified degree of detail. Langer's *Encyclopedia of World History* might constitute a preliminary working inventory of such states. However, Langer had no such inventory in mind; he was cataloguing *events*, not polities. And serious interdependence problems would arise in many studies since states belonging to the same great cultural tradition or higher civilization would at any given point in time have many common characteristics reflecting in essence their unity as an intellectual community (for more about interdependence, see p. li below). Furthermore, Langer tends to give more attention to states which are nearer to the Western world in time or space than to those more distant. By using the paideia as a preliminary sampling classification (i.e., a sampling stratum criterion) and sampling separately from Langer paideia by paideia and century by century, one could compensate for this bias of his.

The comparativist will usually be faced with difficulties of inequalities of documentation. The history of ancient Athens is much better preserved than that of ancient Corinth. If one were to take a random sample of ancient Greek city-states, he might well come up with Megara as a random choice—only to find that for the period of time selected nothing useful is known about that city.

Comparative ethnology has had to face just the same problem. Take a random sample of South American tribes, and the chances will be that of one tribe in every four or five so picked nothing much is known about it beyond its name, its location, and its mode of subsistence. George P. Murdock finally solved this problem for anthropologists by compiling lists of substantially all the tribes on which fairly detailed descriptions exist.

In this study, we solve the problem by focusing on the most *conspicuous* state in the whole paideia during the century in question. That state is defined as the one whose rivalries are given most attention by Langer. Naturally, it is invariably one whose affairs are among the best recorded of any in that civilization at that time. This sort of selection procedure does introduce a serious bias. The most conspicuous states are by no means the most typical or representative ones. For the present study we did not mind this bias, but where such a bias would interfere with the validity of the findings it would be best to establish some simple and easily applied criterion of wealth of documentation. Then for each civilization in each century one might sample randomly and check the choice for acceptability of documentation. If this should prove unacceptable, another random selection may be made and the process continued until an acceptable state is chosen. Finally, the relative wealth of description of each selection is measured and bibliographic quality control is applied to measure selection bias (see Naroll 1967).

ACCURACY OF DATA

The problem of accuracy of data is more serious for cross-historical surveys than for cross-cultural surveys. But it is not nearly so serious as professional historians of today are likely to assume. The writing of accurate reports of the past is a sacred task for historians. They at once assume this definition of their activity as the chief virtue of the profession and at the same time they despair when they realize that no matter how skillfully they try, the achievement of a completely faithful record is beyond them.

I again remind my readers of the crucial distinction between our goal and that of a historiographer. We look for general principles and expect to find only tendencies. He looks for specific events and expects—to at least try—to report them precisely. Our data accuracy task is an entirely different one from his; in many ways it is a markedly easier one. Like the historiographer of classical antiquity who painstakingly sifts and compares his few sources but by entirely different devices, we claim to be able to draw *trustworthy* conclusions from *untrustworthy* sources.

The Historiographic Tradition.

Professional historical research standards involve careful critical examination and comparison of primary sources together with consideration of earlier reviews of these sources by other professional historians. The end product of these labors are secondary historic surveys by experts and, finally, tertiary encyclopedic compilations like that of Langer. But each professional historian working on original research begins anew with the primary sources.

The contrast between the viewpoint of the comparativist and that of the highly trained professional historian looking at the history of a particular nation during a particular period cannot be better illustrated than by my correspondence with Professor Marc Sieber of the University of Basel. I asked him to review our three chapters on Swiss history and to give us a critique of them. He replied:

> I looked over the three essays, and must to my great regret inform you that it will not be possible for me to prepare critiques. With a single exception, these works rest entirely upon secondary sources, sources which in great part must be termed dated and obsolete. Since the new *Handbuch der Schweizer Geschichte* (Zürich: Bericht Haus) although prepared has not yet been published, it will be necessary in the meantime to make use of the numerous monographs and especially of the articles in historical journals, like the *Schweizerische Zeitschrift für Geschichte*, that have appeared since Dierauer. Indeed, for some chapters, like for example "The Golden Sword," it would be absolutely essential to consult also primary sources, historiographical witnesses. (For a bibliography of these, see F. Feller and E. Bonjour, *Geschichtsschreibung der Schweiz* [Basel and Stuttgart: 1962, 2 vols.]). The picture of events which you will thus gain will differ so fundamentally from that presented in your chapters, that it simply would not be possible for me to contribute anything useful by making individual comments here and there. I can only advise you to broaden the source material on which you rely, being guided in their selection by *Bibliographien zur Schweizer Geschichte* which have appeared since Dierauer's time and also consulting the above-cited survey by Feller and Bonjour. Only in this way can you

present an account which will correspond to the state of knowledge of the present day.

To this I replied:

I appreciate the trouble you took and quite understand your view point. You are not the only one of our readers who has reacted similarly; and I do not doubt that a great many specialists will be equally unhappy with our treatment of the seventeen other chapters which constitute the case studies in our book.

Our task, however, is not the traditional historian's task of restoring the past for its own sake; nor do we claim to carry out original studies which base themselves upon primary sources, which consider the relevant current professional discussion, and which try to move the understanding of the expert a little further. Our goal is not to understand a little better the relationship of Charles the Bold of Burgundy and Louis XI of France to the Swiss Confederation. Our goal is rather to see whether statistical correlations exist among certain variables. The function of our narratives is simply to set these variables in their historical context as we understand it. Such a setting helps the reader completely unfamiliar with Swiss history to understand the coding, even if the setting as we describe it turns out to be somewhat distorted.

Now unfortunately it is not possible for us to take the obviously excellent advice you have given us. If we wished to become experts on Swiss history, of course, we would have to do just what you say, but that is not our goal. Our goal is that of comparative study for hypothesis testing. We need to know something about each historical period to code it, but we need not know everything. To drive on the highway from Zürich to Bern, a good road map is essential; but a detailed topographical map is not needed. To *build* that highway, the engineer needs a good topographical map, showing fine detail accurately. The kind of map you need depends upon the use you plan to make of it.

If you think that Swiss historians will be outraged at our failure to consider any of the research since Dierauer, can you imagine how Chinese historians will react? Our main source of data for ancient and medieval China was an eighteenth-century French translation of a sixteenth-century Manchu translation of a twelfth-century Chinese compendium—again a secondary work. All the while magnificent primary sources are readily available to anyone who reads literary Chinese, and there are libraries of critical scholarship interpreting these sources. We look at primary sources only if they are more accessible (in

English, French, German, or Spanish) than secondary works—
and this means that their organization must be such that we
can readily find our way through them. We make no attempt
to familiarize ourselves with scholarly discussion. If we are very
fortunate, there may be a scholarly survey which does all that
for us—as Dierauer's did in his day for his generation.

The standards of scholarship for comparative studies, I submit,
are quite different ones than the standards for monographic
original investigation. Nevertheless, we have been saved from the
worst consequences of our necessarily superficial approach by
the kindly and tolerant help of many colleagues who called our
attention to many errors of fact or interpretation. The important
thing for us is that so far, no one has challenged *any* of our trait
codings!

Data Quality Control

For cross-historical surveys, data accuracy is an entirely different
sort of problem than it is for historical monographs. Of course, we
want all our data codings to be accurate. But in our situation,
unlike that of the historiographer, it is *not* true that the greater
the proportion of inaccurate data, the less trustworthy are our final
results. This last statement is immensely important.

Let me explain. In cross-historical surveys, we seek correlations. The higher the correlations, the more useful our results.
The more random error, the lower the correlations. Hence, with
us, instead of saying the less accurate the data, the less trustworthy
are its results, we say instead, the less accurate the data, the less
impressive are its results. For our correlations reflect the degree of
accuracy of our codings and of the data on which they are based.

This brings us to an apparent paradox. If a cross-historical
survey results in high correlations—correlations very unlikely
to have occurred by chance—then any evidence of random error in
the work does not *decrease* our confidence in its results, it *increases*
them. I repeat: evidence of random error in such a case does not
decrease our confidence in its results, it *increases* them. Since random
errors tend to lower correlations, such evidence of random error
tends only to make us believe that the true correlations must be
even higher. If we get results this impressive despite such random
error, how much more impressive would not an accurate study have
been?

Thus there are only two criteria of data inaccuracy in a cross-historical survey: statistically impressive results which are most unlikely to have been produced by chance, and absence of evidence of *systematic* nonrandom error.

While random errors tend to lower the magnitude of correlations, systematic errors sometimes can raise it. Thus a correlation can seem to reflect the behavior of the people studied, while in fact it only reflects consistent tendencies in the kinds of mistakes made—or lies told—in the historical records.

Therefore, our chief effort should be directed at detecting systematic errors. (For a full discussion of this topic, see my book on *Data Quality Control* [1962] and my chapter on that subject in Naroll and Cohen [1970].) Here let me briefly summarize the methods used to detect them. These can be detected if some sorts of historical reports are known to be more accurate, less subject to such errors, than other sorts of historical reports. For example, primary sources may differ in this respect from secondary sources. More recently written secondary sources may differ in this respect from those written several centuries ago. Sources written by participants may differ from those written by nonparticipating observers. More highly respected historical sources, like Thucydides or Polybius, may differ from less highly respected historical sources like Herodotus or Livy. Sources written by members of the society being described may differ from those written by outsiders. If there are systematic errors in any given trait (or variable) then there should be correlations between that trait's codings and classifications of historical source type. We offer several examples of this sort of test later in this book.

CONCEPTUALIZATION, CLASSIFICATION, AND CODING

Every competent historian who works in the history of a culture much removed from his own native culture in time or space is keenly aware of the problem of historical context. Anachronism in thinking is an error he frequently has occasion to correct in the work of his younger seminar students. One student writes of the fourteenth-century English parliament as though it were much the same sort of institution as the twentieth-century English parliament. Another student speaks of an Athenian law court as though it were administered by professional jurists with a vast body of written precedent governing both their procedure and their interpretation of law. A third student thinks of a Chinese princess of the Han dynasty as though she were a European princess of the eighteenth century.

Any cross-historical survey is faced with the problem of developing concepts and classification and coding rules which make its hypothesis test sensible in *any* historical context. But here I must say that however urgent this task may be for comparative historians, it is substantially easier than is the same task for anthropologists making cross-cultural surveys. The anthrolopologist deals with a far wider range of behavior. For example, the comparative historian need understand essentially only two kinship systems—the bilateral system of modern Europe and the patrilineal system of the Far East, India, the Middle East, and ancient Rome. The comparative anthropologist must work not only with these two types, but also with matrilineal systems, double descent systems, and Australian sections. The comparative historian has again fundamentally only two types of political systems to work with: Western constitutional systems (including limited monarchies) and so-called Oriental despotisms. The comparative ethnologist must deal not only with these two systems but also with segmentary opposition systems, and with acephelous systems (each of these major types can of course be subdivided into many subtypes). Ethnologists thus deal with a wider range of types than do historians. Within the historical profession there may remain a few unenlightened souls—like those who still explain personal habits of historical figures by genetic inheritance—who suppose that primitive societies are merely simpler versions of our own, or that primitive societies all form a single type. Each individual primitive society *is* indeed in several important ways simpler than any individual civilized society. But the range of cultural variation among primitive societies as a whole is far greater than that among civilized societies.

Therefore, a comparative historian cannot better prepare himself for conceptualization, classification, and coding than by studying some comparative ethnology. If his interest is in political affairs, he does well to study primitive political systems. If his interest is art, he does well to study the art of primitive peoples.

Also, no person is prepared to do cross-historical surveys until he has studied the main characteristics of the social, political, religious, and cultural affairs of the nine paideias listed above, during each of its major historical periods.

The result of such preparation is to make a comparativist clearly aware of the range of variation of human behavior among civilized societies. Thus he avoids the deadly trap of unthinkingly applying the concepts of his own culture—or that of some other favorite object of his study, like Toynbee's Hellenic Civilization—to foreign times and places.

Yet again I remind my reader of Goodenough's rule. What we do as historiographers is and must be kept independent of what we do as comparative historians. A historiographer is constructing a theory that will make intelligible what goes on in a particular historical period at a particular time and place. A comparative historian is trying to find patterns common to many different times and places. His data are not the primary sources of the historiographer but the patterns governing each particular historical period as the historiographer formulates them. It is by noting how these patterns vary from one period to another, and under what conditions, that the comparative historian arrives at a statement of laws governing the separate sets of laws which in turn governed the events in the respective historical periods.

With these general considerations in mind, a comparative historian with a hypothesis to test in a cross-historical survey begins by formulating a tentative definition of the variables involved. For our study here, these variables include such things as *peace, deterrence, territorial growth, cultural exchange,* and so on. To begin with, his definitions should not be precise, but vague and intuitive. Next, he needs a pilot sample of perhaps twenty historical periods widely scattered in time and space (this book is the report of such a pilot sample). He seeks to apply his tentative concepts to each such period. He collects statements in the source materials relevant to his concepts. Only then is he ready to define his concepts precisely.

There are at least four major approaches to concept definition in comparative historical studies. The *straightforward* approach measures the variable of interest directly. Our measure in this study, months of war, is an example. Wherever it is feasible to use the straightforward approach, it is preferable to do so. Use of less direct but more ingenious approaches is culpable bravura unless unavoidable.

The *event indicator* approach measures some related historical event instead of measuring the variable of interest directly. Of course, one uses this second approach when it is feasible and the first approach is not. For example, debasement of coinage can be used as an indicator of financial difficulties of the regime concerned.

The *impressionistic* coding approach uses the coder's vague, general impression as the measure of the variable. When such measures are used, it is important that they be carried out by naive coders (those who are ignorant of the hypotheses being tested). Further, these ratings should be repeated two or three times by as many independent coders. Formally measuring coder agreement then constitutes the indispensable test of reliability. The trait "Cultural Exchanges" (described on pp. 22–23 below) was coded impressionistically for this study; in other words, coders simply recorded whether, by and large, it seemed to them such exchanges were frequent or rare. (We did not run proper reliability tests for this study because this is only a pilot study and its theoretical results are inconclusive.)

The *reactive* coding approach uses the impressionistic reactions of authors of historical sources. Thus our measure of the importance of a state was the amount of space given to it in Langer.

All indirect measures require tests of *validity*. But the successful test of the hypothesis being studied itself provides a presumption of validity. Such a success requires explanation. The hypothesis being tested is one possible explanation. Indicator validity tests then direct themselves at plausible rival explanations.

For an example of the use of indirect measures to estimate the strength of a variable which could not be measured directly, see Naroll 1969. Here the relative attention given to suicide by ethnographers is shown to be a valid measure of suicide frequency among primitive tribes. This validity is, on the face of it, not at all plausible; surely it depends a great deal upon the personality of the ethnographer, how much attention he pays to suicide. But how explain the fact that in tribes whose divorce rules make divorce easy, ethnographers tend to give relatively more attention to suicide than in tribes where divorce rules are strict? How explain the fact that in tribes where marriages are usually arranged by others, ethnographers tend to give relatively more attention to suicide than in tribes where marriages are arranged by the bridal pair themselves? How explain the fact that in tribes where wars are reportedly frequent, ethnographers tend to give relatively more attention to suicide than in tribes where wars are reportedly rare? And so on for witchcraft attribution, wifebeating, homicides, and drunken brawling. For a full discussion of concept definition and coding see Naroll and Cohen (1970: chapters 1, 36, 37 and 38).

CHANCE AND TESTS OF SIGNIFICANCE

Correlations and other measures of association are conventionally measured on a scale running from +1.0 through zero to -1.0. Here +1.0 means perfect positive correlation; zero means no association; and -1.0 means perfect negative correlation—that is, the more of one, the less of the other. This measurement of relationship is part of the descriptive branch of mathematical statistics.

But given a certain correlation from a certain sample, what is the likelihood that such a correlation would occur purely by chance? Technically, the question is: In a universe where the correlation is zero, in what proportion of random samples would we except to obtain a correlation at least as large as this? Answering this question is part of the inferential branch of mathematical statistics. The question itself is called the test of significance. The null hypothesis is the hypothesis that there is no relationship in the universe—that the true correlation there is zero. The significance level produced by the test is the proportion of random samples which we would expect to yield so great a correlation if the null hypothesis is correct. If we say a correlation is significant at the 5% level, we mean that we would expect so great a result in *less* than 5% of random samples from a universe with a zero correlation.

The mathematical model deals with strictly random samples. Hence some people make the mistake of supposing that if in fact a sample is not random, a significance test is not applicable. Even if a sample is not random, we still require such a test. A significance test which fails to refute the null hypothesis is just as deadly in a nonrandom sample as in a random one. If our sample departs from randomness, however, we have an additional rival hypothesis to deal with as well. If a significance test shows that we would not often expect a result as unusual as the one we have, the null hypothesis is refuted whether the sample is random or nonrandom. We see that our results are not such as we would expect from *mere chance*. But if our sample departs from randomness, we must deal with an additional rival hypothesis—the hypothesis that our results reflect sampling bias (see the discussion of sampling above).

For more on measurement of association and tests of significance, I have already suggested that the reader consult Freeman (1965), Blalock (1960), Siegel (1956) and Kendall (1962).

The Combining, Dredging, or Mudsticking Problem

The *combing*, *dredging*, or *mudsticking* problem is that of group significance. When, as in this study, dozens or even hundreds of correlations are computed, would we not expect many of them to be nominally significant from mere chance alone? Would we not expect five correlations in one hundred to be significant at the 5% level, by definition? For technical reasons, discussed in Appendix D below (pp. 377–387), the answer to that question is not always simple. Certainly, we would never expect *more* than 5% to be significant at the 5% level; but in certain kinds of situations we know that as few as 2.5% may in fact be all we would expect.

The solution to the mudsticking problem then involves two steps. *First step :* Determine the expected frequency of nominally significant correlations at a given level. For technical reasons, it may be convenient for that level to be not much more than 1%; then the Poisson tables of Molina can be confidently and conveniently used in the second step. If the variables in the study are all continuously distributed and the statistical measures likewise are continuous distribution measures (e.g., product moment correlations, t tests), then the expected frequency may be taken as nominal. If not (e.g., if we are using four-fold contingency tables, or tau, gamma, lambda, or dx measures of association), then the "whiskers" method of Banks and Textor (1963:51) must be used. Dummy variables are set up (Banks and Textor named these "nations with red whiskers," "nations with green whiskers," and so on). Periods in the sample are given "whiskers" scores from tables of random numbers. These whiskers scores then are precisely the sort of measurement which the null hypothesis has in mind — a purely random one. No correlations between whiskers variables and any other can have any meaning at all; such a correlation can result only from pure chance and must be meaningless.

The important technical point is that the whiskers variables must be given mathematically the same distribution as the real measuments. This requirement can be satisfied by treating in turn each set of real codings. Each score should be randomly reassigned to another period in the sample. Needless to say, a different series of random numbers (a distinct line or column) should be used for each such variable.

The real variables are then correlated with the whiskers variables. The proportion of correlations significant at the given level—say 1%—is the required result.

The thoughtful reader will perceive that this method of solving the mudsticking problem is quite expensive if the calculations are done by hand. However, it is simple enough and cheap enough if the calculations are done by a computer.

If the investigator computes only a small number of real correlations, the mudsticking problem is unimportant and this step can be skipped. If he computes a large number, it will certainly pay him to use a computer in any case and so this step will not be a great deal of additional trouble.

Second Step: Multiply the number of meaningful correlations (not whiskers correlations) by the fraction found to be significant among the whiskers correlations. The result gives the expected frequency of significant meaningful correlations under the mudsticking null hypothesis. Call that result a. Note the number of meaningful correlations significant at the given level and call that result c. In table 2 of Molina (1942) look up the probability of obtaining c significant correlations when a are expected. The table entry gives the proportion of studies, or groups of correlations, which could be expected to yield at least that large a number by chance alone. If that proportion itself is less than .010000, then the mudsticking hypothesis is refuted. Then correlations as a group are significant. At least some of them, presumably those with the smallest significance levels, cannot be then explained by the null hypothesis—by chance. (Note that where the number of meaningful correlations is not more than 100, it is better to use the tables of Weintraub [1963]).

GALTON'S PROBLEM

All the statistical tests of significance we have been discussing assume independence of cases. That is, each of the historical periods in the cross-historical survey is mathematically treated as though it were a completely fresh, independent experiment not in any way influenced by the events of any of the other historical periods in the study. Similarly, it is assumed that no two historical periods in the study are influenced in common by any single event or situation not there considered.

In fact, of course, these mathematical assumptions are surely known to be invalid. How then can we test the significance of our results? Anthropologists call this the problem of cultural diffusion. Culture traits are widely spread by borrowing or migration. In this way, very high cross-cultural correlations can be produced. For example, among California Indians there is a perfect correlation in the distribution of patrilineal-totemic clans, flageolets, carrying frames made of sticks and cords, oval plate pottery, large fish scoops, squared mullers, and preference for twins. These seven traits are all found among the three Yuman tribes of the southeast corner of the state but nowhere else in aboriginal California. Such correlations are clearly to be explained as mere artifacts of joint diffusion and tell us nothing about functional relationships among them.

This same problem of diffusion of culture traits faces the comparative historian. But for him it is many times more intense. At least the anthropologist only counts each tribe once. But in a cross-historical survey like this one, we may count the same nation several times, once in the third century B.C., again in the second century after Christ, and so on. Clearly many traits which were present in Rome in 150 B.C. continue to be present in Rome in A.D. 250. Cultural characteristics obviously diffuse in large numbers from ancestors to descendants.

Half a dozen solutions to this problem have now been worked out. They all depend upon the assumption that as a rule, cultures nearer to one another in space (or time) are more likely to be influenced by diffusion than those more distant. The simplest and most convenient solution is the linked pair test, which is applied and explained in this study on pages 33 through 36 and 351 below (for a full discussion of the problem, see Naroll and Cohen 1970: chap. 47).

Causal Analysis of Correlations

The danger of making hasty causal inferences from statistical correlations is one of the first things taught to students of statistical inference. To show that A is correlated with B is far from enough to establish that A is the cause and B is the effect. Every instructor has his favorite example of a nonsense argument of this sort as a warning. My own is this one: there was a high correlation between the price of rum in Havana and the salary of Congregational ministers in New England throughout the seventeenth and eighteenth centuries. What a fascinating theoretical bubble of triangular trade in African slaves, West Indian rum, and Spanish gold this correlation blows up. However, the bubble bursts as soon as one reflects that because of general price rises there is, over a long period of time, a correlation between the price of almost anything and the price of almost anything else.

It is well to begin by defining exactly what I mean by cause and effect. In order to speak of a variable as a possible cause, it is necessary to recognize the possibility that, at least in imagination, some actor might vary the state of the cause. Thus I can imagine Archimedes, given a sufficiently long and weightless lever and a place to set it, out there in a space-suit, moving the world. From this model of an actor manipulating the supposed cause comes this concept: if the causal variable is varied, any other variables whose probabilities are *thereby* changed, are defined as effects. When I change the supposed cause, does this change affect the odds on the supposed effect? Does this change make the supposed effect more likely—or less likely—to exist at all? or does this change make some dimension of the supposed effect likely to increase or likely to decrease?

The problem of causal analysis of correlations is usually thought of as the two-variable problem. If A and B are correlated, is A the cause and B the effect? Or is B the cause and A the effect? Or are they both common effects of some third factor—one not involved in the study—about which we know nothing? This third factor, this hypothetical unknown general cause, is sometimes called a *lurking variable* because it lurks in the theoretical darkness, ready to spring upon our naive causal theories and gobble them up.

However, in recent decades and especially in the past ten years, a number of new methods have been developed to deal with the problem of causal analysis of correlations. All these methods must have more than two variables to be of any use. None are generally applicable in all situations to all problems; all impose limitations and restrictions of one kind or another. Most of them do *not* involve time sequence, and the application of these to cross-historical surveys would not differ from their applications to other kinds of data (for a detailed review, see Naroll and Cohen 1970: chaps. 4, 5, and 6).

However, the cross-historical survey method opens up special possibilities of causal analysis not open to many other kinds of behavioral science studies. Since its data is chronologically ordered, it is specially convenient to study time sequence. Let us then look at the problem of causal analysis of correlations when time sequence can be established between the variables.

Here we immediately remind ourselves that from the beginning of formal logic, philosophers have warned against the fallacy of *post hoc ergo propter hoc*. Sequence by itself does not establish cause-effect relationship any more than does correlation by itself. But what about a combination of the two? Suppose we can say of variable *A* and variable *B* that not only are they highly correlated, but also that *A* usually precedes *B*?

Such a sequential tendency certainly offers formidable support for a cause-effect relationship. If, time and again, when *A* happens, then a few years later you can usually look for *B* to follow, it certainly suggests a cause-effect relationship. True, such a relationship is not a sure and certain proof of causation. Consider a common electric toaster. Put two pieces of bread in the top, push down, and on the side a telltale red lamp lights to warn the housewife that the toaster is heating. Some minutes later, when the bread has browned, the machine pops up the toast, turns itself off and there you are! Now notice that there is a perfect correlation between the lighting of the red telltale lamp and the toasting of the bread. Furthermore, the lamp always lights up first, the toast always pops up sometime later. Perfect correlation plus prefect sequence. Yet there is of course the lurking factor of the electric current, which not only lights the telltale lamp but also heats the elements which actually toast the bread.

So, with this model fallacy of the toaster's telltale lamp in mind, we must curb our enthusiasm about the combination of correlation with sequence.

And yet, in the toaster example, there is not merely a simple lurking variable involved, but rather a whole system: the electric current, the electric cord, the wiring, the switches, the heating elements, the sensors—an elaborate system.

Again, consider another example. Among human males, at the onset of adolescence, the voice changes, becoming deeper in tone. Sometime later, the beard grows out. Now again we have perfect correlation together with perfect sequence. An idiot scientist, given this perfect correlation together with perfect sequence, might infer that the voice change was the cause and the later growth of beard, the effect. But again we have a lurking factor — this time the maturation process.

Again in the voice-and-beard example, we have another system, the entire maturation system of the organism, governing its whole whole growth and development.

I submit that where there is a high correlation together with a strong sequential tendency the rival hypothesis of a lurking variable is on the face of it rather weak. For we must suspect here not merely some single unobserved factor, but an entire, unobserved *system*. For this reason, to establish the combination of correlation-and-sequence creates a strong presumption in favor of the causal hypothesis that the precedent variable is the cause and the subsequent variable the effect.

To measure the conjuction of correlation and sequence, Campbell's cross-lagged correlation (Rozelle and Campbell 1969; Pelz and Andrews 1964) is a convenient device. Figure 1 is a diagram of the model.

EARLIER TIME   LATER TIME
A   A'

B   B'
                          Fig. 1

Let A be the supposed cause, for example, a change in the value system. Let B be the supposed effect, for example, frequency of civil wars. Suppose, as in the model cross-historical survey sketched at the beginning of this preface, we survey 100 sample paideia-centuries. In each such century, for each such paideia, we take a look at the first decade and the sixth decade. In each of these two decades, we measure Instability of Values and Frequency of Civil War. The first decade is our *Earlier Time*; the sixth decade is our *Later Time*. We correlate the Earlier Time Instability of Values with the Later Time Frequency of Civil War $(r_{AB'})$. We also correlate Earlier Time Frequency of Civil War with the Later Time Instability of Values $(r_{A'B})$.

If when Instability of Values increases, this tends to make Frequency of Civil War increase, we expect the first correlation $(r_{AB'})$ to be significantly higher than the second correlation $(r_{A'B})$. If so, this supports the hypothesis that A tends to precede B.

To establish this much is not to prove with certainty the correctness of Sorokin's hypothesis, but it does establish a presumption far stronger than that upon which human beings are accustomed to conduct most of their practical affairs—like civil wars and values assumptions themselves. Such a presumption would remain established until a critic could suggest a plausible rival explanation—most likely not a simple lurking variable but a complex lurking system.

Paucity of Relevant Data

Historical literature yields most abundant materials on warfare, politics, religion, and the arts. Economics and sociology are less richly documented even though here, too, much information is available. Least documented of the major behavioral sciences is psychology. But even here there is a rich biographical literature not only in the West but also in China. (Although this biographical literature is simply raw data; almost no biographical studies of people who lived more than 100 years ago have been carried out by people with any formal training in psychology.)

Thus there are tens of millions of words of data about the past life of ten or twelve paideias, covering one or a dozen centuries each. Still, the comparativist frequently will find that the topic he wishes to study is recorded so indirectly or so inaccurately that he cannot measure his variables directly. He must then seek to devise indirect measurements. Such devices are a fertile field for ingenuity. In decades and centuries of comparative historical scholarship to come, the chief problem of cross-historical surveys doubtless will become this one. Most other problems of cross-historical method are susceptible of clear and final solution. But the problem of indirect measurement seems to be one which, generation after generation, will challenge the ingenuity of comparative historians. I hope that, generation after generation, ever more novel and ingenious devices of this sort may be developed.

Two examples can illustrate the kind of device for the indirect measurement I have in mind. Whiting and Child in a cross-cultural survey measured "generalized fear of human beings" by rating the importance of psychological fixations of witchcraft (1953); they measured many other pervading underlying subconscious fears of people from tribe to tribe by rating their theories of illness and their therapeutic practices. Naroll compared suicide frequencies cross-culturally by comparing relative attention to suicide by ethnographers (1969). For a comprehensive survey of the use of indirect measurements in the behavioral sciences see Webb, Campbell, Schwartz, and Sechrest (1966).

Such indirect measures, as I said earlier in the section on conceptualization, create a need for validation. If suicide frequency is measured indirectly through comparing the attention given to it by ethnographers, how do we know that it is measured accurately? or indeed that it is measured at all? There are at least three main validation strategies. The first would be to develop more than one indirect measure of the same variable and compare results. The second would be to consider the possible sources of distortion or bias and measure these. For example, attention to suicide among primitive tribes may be biased by the ethnographer's own personal tendencies toward suicide. This tendency could be measured by comparing the suicide wordage ratio of ethnographers who later in fact committed suicide with those who did not. Again, attention to suicide among primitive tribes may be biased by the natives' attitude toward suicide; if they disapprove of it, they may talk less about it and hence provide the ethnographer with less material for his report. This native attitude may itself be measured.

These measures of possible sources of bias are nothing but specific data quality control factors. That is to say, they are data quality control factors useful only for this special measure—suicide wordage ratio—rather than being useful in general. Like other data quality control factors, they can provide reassurance in two ways. If there is no relationship between the control factor and the measure, the hypothesis of bias may be considered implausible and may be rejected. Thus, if ethnographers who later commit suicide do *not* differ significantly in their attention to suicide from those who do not later commit suicide, the hypothesis of ethnographer's bias is not supported. If, on the contrary, there is indeed a relationship between the control factor and the measure, the control factor may still reassure the investigator and his readers such a bias has not actually affected the conclusions of his study. Such reassurance might arise for example in the following situation. A cross-cultural survey might establish that suicide wordage ratio is indeed positively related to suicidal tendency of the ethnographer. It might also establish that tribes where divorce is reportedly easy attract more attention to suicide by their ethnographers than tribes where divorce is reportedly difficult. Finally it might also establish that while suicidal ethnographers do devote more attention to suicide than nonsuicidal ethnographers, they do not differ in their reports on divorce. That is to say, the proportion of reportedly easy divorce does not differ significantly between suicidal ethnographers and nonsuicidal ethnographers. Given this set of conditions, it would appear that the suicide wordage ratio is indeed a biased measure. But it would also appear that this bias does not affect the validity of its use in a test of correlation between suicide frequency and divorce frequency. For further discussion of the use of control factors in data quality control, see Naroll and Cohen (1970: chap. 44).

The third validation strategy is the one actually used in Naroll (1969) to validate suicide wordage ratio as a comparative measure of suicide frequency. This strategy consists in showing that hypothetical sources of bias of the indicator seem most unlikely to be related to the other variables, even though such a bias is not actually measured. Suicide wordage ratio among primitive tribes is not only correlated with divorce rules, but also with marriage arrangement practices, homicide frequency, wifebeating, witchcraft attribution, drunken brawling, and frequency of warfare. It makes less sense to explain *all* these correlations as artifacts either of the ethnographer's tendency to suicide or the tribe's attitude toward suicide. It makes more sense to explain them as reflecting variations in actual suicide rates.

REGIONAL AND TEMPORAL VARIATION

It is possible that a given correlation may reflect only the special circumstances of a given paideia, or a given era in the world's history. Therefore, a cross-historical survey would rerun its main hypotheses tests separately for each paideia and each major time block (e.g., a 500-year period). Correlations relied upon in the main test should be present in all these reruns as well (in the reruns, of course, because of much smaller sample sizes, significance tests will be pointless). An alternate method used in chapter 24 is simply to correlate each regional and temporal control with each theoretical variable. Where these correlations are small and nonsignificant, regional or temporal differences cannot be very important.

DEVIANT CASE ANALYSIS

The computer program which is used to run the main hypothesis tests should not only compute associations and test them for significance. It should also print out scatter diagrams. These diagrams show the particular instances which tend to support the hypothesis best and those which are most inconsistent with it. Those instances which are most inconsistent with the hypothesis should be studied for explanation of their departure from theoretical expectations. (By an instance, of course, I mean here a particular paideia-period).

Deviant case analysis in cross-cultural surveys has been thoroughly reviewed by Köbben (1967). Köbben's categories of deviant cases may be grouped into two main types. The first type consists of causal patterns requiring multivariate analysis. For example, there seem to be many reasons why primitive societies vary greatly in suicide frequency. One of these reasons seems to be variations in case or difficulty of divorce. Another seems to be variations in the freedom of young people to arrange their own marriages without interference by relatives or customary proscriptions. Thus it is that a cross-cultural survey may turn up a very high correlation between divorce freedom and suicide frequency. Yet there can be striking exceptions. In Tribe X, say, divorce is impossible. Yet nevertheless in Tribe X there is much suicide, for here marriages are arranged for young girls by their parents; and these arrangements look chiefly toward a generous bride-price. A generous bride-price is most often offered by older, sexually unattractive men, and many young girls hang themselves to avoid such marriages.

The second major type of deviant case reflects one of the methodological problems already discussed. The data may be erroneously recorded, or reported, or coded. Cultural diffusion may have led to cultural lag. Or there may be trouble with the comparativist's concepts: conceptualization, classification, coding, or indicator problems.

GENERATIONS OF CROSS-HISTORICAL SURVEYS

Three major cross-historical surveys can be classed as first-generation cross-historical surveys. As such they made no use of sampling, nor correlational measurements, nor statistical inference. Like first-generation cross-cultural surveys, they thought in terms of encompassing all relevant data (though only one of them actually made all the main Old-World higher civilizations its universe of study).

The studies I have in mind are Sorokin (1937-41), Kroeber (1944), and Eisenstadt (1963). The distinguishing marks that make all of these studies crude cross-historical surveys are three: First, they thought in terms of formal hypothesis testing over "all history." Second, they collected and formally coded all the data that seemed relevant, whether it fit their hypothesis or was inconsistent with it (this fact is in crucial contrast with most philosophers of history like Toynbee, Spengler, Quigley, or Coulborn, who present only data which supports their hypothesis). Third, they measured and counted.

I myself have had a hand in three cross-historical surveys (Naroll 1967, Naroll et al. 1971, and the present study). These three might well be classed as second-generation cross-historical surveys. They use formal sampling methods, they use controls for cultural diffusion, and two of them have formal data quality controls. All three use formal statistical inference; all use formal and objective unit definitions; and two of them test correlational hypotheses. However, none of the three carry out all of the methodological procedures here recommended.

Plans for a third-generation cross-historical survey are being developed in the Department of Anthropology at the State University of New York at Buffalo by me and two of my students. Let us hope that the developing interest in cross-cultural and cross-national surveys will stimulate many other such studies by other behavioral scientists.

Raoul Naroll

★ ★ ★

ACKNOWLEDGMENTS

THE PRESENT VOLUME is a completely revised, recoded, recalculated, and much expanded version of "Deterrence in History," by Raoul Naroll.*

Our largest debt is owed to Thomas W. Milburn, director of Project Michelson at the Naval Ordnance Test Station, China Lake, California. He suggested the research, proposed the Palo Alto conference on our research design, and gave freely of his counsel throughout the project. Through Milburn and Project Michelson we are indebted to the United States Navy for its support of the entire project. Presumably the naval authorities must have hoped — as we ourselves had hoped — that our findings would have solidly supported the deterrence hypothesis. But when on the contrary we found deterrence apparently an unsuccessful strategy, there was never the slightest hint on the part of anyone concerned that we might hedge our report or shade our findings. In these times when support of social science research by the Department of Defense is frequently challenged, we would like to record our appreciation for generous funding and a completely free hand in our scientific policies, our interpretations and our publication of results.

The research was conducted partly under the auspices of the San Fernando Valley State College Foundation, partly under those of Northwestern University, and partly under those of the Institute for Cross-Cultural Research. Final computer runs and manuscript preparation were supported by the State University of New

* In *Theory and Research on the Causes of War*, ed. Dean G. Pruitt and Richard C. Snyder (Prentice Hall, 1969), pp. 150—64.

York at Buffalo. The Council for International Studies and World Affairs at this university gave additional help.

For their contributions to this research through their role as trustees of the Institute for Cross-Cultural Studies, we are grateful to David G. Hays, Alfred Goldberg, Martin Katz, Bess Kaufman, the late Carl D. Strouse, and the late Alexander Cole.

Our research design was greatly stregthened as the result of a conference on the project held at Palo Alto in October 1961. Participants included Chairman Richard C. Snyder, Richard A. Brody, John P. Gillin, Edwin Lieuwen, Lincoln Moses, George E. Mowry, Robert C. North, Philburn Ratoosh, and Richard N. Rosecrance.

We also thank Richard Brody, Lincoln Moses, and T.A. Tatje for their suggestions on statistical methods. People who have read and commented upon all or part of the first draft of the book include Marjorie Berlincourt, Kenneth Boulding, Donald T. Campbell, Allen Dirrim, Robert Heath, George Hourani, Karel Hulicka, Darrel Morse, John Roberts, Laurence A. Schneider, Marc Sieber, and John Sirjamaki.

Research assistants who made substantial contributions to the study include Gail Belanger, Enid Margolis, Eva Pfister, Lucille Rosenzweig, Maria Rudisch, and Ola Vorster. The maps were drawn by Gordon Schmahl.

Needless to say, the authors alone are responsible for errors and shortcomings.

CHAPTER 1

★ ★ ★

MILITARY DETERRENCE,
NATIONAL EXPANSION, AND PEACE

INTRODUCTION

THIS STUDY is an investigation of the use and purpose of military forces in civilized societies whose histories are largely histories of warfare. True, there are some peaceful civilized societies, but these are few in number, and even they are societies with a history of warlikeness. Consider three societies most conspicuous for their peaceableness in the twentieth century: Tibet, Switzerland, and Sweden. During the T'ang dynasty, Tibet was the scourge of China (see chapter 5). The Swiss won their independence through much hard fighting; in the sixteenth century they were considered by many to have the finest infantry in Europe, and in the seventeenth and eighteenth centuries mercenary Swiss regiments were a major Swiss export. During the Thirty Years' War (1618–1648), under Gustavus Adolphus, Sweden became for a time the dominant military power in northern Europe.

Comparative studies of primitive societies lead to the general conclusion that the scope of warfare broadens as the level of civilization rises. Among most of the simplest hunting and gathering tribes, warfare functions chiefly as a mechanism to revenge homicide or to defend territory from incursions. Further up the scale of social evolution, its scope broadens to include next booty, then prestige for warriors, and finally political control (see Wright 1942, Otterbein 1970, and Naroll 1964a, 1966).

It is not too much to say that the rise and fall of empires is the most prominent feature of recorded history. Of the twenty-nine most conspicuous empires in the Old World during the last five thousand years, all but one were established by force of arms (Naroll, 1967).

Almost all known human societies are prepared to go to war to defend their territories. The few exceptions fall into two classes: the peaceful, simple hunting and gathering societies which inhabit the mountainous jungle on the fringes of large, powerful civilizations, avoiding outsiders and fleeing if trespassers invade their territories; and the few peaceful peoples who were so geographically isolated and unthreatened for so long that they forgot about the possibility of invasion. The best-known examples of the first group are the Semang of Malaya, and the best-known of the second group are the Moriori of Chatham Island and the Polar Eskimos of northwestern Greenland.

These rare cases of peoples among whom war is unknown, or nearly so, suggest two important messages for us as we consider the problem of the function of military force. First, and most obvious, is that territorial security does not exist. Hardly any people expect to be left in peace (the Moriori did, but a handful of warlike and cannibalistic Maori ate them). Second, and less relevant to our present inquiry, the complete absence of any kind of organized combat among a few isolated human groups suggests to us that people may not be genetically warlike.

Today those of us who watch international affairs are uneasily aware that military strength is a leading factor in a nation's influence on world affairs (economic wealth and ideological leadership are likewise important, needless to say). Furthermore, it seems plausible to suppose that the stronger the military forces of a nation, the more securely it holds its territory. Presumably for most cultures the maintenance of political independence is essential to the maintenance of the culture pattern. We do intend to investigate here the relationship between the strength of armed forces and the gain or loss of national territory. We naturally supposed that the larger, stronger, and better the quality of a nation's armed forces, the more likely a nation would be to gain territory, or at least to maintain territorial stability. But most important, we are studying the arguments concerning the merits of military strength as a factor in maintaining peace.

Deterrence Theory

Such merits are urged by the proponents of the *deterrence theory* of military preparation who argue, "We are peaceful, but we are menaced by hostile aggressors. If we are strong, we can remain at peace; but if we are weak, we invite attack." The deterrence theory thus holds that military preparations make for peace by forcing would-be aggressors to consider the cost. The advocates of deterrence argue that it reduces the probability of enemy attack by making clear the net loss or lower net gain that the attack would cost. They point out that there is no defense against a nuclear war, and consequently our best hope is for a stable, credible deterrent.

This point of view has been expressed in one form or another by P. H. Backus (1959:23–29), Glenn H. Snyder (1959:457; 1960: 163–78; 1961:10–15, 43–45, 266, 287, 289), Arthur T. Hadley (1961), Charles G. McClintock and Dale J. Hekhuis (1961:230–53), Thomas W. Milburn (1959:138–45), Herman Kahn (n.d., 22–55), Dexter Perkins (1960), and Lawrence S. Finkelstein (1962), among a large group of others. In addition, Richard Brody (1960:443–57), and Richard C. Snyder and James A. Robinson (1961) have abstracted much literature on deterrence.

For a deterrent to be stable it must be invulnerable so that increased effort against it would be futile. The advocates of this point of view feel that mutual invulnerability would stabilize the arms race, resulting in a so-called balance of terror. This balance presumably would allow conflicts to shift to limited wars, and from there to an eventual stabilization, and finally to the reduction in the number of wars. Since all these aspects are negative, a feeling has developed that positive aspects of deterrence also should be employed wherever possible to reinforce the negative aspects (Milburn, 1959; Richard C. Snyder and James A. Robinson, 1961: 133; Glenn Snyder, 1960:163). Positive deterrence might be accomplished by providing an aggressor with an area where he may practice harmless aggression or where he may win prestige. Alliances and treaties, trade agreements, and sharing new scientific gains with an aggressor are cited as examples of positive deterrence. Since the recent findings of learning theory show that punishment alone does little to change the basic motives of behavior, but that punishment combined with reward can be effective in changing behavior, the proponents of positive deterrence think that further study should be given to its use as a supplement to negative deterrence.

Arms Race Theory

Directly contradicting these deterrence theorists are the proponents of the *arms race theory*, who argue that an increase in armaments by any one nation only leads to an increase of armaments by its potential rivals.

Thus, at best, there is a vicious cycle of an ever-increasing proportion of wealth being sunk into wasteful weapons systems; at worst, the race culminates in a war to dissipate the ever-increasing tension.

The arms-race theory has been a popular topic in recent years and there is a large body of literature on it. The point of view that military preparations tend to make war more likely has been expressed by Quincy Wright (1942, Vol. 2:690–91), Arthur Lee Burns (1959:326–42), Mulford Sibley (1962), J. David Singer (1962:169–71), Henry A. Kissinger (1957), Sidney Lens (n.d.), and D. F. Fleming (1962), among others. These men all hold that in an arms race each side strives for military superiority. It is not enough to have parity, for the dangers of underestimating the strength of the rival and of his achieving a technological breakthrough still remain. Each side may interpret his rival's capability as intent. Thus, the arms race becomes circular and self-generating and continues to grow more dangerous. Since the deterrent cannot remain truly stable, no real security is gained by an arms race. Only one resolution to the problem seems to occur to these authors, and that is some system of arms control or disarmament.

Hypotheses Tested

To test these theories of military purpose, this study measured correlations among thirty variables. Our original aim was to test the relationships between three dependent variables and six groups of independent variables (a total of twenty-seven). It turned out that we learned as much from the correlations among the independent variables as from the hypotheses we originally planned to test.

Our three dependent variables were: (1) Frequency of War (2) Territorial Growth, and (3) Territorial Instability. We tested hypotheses related to these variables to: (1) the Defensive or Offensive Stance of the state studied, (2) military situation (five measures of military preparation which constitute our measures of deterrent strength), (3) three measures of geographical situation, (4) six measures of the diplomatic situation, (5) four measures of the general cultural situation, and (6) six measures of the admisitrative situation, i.e., political characteristics of the state studied. In other words, not only did we directly investigate the relationship of military preparation to war frequency and territorial change, we also investigated the relationship of a variety of other factors that seemed conceivably relevant.

Our basic prediction was that states assuming a defensive stance with strong military preparations and favorable diplomatic, geographic, political, and cultural circumstances would tend to avoid war (see table 1).

We were looking, in other words, for a formula of *peace and stability through strength*.

Let us turn now to these variables whose correlations we hoped would yield such a formula.

VARIABLES STUDIED

All variables are studied from the point of view of a particular state (or, as in chapter 22, a particular coalition), called the *Conspicuous State*. Furthermore, the international military, political, and cultural relations of that state are studied from the point of view of its relationships to one other state, called its *Conspicuous Rival*.

By Conspicuous State we mean that state which is considered to have been most active in international situations of conflict (war, diplomatic negotiations) in the paideia concerned during the decade in question (see chapter 2 for criteria of choice). By Conspicuous Rival we mean that state which is considered to be the most active diplomatic or military opponent of the Conspicuous State during the decade in question (see chapter 2 for criteria of choice).

TABLE 1.1

HYPOTHESES TESTED

Key

CS = Conspicuous State of each period sampled

CR = Conspicuous Rival of CS (i.e., in Europe, from 1675 to 1685, France would be the CS and Austria the CR)

Test No.	Independent Variables	Dependent Variables		
		CS & CR have peace	CS has Territorial Stability	CS has Territorial growth
1.1	CS has stronger Armed force than CR; CS in Defensive Stance	Yes	—	—
1.2	CS has stronger Armed force than CR; CS in Defensive Stance	—	Yes	—
1.3	CS has stronger forces than CR; Stance Immaterial	—	—	Yes
2.1	CS has more mobile army than CR; CS in Defensive Stance	Yes	—	—
2.2	CS has more mobile army than CR; CS in Defensive Stance	—	Yes	—
2.3	CS has more mobile army than CR; Stance Immaterial	—	—	Yes
3.1	CS has better quality Armed Force than CR; CS in Defensive Stance	Yes	—	—
3.2	CS has better quality Armed Force than CR; CS in Defensive Stance	—	Yes	—
3.3	CS has better quality Armed Force than CR; Stance Immaterial	—	—	Yes
4.1	CS has extensive Border fortifications; CS in Defensive Stance	Yes	—	—
4.2	CS has extensive Border Fortifications; Stance Immaterial	—	Yes	—
5.0	CS announces intention to respond to CR's threats; Stance Immaterial	Yes	—	—
6.0	CS joins coalition against CR; CS in Defensive Stance	Yes	—	—
6.1	CS joins coalition against CR; CS in Defensive Stance	—	Yes	—

Test No.	Independent Variables	Dependent Variables		
		CS & CR have peace	CS has Territorial Stability	CS has Territorial growth
7.1	Diplomatic negotiations between CS and CR comparatively *active*	Yes	—	—
7.2	Diplomatic negotiations between CS and CR comparatively *intense*	Yes	—	—
8.0	CS and CR have comparatively active Cultural Exchange (students, missionaries, entertainers)	Yes	—	—
9.0	CS gives CR Benefits or vice versa (subsidies, women, honors)	Yes	—	—
10.1	CS ruler has had long experience in office	—	—	Yes
10.2	CS ruler is over forty-five years old	Yes	—	—
10.3	CS ruler hereditary monarch; aged twenty to forty at beginning of decade; CS is centralized state	No	—	—
10.4	CS ruler hereditary monarch	No	—	—
10.5	CS ruler hereditary monarch	—	No	—
11.0	CS has internecine civil violence	Yes	—	—
12.0	CS and CR are comparatively close to one another geographically	No	—	—
13.0	According to rating of secondary source, CS is markedly greater power in international affairs than CR	Yes	—	—
14.0	CS and CR have previous history of war with each other	No	—	—
15.1	Natural barriers (mountains, deserts, unfordable bodies of water) separate CS from CR	Yes	—	—
15.2	Natural barriers separate CS from CR	—	Yes	—
16.0	Chief cities of CS are relatively close to the frontier	No	—	—
17.0	CS a more highly centralized state than CR	—	—	**Yes**

Dependent Variables

War Frequency (Months of War, Variable Code Number A732)

For how many months in the decade studied was the Conspicuous State at war with its Conspicuous Rival? This basic question is simple enough, but the question of the precise definition of a state of war and a state of peace, and the related question of how we might infer the existence of either, proved to be the difficult problems. The following definitions make up our solutions to these problems.

RULE 1.0. A State of War begins with any Warlike Act (unless the act is disavowed by the leaders of the armed groups involved) and thus ends a state of peace. For example, in 1937, Japanese troops shelled and sank the American warship *Panay;* but the Japanese government later apologized for this act and paid indemnities, thus disavowing the acts of its soldiers.

DEFINITION 1.1. A Warlike Act is defined as the commitment of one or more of the following acts:

    1.11 Open Combat between territorial teams or parts of them.

    1.12. Open Invasion by an armed group of one territorial team of another group's territory without the consent of that group.

    1.13. A Public Declaration by the leaders of one territorial team that a state of war exists between that territorial team and another.

DEFINITION 1.2 *Open Combat* is defined as licit, public, lethal group conflict.

RULE 2.0. *A State of Peace* between two territorial teams is established by any one of the following acts or conditions:

DEFINITION 2.1 A *Newly Established Territorial Team* is considered to be at peace with any other territorial team until one of them commits a warlike act against the other.

RULE 2.1. The conclusion of a peace treaty or armistice by the leaders of two territorial teams at war with each other establishes peace between them until the next warlike act occurs.

DEFINITION 2.21. A *Peace Treaty* is an agreement between opposing forces hitherto engaged in open combat to refrain from such combat for an indefinite period of time.

DEFINITION 2.22. An *Armistice* is an agreement between leaders of opposing forces engaged in open combat to refrain from such combat for a stated period of time.

RULE 2.2 If a truce occurs between two territorial teams at war, peace is presumed to exist beginning two years after the beginning of the truce and continuing thereafter until the next warlike act.

DEFINITION 2.31. A truce is an actual suspension of open combat between opposing forces previously engaged in open combat, without any explicit agreement to do so. This definition departs from one commonly used meaning of the word *truce*. Soldiers often use truce to mean a formally agreed upon but brief and temporary cessation of hostilities, for example, to bury the dead or to celebrate a holiday. We use it here to mean a tacit agreement to stop fighting for an indefinite period, in contrast to a peace treaty which is an explicit agreement to do the same thing.

Note well that the distinction we make here between the words *truce* and *armistice* is made by us only in our discussions of the codings in part 2 of each chapter. In part 1 of each chapter we have tended to use the language of our sources where this distinction is not usually made, and the two words are used interchangeably.

Since the sources we used did not always report the precise date of events which constituted the begining or ending of a war, we have the following eight rules for approximating the war frequency count.

RULE 3.1 The war frequency count is rounded off to the nearest month. Fractions of less than half a month are dropped; those of more than half a month are counted as a whole month; if exactly half a month is reported, the count is rounded off to either the next lowest or highest whole number to make an *even* number of months (for example, 13 3/4 months are counted as fourteen months; 14 1/2 months are also counted as fourteen months).

RULE 3.2. Accounts were kept in terms of the calendar used by the source being followed. Errors which result from varying definitions of the month were ignored.

RULE 3.3. Where the year in which a war begins is not specified or implied, it was presumed to have begun in the first year specified or implied in a report of a warlike act. Where the year in which a war ends is not specified or implied, it was presumed to end two years after the last year specified or implied in a report of a warlike act.

RULE 3.4. Where the day or week, as well as the month and year *in which a war begins or ends was specified or implied, the month* was treated as one of war or one of peace according to rule 1.0 above.

RULE 3.5 Where the month, but not the day or week, of change is specified or implied, the condition existing at the end of the month was counted for the month as a whole: a month in which war begins is a month of war; a month in which war ends is a month of peace.

RULE 3.6. Where the season of the year, but not the month, is specified or implied, the season was treated as a three-month period; a season in which war begins is a Season of War; a season in which peace begins in a Season of Peace.

RULE 3.7. Where the year, but not the season or the month, is specified or implied, the year in which war begins was treated as a Year of War; the year in which peace begins was treated as a Year of Peace.

RULE 3.8. Where portions of a year can be excluded, since a season, month, week, or day preceding or subsequent to the event in question is reported, even though the corresponding season, month, week, or day of the event itself is not reported, the remaining fractional period is used. For example, if war is known to have begun sometime in October after the twentieth of the month, October was treated as a month of peace; if war is known to have begun sometime after the spring of the year 1180 (perhaps in the summer, perhaps in the fall or winter), 1180 was counted as having nine months of war, three months of peace.

DEFINITION 4.0. A *Declared Alliance* is a publicly announced association for the purpose of waging war.

Statistical Transformation. For statistical purposes raw scores of all three dependent variables were transformed mathematically in order to produce transformed scores in standard form. The resultant Transformed Score has what might be called a pseudo-normal distribution. With respect to both skewness and kurtosis, it tests well within the normal range of Geary's and Pearson's tests for normality (n.d.)—the most spohisticated of such tests. However, the Transformed Scores do depart from normality in that they have a discrete rather than a continuous distribution. This fact tends to *decrease* the significance in group tests of statistical significance and hence is a conservative error. The transformation had two steps. For War Frequency there were: step 1, where X equals the raw score and Y equals the first transform, is expressed as

$$Y = 2 \left(\text{Arcsine} \sqrt{\frac{X}{100}} \right)$$

and step 2, the Y scores were put into standard form with a mean of 50 and a standard deviation of 10, by the following formula, where T equals the final transform and Y equals the first transform:

$$T = 50 + 10 \left(\frac{Y - \overline{Y}}{\sigma_Y} \right)$$

Territorial Gain (Variable Code Number A730) and Territorial Instability (Variable Code Number A731)

Here again the determination of our second dependent variable is simple enough. During the decade studied, by what proportion did the Conspicuous State we studied expand or contract its territory? Again, the measurement of its boundaries and their change, with the evidence at hand, at times proved a difficult problem. Here is how we handled that problem.

Territorial Change. Territorial Change refers to the area of territory gained or lost by the Conspicuous State from or to the Conspicuous Rival and/or its declared allies. (This policy of counting only change affecting both the Conspicuous State and its Conspicuous Rival means that we ignore territorial changes during the decade which affect the Conspicuous State but which do not affect the Conspicuous Rival or any of its allies; and similarly we ignore territorial change which affects the Conspicuous Rival or any of its allies but not the Conspicuous State. It also means that we ignore changes affecting the allies of the Conspicuous State unless they also affect the Conspicuous State itself.)

In trying to find out the area actually controlled by the rulers of a Conspicuous State, two contrasting questions arise. On one hand, it is usually easy to find out what territories the rulers of the state claimed, what cities and fortifications their troops actually held, and what areas were occupied by the troops of their declared rival states. And these things together make up the image of the international arena which guide mapmakers, even today. On the other hand, the peasantry of the countryside may often be effectively not subject to control, as in the case of nomadic tribesmen of deserts, hills, or jungles—but as long as these people do not take a hand in the game of power politics between the rulers of states and cities, their lack of subordination is commonly ignored. For instance, an international dispute took place in 1963 between the Netherlands and Indonesia over the "control" of western New Guinea, much of which was still occupied by tribal peoples who in fact are independent, war-making groups.

Furthermore, the actual degree of subordination of reputed subordinate officials is often difficult to determine, and may not really be clear even to the subordinate officials themselves until there is some kind of showdown.

To deal with these problems, we have adopted the following six rules:

RULE 4.1. For the purpose of the present study, a civilized state is considered to occupy territory which it publicly claims, from which it excludes the armies (armed, organized, publicly declared adherents) of other civilized states, and over which it exercises reputed control of the cities and fortifications of the civilized inhabitants.

RULE 4.2. A person is considered civilized if he is the domestic speaker of a dialect which is mutually intelligible with a dialect which is the usual domestic speech of the majority of the inhabitants of any city. A city is defined as a collection of dwellings within six kilometers of a central point containing at least ten thousand people.

RULE 4.3. A civilized state is a territorial team whose leaders both claim and exercise the exclusive right to wage armed, licit, lethal public combat over an area which includes at least one city.

RULE 4.4. Once a state is known to exercise actual control over a city or fortification, it is presumed to retain such control as against dissident or disobedient subordinate officials or rebels until the officials in control of the local military forces publicly repudiate the authority of the state, or until it becomes notorious that they ignore the orders of its officials.

COROLLARY 4.5. The study ignores rural bands of civilized people not in control of a city or a fortification; and the study also ignores uncivilized people (even if in control of a fortification) if not in control of a city.

RULE 4.6. Nominally subordinate civil and military officials are presumed to be obedient unless some report to the contrary appears in the sources.

Territorial Change is treated as two dependent variables, differing by sign, as follows:

1. *Territorial Growth* (A 730). The percentage of Territorial Gain or loss enjoyed or suffered by the Conspicuous State from or to its Conspicuous Rival or its allies.

Statistical Transformation. Like the other dependent variables (see p. 11), the raw score of territorial gain was mathematically transformed for technical reasons. Again, the transformation had two steps: Step 1, where X equals the raw score and Y equals the final transform:

$$Y = \text{Arctangent} \sqrt{X}$$

For step 2, See Formula (1.2), p. 11 above.

Territorial Instability (A 731). The measurement of Territorial Instability follows directly from the measurement of Territorial Gain. It is merely Territorial Gain without any plus or minus sign; as the mathematicians would say, it is the absolute value of Territorial Gain. If a state expands by 20%, its Territorial Gain raw score is +20. That gives it a transformed score of 62. It if contracts by 20%, its Territorial Gain raw score is -20, which gives it a transformed score of 34. In both these cases the raw score of Territorial Instability is the same, 20, and the transformed score is 60.

Statistical Transformation. Once more, as with the other two dependent variables, the raw score of Territorial Instability was mathematically transformed for technical reasons. Again, the transformation had two steps: Step 1 is where X equals the raw score and Y equals the first transform

$$Y = \sqrt{\overline{\ln X}}$$

For step 2, see Formula (1.2), p. 11, above.

Defensive Stance (718)

This variable, Defensive Stance, was coded separately, and also used as a factor in the coding of five other variables (B701, B702, B703, B704, A706). Defensive Stance was considered present when some indication appeared that the Conspicuous State did not intend to attack the Conspicuous Rival if they were at peace throughout the decade; or in fact had not begun the war, if at war at any time during the decade. Since the Conspicuous Rival was selected because of indications of military or diplomatic conflict between it and the Conspicuous State, the Conspicuous State would most often be coded as in a Defensive Stance because of evidence that the Conspicuous Rival had attacked it. This variable was coded absent when some indication appeared that the Conspicuous State *did* intend to attack the Conspicuous Rival, if at peace; or in fact had begun the war, if at war. In three of the periods studied, the evidence was ambiguous, and here this variable was coded *no data* (England vs. France, 1376–1385; Byzantine Empire vs. Persia, 576–585; Swiss Confederation vs. Burgundy, 1476–1485).

Military Factors

Relative Strength of Armies, Stance Immaterial (A701)

This variable, A701, was coded *present* if the Conspicuous State reportedly had larger armies than the Conspicuous Rival during the period studied. The term *strength* is here used in its technical military sense, as in the phrase "strength return," to refer only to the number of soldiers in the armies involved. No considerations of military quality are involved, neither state of training, mobility, discipline, equipment, supplies, nor leadership are considered—only sheer numbers. If the Conspicuous State and the Conspicuous Rival were at war during the decade, then the comparison sought was between the average size of armies in the field of operations during the war; if the two were at peace with one another throughout the decade, then the total reported size of all the armies, rather than merely those present in the field of operations, was the comparison sought.

In chapter 15, the comparison lies between France and England in the decade from 1276 to 1285. The two powers were at peace with one another. They had no standing armies and fought with feudal levies when at war. Nearly all the people of both countries were rural and organized for war under the feudal system. At this time France had more people than England; consequently, we presumed that the feudal levies of France would have been more numerous than those of England.

Military historians are much concerned about the problem of trustworthiness in reports on strength of armies. They are aware, for example, that it is impossible to determine with any precision the strength of armies engaged in particular battles of the American Civil War, even though we often possess the official strength returns of the commanders on either side, in which they confidentially reported their strength to their own military superiors. There are nagging problems of definition: Does one count all soldiers on the rolls of the units engaged, including those absent from the theater of operations, in hospital or on leave or absent without leave? If not, does one count all soldiers present for duty in the theater of operations, including those not actually on the field of battle because of detached service? The kinds of reports we deal with in this comparative study are far less precise, far less trustworthy than the Civil War records and modern histories based on them. The variable coded throughout this study is the historical report. What the true facts were, we shall never know. The working hypothesis of this study is the hypothesis that the historical records (primary sources) and the modern histories written from them (secondary sources) have been often strongly influenced by the facts they purport to record—that there is often some relationship between what the historians said happened and what actually did happen.

Consequently, though we do not look upon reality through historians' eyes, we often look upon a distorted shadow of it. For a further discussion of this problem, including the measures we have taken to guard against spurious correlations reflecting source bias, see the Preface and chapters 2 and 24.

In only one period (Byzantine Empire vs. Persia, 576–585) did the reports available to us fail to indicate that one or the other side had larger armed forces; this period was coded *no data*.

Relative Strength of Armies, Defensive Stance ($B701$)

This variable was coded *present* if Relative Strength of Armies, Stance Immaterial and Defensive Stance both were coded *present*. If either of these variables was coded *absent*, then this variable too was coded *absent*. In the same period (Byzantine Empire vs. Persia, 576–585), the Relative Strength of Armies was unascertained and the stance was ambiguous—this period was coded *no data*.

Relative Mobility of Armies, Stance Immaterial ($A702$)

One army was considered more mobile than the other if it enjoyed a clear advantage in speed of movement because of superior transportation facilities. In practice, only two types of superior transportation facilities proved to be involved—horses and ships. If one army had a markedly greater proportion of cavalry to infantry than the other, or had fleets of transports and control of the sea, it was considered more mobile. However, if its naval superiority did not seem to be relevant to the tactical military situation, as in the Second Punic War during the decade 225 B.C. to 216 B.C., it was ignored. Where there was data on the mobility of each army and the reported relative advantage or disadvantage of each side nevertheless appeared doubtful, this variable was coded absent. In other words, the variable was coded present only if, when we acted according to the reports at hand, it seemed quite clear that the Conspicuous State had a more mobile army than the Conspicuous Rival. In two periods (Sung dynasty vs. Tanguts in China; Abbasid Caliphate vs. Byzantine Empire) we lacked any data on the mobility of at least one contestant and accordingly coded these two periods *no data*.

Relative Mobility of Armies, Defensive Stance (B702)

This variable, B702, was coded *present* if both Relative Mobility (A702) and Defensive Stance (718) were coded *present*. This variable was coded absent if either of these was coded *absent*.

Relative Quality of Armies, Stance Immaterial (A703)

This variable, A703, was coded *present* if later historians considered that the army of the Conspicuous State was of better quality than that of the Conspicuous Rival. References to tactical skill, discipline, equipment, and ability of generals were all considered. Commonly, only one or two of these factors were discussed at all. It rarely happened that historians reported one side to enjoy an advantage with respect to one of these factors while reporting the other side to enjoy a compensating advantage on the other side; but each factor mentioned was considered for coding purposes to have equal weight. In only one period did it prove impossible to form an opinion (Sung dynasty of China vs. Tanguts, 1076–1085) and this period was coded *no data*.

Relative Quality of Armies, Defensive Stance (B703)

This variable was coded *present* if both Relative Quality (A703) and Defensive Stance (718) were coded *present*. This variable was coded *absent* if either of these was coded *absent*. The three periods in which stance evidence was ambiguous were all periods in which Relative Quality (A703) was coded *present*; consequently these three periods were coded *no data* here.

Border Fortification, Stance Immaterial (A704)

This variable, A704, was coded *present* if the Conspicuous State had conspicuous, extensive border fortifications on the frontier it shared with the Conspicuous Rival. It was also coded *present* if no such border fortifications were reported, but if the two states were at war at any time during the decade and the war itself was chiefly siege warfare in which one army spent most of its time and effort besieging rival fortifications. Since throughout nearly all the periods studied nearly all cities were walled, city walls were ignored in these codings. Instead, we looked for walled borders like the Roman and Chinese walls, and for special fortifications built to command passes, river crossings, or the like. In one period (Rome vs. the Visigoths, A.D. 376–385), data was ambiguous: the normal northern frontier was indeed fortified, but the Visigoths were peacefully and voluntarily admitted through the frontier defenses by the Roman authorities. Only sometime after peacefully passing through these defenses did the Visigoths become hostile to the Romans; consequently, this period was coded *no data*.

Border Fortifications, Defensive Stance (B704)

This variable was coded *present* if both Fortifications (A704) and Defensive Stance (718) were coded *present*. It was coded *absent* if either of these traits was coded *absent*. As in coding Relative Quality, Defensive Stance (B703), the three periods in which stance was ambiguous were periods in which frontiers were fortified; these three periods were therefore again coded *no data* as was the Rome-Visigoth period mentioned above.

Prestige of Armed Forces (713)

Since the Conspicuous State in troubled, warlike times (as most of these periods were) would be conspicuous for its prestige as much as for its conflicts, the variable here is not merely the difference between the Conspicuous State and its Conspicuous Rival, but rather the size of the gap between them. We have coded this trait *present* where it seemed clear to us that the Conspicuous State was not merely the first among equals but in a class by itself in terms of military prestige, not only in the eyes of its own people, but in those of its Conspicuous Rival and of historians today. We have coded this trait *absent* where there was any doubt of this or where the lead seemed slight.

Geographical Factors

Propinquity (712)

This variable, 712, was coded *present* if the Conspicuous State and the Conspicuous Rival had a common land boundary. It was coded *absent* if they had no such boundary. It was also coded *absent* in two ambiguous cases where an army occupied territory adjacent to the rival without effectively incorporating this territory into its political system (Spain vs. the Netherlands, 1576–1585; the Swiss Confederation vs. Burgundy, 1476–1485).

Natural Barriers (715)

This variable, 715, was coded *present* if some sort of natural barrier occurred along more than two-thirds of the frontier between the Conspicuous State and its Conspicuous Rival. Mountains with height over three thousand feet, deserts, and unfordable bodies of water were considered natural barriers. This trait was coded *absent* where such barriers occurred along less than *one-third* of the frontier. No cases were found of pairs of rivals with such barriers along more than one third but less than two-thirds of the frontier. Thirteen of the pairs proved to have such barriers along their boundaries. Two ambiguous cases were coded *trait absent*: Rome vs. the Visigoths (376–385) where the Visigoths were peacefully and voluntarily admitted across the Danube; and France vs. England (1276–1285)—for although, of course, the English Channel separates England proper from France, the English king had extensive holdings on the French mainland.

Capital City Location (716)

This variable, 716, was coded *present* if the capital city of the Conspicuous State was within three hundred miles of the nearest point on its frontier with its Conspicuous Rival, and coded *absent* if the capital city was three hundred or more miles away. For Chapter 10 this variable was coded *present* because Rome was near the seacoast and Carthage was a naval power. In considering the Swiss Confederation, we realized that the Confederation as such had no capital city. For the period from 1376 to 1385 (Switzerland vs. Kiburg) Bern played so predominant a role on the Swiss side that we counted Bern as the Swiss capital. In the other two periods of Swiss history studied this trait was coded *no data*.

Diplomatic Factors

Announcements of Intention (A705)

This variable, A705, was coded *present* if the tactical aggressor who began the war between the Conspicuous State and its Conspicuous Rival had formally announced an intention (perhaps in the form of a warning or ultimatum) to attack before actually beginning or declaring war. This trait was coded *absent* if no such formal announcement was made, whether or not the attack came as a strategic surprise. This trait was also coded *absent* if war began in circumstances suggesting awareness by a tactical defender of impending attack by a tactical aggressor in the absence of any discussion of announcements or in circumstances suggesting suprise in the historical sources consulted. This trait was coded *no data* if no war began during the period studied, either because the rivals were already at war when the period began (China vs. Tibet, 776–785; China vs. Huns, 126–116 B.C.) or because they never made war upon each other during the period (France vs. England, 1276–1285; Protestant Swiss vs. Catholic Swiss, 1576–1585; Rome vs. Parthia, 25–16 B.C.).

Surprise Attack (B705)

This trait is almost the mirror image of the foregoing one. It was coded *present* if the aggressor had both tactical and strategic surprise with no hint of intentions being given or received. It was coded *absent* if some sort of warning was mentioned or inferred by the coder, who does not believe that the defender was entirely surprised, both tactically and strategically. Note that periods in which the tactical aggressor made no announcements of his intention, but in which, nevertheless, the coder does not believe that he gained strategic surprise—that his attack was entirely unexpected —would be coded as *trait absent* both in this trait and in the preceding one. Hence the coding of this trait cannot always be inferred from the preceding one. The five periods coded *no data* in the preceding trait were also coded *no data* on this one.

Alliances, Defensive Stance (A706)

This trait was coded *present* if the Conspicuous State was a member of a coalition directed against the Conspicuous Rival and if, furthermore, Defensive Stance was coded *present*. The trait was coded *absent* if historians made no mention of any coalition or alliance adhered to by the Conspicuous State and directed against the Conspicuous Rival. Regardless of coalition or alliances, this trait was coded *absent* if Defensive Stance was coded *absent*. The three periods of ambiguous stance were also periods in which Conspicuous States were members of pertinent coalitions; these periods were coded *no data*. In considering France vs. England (1276–1285), stance was defensive and France was allied with Sicily, but it is ambiguous whether this alliance was directed against the English; consequently this period was coded *no data* also. Permanent confederations were not considered alliances or coalitions but rather, single states.

Active Diplomacy (A707)

This variable was coded *present* if more than one diplomatic mission was reported either explicitly or by clear implication. It was coded *absent* if less than two diplomatic missions were reported or if no mention of diplomatic communication was made in the historical sources studied. In very few of the periods studied did the rivals maintain permanent diplomatic missions at each other's capitals; if they did, the variable was coded *present*. Where either or both the rivals belonged to rival alliances or coalitions, missions between any allied power and any of its rivals are counted; in other words, we counted diplomatic missions between any of the rivals involved, but not between allies.

Intense Diplomacy (Treaties) (B707)

This variable was coded *present* when agreement was reached on a substantive issue between the parties. The most common such agreement was the conclusion of a peace treaty between the rivals. The variable was coded *absent* when no negotiations were reported or if any were reported when no agreement was reached. Take careful note that the conduct of diplomacy could readily be scaled thus: (1) no negotiations; (2) negotiations but no agreements; (3) negotiations and agreements on minor matters not affecting war/peace status, territorial or military alliances, but not agreement on major matters as just listed; (4) negotiation and agreement on major matters.

Previous History of Conflict (714)

This trait was coded *present* if a previous war (including a peace or truce) was reported between the Conspicuous State and its Conspicuous Rival, a war which came to an end during the century preceding the beginning of the period being studied. The trait was coded *absent* if no war took place during that period, or if a war began before the beginning of the period but continued on into the period being studied. Thus the trait being studied was the existence or nonexistence of a previous conflict antedating any war in which the two rivals were involved during the period being studied.

Cultural Factors

One-Sided Benefits (A709)

This variable was coded *present* if any sort of benefit (subsidy or women or honors) was onesidedly conferred by either state upon the leader or other officials of its rival. By a subsidy we mean a payment of valuable goods without expectation of an economic return: such a payment might be thought of as bestowal of gifts by a stronger state on a weaker one, or payment of tribute by a weaker state to a stronger one. By bestowal of women we mean the delivery of a woman for the enjoyment of her personal favors and would include delivery of a woman of high status in an arranged dynastic marriage or delivery of a woman of lower status to serve as a concubine. By honors we mean tokens of status which do not involve economic wealth or political authority and would include, for example, honorific titles or seals bestowed by Chinese emperors on neighboring states as well as awards of decorations or titles of honor by European states. In chapter 17, we coded this variable *absent* even though Philip II of Spain conferred benefits on former rebels who returned to his allegiance. The point here is that we are looking for benefits conferred upon rival leaders to influence the conduct of the affairs of that rival; we are not looking for benefits conferred upon individuals to induce them to change sides.

Cultural Exchange (A708)

We coded this variable *present* if cultural exchanges seemed frequent; we coded it *absent* if cultural exchanges seemed infrequent. This was impressionistic coding; in one period (Switzerland, 1576–1585) not enough information to permit coding was found in the sources consulted, and this period was coded *no data*. By cultural exchange we mean exchange of culture bearers, so that the elite of one society is brought into close contact with the culture of its rival society and thus gains familiarity with it. Such culture bearers could include visiting teachers, students, missionaries, women exchanged in marriage, entertainers, or hostages.

However, exchanges of slaves or war captives or craftsmen are not considered cultural exchanges. The point we are making here is that there is communication among the elite of different societies. In two cases the variable was coded *present* because the elite among the rivals was deemed to share a common culture and to be part of a common cultural elite. The first case was England and France, 1276 to 1285. Here, England was ruled by French-speaking Normans who had large possessions in France. Not until the following century did the Norman court and nobility take up English speech in place of French. The second was Switzerland, 1576 to 1585. Here the rivalry was between coalitions of cantons, Protestant versus Catholic. In each coalition, the leaders were German (Swiss-German) speakers and so here too we have considered them to share in a common culture. Needless to say, as in the rivalry between Muscovy and Novgorod, where not merely the two elites but all the people of both rival societies spoke mutually intelligible dialects of the same language, they were considered to share a common culture. (For a discussion of what defines a culture, see the references to discussions of the problem of ethnic unit definition in Naroll and Cohen 1970, Chapter 39).

On the other hand, the exchange of elite hostages who lived in the rival court as high-ranking guests was counted as a cultural exchange. Furthermore, one-sided exchanges, in which hostages or other culture-bearers went from one rival to another without any like movement in the opposite direction, were also counted as cultural exchanges.

Trade (A708)

This variable was coded present if commercial trade seemed relatively extensive; it was coded *absent* if commercial trade seemed relatively restricted. Again, this was an impressionistic coding. Not enough information to permit coding was found in the sources consulted on six periods: Switzerland, from 1576 to 1585; China, from 125 to 116 B.C.; China, from 25 to 16 B.C.; China, from A.D. 776 to 785; Rome, from 225 to 216 B.C.; Caliphate, from A.D. 776 to 785; these six periods were accordingly coded *no data*.

General Exchange (*C*708)

This variable was coded *present* if either Cultural Exchange (A708) or Trade (B708) was coded present; it was coded no data if both these traits were so coded; otherwise it was coded *absent*.

Administrative Factors

Experience of Ruler (*A*710)

This variable was coded *present* if the ruler of the Conspicuous State came to power at least ten years before the beginning of the decade and furthermore continued to rule at least six years after that. It was coded *absent* if the incumbent ruler at the beginning of the decade had been in power less than ten years. It was also coded *absent* if the incumbent ruler died in office at the beginning of the decade or within six years after the beginning of the decade. The year in which a ruler acceded to power is counted as a year in office where information on month and day of accession was not available. Periods of regency were not counted as experience for a minor. This variable was coded *no data* for the Roman Republic (225–216 B.C.) as well as for the Swiss Confederation, since these states were controlled by collegial bodies rather than by individuals. The variable thus distinguishes between sole rulers who have long experience in office and those who lack such long experience.

In chapter 5 this variable was coded *absent*. Here, in T'ang China, there were two rulers in succession. T'ai Tsung ruled for three years, then he died and was succeeded by his son Te Tsung, who ruled for the remainder of the decade. Since Te Tsung ruled for more than half the decade, it is *his* experience (or lack of it) which we coded.

In chapter 7, the variable was coded *present*. Here, in Ming China, the ruler was the Hung Wu emperor, who had been formally enthroned as such for less than ten years (since 1369) at the beginning of the decade. However, for many years previously he had been the ruler of an independent rebel band which gradually was gaining control of all China (as early as 1356 his band captured Nanking, for example).

Youth of Ruler (B710)

This variable was coded *present* if the ruler was less than forty-five years of age at the begining of the decade. It was coded *absent* if the ruler was forty-five years of age or more at the beginning of the decade. It was coded *no data* if the state was ruled by a collegial body.

In chapter 12 the variable was coded *present*. Here, in the Roman Empire in the second century after Christ at the begining of the decade the Emperor Marcus Aurelius was ostensibly sharing the supreme authority with his son Commodus. Commodus acceded to sole power at the death of Marcus Aurelius in the year 180, when he was nineteen years old. Since Commodus was sole ruler for more than half the decade (176–185), we considered his age at the time of his accession to sole rule.

Unbridled Ruler (C710)

This variable was coded *present* if the ruler was a hereditary monarch, twenty to forty-five years of age at the beginning of the decade, and ruled a centralized monarchy. It was coded *absent* if any one of these conditions was absent. It was coded *no data* if needed information was lacking on one of these conditions while information on the others was present.

Hereditary Monarchy (D710)

This variable was coded *present* if the ruler of a Conspicuous State was a hereditary monarch. A hereditary monarch is one who obtains his office by virtue of his kinship status rather than by virtue of his achievements. Where the incumbent monarch customarily designated a particular successor from among his close relatives (commonly his sons) the variable was coded *present*. The variable was coded *absent* where the state had a republican organization; where the monarch was chosen not by the previous monarch but by some collegial body, e.g., a council of notables; or where collegial succession held, i.e., where the monarch customarily appointed an unrelated official as his successor. A successful rebel who founded a dynasty of hereditary monarchs was not himself considered a hereditary monarch. The dynastic situation in Rome. A.D. 176–185 was so ambiguous that the variable was coded *no data* for this period.

Civil War (711)

This variable was coded *present* where there were reports of civil wars or lethal riots, i.e., public defiance of the de facto authorities in which someone was killed. It was coded *absent* where no reference to civil disturbances was found in the historical sources consulted. It was coded *no data* where civil disturbances were not reported in sufficient detail to permit an inference about bloodshed therein (Russia, 1476–1485; Rome, 576–585; Switzerland, 1476–1485). This variable was also coded *no data* for Spain vs. the Netherlands (1576–1585), since the war itself was a civil war while the purpose of this variable was to consider the effect of a civil war as a *third* factor upon the rivalry between a Conspicuous State and its Conspicuous Rival.

Centralization of Power (717)

This variable was coded *present* if the Conspicuous State clearly had a more highly centralized plan of government in ostensible effect than did its Conspicuous Rival. It was coded *absent* if the two states seemed about equal in ostensible centralization, or if the Conspicuous Rival seemed ostensibly more highly centralized. We would have preferred to code actual rather than ostensible centralization but we feel that the reports at hand do not permit such classification. In this variable, we were concerned first with the authority of the central government of the state over its territorial subdivisions; and second, within the central government, we were concerned with the degree of concentration of authority into few or many hands. We were not concerned with the degree of cultural homogeneity of the state, nor with the administrative difficulties faced by the central government which might to a greater or lesser degree hamper its exercise of authority (e.g., communication facilities), nor with the relative conformity of the actual operating system to the ostensible and publicly announced plan of government.

CHAPTER 2

★ ★ ★

METHOD OF STUDY

THE NOVEL ORIENTATION of this study, its background in the cross-cultural survey method of anthropology, its focus on cross-historical correlations, and its aim of discerning laws of history through causal analysis of these correlations have all been set forth at considerable length in the Preface. In this chapter we shall spell out the details of our procedures. These were planned nearly ten years ago and were nearly all carried out from 1962 to 1964. Hence we do not always do as we advise in the Preface. Thirty years ago, one of us was a young army recruit. His sergeant told him and his fellow recruits, "Don't do like I do. Do like I say do." In this spirit, if discrepancies arise between our practice and our preaching, we request our readers similarly not to do as we do, but to do as we say to do.

UNITS OF STUDY

Our concept of the higher civilization, or paideia, is defined in the Preface, in terms of its dominant body of literature. In each paideia, the particular periods of time were chosen, as is described under "Sampling Methods" (pp. 28–30 below). In each such paideia, for each century chosen, two states were selected for attention, a *Conspicuous State* and its *Conspicuous Rival*. The Conspicuous State was thought of as the state whose diplomatic or military rivalries with other states had attracted the most attention among modern historians. Its Conspicuous Rival was thought of as that state most often the military or diplomatic rival of the Conspicuous State. Appendix A presents a detailed content analysis protocol for designating the Conspicuous State and its Conspicuous Rival by content analysis of references in standard encyclopedic histories such as Langer (1948). This objective procedure proved, however, too time-consuming to apply in this pilot study. Each investigator subjectively designated the Conspicuous State and its Conspicuous Rival in accordance with his idea of the attention given by encyclopedic historians to international rivalries in the paideia during the period in question.

SAMPLING HISTORICAL PERIODS

The Extended Sampling Plan

How might particular historical periods be chosen for study as a representative sample of all recorded history? The present study is the result of a makeshift compromise, in which twenty particular historical periods were rather arbitrarily chosen from a much longer list—that of the extended sampling plan.

This plan called for studying one decade in each century for which usable historical records survive from each of these nine paideias. Very roughly, there are 120 sampling periods from which sufficient historical materials survive to permit the comparative historian to work. For example, although the Egyptian paideia lasted about twenty-five centuries, it is doubtful if records for more than half of those centuries survive in sufficient detail to permit study. During Egypt's periods of union under powerful central rulers, as in the Third through the Seventh, the Eleventh through the Twelfth, and the Seventeenth through the Eighteenth Dynasties, monumental inscriptions were more frequent, and, consequently, better records of events have survived than for the periods in between. A very rough estimate of the extended sampling universe might allot one hundred and twenty centuries among our nine paideias, as shown in table 2.1.

A ten percent sample of the universe in table 2.1 can be designated simply by selecting a particular decade in each successive century. For the purpose of the present study, using a random numbers table, the decade — A.D. 76 to — A.D. 85 (i.e., A.D. 76 to A.D. 85, A.D. 176 to A.D. 185, etc.) was chosen. (This corresponds to the decades 25 B.C. to 16 B.C., 125 B.C. to 116 B.C., and so forth).

TABLE 2.1

EXTENDED SAMPLING UNIVERSE

Paideia	Lenth of Record	Allotted Centuries
Mesopotamian	*2500-600 B.C.	8
Egyptian	*3000-600 B.C.	12
Hebrew	**900-600 B.C.	4
Islamic	A.D. 600-Present	13
Greco-Roman	600 B.C.-A.D. 450	25
Western	A.D. 450-Present	15
Russian	A.D. 1350-Present	6
Hindu	*300 B.C.-Present	12
Chinese	***600 B.C.-Present	25
Total		120

*The many gaps in the record must be taken into account here
**The Maccabean monarchy (142-63 B.C.) has been considered part of the record here.
***The record tends to go back beyond this date.

Sampling Plan of the Present Study

The Sampling of the present study departed in two ways from the ideal set forth in the extended sampling plan description just given. First, the plan of the present study called for case studies based chiefly on secondary sources to be written on each decade studied. This commitment involved an important restriction to twenty as the total number of periods which could be studied in the time available.

Second, sponsors were especially interested in the possible applications of its findings to present-day international affairs. The twentieth-century world emphasizes loose international associations of republics, whereas most of the cross-historical universe is populated by monarchies; therefore, the Swiss Confederation was introduced as an additional tradition, even though in fact the confederation is a comparatively minor element of the Western paideia. We decided to treat it as though it were a distinct paideia of its own purely for comparative purposes.

Our final selection of periods to be studied is set forth in table 2.2. The arbitrary inclusion of the Swiss tradition and the arbitrary choices of particular centuries (reflecting convenient accessibility of data) severely restricted the validity of the results from a sampling point of view. The extent to which the results of the present study can be generalized to the whole cross-historical universe cannot be inferred by statistical theory but must remain a matter of the individual reader's judgment. However, if we had studied a purely random sample from these 120 centuries (or a sample stratified by paideia), then the theory of mathematical statistics would have permitted us to generalize rigorously to the universe from such a sample.

If we pursue the present study, the next step might well be to study a stratified random sample of the remaining 103 paideia periods in order to see whether the results of the present preliminary survey are thus confirmed. In order to estimate the applicability of these findings to republics, a separate sampling of another universe should be made—a universe of Western republics, whether from classical antiquity or medieval Italy or Germany or Russia. While republican forms of government are common among primitive peoples and are reported from early India and from the higher civilizations of pre–Columbian Mexico, there is hardly any documentation for them outside the Greco-Roman tradition and its Western and Russian offshoots.

DATA ACCURACY

In the discussion of data accuracy in the Preface, it was pointed out that our problem of data accuracy differs markedly in its implications from that of conventional historical work. We are concerned solely with errors in our codings. Our sole object is to seek and analyze correlations among these codings. The introductory historical sketch for each historical period studied is offered only to provide a reader with some general idea of the situation being coded. Furthermore, errors in our codings may have diametrically opposite effects upon our confidence in the correlations, depending upon whether they are random or systematic errors. Paradoxically, random errors tend to increase our confidence in our correlations, for the effect of random errors is to lower correlations. Consequently, evidence of random error tends to *increase* our confidence in the correlations we find. If the correlations are this high despite random error, we would expect them to be even higher without any random error. But the effect of systematic error may be to increase correlation. If there were parallel systematic errors in both variables being correlated, a spurious correlation might be created. Such a spurious correlation could deceive us into believing that we had learned something about deterrence theory when, in fact, all we had learned was something about the kinds of errors made by historians or by us comparativists.

Random Error

To measure *random* error by comparativists, we compare two codings by coders and we report coefficients of reliability. These codings should have been independent but were not.

Systematic Error

To measure *systematic* error, we look at conditions under which historical data was compiled; We call these conditions *control factors*; these control factors are then systematically correlated with each of the theoretical variables set forth in Chapter 1. Any evidence of a correlation between our theoretical codings and our control factors is grounds for suspecting systematic error in our sources or in our own coding work. Five control factors were used in this study. Two of these were coded twice in slightly different ways, giving us then a final total of seven control factor codings.

Publication Year (A 424)

Rationale. We assume that secondary sources written by modern, professionally-trained historians would be less biased and more accurate than other sources of information.

This control factor was coded *present* if the leading source had been written after 1850 and coded *absent* if written before 1850. Two periods (Switzerland, 1376–1385; Islam, 776–785) were coded *no data* because works we relied heavily upon were written partly before and partly after 1850.

Primary Source (*B* 424)

Rationale: secondary sources presumably have less, and different biases from primary sources.

If our data for a period was chiefly taken from primary sources, this control factor was coded *present*; if chiefly taken from secondary, it was coded *absent*. Islam (776–785) was coded *no data* because the situation was ambiguous—we relied about half and half upon primary and secondary materials. By a primary source is meant one which *today* is as close to an original participant or eyewitnes account as it is possible to get, including so-called derivative sources—secondary sources compiled from primary materials which are now lost. For example, the Chinese standard histories of the Han and T'ang dynasties were classed as primary sources. (For a manifold classification of primary and secondary sources, see Naroll 1962: 31-32.)

Authors' Associations (*A*425)

Rationale. An author sympathetic to the Conspicuous State might be suspected of permitting this bias to affect his reporting in some consistent way.

If the author or authors of our leading sources were associated with the Conspicuous State, this control factor was coded *present*; if associated with the Conspicuous Rival, it was coded *absent*; if some were associated with one and some with another, or they were associated with neither, the control factor was coded *no data*. An author's assocation means his membership in a social or cultural group which has social or cultural ties with one or the other state unequally. Thus, in considering the Chinese versus the Mongols, a Japanese author would have been classed as having Chinese associations, since Japan traditionally had many more intellectual links with China (as a member of the Chinese paideia) than with the Mongols. A Protestant English author would be coded associated with Protestant Swiss rather than with Catholic Swiss. But a Japanese Buddhist author writing on the Swiss reformation would be classed as having associations with neither. Most of these classification decisions seemed both easy and obvious.

Authors' Associations (*B*425)

This control factor is the same as the preceding one, except that periods coded *no data* in A425 were coded *association absent* here. This variant coding produced lower correlations than those nominally significant at the 10% level or better for coding A425. Hence, B425 does not seem to have been useful.

Authors' Sympathies (A426)

Our rationale is the same as our rationale for authors' associations. This factor substitutes a subjective impression of sympathy for an objective associational link.

This control factor was coded *present* if the comparativist subjectively rated the leading sources as being sympathetic toward the Conspicuous State and was coded *absent* if he subjectively rated the leading sources as sympathetic toward the Conspicuous Rival; It was coded *no data* if the sympathies seemed unclear or impartial.

Authors' Sympathies (B426)

This control factor is the same as the preceding one, except that here, where the sympathies seemed unclear, or impartial, the period was coded *sympathies absent*, i.e., the sources lacked sympathies favoring the Conspicuous Rival.

Proximity (427)

Rationale. Authors writing when the events concerned were still comparatively fresh in people's minds might be supposed to have stronger concerns and thus stronger biases than those writing later, when the events had lost interest to all but scholars.

This control factor is coded *present* if leading sources were written within a hundred years of events described and coded *absent* if written more than a hundred years later. The leading source for China from 25 to 16 B.C., was coded *no data* because we were unable to learn exactly when Pan Ku's history was written.

GALTON'S PROBLEM

The Linked Pair Test

As explained in the Preface, cross-historical correlations might well be simple artifacts of cultural diffusion. In order to guard against this possibility, such diffusion is directly measured. In this study, we use Naroll's Linked Pair method (Naroll 1964b) of

TABLE 2.2

LINKED PAIR TEST FOR CULTURAL DIFFUSION
OF DEFENSIVE STANCE (No. 1)

Area-Time Alignment

(1) Period	(2) Conspicuous State	(3) Own Defensive Stance Score	(4) Neighbor's Defensive Stance Score
Graeco-Roman			
1. 225 B.C.	Rome	A	P
2. 25 B.C.	Rome	P	P
3. A.D. 176	Rome	P	P
4. 376	Rome	P	O
5. 576	Byzantium	O	P
Western			
6. 1276	France	P	O
7. 1376	England	O	P
8. 1576	Spain	P	A
9. 1676	France	A	P
10. 1776	England	P	P
Swiss			
11. 1376	Swiss Confederation	P	A
12. 1476	Swiss Confederation	A	P
13. 1576	Swiss Protestants	P	P
Russian			
14. 1476	Muscovy	A	A
Islamic			
15. 776	Abbasids	A	A
Chinese			
16. 125 B.C.	Former Han Dynasty	A	A
17. 25 B.C.	Former Han Dynasty	A	P
18. A.D. 776	T'ang Dynasty	P	A
19. 1076	Sung Dynasty	A	A
20. 1376	Ming Dynasty	A	A

$\Phi = $ .05

P = .60

(By Fisher's Exact Test)

measuring cultural diffusion. This method assumes that usually, much more often than not, similarities between historical periods which result from diffusion are most likely to occur between neighbors in time or space. The Linked Pair method measures the similarities between such neighbors in this sample. The twenty periods in the sample are arranged in such a way as to put neighbors together. These arrangements are called alignments. The Linked Pair Test for diffusion of any trait is simple. The score on that trait of each historical period is called *Own Score*. The score on that trait of the next period in the alignment being used is called *Neighbor's Score*. The test simply consists in correlating Own Score and Neighbor's Score. If in fact there are strong diffusional influences leading to marked resemblances between sample neighbors in time or space, then there will be a high correlation between Own Score and Neighbor's Score. Table 2.2 illustrates the application of the Linked Pair method using the Area-Time Alignment to the trait Defensive Stance. Notice that the scores in column 4 are identical with the scores in column 3 on the following line. Correlating the scores in column 3 with the scores in column 4 constitutes the Linked Pair Test for cultural diffusion.

Alignments Used

Area-Time Alignment (560)

The entries in Table 2.2, column 3, show the order in which the periods were taken for the alignment. Each area tradition was considered separately in turn, moving from general paideia to special tradition and from west to east. Within each area tradition, the periods were taken in chronological order. Thus, first all the general Greco-Roman periods were taken in chronological order, then all the general Western periods, then all the Swiss. and so on.

Time-Area Alignment (561)

The entries in Table 2.3 show the order in which periods were taken for this alignment. This alignment takes time periods, century by century, from the earliest to the latest. Within each time period each area tradition was considered in turn, as in the Area-Time Alignment, moving from general paideia to special tradition and

TABLE 2.3

LINKED PAIR TEST FOR CULTURAL DIFFUSION
OF DEFENSIVE STANCE (No. 2)
Time-Area Alignment

(1) Period		(2) Conspicuous Stance	(3) Own Defensive Stance Score	(4) Neighbor's Defensive Stance Score
1.	225 B.C.	Rome	A	A
2.	125 B.C.	Former Han Dynasty	A	P
3.	25 B.C.	Rome	P	A
4.	25 B.C.	Former Han Dynasty	A	P
5.	176 A.D.	Rome	P	P
6.	376	Rome	P	O
7.	576	Byzantium	O	A
8.	776	Abbasids	A	P
9.	776	T'ang Dynasty	P	A
10.	1076	Sung Dynasty	A	P
11.	1276	France	P	O
12.	1376	England	O	P
13.	1376	Switzerland	P	A
14.	1376	Ming Dynasty	A	A
15.	1476	Switzerland	A	A
16.	1476	Muscovy	A	P
17.	1576	Spain	P	P
18.	1576	Swiss Protestants	P	A
19.	1676	France	A	P
20.	1776	England	P	A

$\Phi = -.29$

$P = .73$

(By Fisher's Exact Test)

from west to east. In other words, the decade from 225 to 216 B.C.
was taken first; next the decade from 125 to 116 B.C; next the decade
from 25 to 16 B.C.; and so on; and where more than one area
tradition was studied during a given decade, the general paideia
was considered before the special one (e.g., Western, 1376–1385,
before the Swiss Confederation, 1376–1385) and the more westerly
before the more easterly (e.g., Rome, 25–16 B.C., before China,
25–16 B.C.).

MEASUREMENT OF CORRELATION

As we stated in the Preface, the main idea of a cross-historical survey is to search for correlations. By correlation we mean a certain relationship between variables. If two variables are positively correlated, then the more we find of one variable in a given historical period, the more we can expect to find of the other. If they are negatively correlated, then the more we find of one, the less we can expect to find of the other. If they are uncorrelated, then learning about one does not tell us anything about the other. There are various measures of correlation (including so-called measures of association). All of them agree in assigning a value of 1.0 to a perfect positive correlation, of -1.0 to a perfect negative correlation, and of 0 to an absence of correlation.

In this study, we make use of two measures of correlation: the point biserial correlation and the phi coefficient of association. All the correlations we found are set forth in Appendix "C".

Normalizing Transforms

The need for normalizing transforms arose from our wish to use as sensitive a significance test as we could. By a significance test in mathematical statistics is meant, of course, a test of the likelihood that the observed results can plausibly be dismissed as mere chance freaks. A significance test of a correlation is a measure which permits an answer to the question: From a universe in which there was no correlation, in what proportion of random samples of so many cases would we expect so high a correlation? For example, in this study we found a correlation of -.58 between Territorial Gain and Active Diplomacy. Our test of significance shows that we should expect so large a correlation in either direction (plus or minus) through random sampling error in less than one random sample out of every hundred, from a universe in which there was no correlation. Obviously, the less likely is a correlation to arise from chance (i.e., random sampling error), the more significant that correlation is.

The mathematics of significance tests is such that more significant results can be expected from our three quantitative variables (months of war, territorial gain, and territorial stability) if they take the mathematical form of a normal distribution.

None of our three variables naturally assumes a clearly normal distribution. By a normal or Gaussian distribution is meant one which does not differ materially from the following formula:

$$Y = \frac{1}{\sqrt{2\pi}} \, e^{-\frac{X^2}{2\sigma^2}}$$

The search for such transformations was based on trial and error, using the IBM 7090 computer to compute eighty-five different tansformations and to test each of these as well as the untransformed data for normality. The tests of normality used in this computer program (see Appendix B for the program itself in FORTRAN program language) were two of those in Geary and Pearson (n.d.). The test for skewness used was the b_1 test, and for kurtosis the a test (mean deviation/standard deviation ratio). Geary and Pearson's work contains tables of values of the sampling distributions of these criteria; following these, for this sample, we took the mean of b_1 at zero and of a at o. 81128, the standard deviation of b_1 by extrapolation at o. 465 and of a at o. 04419.

These tests were used rather than the more common chi-square test, because for small samples the results of the chi-square test seem to be too dependent upon the manner in which the data is grouped; furthermore, for small samples it is difficult to construct a meaningful chi-square test of normality without involving dangerously small expected frequencies.

For a more general discussion of the topic of tests of normality, the reader is referred to chapter 27 of Duncan (1959).

For the transforms used, see the computer program in Appendix "B".

As will be seen from table 2.4, this trial and error method, involving so much calculation that it would not have been feasible without a computer, was successful in finding transformations which evidently are close approximations of normal distributions. The measures of normality fall well within the range of chance variation expectable from a normal distribution. Needless to say, these tests of normality do not demonstrate that the transformations

TABLE 2.4

EFFECT OF NORMALIZING TRANSFORMATIONS

	Territorial Gain	Territorial Stability	Months of War
Transformation Used	Arctangent of Square Root	Square Root of Natural Logarithm	Twice the Arcsine of Square Root of One One-Hundreth
Skewness			
Gamma scores:			
Raw Data	3.79	3.90	0.559
Transformed Data	0.26641	0.18131	0.35718
Two-tailed Probabilities:			
Raw Data	10^{-15}	10^{-15}	.33
Transformed Data	.57	.70	.44
Kurtosis			
a scores:			
Raw Data	0.43326	0.47532	0.85164
Transformed Data	0.84284	0.85165	0.83975
Two-tailed Probabilities:			
Raw Data	10^{-15}	10^{-15}	.36
Transformed Data	.48	.36	.52
Parameters			
Means:			
Raw Data	10.707	19.654	44.470
Transformed Data	0.10624	1.0350	1.3763
Standard Deviations:			
Raw Data	56.703	54.225	40.942
Transformed Data	1.0434	0.73341	1.0957

actually constitute normal distributions, but they do show that departures from normality are not great, and that consequently they offer assurance that statistically significant results from statistical tests based on the assumption of normality of distribution must chiefly reflect actual relationships of the data and can be but trivially influenced by departures of these transformed distributions from normality, since these departures are so slight.

(In addition to these regular transformations, an Edgeworth

correction retransformation was programmed and tried. Theoretically, the Edgeworth correction will make an approximately normal distribution a still better approximation. In every case where tried, the Edgeworth correction did improve the transformation—but slightly, so very slightly as not to make the change worth the trouble of using it.)

Standard Scores

Tables 2.5 through 2.7 show the standard scores ready for use in significance tests. These standard scores are derived from the transformations listed in table 5. The transformed score is standardized in the usual way: each transformed score is subtracted from the mean of the transformed score and divided by the standard deviation of the transformed scores; the result is multiplied by 10 and added to 50—thus giving us a standard score with a mean of 50 and a standard deviation of 10.

TABLE 2.5

STANDARD SCORES — TERRITORIAL GAIN

Raw Score	Standard Score
— 39	34.1728
— 25.6	34.3013
— 19.9	34.4083
— 2.27	37.9040
— 1.4	39.8717
0	48.9818
0.01	49.9370
1.5	57.4741
3.6	59.3877
4.0	59.5928
6.0	60.3217
11.5	61.2882
12.0	61.3430
13.0	61.4435
252.0	63.4335

TABLE 2.6

STANDARD SCORES — TERRITORIAL STABILITY

Raw Score	Standard Score
0	36.3190
0.01	37.3141
1.3	48.3350
1.4	48.6487
1.5	48.9426
2.27	50.7312
3.6	52.7329
4.0	53.1868
6.0	54.9088
11.5	57.5577
12.0	57.7253
13.0	58.0385
19.9	59.6605
25.6	60.5855
39.0	62.0759
252	67.9617

TABLE 2.7

STANDARD SCORES — MONTHS OF WAR

Raw Score	Standard Score
0	37.4389
1.0	39.2672
6.0	41.9559
12.0	43.8958
16.9	45.1719
34.0	48.8021
37.0	49.3744
45.5	50.9524
51.0	51.9574
66.0	54.7477
67.0	54.9711
72.0	55.9330
90.0	61.1206
105.0	66.1109*
120.0	66.1109*

* These values are identical because in this transformation all values over 100 are treated as 100.

Point-Biserial Correlations

For correlations between each of three quantitative dependent variables on one hand, and each of the remaining independent variables as well as the quality control tests, the point biserial coefficient of correlation was used as set forth in Walker and Lev (1953:262, 265–66). This correlation is a form of the product moment correlation and its values are thus comparable with ordinary product moment correlation coefficients. It is suitable for use in correlating one quantitative variable with another dichotomized variable. (In this study, for example, all variables except the three dependent variables are scored either *present* or *absent*. A score of o does not mean that data have been ignored in the statistical computation; such cases simply have been skipped and not counted.)

Phi Coefficients

When one dichotomized variable is correlated with another dichotomized variable, a fourfold contingency table results. In this study, we measured correlation in all such cases by the phi coefficient *with Yates's correction* (Walker and Lev, 1953:272–13).

TESTS OF SIGNIFICANCE

Individual Correlations

As noted above, a test of significance of a coefficient of correlation is a test of the hypothesis that a correlation as different from zero as that correlation might well occur by chance. The significance level of a correlation, thus calculated, is the probability that so high a correlation would occur by chance through a random sample from a universe in which there was no such correlation.

Point-biserial correlations are tested for significance by the t test of significance between means (Walker and Lev, 1953:265). Significance levels of t were obtained from the tables of Hartley and Pearson (1950: 168–169). Phi coefficients are tested for significance by Fisher's Exact Test (Kenney and Keeping 1951: 230–233). While this test is most tedious to compute by hand, all the tests for this study are tabled by Lieberman and Owen (1961).

These authors explain the use of their tables for Fisher's Exact Test on pp. 9–10 of their book. Both kinds of significance tests are set forth in Appendix "C" below.

The Correlations as a Group

These tests concern the so-called dredging, mudsticking, or combing problem, discussed in the Preface. The results of the group significance hypotheses tests are set forth in Appendix "D," below.

In the discussion of the second step of the test for the mudsticking hypothesis, p. l-li above, the use of Molina's (1942) Poisson tables was proposed in order to estimate the probability of getting so large a group of individually significant correlations by chance. The method there proposed is general in application. If significance levels of o. 01 or less are used, the error of the group significance test thus proposed on groups of 10 or more is less than o. 002 (see Smith 1953:32).

Another, more exact procedure is available for significance levels of 0.10 or less and groups of tests of 100 or less. That more exact procedure is the one we actually used whenever we could. It involves using the tables of Weintraub (1963), setting forth the exact probabilities of the cumulative binomial probability distribution. For example, we ran a total of twenty-nine point-biserial correlations involving Territorial Instability. Of these, nine proved individually significant at the 10% level. Using Molina's Poisson tables, as proposed on p. l-li above, results in an estimate that the probability of getting nine nominally significant correlations when 2.9 are expected is only o. 003058. That is, according to Molina (1942: Table II, p. 4), we would expect so many individual correlations significant at the 10% level or better in less than four groups of twenty-nine out of 1,000 groups ($a = 2.9, c = 9$, tabled value in Molina is o. 003058). Using Weintraub for the same problem, we have $N = 29$, since there were twenty-nine individual significance tests in the group. We have $P = 0.10$, since the significance tests counted were those significant at the 10% level. We have $R = 9$, since nine individual tests proved significant at the 10% level. On page 155 of Weintraub (1963) we find that the exact probability of getting by chance alone through random sampling nine or more individual correlations

significant at the 10% level in a group of 29 trials is exactly
0.0015501868.

REGIONAL ANALYSIS

The purpose of regional analysis is to inquire whether the significant correlations discovered are found in all regions studied or whether instead they reflect the influence of only a single region. In the present study, we looked at three paideias for that purpose, the Greco-Roman, the Western, and the Chinese. For purposes of regional analysis, the three special Swiss studies were included in the Western paideia.

Our group significance tests (Table 24-9, below) showed evidence of significant results among five variables: (1) Propinquity (712), (2) Active Diplomacy (A707), (3) Hereditary Monarchy (D710), (4) Centralization (717), and (5) Quality of Armed Forces, Defensive Stance (B703).

Each of these five variables is separately correlated with each of the three paideias in order to see if there is any special tendency for any of the paideias to have any particular coding of any of the six traits. Where any such correlations are individually significant at the 0.10 level, partial correlations could be computed to see if controlling for the regional association affects the substantive correlation.

DEVIANT CASE ANALYSIS

For each of the five most significant correlations, we looked for deviant cases. By singling out the chief exceptions to the rule we had discovered, we might hope to suggest possible limitations on that rule. Deviant case analysis involves no formal procedures. It consists of reviewing the leading events of the decade involved, in the hope that some plausible explanation of the deviation will suggest itself.

Three of the five most significant correlations involved territorial instability, and in two of these, there were *no* markedly deviant cases. All the extreme values conformed to the overall pattern. In these instances, we nevertheless looked at the single most deviant case. In the other instances, we looked at all the deviant cases to see what might turn up. In these five highly significant correlations, as might be expected, there were in any event no more than two or three deviant cases each.

CAUSAL ANALYSIS

No formal causal analysis methods were applied to this data. For each plausible correlation, we tried to survey only the possible causal explanations. As it turns out, it might have been useful to do a matrix analysis of the interrelationships between Territorial Instability and other variables. We regret the failure to provide for some kind of cross-lagged correlation in our research design. We now think that the use of such correlations would have offered the best hope of explaining causal relationships.

CHAPTER 3

★ ★ ★

THE CLIMAX OF THE BORDER WAR

125-116 B.C.: Conspicuous State, Former Han Dynasty;
Conspicuous Rival, The Huns.

THIS randomly chosen decade proves to be the turning point in the long struggle on the northwestern frontier between the Chinese emperors of the Han dynasty and the Huns. For almost four hundred years the Huns had conducted devastating raids into China, pillaging, burning, and taking slaves. Their victims did not desire the Hun territory for its own sake; their problem had been to deter these raiding nomads. Thus, the Chinese had been continually in a defensive stance. In previous years they had tried everything they could think of to pacify the Huns: they had built the Great Wall, sent their princesses to marry Hun leaders, made alliances with third parties, paid the Huns subsidies. But nothing had worked for long. Now, under the great Han Emperor Wu Ti, the Chinese resolved to protect their frontiers by smashing and utterly destroying the power of the Huns, and in a series of brilliantly conducted campaigns, inflicted great injuries on them. But heavy losses, especially of horses, kept the Chinese from following up their victories and achieving their goal of utter destruction of the Huns. As the decade ended, a hard-won truce held along the frontier while both sides were recuperating. In the coming decades repeated Chinese attacks upon the Huns were at last to bear fruit, but that is beyond the scope of our study.

The empire of the Huns and the Han dynasty were established at almost the same time. The consolidation of the Huns into an empire began about the year 215 B.C., when their leader, Touman, was forced by the Chinese to withdraw northward into Outer Mongolia, where the Huns would be beyond reach of the Chinese. At that time the Ch'in Dynasy (predecessor of the Han Dynasty) was in its decline, and for the next few years the Chinese were concerned with domestic problems and were unable to give attention to the Huns. In 209 B.C., Touman led his forces southward and recon-quered his previously held territory in Inner Mongolia, where he was able to form a strong political organization. Under his son, Maodun, the Huns became a military power which seriously threatened the Chinese. Maodun annexed Eastern Mongolia and Western Manchuria, occupied the Orkhon and Selenga basins of Outer Mongolia, and took possession of Kashgaria. Then he turned to the Chinese and almost succeeded in defeating them. Narrowly avoiding this defeat, the new Han dynasty retained its independence and gradually grew stronger. The Hun empire, having reached its zenith, began to decline.

The Huns were nomadic peoples, living in large part on the products of the horse; they drank its milk, made felt dwellings from its hair, and used it for transportation. But the Huns desired other things not found on the steppes: grains and silk and jewels. If they wanted to, they could sell their horses to the sedentary peoples around them, and then buy the foods and luxuries they wished to enjoy. But it was easier and more exciting to take what they wanted. Thus periodic raids upon the Chinese became a part of the Hun economy and way of life.

After Maodun's death the Hun Empire remained strong for some time, with the balance of power between the Huns and the Chinese being almost equal. The Chinese tried in every way they could to deter the Hun raids. In 197 B.C. they delivered gifts of silks, wine, and rice and sent a princess to be a Hun bride. In 178 B.C. they sent another princess. In 156 B.C. they sent gifts and a princess once again. In 165 B.C., and again in 127 B.C., they settled colonists on the frontier. In 126 B.C. they attempted to foment civil war among the Huns. Although some of these measures often conciliated the Huns, and once for twenty years (158–138 B.C.) brought a period of virtual peace, the Huns continued to be a constant threat to the Chinese northern frontier.

When Wu Ti became emperor in 140 B.C. he made up his mind

to reduce the Hun threat. He determined to mobilize Chinese resources and deliver a powerful blow against the Huns. Wu Ti was a strong and capable ruler who transformed the Chinese Empire. He consolidated a number of vassal states into a central government. He made the Han emperor an absolute ruler. He expanded to such an extent that by the end of his reign the Chinese held three times as much territory as they had at the beginning of it. Early in his reign he turned his attention to the territory of the Huns, and began to plan campaigns to drive them northward. Thus, for the first time in many years the Chinese under Emperor Wu Ti were on the offensive against the Huns. By the beginning of the decade under study, the twenty-year interlude of peace had given way to renewed constant wars between the Huns and the Chinese; the balance of power continued to be about evenly divided between them.

But during the decade from 125 to 116 B.C. the balance of power shifted. The Chinese waged four smashing campaigns; each one left the Huns weaker. And in addition, two important Hun vassals defected to the Chinese, taking their people with them. At the end of the decade the Chinese had succeeded in crippling, but not destroying, the Hun power.

The first of these campaigns took place in 124 B.C., triggered by Hun raids the year before. When it was over the Chinese had weakened the Hun holdings in the area of Kashgaria to the northwest and convinced the Huns that they were now fighting a powerful opponent. The campaign was led by Generalissimo Wei Ch'ing, who had six armies under him with a combined force of more than a hundred thousand troops. His adversary, the Hun viceroy of the west, relied on the comforting thought that the Chinese could not reach him, and on the eve of the battle he got roaring drunk as the Chinese army encircled him in the dark. The Hun viceroy was warned by his people in time to flee to the north, but he was able to take with him only his wife and several hundred cavalry troops. He left behind him ten princes, over fifteen thousand people, and more than a million domestic animals, all of which the Chinese seized.

In the fall of the year 124 B.C. the Huns returned and raided the area once more. The Chinese retaliated in the spring of 123 B.C. by waging a second campaign against them. In this campaign Wei

Ch'ing was again the leader, and again he had under him a force of a hundred thousand cavalry. On his first encounter with the Huns he killed three thousand of them, then withdrew to give his troops a chance to rest up. All in all the Chinese lost three thousand cavalry, and the Huns lost nineteen thousand men by death or capture. Although the Chinese losses were heavy, the Hun losses were even heavier. When the fighting was over the Huns moved their capital north to Urga in the Orkhon basin; it was the first sign they had given of their weakening position. One of the Chinese generals, Chao Hsin, gave himself up to the enemy, and another was captured but escaped. Chao Hsin had formerly been a prince of the Huns whom the Chinese had captured and then given the command of an army. When the Huns recaptured him, it was he who advised the Hun leader to go north across the desert in order to lure the striking force of the Chinese there, exhaust them, and take them prisoners. He indicated how unwise it was for the Huns to remain any longer in the vicinity of the wall.

In the fall of 122 B.C. the Huns raided again, and in the spring the Chinese struck back in a third campaign. This time General Wei Ch'ing took with him his young nephew, Ho Ch'ü-ping, who, with a force of eight hundred, ranged ahead of the main army and killed or captured 2,028 of the Huns. Although Ho Ch'ü-ping was only twenty years old, he had been commanding troops for two years and had already shown great military prowess.

At this time two vassal kings of the Huns went over to the Chinese. The Hun leader had become angry with these two kings of Hun-yeh and Hsiu-t'u for losing thousands of their people to the Chinese. He decided to punish them, and summoned them. They became terrified, made plans to join the Chinese, and notified the emperor of their intentions. The emperor sent Ho Ch'ü-ping to bring them to him. But before Ho Ch'ü-ping arrived, the king of Hun-yeh killed the king of Hsiu-t'u and joined their two forces together. When Ho Ch'ü-ping, with a force of Chinese soldiers, rode to within sight of the Hun-yeh army, rebellion erupted. Several of the subordinate generals under the Hun-yeh king opposed surrender to the Chinese, and many of the soldiers fled. Thereupon Ho Ch'ü-ping galloped into their midst and cut down eight thousand of the fleeing men. The Hun-yeh king and the remainder of his forces, forty thousand men, then completed their surrender to the Chinese. The effect of this submission was to decrease Hun raids in the area west of the Huang-ho, thus enabling the Chinese to cut the garrison strength there.

In the same year (122 B.C.) the emperor sent another general, Li Kuang, on a campaign against the Huns. Li Kuang, leading four thousand cavalry, was to rendezvous with Chang Ch'ien, who set out on a different route with ten thousand cavalry. Chang Ch'ien, who had won renown as an envoy, was familiar with the water and pasture lands in Hun territory, where he had been detained by the Huns on his diplomatic missions. Li Kuang, however, was surrounded by the Huns with a force of twenty to thirty thousand cavalry before Chang Ch'ien could join him. Greatly outnumbered, Li Kuang fought bravely, inflicting heavy losses on the enemy. In the process he is said to have lost most of his men. After two days of battling with the Huns, Li Kuang's army was joined by Chang Ch'ien, and the Huns withdrew, defeated. When Li Kuang and Chang Ch'ien returned to the capital, both commanders were called to account. Li Kuang was given no reward, as it was considered that his brave fighting and the tremendous loss of men cancelled each other out. Chang Ch'ien was condemmed to death for failing to keep his rendezvous with Li Kuang in time. However, the emperor permitted Chang Ch'ien to pay a fine instead, and reduced him to the status of commoner. (In later years Chang Ch'ien was acclaimed for his diplomatic feat of opening the way for relations between the Han and the lands of the barbarians to the southwest.)

In 119 B.C., in the fourth campaign against the Huns, Wei Ch'ing and Ho Ch'ü-ping delivered decisive blows and effectively weakened the power of the Huns. The emperor had resolved that in this campaign his armies would penetrate across the Gobi desert. He furnished two armies, each one equipped with fifty thousand cavalry, foot soldiers, and a large number of chariots filled with grain and other supplies. Wei Ch'ing, commanding one army, and Ho Ch'ü-ping, commanding the other, set out along different routes. Ho Ch'ü-ping encountered and defeated the Hun viceroy of the east, killing or taking prisoner more than seventy thousand men. The Huns were hit so hard that they did not dare cross the Gobi desert for some years nor raid the frontier borders.

Wei Ch'ing meanwhile pushed across the Gobi desert, and in spite of the scarcity of water was able to reach the Hun leader and engage him in a grueling battle. He encircled the battle field with his war chariots,

> but a windstorm arose in the west which whirled so much sand in their faces that neither army could see the other. When the Chinese committed the right and left wings to the attack and encircled the Hun leader, he perceived that the Chinese striking power outnumbered his and the cavalry were still fighting vigorously, putting the Huns at a disadvantage. In the twilight he mounted a wagon drawn by six animals and with a hundred strong cavalry pushed through the Chinese enclosure and fled to the northwest while in the dark the opponents sought wildly for prisoners, killing and wounding in equal numbers. Thus the left flank was seized by the Chinese and from it they learned that the Hun leader had fled before daybreak. The Chinese army during the night followed up the pursuit with light cavalry, and the Generalissimo's forces came behind them, while the Hun forces fled after each other. [De Groot, 136; *Translated by Raoul Naroll*]

This battle broke the power of the Huns for several years. Although they still retained much land, they were confined to the north and made few attacks on the Chinese frontier. But their victory had cost the Chinese much. They were in a poor position to fight further; they had captured nearly a hundred thousand Huns, but they had lost almost as many of their own troops; furthermore, out of one hundred forty thousand horses they were left with but thirty thousand, and no way to obtain others. When Ho Ch'üping died two years later at the age of twenty-four, the Chinese forces were even further weakened. He had been their greatest general; without him the Chinese were unwilling to continue their offensive against the Huns. Both sides now needed time to recuperate.

This was the decade when the Han dynasty finally crippled the Huns. The Huns suffered four severe defeats in a six-year period. They lost more than one-hundred fifty thousand people and 1.5 million domestic animals. They were driven far across the Gobi desert. Two important Hun vassals, seeing how the tide was turning, went over to the Chinese, giving them not only moral encouragement but a zone of protection against the Huns on the western frontier. If the Chinese had not lost so many horses, and if their

MAP No. 1

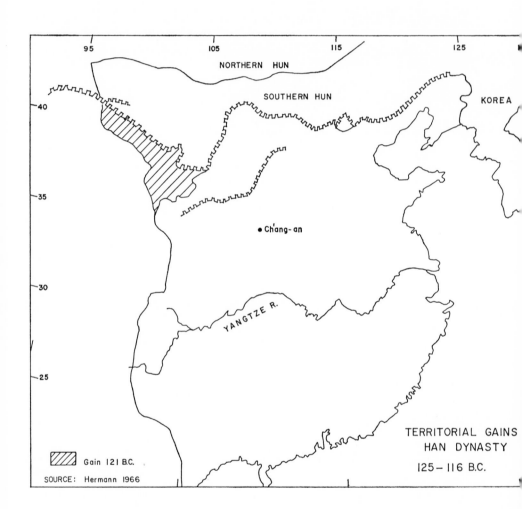

brilliant young field commander had not died, the Huns might well have been destroyed altogether. Even though the Chinese had sixty-five years of hard fighting before them, they had finally succeeded in gaining the upper hand over the Huns.

PART 2: SURVEY OF VARIABLES (CODED FOR CONSPICUOUS STATE, FORMER HAN DYNASTY)

Dependent Variables

Months of War. There seems to have been about one hundred and five months of war and fifteen months of peace during the decade. The last mention of fighting between the Chinese and the Huns is in the summer of 117 B.C., and we have therefore considered the beginning of the peace period as the fall of 117 B.C. The raw score of 105 yields a standard score of 66. For method of transformation see p. 11.

Territorial Change. The Chinese made a permanent Territorial Gain of 3.6 % during the decade in the area south of the Huang-ho, in present-day Kansu (see map 1). The raw score of 3.6% yields two standard scores: Territorial Gain 59, and territorial Stability 53. For method of transformation see p. 13f.

Military Variables

Defensive Stance. Although the Huns had historically been on the offensive, by the time of the decade in question the Han Dynasty did not adopt a purely defensive stance. They assumed the initiative, attempting to smash the Hun empire decisively. Coded *absent*.

Strength of Armed Forces. The Han Dynasty had numerical superiority. The Chinese fought most of the campaign of the decade with large armies: in 124 B.C. General Wei Ch'ing commanded 30,000 cavalry and the next year he led six divisions with more than one hundred thousand troops; in 119 B.C. General Wei Ch'ing and General Ho Ch'ü-ping each commanded an army of 50,000 cavalry. The size of the Hun armies is not given in the sources, but there is mention of as many as seventy thousand Hun prisoners being taken by Ho Ch'ü-ping in 119 B.C. More often, however, the number of the Hun prisoners taken is given at between three and ten thousand. The Chinese probably had numerical superiority over the Huns. Coded present.

Mobility of Armed Forces. Neither side appeared to be decidedly more mobile than the other. General Ho Ch'ü-ping used fewer heavy war chariots than was customary in the Chinese campaigns and introduced instead the light cavalry brigade. For the first time the Chinese army was as mobile as the opponent's. However, the Chinese lost one hundred ten thousand of the one hundred forty thousand horses used during the decade, and thus paid a very high price for their newly won mobility. Since it was impossible for the Chinese to replace these losses they were unable to follow up their victories against the Huns and to break their power completely; as neither side had a clear advantage this was coded *absent*.

Quality of Armed Forces. During the decade under study China had two generals of outstanding ability, the commander-in-chief, Wei Ch'ing, and his nephew, Ho Ch'ü-ping. When Ho Ch'ü-ping died in 118 B.C. at the age of twenty-four, he had never lost a battle, and his death was a severe military loss to the Chinese Empire. In contrast, the Huns appeared to have had no outstanding generals during this period. Since the Chinese weapons had always been of superior quality, the Chinese army during the decade from 125 to 116 B.C. had a formidable advantage over the Huns, and was able to weaken their power greatly. Coded *present*.

Fortifications. The Chinese during this period were building a wall to fortify the highland of the Huang-ho River. When the Han forces weakened the power of the Huns at the end of the decade, the Chinese were able to reduce the garrisons there and settle colonists in the area. Coded *present*.

Prestige. The prestige of the Chinese court under Emporer Wu Ti was on the rise, whereas the Huns, in the process of being reduced to a defensive position, were beginning to lose prestige. Nevertheless the Han military prestige was not in a class by itself. Hence it is coded *absent*.

Geographical Variables

Propinquity. The Hun Empire was northwest of China, in what is now Mongolia, Turkestan, and southwestern Siberia. Coded *present* because the Han Dynasty shared a common land border with the Huns.

Natural Barriers. The most formidable barrier between the Huns and the Chinese was the Gobi desert. In the desert it was extremely difficult for the Chinese to obtain the food and water they needed to pursue the Huns; thus, when the Huns retreated to the north of the desert they were out of reach of the Chinese forces. Coded *present.*

Capital City, The Chinese capital, Ch'ung-an, was 315 miles from the nearest point on the outer wall. During the decade from 125 to 116 B.C. the Huns moved their capital north to Urga, in the Orkhon River basin, 575 miles from the nearest point on the Great Wall. Coded *absent.*

Diplomatic Variables

Announcements. No announcements of Chinese intentions to attack the Huns were mentioned during the decade. Coded *no data.*

Surprise Attack. There is not enough information on this variable. Coded *no data.*

Alliances. The Wu-sun people appear to have been the ally most sought after by both the Huns and the Chinese. The king of Wu-sun had been a tributary of the Huns, and had freed himself. The Huns tried unsuccessfully to force him to resume this role. The Chinese used gold, silver, silks, and jewels to win him over. The Chinese envoy visited the Wu-sun court, where he was respectfully received. The king of Wu-sun even had him accompanied to the frontier with an escort of thirty horses. But the king of Wu-sun refused to submit to the emperor. Neither the Huns nor the Chinese could coax him into an alliance. Coded *absent.*

Active Diplomacy. There is mention of only one attempt at negotiation during the decade—the peace mission sent by the Huns to the emperor at the end of the decade. The Huns had already withdrawn to the north of the desert, their striking force greatly weakened. Although the Chinese now had too few horses to pursue the Huns, they had succeeded in putting them in a defensive position. When the Hun envoy arrived at the Chinese court, the emperor referred the peace mission to his council. Some of the members were in favor of establishing peaceful relations with the Huns, but others thought the time propitious for bringing the Huns to submission. The emperor decided on the latter course, and sent an envoy to tell the Hun leader to subject himself and appear at the border for an imperial audience. The Hun leader was furious when he received the summons, and in reprisal, detained the Chinese envoy. Coded *absent*.

Intense Diplomacy. There were no formal treaties concluded during the decade. Coded *absent*.

Previous Conflict. For almost a hundred years before the decade from 125 to 116 B.C., the Han emperors had been protecting their northwestern territories against the Huns, who continually made devastating raids from their lands in the steppes of Mongolia, Turkestan, and southwestern Siberia. When they were pursued by the Chinese, the Huns withdrew their families and herds beyond the Gobi desert, out of reach of the Chinese forces. But after a hundred years of fighting, the military power of the Huns began to decline. In contrast, under the leadership of the Han Emperor Wu Ti, the power of China was both consolidating and expanding. During the decade under study the Chinese finally became strong enough to cripple the Huns and restrain them north of the Gobi desert. Coded *present*.

Cultural Variables

Benefits. In addition to the high rank the emperor had bestowed upon the Hun princes Chao Hsin and Mi-ty (see "Cultural Exchange," below), the emperor planned a splendid reception for the king of Hun-yeh when the latter submitted his own and the king of Hsiu-tu's troops (see "Civil War," below). The emperor ordered twenty thousand chariots to be sent ahead to greet the king of Hun-yeh. Unfortunately, there were not enough horses to pull so many chariots, nor was there enough money to buy horses. Owners of horses did not want to lend them for this purpose and hid them. The emperor's advisors finally urged him to abandon this elaborate escort plan, and the emperor agreed to do so. But he rewarded the king of Hun-yeh with a domain of ten thousand families, and bestowed upon him the rank of a vassal prince. He had the king's followers released on the frontier and allowed them to live in freedom and follow their own customs. Coded *present*.

Cultural Exchange. There was no direct cultural contact between the Chinese and the Huns. Probably the most common basis of exchange was through military prisoners. When the prisoners were of high rank they were often given a position of corresponding prestige by their new host. In the decade under study Chao Hsin, a prince of the Huns who had given himself up to the Chinese in battle, received from them a title and the command of a Chinese army. Then, when he later engaged the Hun forces in battle and was defeated by them, the Huns recaptured him, gave him a rank immediately below the Hun leader's, and married him to a Hun princess. It was this Chao Hsin who advised the Huns to go north across the desert and leave the area of the great wall permanently. The Hun leader presumably respected what Chao Hsin had learned from his Chinese contacts, for he followed his advice. And when Chao Hsin advised the Hun leader to send a peace mission to the emperor he again followed his advice.

Another hostage of high rank was the Hun prince Mi-ty, the oldest son of Prince Hsiu-t'u (see "Benefits," above.)

> He was a young man, tall, well-built and handsome, and his face seemed to reveal the finest qualities. He was among those chosen by the mandarins for service at the court. This young Hun was put in charge of the emperor's stable, and he did his job well; the horses had never looked so well cared for.
> Mi-ty considered himself born to better things and tried to make himself known to the emperor. One day, when the occasion was appropriate, Mi-ty paraded the horses before him. The emperor, charmed to see the horses so well groomed, and realizing that he was the son of a prince, thereupon made him a mandarin... From that time on the emperor treated him with distinction. [De Mailla, 46; *translated by* FRADA NAROLL]

But the hosts did not always treat their guests with such consideration. When the peace mission which the Huns sent to the Chinese returned with the emperor's reply, the Hun leader became so enraged that he detained the Chinese envoy, a practice which was not at all uncommon. When Chang Ch'ien was sent as an envoy and then detained by the Huns he was able to bring back to the emperor information that he had gathered in Hun territory, and in outlying barbarian states. Coded *absent* because there was no direct cultural contact.

Trade. There was no information available on this variable. Coded *no data.*

General Exchange. Coded *absent* (see "Cultural Exchange" and "Trade", above).

Administrative Variables

Experience of Ruler. Emperor Wu Ti commenced his reign in 141 B.C., at the age of seventeen and was thirty-three years old in 125 B.C., when the decade began. Coded *present* because the ruler came to power more than ten years before the decade began and ruled for at least six years longer.

Youth of Ruler. Wu Ti was born in 158 B.C. He was thirty-three years of age when the decade began. Coded *present* because the ruler was under twenty-five years of age at the beginning of the decade.

Unbridled Ruler. Coded *present* because Wu Ti was a hereditary monarch, was thirty-three years old and ruled a centralized monarchy.

Hereditary Monarchy. Coded *present* (See "Unbridled Ruler" above).

Civil War. Among the Chinese at this time there was none; Emperor Wu Ti was one of the strongest ever to rule China. The Huns, however, were involved in internal strife. The sources relate one incident, which took place in 121 B.C., when the leader of the Huns got angry because the kings of Hun-yeh and Hsiu-t'u had lost many thousands of men to the Chinese forces in the west. When the Hun leader decided to punish them, these two kings became frightened, and made plans to submit to the Chinese. In the meantime the king of Hun-yeh killed the king of the Hsiu-t'u and combined both their forces. Before the king of Hun-yeh could submit to the emperor, some of his subordinate generals fled in disorder not wanting, after all, to submit to the Chinese. Ho Ch'ü-ping, the Chinese warrior, cut them down. The Hun-yeh king and his remaining soldiers then gave themselves up to the Chinese, as they had planned. Although this is only one instance of internecine strife during the decade under study, it followed the successful revolt of the Hun viceroy of the west against his uncle, the Hun leader, in 125 B.C. Coded *absent* because there was no civil war among the Chinese.

Centralization. China under Emperor Wu Ti was emerging from a group of vassal states, each with its own ruler, into a strong power with a central government which directly administered the provinces. According to McGovern (pp. 117–18) the Huns were less highly centralized than the Chinese. Coded *present*.

PART 3: DATA QUALITY CONTROL

The primary sources on the Huns of this period have been collected and translated into German by J.J.M. de Groot *Chinesische Urkunden zur Geschichte Asiens* (Berlin: de Gruyter, 1921), vol. 1. From these sources in De Groot we have made use of the *Pen Ki* (*Annals*) and chapters 110, 116, and 123 of the *Shih-chi* (*Historical Records*) by Ssu-ma Ch'ien, as well as the *Pen chi* of the *Hou Han Shu* (*History of the Former Han Dynasty*) by Pan Ku. We also consulted Burton Watson, trans., *Records of the Grand Historian of China, Ssu-Ma Ch'ien* (New York: Columbia University Press, 1961), vol. 2. Ssu-ma Ch'ien was a contemporary of the decade. Pan Ku wrote in the first century after Christ, 200 years after the events described.

The secondary works consulted include Joseph A.M. de Mailla, *Histoire Générale de la Chine* (Paris: D. Pierres, 1777), vol. 3; and William McGovern, *The Early Empires of Central Asia* (Chapel Hill: University of North Carolina Press, 1939). De Mailla's work is an eighteenth-century translation into French of a classic survey of Chinese history written in the eleventh century by Ssu-ma Kuang, and edited in the twelfth century by the philosopher Chu Hsi. McGovern's work is a contemporary survey of Chinese-Hun relations, a masterly work which has taken into account all the Chinese sources as well as subsequent works on the Huns by later scholars.

Publication Year. The sources that are coded are Ssu-ma Ch'ien and Pan Ku (Ssu-ma Ch'ien was a contemporary during the decade and Pan Ku wrote in the first century after Christ). Coded *absent* because all authors who wrote prior to 1850 are so coded.

Primary Source. Coded *present*. Ssu-ma Ch'ien is a primary source.

Authors' Associations. The Chinese authors Ssu-ma Ch'ien and Pan Ku were court historians, favorably disposed toward China. Coded *present*. De Mailla had a mandarin's status at the Manchu court, but was not a real Chinese scholar. We are not in a position to detect his bias. *Not coded* in this chapter. McGovern was a professor of political science at Northwestern University. He lived in China when he was young and had taught Chinese (*not coded*).

Authors' Sympathies The Chinese court historians Ssu-ma Ch'ien and Pan Ku were understandably pro-Chinese and anti-Hun. Coded *present*. De Mailla does not reveal any special sympathy for either side during the events of the decade, nor does McGovern; *not coded*.

Authors' Proximity. Ssu-ma Ch'ien was twenty years old when the decade began. However, it is not known when the chapters of the *Shih-chi* which we used were written. Pan Ku wrote two hundred years after the events described. Coded *present*. De Mailla wrote about nineteen hundred years after the events, and McGovern about twenty-one hundred years after them; *not coded*.

CHAPTER 4

★ ★ ★

A LULL ON THE NORTHERN MARCHES

25-16 B.C.: Conspicuous State, Han Dynasty; Conspicuous Rival, the Huns.

PART I: SKETCH OF HISTORICAL SETTING (CHIEFLY AFTER PAN KU)

THE RANDOMLY chosen decade from 25 to 16 B.C. was one of the quietest in the struggle between the Chinese emperors of the Han Dynasty and the nomadic Huns who periodically raided their northwestern frontier. The struggle had begun in 220 B.C. During this period of more than two hundred years, the emperors of the Han Dynasty had tried in every way possible to protect their frontiers against the Huns. Sometimes they were successful, but whenever they were, the Huns retreated beyond the Gobi desert, where it was almost impossible for the Chinese to pursue them. During most of the long struggle, there was continual fighting, but there was one extended period of peace, from 51 B.C. to A.D., 9, and the decade under study took place during that long period when both sides were more concerned with internal than with external problems.

The partial peace which was established in 51 B.C. was completed in 36 B.C., and allowed the Chinese to relax somewhat their constant vigilance over the northwest. By 25 B.C., the former Han Dynasty had begun to crumble. Imperial power had been weakening from the time of the Emperor Wu Ti partly because of the incompetence of the rulers and partly because of the corruption which had infested the administrative system. Emperor Ch'eng Ti, who acceded to the throne in 32 B.C. was devoted to pleasure, and preferred to leave imperial duties to the most able and willing of his maternal uncles. Consequently, the power of his uncle and his mother's lineage increased until they held power in fact if not yet in name, and by A.D. 9 Ch'eng Ti's (maternal) nephew actually seized the throne.

A century before, China's formerly continual defensive stance had been abandoned under the great Han Emperor Wu Ti in favor of a series of offensive campaigns to drive the Huns northward and weaken their striking power. A balance of power which had been initially almost equal shifted in the first half of the century after the Chinese waged four victorious campaigns, each one of which left the Huns weaker than before. Thus, by 51 B.C. the Huns were ready to submit to the Chinese, at least for a while. Civil discord among the Huns contributed substantially to this temporary victory for the Chinese. The Huns split into two rival factions—the Southern Huns under Hu-han-yeh, and the Northern Huns under his brother Chih-chih. Hu-han-yeh sought protection from his brother's forces by turning to the Chinese, and was given the status of a subordinate ruler by them.

Chih-chih did not submit to the Chinese, but he did enter into friendly relations with them. He sent his son to the Chinese court as a hostage and periodically had his envoys bring tributary gifts to the emperor. He apparently hoped to weaken the ties between Hu-han-yeh and the Chinese, but when it became clear to him that he was succeeding he began to expand westward. He absorbed numerous petty kingdoms, some of which had attachments with the Chinese. In 44 B.C. Chih-chih requested the return of his son from the Chinese court, and the boy was duly sent home under the escort of a high Chinese official. When they reached the Hun capital Chih-chih had the Chinese envoy killed. Then, in order to strenghten himself against Chinese retaliation, he allied himself with the K'ang-chü, a small kingdom to the southwest, and the K'ang-chü soon followed Chih-chih's example, and began to treat the Chinese officials disrespectfully.

During this time Chih-chih built a huge walled city, the first in Hun history. The Chinese were so concerned with their internal problems that decisive action against the Huns might have been still further postponed had it not been for an unusually bold and aggressive Chinese military officer, Ch'en T'ang. Attempting to convince his superior, the protector general of Kashgaria, of the necessity for an immediate offensive campaign against the Huns, Ch'en Tang pointed out that if Chih-chih were allowed to become any more powerful, he might invade all the Chinese colonies formerly attached to the Greater Hun Empire and then declare himself the ruler of all the Huns. Ch'en T'ang thought it was necessary to give Chih-chih as little time as possible to fortify himself in his walled capital. He accordingly organized a large army of Chinese colonists and Kashgarians, forcefully overcame his superior's objections, and, without the emperor's knowledge, set out for the rebel capital.

On the way Ch'en T'ang encountered a detachment of K'ang-chü cavalrymen who captured his baggage train. But he was able to rally his troops and defeat the K'ang-chü. Realizing that Chih-chih's arrogance had alienated many of the K'ang-chü, Ch'en T'ang had hopes of luring them from their alliance with the rebel Hun leader. He therefore dealt with the K'ang-chü very carefully and was able to induce the K'ang-chü leaders to cooperate with him. He then proceeded toward Chih-chih's fortified capital and his army of more than forty thousand encamped outside of the city.

Chih-chih sent an envoy to demand the reason for this show of force. Ch'en T'ang replied that they were demanding satisfaction for his oppression of their tributary, the kingdom of K'ang-chü. However, the envoy was assured that the Chinese would move no closer to the city while they awaited Chih-chih's response. Chih-chih did not feel in a strong enough position to attack and began negotiations with the Chinese. But the Chinese troops approached during the night and invaded. They made a bonfire outside the walls and watched the wind carry the flames to the side of the fortress, and then to the houses within. During the ensuing disorder, they stormed the palace where Chih-chih was hiding and killed him.

The death of Chih-chih and the destruction of his kingdom as an important political unit strengthened Hu-han-yeh's position greatly, but he was still intimidated by the striking power of the Chinese. Accordingly, he immediately petitioned the Chinese court for an imperial audience and the opportunity to renew his homage. For their part, the Chinese received Hu-han-yeh with as much regard as they had upon his first submission. They gave him twenty thousand pounds each of raw and woven silk, among other gifts, and at his request granted him a wife–a highborn lady of the emperor's own harem. It is obvious that the Chinese were anxious to conciliate the Huns at this time.

Before Emperor Ch'eng Ti commenced his reign in 32 B.C., his father had had high hopes for him. Ch'eng Ti had been a studious youth but his overindulgences made his father increasingly hesitant to name him heir-apparent. Finally, on the basis of a promise to change his ways, he was named crown prince.

The Chinese family system is patrilineal. People related by common descent through males are associated in corporate family groups (for a full description of this intricate and important aspect of Chinese society, see Francis L.K. Hsu, *Clan, Caste and Club*, pp. 60–78).

The Emperor Ch'eng Ti had no interest in public affairs, wished to continue to enjoy the perquisites of his office and simultaneously have its duties and responsibilities carried on by others. Members of his mother's patrilineal lineage, the Wangs, were only too glad to cooperate. Scarcely had Ch'eng Ti ascended the throne when he entrusted all authority to his maternal uncles. Natural disasters occurred repeatedly during his reign, and repeatedly he sought the interpretations and advice of the sages. But he ignored their advice. He bestowed titles of eminence on the brothers of the queen mother even though they had not distinguished themselves through service to the state. He pursued pleasures in a manner which the Chinese considered unbecoming in an emperor and displeasing to Heaven, and he could not be persuaded to renounce his excesses.

In the eighth year of his reign (24 B.C.), Ch'eng Ti was becoming dissatisfied with seeing his uncle Wang Feng rule in his place. He was delighted to be presented with a memorandum condemning Wang Feng's abuse of authority and had hopes of seizing the power for himself. Before Ch'eng Ti could dismiss Wang Feng, however, the uncle had the queen mother plead on his behalf and succeeded in remaining in power. Ch'eng Ti lacked the forcefulness to prevent the further advance of the Wang family, and by the following year the five princes of the family were in control of the court and virtual masters of the Chinese empire. When Wang Feng lay on his deathbed he chose his own successor, and Emperor Ch'eng Ti was unable to oppose him.

Although Ch'eng Ti did try to reassume imperial responsibilities after Wang Feng's death, he was still too interested in debauchery

MAP No. 2

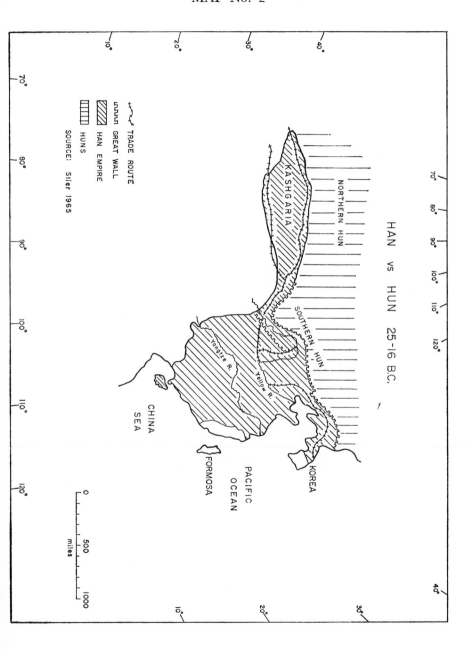

to pursue the fight for power. The rest of his reign witnessed such degrading insults to the dignity of the throne as the replacement of the reigning empress by a comedienne of humble origins and questionable morals. Ch'eng Ti gradually ceased to function as an effective political leader.

Thus, the decade from 25 to 16 B.C. was concerned with the internal problems of the Chinese court. The weakening former Han Dynasty never recovered its strength, and twenty-five years after the decade ended, Wang Mang, the son of one of Emperor Ch'eng-Ti's uncles, seized the throne and tried to found a new dynasty. He also ended the sixty-year peace between the Chinese and the Huns. During this period of sixty years the Huns desisted from raiding the Chinese borders, and the Chinese conciliated the Huns. The Chinese were anxious to maintain the peace because of their internal problems. The Huns were grateful for an opportunity to rebuild their forces.

PART 2: SURVEY OF VARIABLES (CODED FOR CONSPICUOUS STATE, HAN DYNASTY)

Dependent Variables

Months of War. There were minor encounters during this decade, but not between the Huns and the Chinese. There were no months of war and 120 months of peace. The raw score of 0 yields a standard score of 37. For method of transformation see p. 11.

Territorial Change. No Territorial Change occurred during the decade. The raw score of 0 yields two standard scores: Territorial Gain 49 and Territorial Stability 36. For method of transformation see. p. 13f.

Military Variables

Defensive Stance. This was an era of peace and diplomacy, and the Huns at this time were apparently content to remain vassals of the Chinese, in a defensive stance vis-à-vis the Chinese. The Chinese are regarded as having maintained an offensive stance. Coded *absent*.

Strength of Armed Forces. No specific data is given on the actual size of forces in this decade, although it is mentioned that the Hun ruler Hu-han-yeh had been greatly intimidated by the crushing blow dealt to his rival, Chih-chih, and by an army of more than forty thousand Chinese. The Han forces seem to have been superior in strength to the Huns, but this advantage was probably precarious. It is noteworthy that the Chinese felt it necessary to send two high military officials back to the border with the Hun ruler after rejecting his offer to defend the Chinese fortifications. Coded *present*.

Mobility of Armed Forces. There is no specific mention of mobility in the Chinese sources of this period; however, it is known that the rebel Hun leader, Chih-chih, used foot soldiers for the first time in hundreds of years, indicating that the Huns may have had very few horses. If this was the case, we can conjecture that the extended period of peace from 36 B.C. to A.D. 9 may have been partly because of decreased Hun mobility. Coded *absent*.

Quality of Armed Forces. There is very little information concerning military skill in the sources of this period. The Chinese general Ch'en T'ang felt that a Chinese soldier was worth five Huns. He described the Hun forces as badly armed, poorly nourished, and underpaid. Soldiers accustomed to cavalry warfare would certainly have been at a distinct disadvantage on foot, especially before constantly renewed Chinese forces. It is clear, however, that the Chinese still had a healthy respect for the Huns' military prowess and were cautious and conciliatory towards them during the entire period of peace. Coded *present*.

Fortifications. At the height of his power Chih-chih, the rebel Hun leader, had a huge walled city built to serve as his capital. This fortress was beseiged and burned by Chinese forces in 36 B.C. His rival, Hu-han-yeh, does not appear to have fortified his capital. The Chinese Empire itself was fortified along the great wall, but there is no evidence that new fortifications were established during this period. Coded *absent* because "Defensive Stance," above, has been coded *absent* also.

Prestige. China was the recognized dominant power, but felt less than secure with respect to certain of the colonies and tried to avoid any situation which would facilitate transfer of loyalties from Han to Hun. Coded *present*.

Geographical Variables

Propinquity. The Huns were northwest of China in what is now Mongolia, Turkestan, and Zungaria. Coded *present* because of common land boundary.

Natural Barriers. The Gobi desert was the most formidable barrier between the Huns and the Chinese, but there is no indication that that barriers were of importance in the decade under study. Coded *present.*

Capital City. Ch'ang-an, the Chinese capital, was 315 miles from the nearest point on the outer wall. The Hun capital at this time was again located in the vicinity of Urga, in the Orkhon River basin, 575 miles from the nearest point on the Great Wall. Coded *absent.*

Diplomatic Variables

Announcements. Since this was a decade of peace, there were none. In the preceding decade, however, when the Chinese forces laid siege to Chih-chih's city (see "Fortifications," above), the Chinese announced their intention to remain where they were encamped. Instead, they advanced, caught Chih-chih off guard and killed him. Coded *no data.*

Surprise Attack. Coded no data. See "Announcements," above.

Alliances. There is no indication that alliances were made by either the Conspicuous State or the Rival in the decade under study. But in the preceding decade the Chinese defeated Chih-chih while he was allied with the kingdom of K'ang-chü. Coded *absent.*

Active Diplomacy. There is no mention of any important negotiation during the decade under study. There were serious negotiations between the Chinese and the Huns before 25 B.C., when the Huns offered to defend the borderlands for the Han Dynasty; after careful consideration, the Chinese turned down the Hun offer in a face-saving manner. Following the decade under study, unsuccessful negotiations were carried on with the Hun ruler by a Chinese envoy to retrieve a strategic strip of land originally ceded the Huns by the Han Dynasty. Coded *absent.*

Intense Diplomacy. There was none during the period studied. Coded *absent.*

Previous Conflict. For more than one hundred and fifty years the Chinese emperors of the Han Dynasty had been struggling to protect their northwestern borders from the devastating raids of the nomadic Huns. After fifty years of intensive fighting the conflict was temporarily resolved when the Chinese subdued the main body of Huns in 51 B.C. A peace was negotiated at this time, but submission of all the Huns was not achieved until 36 B.C., when the rebel Hun leader Chih-chih was defeated. The peace which then followed lasted until the end of the former Han Dynasty in A.D. 9. Coded *present.*

Cultural Variables

Benefits. No honors seem to have been awarded in the decade under study; however, in the preceding decade an advisor to the Hun ruler defected to the Chinese and was made a feudal prince and given a seal. In 33 B.C., when Hu-han-yeh appeared at court, he was given sixteen thousand catties of silk floss and eighteen thousand pieces of silk fabrics. The subsidy actually went up in the recorded transactions of 25 B.C. (twenty thousand of each) and in 1 B.C. (thirty thousand of each). Coded *present.*

Cultural Exchange. In general, cultural exchange was not frequent. Both during and after the decade from 25 to 16 B.C., high-ranking Huns came for audiences at the Chinese court. In 33 B.C. the Hun ruler, Hu-han-yeh, appeared at court. He was greeted with much ceremony, given gifts and, at his own request, a highborn wife—a woman of the emperor's own harem. This wife was known as the Consort Who Brought Peace. Coded *absent* because instances of Cultural Exchange were rare.

Trade. We found no information available on this variable. Coded *no data.*

General Exchange. Coded *absent* because "Cultural Exchange," above, is coded *absent.*

Administrative Variables

Experience of Ruler. Emperor Ch'eng Ti commenced his reign in 32 B.C. at the age of nineteen and was twenty-six years old when the decade began. Coded *absent* because Ch'eng Ti had not been in power for ten years when the decade began.

Youth of Ruler. Emperor Ch'eng Ti was born in 51 B.C. Coded *present* because he was less than forty-five years old at the beginning of the decade. See "Experience of Ruler," above.

Unbridled Ruler. Ch'eng Ti was a hereditary monarch who ruled a centralized state, and was between twenty and forty-five years old at the opening of the decade. Coded *present* (see Hereditary Monarchy, below).

Hereditary Monarchy. Ch'eng Ti was chosen from the eligible princes by his father. Coded *present.*

Civil War. In China, the Conspicuous State in this decade, there were perpetual court intrigues between the family of the queen mother and the family and followers of the emperor. However, there was no actual war between the two factions. There is no mention of strife among the Huns after 36 B.C., when Chih-chih's rebellion was finally brought to an end with his death. In 31 B.C. Hu han-yeh died, and for the next seventy-six years his many sons ruled, one after another, apparently without strife. Coded *absent.*

Centralization. In spite of the internal problems which beset the Han dynasty as this time, China still had a strong central government and was directly administering the provinces. As to the Huns, the destruction of Chih-chih's forces in 36 B.C. made the Huns a united group once again. However, there were still many Huns who did not immediately submit to Hu-han-yeh, and it is difficult to see how a force which had been so sharply divided could be directly administered so soon after reunion; thus, it appears that the Chinese were probably much more highly centralized than the Huns. Coded *present.*

PART 3: DATA QUALITY CONTROL

The primary sources concerning the Huns of this period have been collected and translated into German by J.J.M. de Groot, *Chinesische Urkunden zur Geschichte Asiens* (Berlin: de Gruyter, 1921), vol. 1. From these sources in de Groot we have made use of the *Pen Ki* of the *Hou-Han shu* in the *History of the Former Han Dynasty* by Pan Ku.

The secondary works consulted (but not coded) include Joseph A.M. de Mailla, *Histoire Générale de la Chine*, (Paris: D. Pierres, 1777), vol. 3; William McGovern, *The Early Empires of Central Asia* (Chapel Hill: University of North Carolina Press, 1939); and Yu Ying-shih, *Trade and Expansion in Han China* (Berkeley, 1967). De Mailla's work is an eighteenth-century translation into the French of a classic survey of Chinese history written in the eleventh century by Ssu-ma Kuang, and edited in the twelfth century by the philosopher Chu Hsi. McGovern's work is a contemporary survey of Chinese-Hun relations, a work which has taken into account all the Chinese sources as well as subsequent works on the Huns by later scholars.

Publication Year. Pan Ku wrote in the first century after Christ, seventy-five to one hundred years after the events described. Coded *absent* because it was written before 1850 (this is the only primary source which has been coded).

Primary Source. Pan Ku is coded *present* because his was as close to an eyewitness account as we can get.

Authors' Associations. Pan Ku was a court historian. Coded *present*. (De Mailla had a mandarin's status at the Chinese court, but was not a real Chinese scholar. *Not Coded*. McGovern was a Professor of Political Science at Northwestern University who had lived in China when he was young and had taught Chinese. *Not coded*.)

Authors' Sympathies. A Chinese court historian would understandably be pro-Chinese and anti-Hun. Pan Ku is coded *present*. (De Mailla does not reveal any special sympathy for either side during the events of the decade, nor does McGovern. Neither is coded.)

Authors' Proximity. Pan Ku lived from A.D. 32 to A.D. 92, and thus wrote seventy-five to one hundred years after the events described. Coded *no data*. (De Mailla wrote about eighteen hundred years after the events, and McGovern about two thousand years afterwards. Neither is coded.)

CHAPTER 5

★ ★ ★

T'ANG CHINA VERSUS TIBET: GRADUATED RECIPROCATION IN TENSION REDUCTION

776-785: Conspicuous State, T'ang Dynasty; Conspicuous Rival, Tibet.

PART 1: SKETCH OF HISTORICAL SETTING (CHIEFLY AFTER LIU HSU AND OU-YANG HSIU)

THE DECADE from 776 to 85 in China saw a new emperor continually threatened by rebellious uprising among his subjects. During most of the decade the emperor had to put down one rebel after another, and not until the decade ended did he finally get firm control of the government. That his primary concern was with his rebellious subjects is obvious, and may explain why he was willing to accommodate the Tibetans and make a peace with them at this time. The Chinese had just defeated the Tibetans twice when the new emperor mounted the throne in 779. But his own civil war soon made him anxious for peace with his neighbors. So having first used force, the Chinese now offered the Tibetans conciliation. For their part, the Tibetans, having suffered two recent defeats, were not adverse to peace and needed only to save face. The T'ang emperor, by conciliating the Tibetans with goodwill gestures, enabled them to do this and thus brought about the peace which both sides now found advantageous.

The events of the decade provide an illuminating case of Charles E. Osgood's graduated reciprocation in tension reduction ("Suggestions for Winning the Real War with Communism," *J. of Conflict Resolution* 3: no. 4 [1959], 295–325). The process works in the following way. In inter-nation conflict, the greater the tension, the greater the likelihood of war (which presumably neither side really wants).

To avoid this type of mounting tension, one side may make a tentative gesture of conciliation in a small matter. If the other side responds by making another small gesture of conciliation, the first nation may be encouraged to make a larger move toward peace, and by a series of gradual unilateral reciprocal steps the tensions are reduced. This is what took place between the Chinese and Tibetans during the decade from 776 to 785.

The T'ang dynasty, regarded by later Chinese writers as their golden age, was in the middle of its three-hundred-year rule in 776. The national system of education had been reorganized, making provisions for graduates of the university to pass into the civil service, and thus assuring an adequate supply of trained civil officials. It had become common for the sons of neighboring rulers to be educated at the Chinese capital and to return home with respect for Chinese culture. The code of laws had been completely revised, with provision made for the extensive foreign trade. The government had become powerful and well organized. But internal and external troubles were frequent during the entire T'ang dynasty with frontier raids, rebellions, intrigues and conspiracies a part of almost every reign. The educational, legal and administrative reforms helped the dynasty survive in spite of the troubles at home and on the frontier. And to the T'ang emperors, the Tibetans were among the most troublesome of the frontier raiders.

By the end of the sixth century the Tibetans were already politically united, and the T'ang rulers had adopted a policy of friendly conciliation towards them. When a Tibetan leader's demand to marry an imperial princess was rejected, and he invaded the empire, the emperor first defeated him and then conciliated him by allowing the marriage. Sometimes the Tibetans fought as allies alongside the Chinese, sometimes they fought as enemies against them. In 670 the Tibetans attacked and captured four towns in Turkestan: Kucha, Khotan, Kashgar, and Karasher. The capture of these garrisons gave them control of the two most important trade routes to the west. In 679, when the western Turks allied with the Tibetans, the Chinese lost Turkestan. But by 692 the Tibetan-Turkish alliance was broken, the four towns were recaptured, and China reestablished control over the trade routes. In 773 the ruler of Kashmir tried to make an alliance with the Chinese against the Tibetans, but the emperor refused. Then the Tibetans allied with the Arabs and were able to undermine Chinese prestige.

By the middle of the eighth century the Tibetans had expanded their territory greatly and had become powerful. In 755, during the reign of the Chinese emperor Hsuan Tsung, the rebellion of An Lu-shan expressed new social and political forces. The two emergent social forces were military satraps and a new group of gentry in the northeast and south of China. They sought to gain political power from the "old gentry" of the Northwest. The resulting gigantic struggle weakened the Chinese state internally and was to force the moribund ruling house to call repeatedly on barbarian mercenaries to fight its battles against these new social forces.

In 763 the Tibetans again raided the T'ang dominions intensively and they made repeated raids until the beginning of the decade from 776 to 785. Thus, from the beginning of the T'ang dynasty the Tibetans were the major foreign problem of the Chinese rulers.

In 776, when the decade began, the Chinese, by allying with the T'u-chüeh, T'u-yü-hun, Ti, Man Ch'iang, and Tanghsiang were able to defeat an army of two hundred thousand Tibetans; in the following year the Chinese captured the Tibetan city of Wanghan. Two years later the Chinese again defeated a Tibetan army of two hundred thousand. Emperor Te Tsung had just succeeded to the throne and he "determined to rule the four quarters with virtue, and collected five hundred of the chained captives, gave to each a suit of clothes, and sent Wei Lun to take them back to their country, and to conclude a treaty of peace, and also commanded the frontier general to put a stop to plunder and invasion." (Bushell, 485). Emperor Te Tsung at this time was also troubled by rebellions in the provinces, and hoped to conciliate the Tibetans by this gesture of good will. That the Tibetans approved of this gesture is shown by their ruler's answer to Wei Lun, the emperor's envoy:

> 'I have three causes of sorrow... I was ignorant of the loss the empire had sustained, and was unable to condole and mourn— this is the first. I knew not the day of the imperial funeral, and was unable to present offerings, and fulfill the proper rites—this is the second. I knew not of the holy and wise accession of the Emperor, my father-in-law, and despatched armies by three parallel roads. The army of Ling-wu, having already heard of your appoinment, has halted. But the army of Shannan has

invaded Fu-wen, and the army of Shu marched past Kuan-k'ou, and they have not yet been overtaken—this is my third sorrow.' He then sent envoys with despatches and presents to the emperor, and in less than twenty days they returned with the imperial commands. [Bushell, 485]

The emperor perceived that this policy of conciliation was mellowing the Tibetans, and he continued it. One of his commanders sent to the Emperor the captives which he had taken in battle, and the officers petitioned that they should be treated in accordance with the old practice, and sent to be slaves, but the sovereign replied, 'Our wish for a treaty is on record, and can our words be double?' He therefore bestowed on each two pieces of silk, and a suit of clothes, and sent them back. [Bushell, 486]

In the same year he sent another mission to the Tibetans with gifts, and the Tibetans entertained them and sent their chief minister with the emperor's answer. The following year the mission to the Tibetans returned with a request that the emperor's official dispatch be changed in wording. The Tibetans objected to some of the language that had been used, especially the phrase "offered as tribute," (which they wanted changed to "presented" (Bushell, 487). The Tibetans also resented being treated as subjects instead of allies by marriage. The emperor acceded to the Tibetans and changed the document as requested. In return, the Tibetans in the following year released 800 captives which they had been holding. Thus, each time the emperor accomodated the Tibetans they responded favorably.

By 783 the formal peace treaty ceremonies were completed, and the document drawn up. The conciliatory policy of the Chinese toward the Tibetans shows throughout. The document first describes the extent and influence of the T'ang dynasty, then turns to relations with the Tibetans:

With the T'u-fan tsanp'u [Tibetan leader] it has made matrimonial alliances to strengthen the bonds of neighborly friendship and unite the two countries, and the sovereigns have been allied as father and son-in-law for nearly two hundred years. Meanwhile, however, in consequence of minor disagreements, their good relations have been broken off by war, so that the borderland has been troubled and without a quiet year. The emperor on his recent accession compassionated his black-haired people, and sent back the enslaved captives to their own country, and the Fan nation [Tibet] has exhibited good feeling and agreed to a mutual peace. Envoys have gone and returned carrying in succession the orders of their sovereign, who has determined to put a stop to secret plotting and put by the chariots of war. They have, with the view of making the covenant of the two countries lasting, proposed to use the ancient sworn treaty, and the government, resolved to give rest to the natives of the border, have alienated their ancient territory, preferring good deed to profit, and have made a solemn treaty in accordance with the agreement. [Bushell, 488–489]

The treaty document discussed the boundaries and gave to each the territory it was then in control of, "each retaining its present possessions, and not seeking to encroach on the other. The places that heretofore have not been garrisoned, shall not have troops stationed in them, nor shall walled cities be built, nor land cultivated" (Bushell, 490). When the ceremony was concluded, and the treaty formally signed, the emperor continued his conciliatory policy and sent back presents with the Tibetan peace embassy. In the last year of the decade the Tibetans helped the emperor subdue a rebellion. In their relations with the Tibetans the Chinese had effectively used first force, then conciliation. They had made a series of unilateral steps toward the Tibetans, each one of which was reciprocated and gave encouragement for a subsequent one.

PART 2: SURVEY OF VARIABLES (CODED FOR CONSPICUOUS STATE, T'ANG DYNASTY

Dependent Variables

Months of War. The decade began with war and ended with peace. The peace negotiations were begun in 780 and concluded in 783. There was a total of fifty-one months of war, sixty-nine months of peace during the decade. The raw score of 51 yields a standard score of 52. For method of transformation see p. 11.

Territorial Change. The peace treaty was a formalization of the status quo, and no territory changed hands. The raw score of 0 yields two standard scores: Territorial Gain 49 and Territorial Stability 36. For method of transformation see p. 13f.

MAP No. 3

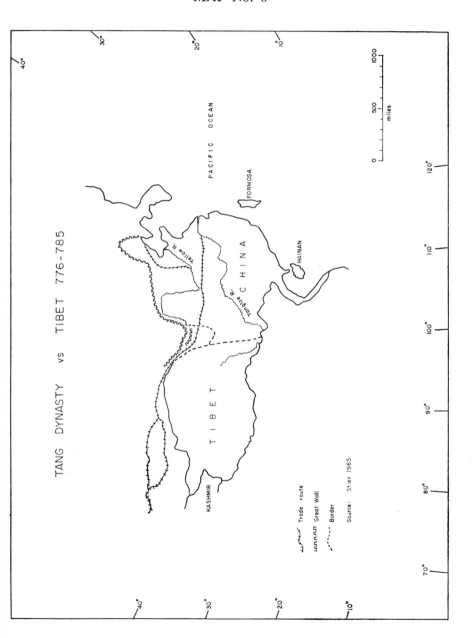

Military Variables

Defensive Stance. The long-term stance of the Chinese was defensive and that of the Tibetans offensive, even though the Chinese at times took the offensive against their invaders. Coded *present.*

Strength of Armed Forces. The dynastic histories never tell us the exact size of the Chinese army. But they do tell us that in 774 the emperor felt the need to reinforce the frontier against the continual attacks by the Tibetans. Consequently, he added two hundred and thirty thousand troops to the existing ones. Two years later, with the help of allies, he defeated a Tibetan army of two hundred thousand. In 779 he again defeated a Tibetan army of two hundred thousand. Although the Tibetans also had additional allied strength, the Chinese reinforcements of two hundred and thirty thousand troops alone were more than the total Tibetan army. Therefore, the Chinese army must have had the numerical advantage. Coded *present.*

Mobility of Armed Forces. Both the Tibetans and the Chinese troops were mounted and thus equal as far as cavalry mobility was concerned. But the Chinese had to keep their troops on the frontier to guard the posts, whereas the Tibetan raiders needed only to advance and withdraw and consequently had the advantage of mobility. The fact that the Chinese twice successfully defeated the Tibetans during the decade under study suggests that mobility may have been less important than other factors in establishing the peace. Coded *absent.*

Quality of Armed Forces. The Tibetan army was probably superior. There are no reports in the dynastic histories concerning the relative quality of the armies, nor do contemporary historians comment on it. But the Chinese were impressed by Tibetan military equipment and Tibetan bravery. The dynastic histories state that the Tibetans considered death in battle more honorable than death from disease. During battle, when the Tibetan front rank was annihilated, the rear still pressed on. Tibetan soldiers wore helmets which left only holes for eyes, and armor which covered the whole body and was very hard to penetrate. The mention of this armor indicates that the Chinese must have had either no armor or armor of inferior quality. Concerning cowardice in battle, the dynastic histories say that "if several generations have been killed in battle the family is ennobled. If any one turns his back on the foe, they hang a fox's tail on his head, to show that he is as cowardly as a fox, and exhibit him in crowded places as a warning to others. They are extremely ashamed of this, and deem death preferable" (Bushell, 442–443).

This emphasis on bravery suggests a culture with a highly developed value orientation toward the military life. Man for man, the Tibetans may have been better soldiers than the Chinese. Coded *absent.*

Fortifications. It is clear that there were a number of fortified posts along the frontier, but no wall. In 774 the emperor had placed two hundred thirty thousand additional troops at the frontier to guard the posts. There is no indication of further fortifications during the decade. In the peace negotiations the Chinese promised not to build any more walled cities nor to garrison places which had previously been ungarrisoned. Coded *present.*

Prestige. Chinese prestige had been high during the first half of the eighth century, but in the decade in question it declined. By 750 the emperor's influence had been strongly established in the north and west, as well as in central Asia. The Tibetans had been severely beaten. But in 751 the Chinese army was defeated by the Arabs, and when the Emperor Hsuan Tsung was faced with a revolution in 756, he had to call on Turkish and Arab troops to save his dynasty. At this time the Shan or T'ai of Manchao (modern province of Yunnan and southern Szechwan) asserted their independence from the T'ang. Then, in 763, the Tibetans reached the T'ang capital, Ch'ang-an, and sacked it. Thus, there had been an increase in prestige of the Tibetans and decrease in prestige of the Chinese at the beginning of the decade 776 to 785. Coded *absent.*

Geographical Variables

Propinquity. Tibet is to the southwest of China and borders China on the provinces of Kunlun to the north and Chinghai and Sikang to the east. Coded *present.*

Natural Barriers. One of the two caravan routes along which goods from China were transported to the markets of the west was the

South Road. The South Road ran along the southern edge of the Takla Makan Desert, and the Tibetans, protected to their north by the almost inaccessible Kunlun Mountains, were so placed that they were able to threaten this important road. Situated high on the plateau, the Tibetans thus had a formidable geographical advantage over the Chinese. Coded *present*.

Capital City. Lhasa, the capital of Tibet, was 1025 kilometers from the frontier. Ch'ang-an, the capital of China during this period, was 560 kilometers from the frontier, and thus much more vulnerable to attack than Lhasa (see A. Hermann, *Atlas of China*, "The T'ang Dynasty, 618–906 A.D.—Boundaries of 700 A.D." p. 40, and *Hammond's World Atlas*, "China and Japan" p. 35). Coded *present*.

Diplomatic Variables

Announcements. There were no annoucements of intention during the decade. Coded *no data* because China and Tibet were already at war when the decade began.

Surprise Attack. Coded *no data*. See Announcements, above.

Alliances. For years the Chinese had been continually raided and plundered by the Tibetans. At the beginning of the decade the Chinese allied with the Tu'-chüeh, T'u-yü-hun, Ti, Man Ch'iang, and Tanghsiang and were able to inflict a defeat on the Tibetans. Then, in alliance with the Nanchao, they defeated the Tibetans again, At the end of the decade, when the peace treaty was in operation, the Tibetans helped the Chinese defeat the rebellious generals Chu Tzu, Han Ming, Chang T'eng-chieh, and Sung Kuei-ch'ao. And while the peace negotiations were being conducted, there were references made on both sides to the two-hundred-year-old alliance between the Chinese and Tibetan ruling families through the marriage of Tibetan rulers to imperial Chinese princesses. Thus, the Chinese clearly benefitted from their alliances during the decade. Coded *present*.

Active Diplomacy. The negotiations during the decade under study were all concerned with the details of the peace treaty. Each side sent large embassies to the other, carrying messages and ceremonial gifts. There was elaborate ritual connected with these negotiations. The embassies would arrive with the messages and gifts and deliver them. The messages would be read, the embassies entertained, and then they would return with the answer; and a new embassy would be sent to conduct the next stage of the negotiations. That a peace was concluded and put into effect during the decade attests to their success. Coded *present*.

Intense Diplomacy. The peace treaty was signed in 783. See "Diplomacy," above. Coded *present*.

Previous Conflict. The decade from 776 to 785 is one small episode in the drawn-out war between the Tibetans and the Chinese which began in the seventh century and was not ended until the middle of the ninth. From the Chinese point of view the Tibetans were but one among many nomads who had to be deterred on the frontier. The Tibetans, for their part, seized the opportunity to make repeated raids on the T'ang dominions during a time when the T'ang dynasty was beset by foreign and domestic problems. The Chinese could not always turn their attention from their internal problems to deter the Tibetans and therefore adopted a conciliatory attitude toward them to prevent the continual raiding. Coded *present*.

Cultural Variables

Benefits. Honors and good will gestures were very important in the policy of friendly conciliation that the Chinese adopted toward the Tibetans. The first embassy from the Tibetan ruler to the Chinese emperor arrived at Ch'ang-an in 634, and was received with marked honor. Four years later the emperor reciprocated by sending an embassy to the Tibetans. The Tibetan ruler, perhaps believing that this reciprocal courtesy indicated a fear or need of him by the Chinese, thereupon demanded the hand of a Chinese princess in marriage. The demand was rejected by the emperor, and the Tibetan ruler then took command of a powerful force and invaded the Chinese empire. The emperor defeated the Tibetans in 641, but conciliated his conquered neighbor by giving to him in marriage a Chinese princess. Although no marriage between a Tibetan ruler and a Chinese princess was contracted during the decade between 776 and 785, one was already in effect.

Throughout the decade there was entertaining and exchange of gifts between the Chinese and Tibetans. But one such exchange caused some hard feeling, and called for a good will gesture by the emperor in his negotiations with the Tibetans. In 781, when a Chinese embassy presented gifts to the Tibetans, together with the dispatch from the emperor, the Tibetan ruler answered the emperor:

> The imperial despatch you bring says: 'The things offered as tribute have all been accepted, and now we bestow on our son-in-law a few presents for him to take when they arrive'. Our great Fan [Tibetan ruler] and the T'ang nations are allied by marriage, and how is it that we are treated with the rites due to a subject? Again, you wish to fix the boundary to the west of Yunchou, but we propose that Holanshan be made the boundary. For the sworn ceremony we propose to follow that of the second year of Chinlung [708], when the imperial dispatch said: 'When the T'ang envoy arrives there, the son-in-law shall first conclude the sworn ceremony with him; and when the Fan envoy arrives here, we, the father-in-law, will ourselves take part in the ceremony with him.' Let them, Wanheng send a messenger to report to the Emperor that he may act. [Bushell, 486]

The emperor, apparently anxious to conciliate the Tibetans, altered the document as requested, the words "offered as tribute" changed to "presented," "bestowed" to "given," and "for him to take" to "for his acceptance," and the following sentences being added: "The former minister, Yang Yen, departed from the old practice, and is responsible for these errors. For the fixing of the boundaries, and the sworn ceremony, everything is conceded" (Bushell, 487). The Tibetan leader had made it clear that it was not the gift but the honor accorded him as a "mark of liberal friendship" that was important to him. And the emperor clearly recognized this attitude and acceded to it.

Another good will gesture was the exchange of prisoners. In 779 the emperor sent 500 Tibetan captives back to their country, each with a suit of clothes, and at the same time urged that a treaty of peace be concluded. The Tibetans were at first "incredulous, but as soon as the Fan [Tibetan] captives entered their borders, were all awed with the power, and grateful for the grace of the Emperor" (Bushell, 485). This act was the beginning of the peace negotiations. To conclude them the Tibetans in 782 released the generals, warriors, and Buddhist monks who had been carried off to the Tibetan country, 800 persons in all, in return for the delivery of the

Tibetan captives. The significance of this gesture of good will toward the Tibetans is difficult to assess, but at least it provided an opening for a peace that had become attractive to both sides. Coded *present.*

Cultural Exchange. The Tibetan rulers had been in contact with Chinese culture for more than two centuries before the decade under study. For at least that long Tibetan rulers had been marrying daughters of the Chinese emperors, and in the very decade under study the Tibetan ruler's wife was a Chinese princess. Early in the sixth century the Tibetans got their first knowledge of arithmetic and medicine from China. Tibetan princes were sent to be educated at the Imperial University. And during the decade under study the emperor sent 500 Tibetan captives back to their country, and the Tibetans reciprocated by releasing 800 generals, warriors, and Buddhist monks who had been carried off to the Tibetan country. Coded *present.*

Trade. Coded *absent* because commercial trade was relatively small in volume.

General Exchange. Coded *present.* See "Cultural Exchange," above.

Administrative Variables

Experience of Ruler. T'ai Tsung became emperor in 762 and died in 779, during the decade. He was succeeded by his son, Te Tsung, Coded *absent* because neither fulfilled the qualification of having ruled ten years prior to the decade and ruling for six years afterward.

Youth of Ruler. Emperor T'ai Tsung was born in 726 and was thirty-six years old when he became ruler. In 776, when the decade began, he was fifty. When he died in 779 he was succeeded by his son, Te Tsung, born in 744, and who was then thirty-five years old. Coded *present* because T'ai Tsung, the older of the two rulers, ruled for only three years of the decade.

Unbridled Ruler. Both T'ai Tsung and his son Te Tsung were hereditary monarchs and ruled a centralized monarchy. Coded *present.*

Hereditary Monarch. The T'ang dynasty was hereditary. Coded *present.*

Civil War. Although the T'ang rulers had been troubled by rebellions in the provinces within their dominion several decades before the one under study, they had been able to inflict severe punishment upon these rebels. Again, twenty years before the start of the decade, Emperor Hsuan Tsung was driven from his capital by the rebellion of An Lu-shan, and his successor saved the dynasty only with difficulty. It was during these times of internal dissension that the Tibetans began to intensify their raids on the Chinese frontier; they even took Ch'ang-an, the Chinese capital, in 763. Similarly, during the decade 776 to 785, there was frequent rebellion. The emperor T'ai Tsung died in 779, and was succeeded by his son Te Tsung. Soon after Te Tsung ascended the throne one rebellion after another broke out among his subjects, and he was not able to quell them until the decade was over. The raids by the Tibetans, then, must have taken second place in his attention, and certainly the Tibetans were able to make many more unhindered raids than if they had been the emperor's only problem. Thus, the internecine strife made deterrence very difficult for the T'ang during this decade and made peace extremely attractive to them. Coded *present*.

Centralization. The Chinese dynastic histories describe the Tibetans as being politically unified by the end of the sixth century. But because they had only part-time specialists and a rural population that was largely nomadic, they were presumably harder to control than the Chinese and thus may have been somewhat less centralized. Coded *absent* because the Chinese were not markedly more centralized than the Tibetans.

PART 3: DATA QUALITY CONTROL

This chapter is based on the translation of S.W. Bushell, "The Early History of Tibet. From Chinese Sources," *Journal of the Royal Asiatic Society of Great Britain and Ireland* (1880) 12 :435–541. It is a translation of books 256 through 257 of the eighteenth-century compendium. This compendium presents together the two standard histories of the T'ang dynasty, distinguished as old and new, and they are numbers 16 and 17 of the twenty-four dynastic histories of the series. The dynastic histories are taken from compilations of events written at the time of their occurrence by officials whose duty was the preparation and custody of historical archives. *The Old T'ang History* was first compiled by Wu Ching and extended from the beginning of the dynasty until 741. Wei Shu copied and added to this. Liu Hsu in the middle of the tenth century reputedly headed a commission which compiled and completed the books. *The New T'ang History* was written chiefly by Ou-yang and Sung Ch'i during the middle of the eleventh century. The two volumes were combined in the eighteenth century (one, a running commentary, appended to the other). Books 256 and 257 of this edition are devoted to Tibet.

Publication Year. Coded *absent* because the compendium was written in the eighteenth century (it was of course, based on even earlier works).

Primary Sources. Liu Hsü is supposed to have compiled *The Old T'ang History* from records by officials working from archives. Ou-yang Hsiu wrote four hundred years after the decade, but worked from primary records. Both are considered primary sources. Coded *present.*

Authors' Association. The authors were Chinese court historians. Coded *present.*

Authors' Sympathies. Obviously court historians would sympathize with the Chinese against the Tibetans. There are no records by Tibetans, consequently it is not possible to check factual information for bias. Coded *present.*

Authors' Proximity. The histories started by Ou-yang Hsiu were taken from the records of the events and were rewritten up until the middle of the eleventh century, and consolidated into one book in the eighteenth century. Thus some of the accounts were contemporary, some were written as much as four hundred years after the events, and finally, some were written eleven hundred years after the events occurred. Coded *absent.*

CHAPTER 6

★ ★ ★

DETERRENCE FAILURE, DEFENSE SUCCESS: SUNG CHINA VERSUS THE TANGUTS

1076-1085 : Conspicuous State, Sung China; Conspicuous Rival, the Tanguts.

PART I: SKETCH OF HISTORICAL SETTING (CHIEFLY AFTER DE MAILLA)

THE LEADING EVENT of the decade from 1076 to 1085 in China was the inability to wrest from the Tanguts lands which the Tanguts (also referred to as Tartars and Hsia) had taken earlier from China during the Sung dynasty. The Tanguts' eastern neighbors, the Khitans, had already been harassing the borders of the Chinese empire when the Tanguts of northern Kansu also began their raids on Sung China earlier in the eleventh century. The Tanguts had begun to make their presence known to the Sung in 1040 when the Tangut ruler sent the emperor a request that he be recognized as the emperor of the Hsia. Since the emperor considered himself the ruler of everything under heaven he was reluctant for anyone else to use the title emperor. The Tanguts attacked and defeated the Chinese forces, and in 1043 the emperor decided to conciliate them; he promised them a yearly payment of valuables: one hundred thousand pieces of silk and three hundred thousand pounds of tea. In 1044 the Tanguts defeated the Khitans as well.

The economy in China during the Sung dynasty was weakened by the cost of defending their territory against the barbarians. At this time a social reformer, Wang An-shih, tried to improve social conditions in China. He was concerned not only with the economic situation but also with threats of invasion from the Khitans and Tanguts. He instituted reforms which lowered the interest rate to farmers, regulated crop prices, lowered the tax on land, and levied a graduated tax on wealth. But he was opposed by conservatives who feared the centralization of authority consequent upon so much state control.

One of Wang An-shih's chief opponents was Ssu-ma Kuang, author of the *Universal Mirror of History*. The neo-Confucian philosophers supported him against Wang An-shih; they felt that Wang An-shih's program was too great a departure from Confucian principles and therefore wrong. When the decade 1076–1085 began, Wang An-shih had just resigned from his post of State Counselor to the emperor. He was named governor of Nanking, then dismissed from his post a few years later. The conservatives who came into power after him did away with all the social reforms Wang An-shih instituted, and the economy of the empire was again imperiled.

By 1080 the emperor was being advised by his ministers to start a war with the Tanguts:

On the fifth moon, Yu-tchong, governor of King-tcheou in Chen-si sent to the emperor the details of what had happened lately in the principality of the Hsia [Tanguts] and proposed to him to retake the towns that these Tartars had robbed from the empire, and he said: 'The spies that I have near the prince of Hsia have warned me that Li-tsing, one of his generals who is of Chinese nationality and comes from Tsin-tcheou, had urged him to invade Honan or the south of Huang-ho; that Leang-chi, mother of Ping-tshang, prince of Hsia, did not want war and having known of it was so annoyed by it that she had Li-tsing killed, and being embroiled with her son over this, she had him put in prison.' Yu-tchong finished by making the emporer feel that this was a favorable time to retake the country that these Tartars had robbed from the empire. The majority of the emperor's council approved Yu-tchong's advice, and said that they could profit from the circumstances. Tchong-ou even claimed rather lightly that the Hsia principality had not a single man and that Ping-tchang was a child whom he could take by the shoulders and lead to the foot of the throne. Sun-Kou, indignant at the weakness of this advice, said that it was easy to raise soldiers and begin a war, but not to finish it, and that it was his feeling that they ought not to undertake it. The emperor objected that if they did not conquer the Hsia, they would attach themselves without fail to the Liao [Khitan], and then, reunited with these enemies of China, they would become a formidable power which would be difficult to resist. [De Mailla 8: 294–95, *this and further excerpts translated by* FRADA NAROLL]

From this information about Leang-chi, mother of the Tangut prince, that the Chinese historians have given us it appears that the Tanguts were not expecting the Chinese to attack them. The queen mother must have felt secure vis-à-vis the Sung if she could indulge in the luxury of killing a general. If we infer that the Tanguts considered their military and natural defenses strong enough to deter the Chinese from attacking them, then the queen mother's attempt to discourage her son from making war is both natural and understandable. However, although the Tanguts may have been content to rely on these military and natural deterrents, they did in fact fail to deter the Chinese.

The emperor decided to make war on the Tanguts. He formed five large army corps, all of which were to enter Tangut territory at the same time and through five different routes. He was apparently unaware of the many advantages that the Tanguts held over the Chinese. The Tanguts were fighting on home territory near their source of supplies, whereas the Chinese were fighting far from their base of supplies. The Tanguts were able to use the waters of the Huang Ho (Yellow River) to flood out the Chinese troops. Tangut terrain had many passes and hills from which they could take the Chinese by surprise. And the Tangut force totaled three hundred thousand, which was a larger one than any single army the Chinese had against them.

The Tanguts defended themselves successfully against three of the five Chinese generals. When the Tanguts encountered General Kao T'sun-yu they lost a town to him. But General Ch'eng-ch'ing cut himself off from his supply lines. He crossed a river and got into sandy country where he could find neither forage for his animals nor food for his men and he lost a large number of both. About a hundred Tangut families in an abandoned town had their stock and provisions taken from them for his troops. But there were still not enough provisions for the Chinese, and when the Chinese general was able to review his army he found that he was missing more than twenty thousand men. This loss and the lack of supplies and equipment caused him to return to China.

When the Tanguts encountered General Li Hsien, who had the troops of seven departments and thirty thousand Tibetans with him, they were followed to a pass. The Chinese general forced the pass and went on to enclose the Tangut town and retake it; the Tanguts were unable to stop him. The general wanted the emperor to rebuild the town so that it could act as a barrier against further border raids. After camping at the foot of a mountain, where he burned a Tangut palace and killed a Tangut officer, General Li Hsien returned to China.

The Tanguts gained an overwhelming victory over the Chinese forces at the Huang Ho. At the beginning of the battle they met General Liu Ch'ang-tso and fifty thousand men at a pass, and were pushed back into a retreat. They regrouped their forces and with a part of their army opened a canal, diverted water from the Huang Ho and inundated the camps of Generals Liu Ch'ang-tso and Kao T'sun-yu. Then they cut off the Chinese supplies. The Chinese were forced to withdraw, after having lost more than two-thirds of their troops.

The Tanguts gained another success in a battle with General Ch'ung Wu when he joined his troops to Sui Te-ching's and attacked a Tangut town. The Tanguts, with an army of eighty thousand came to aid the town; Ch'ung Wu put them to flight and captured it. He advanced into Tangut country, where he took another town and then went on, only to be surprised by the Tangut army, which killed more than half of his men; he returned to China with a force of less than thirty thousand.

> The Tanguts had already decided to put forth their best effort: When the court of the Hsia had been apprised of the powerful armament of the Chinese the courtiers advised Leang-chi, mother of the young prince, to make all the youths take up arms. There was only one old officer who persisted in saying that it was not only necessary to think of maintaining the defensive and ruining all the ways through which the Chinese could advance. He said that it was also necessary to put the best troops in the Ling-tcheou and Hsia country and, from temporary camps, to prevent the imperial troops from rejoining; he added that it was no longer necessary to break their plans and make them return on their footsteps. The princess followed this advice, and its success made it evident that it was the best that there was to follow. The defense plan was the same that the Hsia had followed in 1044, against the Khitan. [De Mailla 8: 298–99]

After the five generals had returned from their campaigns, the emperor decided to build a town at Heng Shan and thus prevent

the Tanguts from raiding the district. He sent Hsiu Hsi there with
a large number of troops to protect the work in case of enemy raids.
The Tanguts sent out several thousand horsemen. Hsiu Hsi advanced against them, but the Tangut forces numbered three
hundred thousand.

> Hsiu Hsi, who had been warned more than ten times, did not
> want to believe he was threatened. However, several prisoners
> that he took confirmed that the Hsia [Tanguts] had come with
> their total forces to prevent him from building the new town, and
> their formidable army that he soon saw appear did not permit
> any further doubts. Kiu-tchen, noticing the fear of the imperial
> troops at the sight of the enemy, advised Hsiu Hsi not to take the
> risk, since he would be beaten without fail, and he would be
> more prudent to withdraw to the town. Hsiu Hsi said that he was
> astonished to hear one of the foremost officers of the imperial
> army talk this way. He placed his army of seventy thousand men
> under the town walls, in battle formation. A corps of enemy heavy
> armed soldiers, the best troops of the Hsia, began to cross the
> Huang Ho. General Kiu-tchen warned Hsiu Hsi and told him
> that if he made them charge when half of them had passed, and
> if he had the good luck to beat them, then he was assured of
> a victory. [De Mailla, 8: 300]

But Hsiu Hsi was obstinate and decided to wait until the entire
army had crossed, and then he charged. The Tanguts resisted his
attack, and further, continually reinforced their lines with new
troops. Consequently, they repulsed the Chinese, who withdrew,
and then the Tanguts enclosed them.

> The Tartars [Tanguts] began by diverting all the water which
> entered the town. The Chinese were forced to deepen the wells,
> but they could not reach any water, and in a few days they were
> in such extremities that more than two-thirds died. The Hsia
> [Tanguts], in order to deprive them of any hope of help, took
> possession of all the passes through which aid could come. It was
> thus simple for the Tartars to take possession of this town. [De
> Mailla, 8:300–301]

The Tanguts took the town, six armed posts, and all the remaining supplies and provisions; and the Chinese lost more than two
hundred thousand soldiers and workers. It was the worst loss that
the Chinese could remember suffering, and the emperor was so
discouraged that he decided to give up the war. Having won such

MAP No. 4

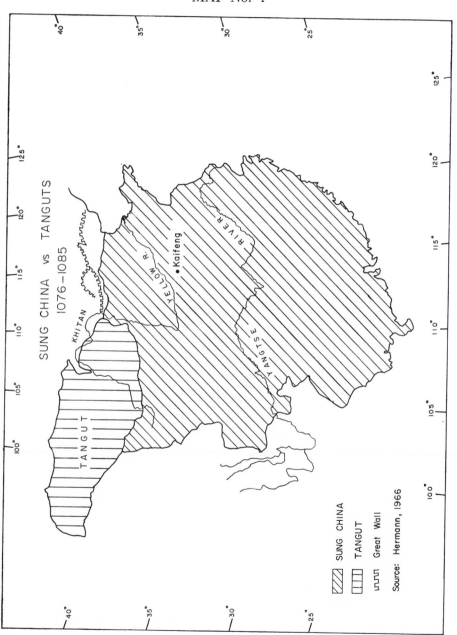

SUNG CHINA vs TANGUTS
1076–1085

KHITAN

TANGUT

YELLOW R.

•Kaifeng

RIVER

YANGTSE

SUNG CHINA

TANGUT

Great Wall

Source: Hermann, 1966

a decisive victory over the Chinese forces, the Tanguts were content to remain at peace on the borders. Deterrence had failed, defense had succeeded.

PART 2: SURVEY OF VARIABLES (CODED FOR CONSPICUOUS STATE, SUNG DYNASTY)

Dependent Variables

Months of War. The Chinese began the war in 1080 and gave up the fight at the end of 1082—there were thirty-four months of war and eighty-six of peace. The raw score of 34 yields a standard score of 49. For method of transformation, see p. 11.

Territorial Change. The Chinese were defeated and unable to regain any of the territory they had lost prior to the decade. The raw score of 0 yields two standard scores: territorial gain 49 and territorial stability 36. For method of transformation see p. 13f.

Military Variables

Defensive Stance. During the decade from 1075 to 1085, the Sung were clearly in an offensive stance, the Tanguts clearly on the defensive. But the long-term stance of the Sung was defensive, and the long-term stance of the Tanguts offensive. Coded *absent*.

Strength of Armed Forces. The dynastic histories do not give the exact size of the Chinese army, but the total forces of the Tangut army is stated as three hundred thousand. Since during the decade the Chinese had five large army corps engaged against the Tanguts, and since, in the last campaign of the decade, two hundred thousand Chinese soldiers and laborers had died, the Chinese must have had the overall numerical advantage. However, in the last battle, a Chinese army of seventy thousand faced a Tangut army of thirty thousand, an overwhelming superiority for the Tanguts, and one of the reasons for their successful defense. Coded *present* because the entire Chinese army was larger.

Mobility of Armed Forces. There is no information concerning the mobility of either the Chinese or the Tanguts. Coded *no data*.

Quality of Armed Forces. There is no information concerning the quality of either army. But the concern which the Chinese felt about the growing strength of the Tanguts, and the emperor's decision to fight them at this time suggests that the Tanguts were excellent soldiers who might become even more formidable. They turned out to be more than a match for the Chinese imperials. Coded *no data.*

Fortifications. The southern boundary of the Tanguts was along the Great Wall, but there is no indication how prominent a part the Wall played during the decade. At the end of the decade the Tanguts took six armed border defense posts, but the dates of their establishment, however, is not given. In the last battle of the decade, when the Chinese suffered such terrible losses, they were building a town at Heng Shan to contain the Tanguts and close the door through which they could easily make their raids. But to prevent the Chinese from building the town the Tanguts mobilized an army of three hundred thousand, diverted the water so that the Chinese died of thirst, and then closed off the passes through which aid could come and took the town. Thus, fortification did not help the Chinese during their battles with the Tanguts. Coded *present.*

Prestige. Although the Tanguts were feared by the Sung, and, with the Khitans, were the most formidable enemies of the decade, their prestige was probably less than the Chinese. The social reformer, Wang An'shih, the famous historian, Ssu-ma Kuang, author of the *Tzu-chih* (or *Universal Mirror of History*), and a revival of interest in philosophy, all brought renewed prestige to the Sung dynasty. Coded *present.*

Geographical Variables

Propinquity. The Tangut, or Hsi Hsia empire was northwest of the Sung empire, between it and the Gobi desert. It occupied northern Kansu as far as Karanor, north of the Great Wall. Coded *present.*

Natural Barriers. These were clearly present. The Tanguts occupied a high plateau, and were separated from the Sung to the south and east by mountain chains. The mountain passes helped them defeat the Chinese. Their location also helped the Tanguts control the caravan routes leading to the west. The Huang Ho, between the Tanguts and the Sung, proved a decisive factor when the Tanguts diverted the water from the river and flooded the imperial troops, causing them tremendous losses. Coded *present*.

Capital City. Kai'feng, capital of the Sung empire, was 330 miles from the border; Ninghia, capital of the Tanguts, was 60 miles from the border and thus more vulnerable to attack. In the decade under study, proximity of largest cities to the frontier does not seem to have been an important one. Coded *absent*.

Diplomatic Variables

Announcements. There were none mentioned. Coded *absent*.

Surprise Attack. The Tanguts considered their natural and military deterrents to be sufficient to discourage the Chinese, and were not expecting an attack. Coded *present*.

Alliances. The Sung emperor feared an alliance between the Tanguts and Khitans and, in order to strengthen his forces against the Tanguts, he used Tibetan troops during the decade. However, this variable is coded *absent* because Defensive Stance has been coded absent for the Sung. (Alliances are coded present only when the Conspicuous State is allied against the Conspicuous Rival *and* if "Defensive Stance" is also coded present.)

Active Diplomacy. There is no mention of negotiations between the Tanguts and the Sung during the decade. Coded *absent*.

Intense Diplomacy. Coded *absent*. See "Active Diplomacy," above.

Previous Conflicts. The Sung dynasty and the Tanguts had been at peace since 1043, when the Chinese had been forced to give this new enemy power annual presents to keep the borders quiet. The Sung dynasty was making similar payments to the Khitans as well. By 1076 the Sung were anxious to regain the territories that the Tanguts had taken from them earlier. The Sung also feared an alliance between the Tanguts and the Khitans. These financial and military pressures helped the emperor decide to take the offensive against the Tanguts. The Tanguts, from their point of view, had no reason to raid the borders as long as they were receiving yearly presents. But if the Chinese started a war, they did not want to emerge the loser. Coded *present*.

Cultural Variables

Benefits. In 1043, when the emperor decided to make peace with the Tanguts, he promised them one hundred thousand pieces of silk and three hundred thousand pounds of tea annually. In 1044, when the Tanguts defeated the Khitans, the emperor was pleased to see two potential allies against him fighting between themselves. He sent the Tangut ruler a golden belt, a beautiful horse, a harness and saddle of silver, 2500 pounds of silver, twenty thousand pieces of silk, thirty thousand pounds of tea, and a seal engraved with the phrase "Seal of the Sovereign of the Kingdom of Hsia." He also promised to defray the costs of the deputies who would be sent to court. Thus, in 1076, the emperor had already paid out large amounts in tribute to the Tanguts, as well as to the Khitans. Coded *present.*

Cultural Exchange. The Tanguts and the Sung dynasty had no direct cultural exchange. However, the caravans which passed through from China to western Asia put the Tanguts in frequent contact with the Sung dynasty, and they had taken on many of the traits of Chinese culture. In 1037 they developed their own script, based on Chinese characters. In the decade of 1076 to 1085 there is no mention of direct cultural exchange. Coded *absent.*

Trade. There was no trade between China and the Tanguts. Coded *absent.*

General Exchange. Coded *absent.* See "Cultural Exchange," and Trade, above.

Administrative Variables

Experience of Ruler. Emperor Chin Tsung mounted the throne in 1067 at the age of twenty. Coded *present* because he ruled for ten years before the decade began and ruled throughout the decade.

Youth of Ruler. Emperor Chin Tsung was born in 1047. In 1076, when the decade began he was twenty-nine years old. He died in 1085, at the age of thirty-eight. Coded *present* because the ruler was less than forty-five years old at the beginning of the decade.

Unbridled Ruler. The emperor was a hereditary monarch, between the ages of twenty and forty-five, and ruled a centralized monarchy. Coded *present.*

Hereditary Monarchy. China was a monarchy and succession was through inheritance. Coded *present.*

Civil War. None is mentioned during the decade. Coded *absent.*

Centralization. The Tanguts had established their independence during the collapse of the T'ang dynasty, and their leader had been given the title Duke of Hsia. They were seminomadic, producing crops and breeding stock, and were presumably harder to control than the Chinese because of their seminomadic population—thus somewhat less centralized. Coded *absent,* because the Sung dynasty did not have a "clearly more highly centralized plan of government".

PART 3: DATA QUALITY CONTROL

This chapter is based on *Histoire Générale de la Chine* by Joseph A.M. de Mailla (Paris: D. Pierres, 1777–1785); it is for the most part a translation of a standard Chinese secondary history, with some quotations from Chinese dynastic histories. There are no Tangut sources available. *A History of China,* by Wolfram Eberhard (Berkeley: University of California Press, 1960) a secondary source, was also consulted, but *not coded.*

Publication year. De Mailla wrote around the year 1730. Coded *absent,* because the work was done prior to 1850.

Primary Source. Coded *absent,* because it was not a contemporary account.

Author's Association. De Mailla had a mandarin's status at the Ch'ing court but was a French Jesuit. Coded *present,* because his cultural ties were to the Chinese, not to the Tanguts.

Author's Sympathies. De Mailla does not reveal any special sympathies for either side during the events of the decade. Coded *no data,* because De Mailla seems to be impartial.

Author's Proximity. De Mailla wrote about six hundred fifty years after the events. Coded *absent.*

CHAPTER 7

★ ★ ★

DETERRENCE NEGLECTED:
MING VERSUS MONGOL

1376-1385: Conspicuous State, Ming Dynasty; Conspicuous Rival, Mongol Yunnan.

PART 1: SKETCH OF HISTORICAL SETTING (CHIEFLY AFTER DE MAILLA)

IN THE RANDOMLY SELECTED DECADE from 1376 to 1385, the most conspicuous rivals of the Ming emperors were the Mongol princes of Yunnan, the mountainous frontier province between southern China and Burma. The Chinese emperor had long contemplated the conquest of Yunnan. But its Mongol ruler had a potentially strong deterrence position, and more than ten years warning. He had an effective, well-trained army of one hundred thousand men, about one-third as many as the Chinese emperor was prepared to throw against him. He could readily raise another one hundred thousand men from the warlike hill tribes of Yunnan, of whom the Chinese were traditional enemies. The Chinese route of advance led through narrow mountain passes in very rugged country; only a comparatively few such passes needed to have been fortified and defended in order to hold the country. This opportunity was neglected.

Thus, the Chinese conquest of Yunnan (1381–1383) presents a number of relevant variables for scrutiny. (Unfortunately, little detail is available in European languages. The European language material for this period is detailed for the Mongols in Mongolia, but not for their isolated cousins on the other side of China in Yunnan.) To begin with, we have a three-cornered culture conflict situation. The Mongols gained control of Yunnan along with the rest of China when, under Kublai Khan, they conquered the

Southern Sungs in 1279. The Mongols were to rule China until 1368. In Yunnan they established their control by importing Moslem administrators who replaced the ethnic Chinese bureaucrats as much as possible. In any case, Yunnan had not then—and has not even to this day—been completely assimilated culturally by the Chinese (the Chinese Communists today call the region "autonomous", a euphemism for ethnically non-Chinese). During the decade from 1376 to 1385, Yunnan's mountainsides were occupied by non-Chinese hill tribes; some Chinese lived in the cities.

In China itself the Mongol rulers of China, the Yuan dynasty, did not become well assimilated to Chinese culture and were for this reason strongly resented. Thus, the rebel, Chu Yuan-chang, was able to form large and effective armies of native Chinese in south China to drive their Mongol masters back to Mongolia and found the Ming dynasty in 1369. But in mountainous Yunnan, supported by the hill tribes, the Mongol princes of the Yuan dynasty held out for another decade. They had more than ten precious years to get ready, but they did not develop a successful deterrence plan.

The possibilities for diplomacy as a deterrence to war were weakened by a new Mongol menace just emerging, in the person of Tamerlane, on the steppes of central Asia. Traditionally the Chinese had chosen between two sharply contrasting policies toward non-Chinese neighbors. If these neighbors seemed hostile or threatening, the Chinese policy had been to attempt to conquer them. But if the neighbors were conciliatory, and willing to acknowledge Chinese suzerainty, then the Chinese policy was to accept the neighbors as "tributary states." This involved a virtual exchange of gifts; however, the tributary state's gift was labelled "tribute." The status of a tributary state was actually a kind of nonaggression pact cloaked in a formula making it palatable to the Chinese. During the Ming dynasty, Burma, Korea, Japan, and Vietnam were all tributary states of this sort. There is no indication that the Mongol princes of Yunan ever considered such a status for themselves. At best, it would have been a temporary solution. The tension of consolidating the Ming regime was exacerbated by the resurgence of Mongol power under Tamerlane. (By 1370—six years before our decade—Tamerlane had conquered Transoxonia and within the next decade added Turkistan, Khwarizm, and Kashgar. There was no doubt that Tamerlane intended to re-constitute the Great Khanate and to repossess China eventually, if he could.)

Yunnan is a mountainous plateau, and the mountain ranges run athwart the line of advance of the Chinese. The terrain afforded the Mongol princes of Yunnan a prime opportunity, but they failed to take advantage of it. This country is extremely difficult even today—it is the same country through which the Burma road was pushed in World War II. Kunming, chief way station on the Burma Road, was, in Ming times, known as Yunnnanfu and was then as now the chief city of the region. It is to be wondered that the Mongol princes did not make more effective use of the natural mountain barriers, but preferred to leave their fate to the outcome of a pitched battle. This mistake of theirs seems plausibly attributable to their own cultural background. Mongol traditions did not encourage the kind of defensive mountain warfare which the situation in 1381 seems to have called for.

Secondly, the Mongol princes clearly neglected a striking opportunity; they had the support of the hill tribes. We may explain this speculatively by supposing that the hill tribes preferred Mongol warriors to Chinese merchants and scholars, finding the former easier to deal with and less exploitative. At any rate, the fact is there. After the decisive battle of Kio-tsing Pass, when it was too late and all the Yunnan cities were opening their gates to the Chinese, the hill tribes responded to Mongol appeals with more than a hundred thousand warriors. Since at Kio-tsing Pass the Chinese barely prevailed against a defending force of one hundred thousand Yunnanese soldiers, they could not have hoped to win against double that number. Had the hill tribes been called upon in good time, so that they could have been organized and trained, the Mongol princes could probably have held Kio-tsing Pass.

Certainly, their optimum deterrence strategy was to: (1) fortify the mountain passes and defend the barriers and avoid a pitched battle in an open field, (2) Recruit and train 100,000 hill tribesmen to double the size of the standing army, and (3) from this position of strength offer to send a "tribute mission" to the Ming emperor (which, however, might only have brought a temporary respite).

From what has been said so far, it is clear that to understand the deterrence problem of the Yunnanese leaders and to evaluate the actual course of events, it is essential that we consider some leading cultural differences between Mongols and Chinese and hill tribes, and their previous history of conflict.

Chinese culture was developed to operate a complex, sophisticated urban civilization. Scholars, farmers, craftsmen, merchants, and soldiers all had their place—but the Chinese traditionally ranked soldiers last. "You don't use good iron to make nails," say the Chinese, "or good men to make soldiers." The affairs of state were traditionally managed by scholars trained in Confucian ethics, history, geography, *belles lettres*, and calligraphy. Learning was venerated. The model for society was seen in the tradition of a past golden age when righteous rulers set the example of paternal love, and society ran smoothly as in a well-orderd Chinese family under the benevolent guidance of the grandfather.

Mongol culture was developed to operate a herding society, in which men had to fight their neighbors to protect their herds and pastures and might hope for wealth and glory by raiding the settled peoples of China. There was not a single town or city among the Mongols when Genghis Khan was a boy; they all moved with their herds, living in their felt yurts as many of them do to this day. The Mongol men prided themselves on their hardiness, bravery, discipline, and virility. The good soldier was their ideal model. They had no interest in books. The Mongols, it is true had, even in Marco Polo's day, assimilated a great deal of Chinese culture; but as a caste of warriors and rulers, their basic values would have remained unchanged from the old days on the steppes.

Marco Polo's detailed account of the court routine of Kublai Khan, greatest of the Mongol emperors of China, shows no interest in scholarship on Kublai Khan's part. Yet scholarship was the dominant value of the administrative civil service that ran China for the Mongols, as it did for the rulers before and after them. Consequently, that civil service would be quick to drop allegiance to the Mongols and switch to a traditional Chinese as soon as it seemed safe to do so.

The conquest of Yunnan was one of the last stages of a great resurgence of the Chinese people against these alien masters, a resurgence which began about the middle of the fourteenth century. Under the great T'ang emperors, four centuries before, all of China proper, as well as some neighboring regions, was under Chinese rule. But with the fall of the T'ang dynasty in 1279, northern strangers got a foothold in China proper by which they gradually extended their power. The Khitan Tartars, who came later, seized the whole northern half of the country, leaving only the part south of the Yangtze to the southern Sung dynasty. But at last the Mongols took this and swept beyond into Yunnan.

By the middle of the fourteenth century, however, the Mongol rulers of China had lost control of much of the rural areas. Bandits controlled large districts. The leader of one of these, a former monk named Chu Yuan-chang, seized the city of Nanking and declared himself emperor. He assumed the throne name of Hung Wu and called the dynasty he was founding the Ming ("Bright") dynasty. The Mongols retreated to the deserts of Mongolia where they have lived ever since. Hung Wu pursued them there and set about enlarging his power. Toward the end of his reign he obtained the submission of both Korea and Burma as tributary countries and during the later course of the Ming Dynasty, Japan and Vietnam also became tributary countries.

When most of the Mongols in China retreated northward to the steppes of Mongolia they left behind in the southern mountains of Yunnan an isolated survival of Mongol power. Here the Mongol officials ruled not over Chinese but over hill peoples like the Lolo and the Miao, who to this day populate rural Yunnan and who, in the time we are studying must have populated its cities and towns as well. For only a hundred years before, Marco Polo had passed through this country. Four chapters of his *Travels* are devoted to the people of Yunnan, and in Marco Polo's day there were no Chinese to speak of in Yunnan. He tells us that in the three main provinces of Yunnan there was not a single medical doctor to be found. Now the Chinese had a well-developed medical profession at that time with a fair knowledge of anatomy and an emphasis on herbal drugs and acupuncture, but in Yunnan the people used only trance shamans whose treatments are described by Polo in great detail. Furthermore, he tells us that in the capital city of Yachi (later known as Yunnanfu and today called Kunming), the

people spoke a strange and difficult language—since he spoke and
wrote Chinese and was an accomplised linguist, this could not have
been a Chinese dialect but presumably was a Tibeto-Burmese
language and thus unrelated to any of the languages Marco Polo
already knew (he must have known a Turkish language and certainly
knew Mongol as well as Chinese). In Zarandan, in what is now
western Yunnan, in the region around Yung-chang, Marco Polo
reported that they had no alphabet or writing system. Since Chinese
characters can be used by speakers of any language (and are used
today by speakers of Korean, Japanese, and Vietnamese) their
absence in Zarandan in Polo's day is clear evidence that the Chinese
had not got there yet in any number.

The penetration of Yunnan by the Chinese, today the dominant
people in the valley cities and towns, has merely been a stage in a
process of southward expansion that has been going on for close
to three thousand years, and is still continuing. In about 1000 B.C.,
the Chinese occupied only the basin of the Yellow River. Later,
they spread into the valley of the Yangtze, pushing the inhabitants
back into the hills of Kweichou and Yunnan. Thus it was that the
Chinese were the traditional enemies of the native Yunnanese.

Furthermore, there were great cultural differences between the
two ethnic groups, which would be likely to make for considerable
friction. A Chinese scholar-official, charged with the administration
of a Yunnanese district, would look with great contempt upon
people who cremated their dead instead of burying them in elaborate and expensive coffins; who permitted strangers openly
to sleep with their wives; who practiced the couvade after the wife
gave birth (the father going to bed for forty days with the infant
beside him); who had no interest in letters or scholarship; and who,
when someone was sick, called in trance shamans to dance instead
of consulting a physician.

The Yunnanese, like the Mongols, were a militarily oriented
people. In the Karajang district, great numbers of horses were
raised for export; like the Mongols, the men were riders who fought
on horseback (as the nomads of neighboring Tibet do today).
They were well-armed riders, wearing leather armor and carrying
spears and shields and, Marco Polo dryly notes, "all their arrows
are poisoned" (*Travels of Marco Polo*, 182). In the Zarandan district,

war was the main business of the men. And in the Toloman district, says Polo, who judges by Mongol standards, the men are "good soldiers." So the Mongols, who valued riding and warfare highly, and trade and scholarship little, would have been far more congenial rulers to the hill tribes of Yunnan than the Chinese, their long-hated enemies. Thus it was that after the decisive battle of Kio-tsing Pass, when the Mongol cause in Yunnan was already hopeless, that a hundred thousand hill tribesmen rallied for a last ditch stand against the Chinese invaders.

In 1381, the Hung Wu emperor collected a task force of three hundred thousand men for the conquest of Yunnan. He entrusted this force to the command of Fou-yeou-te, assisted by three subordinate generals, Mou-yn Lan-yn and Ko-yn. Fou-yeou-te divided his forces into three columns, a main body of perhaps two hundred thousand men and two large detachments of perhaps fifty thousand men each. The Yunnanese concentrated their army of one hundred thousand men under their general Talima at the key pass of Kio-tsing. Fou-yeou-te was joined at Kio-tsing by a large portion of one of his detachments, and so had some two hundred twenty-five thousand troops for the attack. According to de Mailla, an expert on Chinese cartography as well as a historian, the natural position of Kio-tsing Pass was so strong that Talima could easily have held it against the more than two-to-one superiority in numbers the attackers enjoyed. But evidently the Yunnanese were concentrated on one side of the narrow pass, the side along which the road ran, beside the Long-kiang River. On the advice of General Mou-yn, the Chinese army crossed the river lower down, cut a new road on the opposite side of the pass, and thus outflanked Talima's defense position. When the Yunnanese forces broke up in confusion, as they sought to regroup themselves to meet this new threat, the Chinese crossed the river and joined battle. The Yunnanese fought so well, despite their disorganization, that for a time they drove the Chinese attackers back into the river. Only by sheer force of numbers did the Chinese army finally prevail.

This battle proved decisive. Many of the leading towns thereafter opened their gates to the Chinese without a fight. When he learned of the defeat, the Mongol ruler of Yunnan and his leading ministers of state committed suicide.

MAP No. 5

MING TERRITORIAL
EXPANSION
1376 - 1385

Expansion into Yunnan

Source: Hermann 1966

Meanwhile, a large detachment of Chinese was entering Yunnan by another route. While no regular Yunnanese forces opposed them, they were much delayed by local levies hastily collected by a Mongol officer. Early defeats suffered by these levies only stimulated more of the tribesmen to join the Mongol forces, which grew to another one hundred thousand men. However, these men were untrained and undisciplined. Although led by an experienced Mongol general, Chepou, they were defeated and broken up by a Chinese detachment of only twenty thousand regular troops. De Mailla says of Chepou, "Although he did everything in this action that could be expected from a tested captain, his troops were recruits who had never seen battle, and consequently they were easily routed. Three thousand men remained on the field and the rest took flight, without listening to Chepou or heeding orders" (v. 10:84).

That was the last real stand of the defenders of Yunnan. In the two years which followed, the Chinese mopped up. They inflicted sharp punishment upon the hill tribesmen who had flocked to the Mongol standard, burning their villages and destroying their granaries—leaving them to face the mountain winter without food or shelter.

Deterrence had been neglected. Disaster followed.

PART 2: SURVEY OF VARIABLES (CODING FOR CONSPICUOUS STATE, MING CHINA)

Dependent Variables

Months of War. The war broke out in the ninth month of 1381 and the main Mongol forces were shattered in that same year. But mopping up actions continued among the hill tribes on into 1383. We counted one month of war. The raw score of 1 yields a standard score of 39. For method of transformation see p. 11.

Territorial Change. This campaign resulted in the incorporation of Yunnan into the Ming empire. Ming China had a territorial gain of 6%. The raw score of 6 yields two standard scores: territorial gain 60 and territorial stability 55. For method of transformation see p. 13f.

Military Variables

Defensive Stance. The Ming rulers were clearly in an offensive stance, the Yunnanese clearly in a defensive stance. However, this stance was one of short-term intentions, not long-term attitudes. The Mongol rulers of Yunnan presumably would have attacked Ming China if they had the resources. Coded *absent.*

Strength of Armed Forces. The Chinese outnumbered the Mongols. Coded *present.*

Mobility of Armed Forces. The Yunnanese must have enjoyed the advantage here, an advantage, however, which they did not make much use of. The Mongol tradition called for fighting on horseback; and at least one of the Yunnanese native tribes habitually fought on horseback. Yunnan was an important horse-exporting center. Coded *absent.*

Quality of Armed Forces. The main Yunnanese force, one hundred thousand strong, was, man for man, evidently superior to the Chinese invaders. Although outgeneraled and taken off-balance, they fought so well against more than twice their number that only the weight of numbers overpowered them. On the other hand, a second Yunnanese army hastily raised among the hill tribes was untrained and undisciplined and easily defeated by a much smaller Chinese force. On the average, then, this variable ought to be scored as a standoff. Coded *absent.*

Fortifications. The main passes protecting Yunnan against invasion from China were not adequately fortified. The decisive battle at Kio-tsing Pass was not fought behind fortifications; it is possible that one side of the pass was fortified but it is clear that the other side, at least, was not. The failure of the Mongols to fortify the passes during the dozen years of grace that they had to prepare for invasion was one of their chief blunders. The Chinese themselves made no use of fortifications in their invasion. Coded *absent.*

Prestige. For 150 years, the international prestige of the Mongols had been enormous. Speaking of Kublai Khan, the greatest of the Mongol emperors of China, who ruled over the greater part of Asia, Marco Polo (*Travels* book 2, chapter 1) truthfully remarked that "he is the most potent man, as regards forces and lands and treasure, that existeth in the world, or ever hath existed from the time of our First Father Adam until this day." In the century which followed, the Mongol Empire broke up into a number of Mongol successor states, and the Ming restoration in China marked the end of their prestige in Eastern Asia. But had this message—this most unpalatable message—penetrated the minds of the rulers of Yunnan? Or did they still see themselves as the inheritors of the power and glory of Genghis and Kublai, and the Ming Dynasty as a mere passing phase? In the eyes of outside observers in 1381, there would have been no difficulty in assessing the relative prestige of Ming China and Mongol Yunnan—the Chinese obviously towered over Yunnan by any standard, whether military, diplomatic, economic, artistic or intellectual. Coded *present*.

Geographical Variables

Propinquity. The River Chiang provided the common border between Yunnan and Ming China during the decade. Coded *present*.

Natural Barriers. Yunnan is a high plateau engirdled by steep mountains. Access to it from China proper is by way of narrow mountain defiles. This is the Burma Road country. Coded *present*.

Capital City. Yunnanfu (now Kunming) is about one hundred miles from the border, a five-day journey in those times. The Ming capital then was Nanking (see map no. 5), about eight hundred miles from the border. Coded *absent*.

Diplomatic Variables

Announcements. It is hard to suppose that the invasion came as much of a surprise to the Mongol ruler of Yunnan, Patchalaourmi. However, there is no suggestion that the Chinese emperor gave any formal warning, or any invitation for Patchalaourmi to submit. Technically, then, announcements of intention must be coded *absent*.

Surprise Attack. The Mings had already expelled all Mongol rule except for Patchalaourmi in Yunnan. It was obvious that the Chinese would attack Yunnan. The attack cannot have been a strategic surprise. Coded *absent*.

Alliances. Presumably Patchalaourmi still considered himself closely bound to the main body of Mongols on the other side of China in Mongolia. However, there is no indication of any communication between them about the war—either in the Chinese secondary work we are following or in Ssanang Ssetsen Chungtaidschi's Mongolian chronicle. The important coalition was, properly speaking, a matter of Yunnan internal politics rather than of international relations—the alignment of the Yunnanese hill tribes with the Mongols against the Chinese. Coded *absent.*

Active Diplomacy. No negotiations at all were reported. It is quite likely that no diplomatic relations existed between the courts at Nanking and Yunnanfu—the Mongols in Yunnanfu may possibly have continued to refuse to recognize the new rulers of China. Coded *absent.*

Intense Diplomacy. There was none. Coded *absent.*

Previous Conflict. A previous history of conflict led directly to this war. From the Chinese point of view it was part of the process of restoring the past by expelling the Mongol invaders, since Yunnan continued to be governed by a Mongol prince. From the Mongol point of view, Chu Yuan-chang, now styling himself the Hung-wu emperor and founder of the Ming dynasty (in 1398), was a rebel upstart. From the point of view of the Yunnan hill tribesmen, the Chinese invasion was a return of the ancient foe. Coded *present.*

Cultural Variables

Benefits. No sums of money, taxes, gifts, or other benefits, were exchanged. The Ming emperor did not need revenues from Yunnan; after the conquest was completed, he lodged the Mongols he captured in Yunnan in great luxury at his capital in Nanking. Coded *absent.*

Cultural Exchange. The Mongol rulers of Yunnan had been exposed to Chinese culture for over a century, but key differences in values remained. Marco Polo, who sees China through Mongol eyes, and who lived in China for decades, never grasped the key elements of the Chinese viewpoint: reverence for ancestors, for scholarship and for the past. This case supports the hypothesis that cultural exchanges do not lessen conflict unless value orientations are reconciled. Exposure of each to the culture of the other was maximum. The Mongols worked closely with Chinese scholars, the "missionaries" of Chinese Confucianism; and Chinese merchants must have dominated trade throughout all of what is today China. Coded *present*.

Trade. There was no significant trade between Yunnan and Ming China. Coded *absent*.

General Exchange. Coded *present* because cultural exchange is coded *present*.

Administrative Variables

Experience of Ruler. While the Ming Dynasty was not formally established until 1369, its first emperor, known as Chu Yuan-chang, had for more than a decade actually functioned as an independent ruler of an ever-growing portion of China. Coded *present*.

Youth of Ruler. The Hung-wu emperor was born about 1318 and so was about sixty-three years old when he sent his armies into Yunnan. Coded *absent*.

Unbridled Ruler. The Hung-wu emperor did not inherit the throne, nor was he between twenty and forty-five years old. Coded *absent*.

Hereditary Monarchy. The Hung-wu emperor was a successful rebel. Outside of Europe the great Empires were ruled by hereditary monarchs, but when a dynasty became inefficient, it was overthrown. The suddenness of the collapse of Mongol power in China seems clear evidence that popular sentiment in China favored the new regime. Coded *absent*.

Civil War. There was none. Chu Yuan-chang was not opposed in consolidating his control of China, nor was there a Chinese fifth column operating inside Yunnan. Coded *absent*.

Centralization. The two states did not differ in formal legal structure. However, Ming China was culturally more unified than Yunnan, a congeries of petty hill tribes speaking several distinct languages and ruled by Mongols who were foreigners to all of them. This contrast must have helped the Chinese in their organization of the war. However, Ming China was not ostensibly more centralized than Yunnan in structure. Coded *absent*.

PART 3: DATA QUALITY CONTROL

This chapter is based chiefly on two works, de Mailla and Marco Polo, although several others were also consulted. De Mailla is the only work in a European language which gives an account of the Yunnan campaign, and Marco Polo is indispensable as a source of information of the ethnic situation in Yunnan in those days. The works of Marco Polo were not coded because they did not shed light on the conspicuous state (Ming China), but rather on its conspicuous rival. Marco Polo visited Yunnan about one hundred years before the events which concern us here. He wrote of his travels in 1298. An official of Kublai Khan, he is considered Mongol in his sympathies and viewpoint. What made him valuable for our purposes was that he was engaged in descriptive geography. He has no theories about Yunnanese ethnology—only data.

He is our authority for the cultural differences between Chinese and Yunnanese at that time. His remarks, however, are strongly supported by present day ethnographers who have described the culture of such Yunnanese hill tribes as the Lolo and the Miao in great detail. Polo is generally considered to be a trustworthy reporter of things he has seen himself though, like many other travelers, he was likely to accept uncritically wild distortions about people he had not seen himself. When visiting Yunnan, Polo was most impressed not by the people but by a peculiar man-eating "serpent" which he described in great detail. Readers will recognize a description of a crocodile. If he got his ethnological points as well as he did his zoological ones, we are in good hands. Wherever we can check him on Yunnanese ethnology, he seems accurate.

Joseph A. M. de Mailla (1679–1748) was a French Jesuit who lived most of his life in Peking. His *Histoire Générale de la Chine*, 12 vols. (Paris: D. Pierres, 1777–1785) is a translation of a standard Chinese secondary history for the most part; but this Chinese work, the *Tung Chien Kang Mu*, ended in de Mailla's day with the fall of the Mongol dynasty, and the *Ming Shih* had not yet appeared. Therefore de Mailla's history of the Ming and Manchu dynasties was based on three other Chinese secondary works, histories of the Ming dynasty (cited in de Mailla, 10:1-3, footnote). De Mailla retained his viewpoint as a French Jesuit; for example, in a special comment, he defended Wang An-Shih against the attacks of traditional Chinese historians. However, the Ch'ing court, at the time de Mailla was in China, closely adhered to Chinese orthodox scholarship.

Publication Year. De Mailla wrote in about 1730. Coded *absent* because de Mailla was published before 1850.

Primary Source. De Mailla is a secondary source. Coded *absent*.

Author's Associations. De Mailla had status at the Chinese court as a mandarin, He translated the *Tung Chien Kang Mu* from a Manchu translation rather than from the original Chinese. There remains the secondary question of whether his sources, written during the self-conscious Manchu regime could escape Manchu biases. Coded *present*.

Author's Sympathies. We cannot detect what de Mailla's sympathies are. Coded *no data*.

Author's Proximity. De Mailla wrote 350 years after the events he recorded. Coded *absent*.

CHAPTER 8

★ ★ ★

BYZANTINE DISTRACTION: THE CALIPHATE VERSUS THE BYZANTINE EMPIRE

776-785 : Conspicuous State, The Caliphate ; Conspicuous Rival, Byzantine Empire.

PART 1: SKETCH OF HISTORICAL SETTING (CHIEFLY AFTER THEO-PHANES AND WEIL)

THIS RANDOMLY CHOSEN DECADE from 776 to 785, in the history of the Caliphate presents the Byzantine Empire as the Conspicuous Rival. By 776 the caliph ruled a much expanded version of the original state of Islam. Muhammed, just before his death in 630, had laid the foundations for a religiously centered political state. At that time Islam dominated one-third of the Arabian peninsula. After Muhammed's death three caliphs were elected in succession. By the year 650, Islam had expanded its territory at the expense of the Byzantine Empire. In 661 the first hereditary dynasty, the Umayyad, was established. From 775 to 785 the new Abbasid dynasty under Mahdi, its third caliph, was in control. From 785 to 786 Hadi was the caliph, and was to rule for only one year. At the time of our decade the Caliphate stretched from Spain eastward to Samarkand. It included North Africa, Syria, Arabia, and Khurasan.

The Byzantine Empire included southern Italy, most of the Balkans, and all of what is present-day Turkey. In the decade concerned, Leo IV reigned from 775 to 780. Irene, his wife, ruled for the rest of the decade for her minor son, Constantine VI.

Both powers—the Caliphate and the Byzantine Empire—had been troubled by internal dissension for some time. Mahdi, the Abbasid caliph, was concerned about his successor and about rebellious subjects in portions of his vast empire. But his problems were not as complex as those of the Greek emperor. The rival Byzantines, distracted by many simultaneous internal difficulties, neglected their defenses against the Arabs for a while. Seizing the opportunity, the Caliphate waged a successful campaign. The Arabs demanded and received a substantial tribute, thus inflicting upon the Greeks a humiliating defeat.

Almost from Islam's beginning as a state it was clear that a desert economy would not support an empire with expansionist aims. The expansion was to be mainly at the expense of the Byzantine Empire. By 650 Syria, Upper Mesopotamia, Palestine, and a portion of North Africa were controlled by the Arabs, who were then confronted with the need to defend their new provinces against Byzantine vessels. The Arabs built a fleet for this purpose, took Cyprus and Rhodes, threatened Italy and Sicily and even Constantinople. The Greeks then found themselves in a much more vulnerable position vis-à-vis the Arabs, especially on their eastern border, and needed to strengthen their forces there. Asia Minor had been districted into military zones (later called *themes*), each under a military commander, as far back as 630 by the Byzantine emperor Heraclius after his victory over the Persians. The military authority in these areas eventually grew at the expense of the civil authority, especially, it is thought, under Leo III (714–741); he probably created two new themes. Although this area was fully incorporated into the empire, it served as a quasi-buffer zone between the Byzantine Empire and the Caliphate. The Arabs, in counter defense, erected a line of fortifications along the frontier from Syria to Armenia.

Although the decade from 776 to 785 was a period of internal dissension for both powers, for the Caliphate it was also a time when Arab society, under a new dynasty, was making impressive intellectual contributions. Not long before, the Arabs had moved their capital eastward from Damascus to Baghdad and were in the process of making it an important and powerful world center, one which would soon equal Constantinople. Mahdi, the third Abbasid caliph, ruled from 775 to 785. At the beginning of his reign he resumed the war which had been going on for more than a century between the Arabs and the Greeks. By the time the peace treaty was signed, in 782, Mahdi had gained new prestige as well as tribute for the Arabs, even though the new territory he conquered was not large.

In Byzantium the internal strife during this period centered around the icons—the question of whether images and pictures of Christ and the saints were to be worshipped. The iconoclastic group, composed for the most part of the ruler, the high clergy, and the army, condemned image and relic worship and were in favor of reducing the number and power of the monasteries. The iconodules, or image worshippers, were largely commoners, women, and monks (of whom there were many). By the time the decade under study had begun, the bitter struggle over the issue of icons had been going on for half a century. There had been breaking, burning, and painting over of icons accompanied by large scale persecution of monasteries and monks; many monks were exiled; others escaped.

In 775 Leo IV became emperor of the Byzantine Empire. He was an iconoclast, but a mild one. His wife, Irene, was an image-worshipper, and when she became the ruler at his death in 780 she began to restore veneration of images. But since the army was largely iconoclastic she had to transfer the iconoclastic troops to Asia Minor and bring iconodule troops from Thrace to defend the capital.

Irene's problem with iconoclasm was not the only one she faced. She had to protect the throne against the attempts of a pretender to seize it, and she also had to divert troops to Greece, where the Slavs were rebelling. Furthermore, the Bulgars were becoming increasingly restless, and there was a rebellion in Sicily.

In addition, the Arabs were attacking on the borders of the Empire. When the Umayyad dynasty had given way to the Abbasid, the Arabs became concerned mainly with the problem of succession; they moved their capital farther away from Constantinople, closer to the centers of population, commerce, and military force which were now in Iraq and Khurasan. Consequently, for the previous twenty years the Greeks had found it an easy matter to protect their border defenses. But now along the boundaries of the Empire, Irene was faced with a consolidated potential striking power.

Thus, when Mahdi became caliph in 775 the Greeks had many things to occupy their attention, and he could attack their borders with a good chance of success. Mahdi assembled an army in Syria and, without announcing his intentions, marched into Asia Minor and took the Byzantine city of Ancyra. Leo IV was busy defending his throne from a group who wanted to install his brother, Nicephorus, as the Byzantine Emperor and thus he was not in a position to fight the Arabs. Pleased with their easy victory, the Arabs marched home. In 777 they attacked the Empire again, took large numbers of prisoners and again returned home. In 778 the Arabs attacked Dabekon in Syria. This time Leo IV sent one hundred thousand troops to fight them, under the command of the famous general of the Thrakesion theme, Michael Lachanodracon. Then the Greeks beseiged Germanikeia, seized the Arabs' camels, and would have taken Germanikeia if the Arabs had not bribed Michael. Instead of resisting, Michael drew back at first and plundered the surrounding area, then returned and finally faced the Arabs, who retreated. After the Arabs had retreated, the Greeks under Michael moved on towards Syria, where they destroyed the Hadath fortress and burned all the Arab land up to the Syrian border.

Against this offensive thrust the Arabs countered with a force of eighty thousand men. They not only recovered the lost areas but also took Phrygia and laid waste all the Greek land as far as the town of Dorylauem (Opsikion theme). The Greeks were ordered to garrison each of their castles with three thousand of their best troops. They succeeded in burning the surrounding meadows so that the Arabs' horses could no longer graze, and the Arabs were forced to retreat, leaving many of their horses behind. On their retreat the Arabs stopped near Amorion (Anatolikon theme) but, finding it well fortified, did not attack it. Thus the Arabs were driven out of Asia Minor in 779.

But the Arabs rebuilt the Hadath fortress in Syria, took the fortress of Semalrum in Armenia, and in 780 they again attacked in Asia Minor. This time Michael Lachanodracon had amassed a large army at the frontier, and the Arabs with an army of only fifty thousand had to draw back. In that same year, 780, Emperor Leo IV died, and his wife, Irene, became ruler for their young son. She ordered the generals of all the themes to guard the passes through the mountains and get ready for an Arab attack. When the Arabs arrived in 781 the Greeks were well prepared and defeated them. But not for long.

In 782 the Arabs returned to Asia Minor with an army of one hundred thousand well-equipped troops. Irene, however, was at the moment distracted by her attempts to secure the throne, to restore the icons, and to keep down the rebellions which had arisen in Greece, Macedonia, and Sicily. It seemed to her that the most urgent problem was the rebellion in Sicily. Elpidios, the governor of Sicily (who supported the claim of Leo IV's brother Nicephorus to the Byzantine throne) had taken this moment to rebel against Irene. She decided to send the bulk of the army to Sicily to quell the revolt there. When the army arrived, and Elpidios saw that he would be unable to resist such a powerful force, he fled to the Arabs, who not only gave him asylum, but even crowned him Emperor of Constantinople.

Irene had quieted the rebellion in Sicily at great cost. While her troops were occupied in Sicily, ninety-five thousand Arabs were meanwhile on the march in Asia Minor. They got as far as Chrysopolis in the north and besieged Nicolaie in Phrygia. In a battle at Darenon against Michael Lachanodracon, the Arabs, with thirty thousand men, killed fifteen thousand Greeks. Even though Irene sent reinforcements from the capital, the Greeks continued to fare badly. The Greek general Tatzates defected to the Arabs and advised them to negotiate a peace treaty.

The Arabs were willing to negotiate, but on their own terms. They demanded an unhampered return of their army, the right to keep all the spoils taken in the war, a free food supply for their return march, and an annual tribute of between seventy and ninety thousand dinars for the next three years. It is not clear why Irene accepted the terms of the peace treaty. Either her military position was so weak that she had to sign the humiliating treaty, or she simply may have wanted to get rid of the Arab nuisance so that she would then be free to turn her attention to the matters of securing the throne and restoring the icons. In any event, Irene agreed to the terms which the Arabs imposed. The Arabs freed the Greek diplomats whom they had taken as hostages, gave up Nicolaie in Phrygia, and marched homeward. The Greeks honored all the terms of the treaty and they even refrained from harrassing the Arabs on their return through the narrow mountain passes. The payment of tribute was followed by a lull in the religious wars between the

MAP No. 6

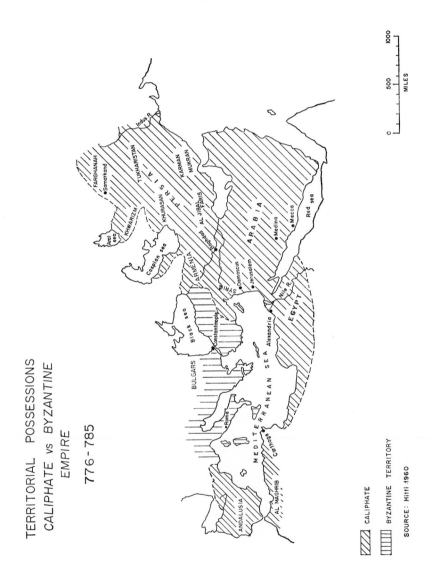

TERRITORIAL POSSESSIONS
CALIPHATE vs BYZANTINE
EMPIRE

776-785

CALIPHATE

BYZANTINE TERRITORY

SOURCE: Hitti 1960

Caliphate and the Byzantine Empire; but it was to be resumed once more in 798, under Mahdi's son.

PART 2: SURVEY OF VARIABLES (CODED FOR CONSPICUOUS STATE, THE CALIPHATE)

Dependent Variables

Months of War. The month in which war ended was not specified in the works we consulted. The fighting began in 775, before the decade, with an Arab invasion of the Byzantine Empire, and ended in 782 with a formal peace treaty. Between the Conspicuous State and the Conspicuous Rival there were seventy-two months of war during the decade and forty-eight months of peace. The raw score of 72 yields a standard score of 56. For method of transformation see p. 11.

Territorial Change. The Arabs gained approximately 0.01% during the decade under study, in the area of Armenia. The raw score of .01% yields two standard scores: Territorial Gain 49 and Territorial Stability 36. For method of transformation see p. 13f.

Military Variables

Defensive Stance. Both Arab and Greek sources agree that without announcing their intentions beforehand the Arabs assembled troops in Syria and marched into Asia Minor. They were on the offensive, the Greeks on the defensive. Coded *absent*.

Strength of Armed Forces. In the ninth century, when the Abbasid Caliphate was its strongest, the standing army numbered about one hundred twenty-five thousand. We can infer then that during the decade under study the Arab army numbered approximately one hundred thousand. At least this is the largest figure mentioned in the sources we consulted, although bands of mercenaries may have augmented the regular troops from time to time. The Greeks also seemed able to raise at the most one hundred thousand men. Most of the campaigns of the decade involved considerably fewer troops than that number. Each side was unable to throw its entire military power against the other, each had to fight other enemies, each was beset by internal troubles. On balance it would appear that the Arab bands throughout the vast empire provided a greater potential source to draw from than the manpower the Greeks could raise. Coded *present*.

Mobility of Armed Forces. The Arabs had cavalry, but it is not clear how much they used horses or camels or both at this time; we are told that they used camels to pull the litters of the field hospitals and we are also told that they used horses at Dorylaeum. Even though the Greeks had cavalry it is not clear to what extent they used it at this time. Consequently it is difficult to assess the relative mobility of the armies. Coded *no data*.

Quality of Armed Forces. Since the Arab army paid its soldiers well, it was an attractive way of earning a living. The army had infantry, cavalry, engineer, and archer groups, as well as field hospitals. The infantry carried spears, swords, and shields; the cavalry wore helmets and breastplates and carried lances and battle-axes; the archers had troops attached to them who threw incendiary bombs. The Arab army was a strongly knit unit with high morale.

The Byzantine army was strictly disciplined and, under Leo III, had been a very strong force. When he died in 741 the army continued its effectiveness under his son, Constantine V. Both men won brilliant victories over the Arabs; Constantine V, using cavalry, defeated the Bulgars in 763, again in 773, and he died fighting them in 775. When Leo IV acceded to the throne at his death, to be followed by a five-year reign (780) by his wife, Irene, acting as regent for their young son, the strength of the army appears to have somewhat diminished. Not much information about the Greek army during the decade under study is found in the works we consulted. Although the Greek generals were able, they accepted bribes and defected to the enemy and thus weakened the morale of their soldiers. The Greek army seems to have been inferior to that of the Caliphate in morale, and probably also in equipment. Coded *present*.

Fortifications. Many ruined Arab fortresses were restored in this era when the wars between the Arabs and the Greeks were resumed. Hitti (p. 299) says that the "Moslem line of frontier fortifications [*thughur*] extending from Syria to Armenia retreated as the Byzantine line opposite advanced." The Greeks destroyed the fortress of

Hadath in 778, but Mahdi soon had it rebuilt. In 779, when the Arabs attacked Dorylaeum (Opsikion theme) with a large army, the Greeks were ordered to garrison each of their castles with three thousand of their best soldiers; the Greeks were able to withstand the Arabs and even captured some Arab horses. On their way back the Arabs tried to take the city of Amorion (Anatolikon theme), but it was too well fortifed, and they left it untouched. In 780, however, the Arabs beseiged the fortress of Semalrum in Armenia and it surrendered to them. Even though fortresses helped hold them back, the Arabs were nonetheless able to inflict a humiliating defeat on the Greeks in this decade. Coded *present*.

Prestige. Although the wealth and power of the Byzantine Empire had long been greatly admired by its neighbors, its prestige was beginning to decline by 776, whereas the prestige of the Caliphate was rising. Northern and central Italy had broken away from the Byzantine Empire. The Franks were growing powerful and aligning with the Pope against Byzantium. The Bulgars were becoming more and more restless. The Arabs as an ethnic group were nearing the end of their military and political domination of the Islamic Caliphate. It was becoming more consmopolitan, and the Persians and Turks would dominate it in the ninth century. During the decade we have studied, the Caliphate was able to exact tribute from the Greeks (see "Benefits," below). Thus, while the Byzantine Empire was rapidly losing prestige, the Caliphate was just as rapidly gaining it. Coded *present*.

Geographical Variables

Propinquity. Both the Caliphate and the Byzantine Empire covered immense areas. They confronted each other on the Mediterranean and Black Seas. On land they bordered at Armenia in the east, and at France and Spain in the west. Coded *present*.

Natural Barriers. The Mediterranean and the Dardanelles had been a protection for Byzantium against the Caliphate until the Arabs built a navy; even with a navy, although the Arabs attacked Constantinople, they never succeeded in taking it. As for land barriers, there were mountains with narrow passes between the Arabs and the Byzantine provinces in Asia Minor; when the Arabs returned through these passes from their campaign in Asia Minor in 782, the Greeks were in a position to harass them but refrained from doing so, because Irene had guaranteed the Arabs an undisturbed return march. Coded *present*.

Capital City. The capital of the Caliphate was moved shortly before the decade in question from Damascus to Kufa, then to Anbar, and finally, in 762, to distant Baghdad. Baghdad was about four hundred fifty miles from the frontier in the province of Armenia. Constantinople, the Byzantine capital, was about four hundred seventy miles from the frontier near the Taurus mountains. Coded *absent* because Baghdad was not within three hundred miles of the border.

Diplomatic Variables

Announcements. Both Greek and Arab sources agree that in this decade the Arabs attacked the Byzantine Empire without any previous announcements of intention. Coded *absent*.

Surprise Attack. The bulk of Irene's army was occupied in Sicily at the time of the Arab march into Asia Minor. Coded *present*.

Alliances. There is no mention of important international alliances made on either side during the decade. Coded *absent*.

Active Diplomacy. The most important negotiations were those concerning the peace treaty (see "Benefits," below). Coded *present*.

Intense Diplomacy. See "Benefits" below. Coded *present*.

Previous Conflict. The caliphs began to wage war with the Byzantine Empire almost from Islam's beginnings in the seventh century. By fighting on land and sea the Arabs gained North Africa, Syria, Upper Mesopotamia, Palestine, and parts of Asia Minor from the Byzantine Empire. Early in the seventh century the Greeks, in defense, strengthened their military zones, each one under a supreme commander. Soldiers in these zones were granted land in return for hereditary military service and thus provided a stable economic and military base for Byzantium. But in spite of reorganization in both provincial and central governments, Byzantium remained vulnerable to the Arabs. Constantinople itself was attacked several times. During the years immediately preceding the decade 776 to 785, however, there had been only small-scale warfare between the Arabs and the Greeks; each power was troubled by internal strife and could not afford to send troops against the other. Coded *present*.

Cultural Variables

Benefits. After the Arabs had waged a successful campaign in northwestern Asia Minor (Thrakesion theme) the Greeks negotiated a peace, and in 782 a three-year peace treaty was concluded. The terms of the treaty required the Greeks to pay a yearly tribute of between seventy and ninety thousand dinars. The Arabs also demanded and got from them the right to all the spoils and prisoners taken in the war, as well as a free food supply on their unhindered homeward journey. There was no further fighting during the decade and peace between the Arabs and Greeks lasted until 798, when fighting was once again resumed. Coded *present*.

Cultural Exchange. The wars which had been raging between Islam and the Byzantine Empire provided little opportunity for official cultural exchange. Nevertheless it is clear that the two sides did influence each other greatly. The Caliphate employed thousands of Greeks for their building programs; although many were prisoners of war and slaves, there were also free workers. And the Caliphate sent both male and female spies into the Byzantine Empire in the guise of merchants, travelers, and physicians. But much more important was the effect of Greek thought on the Arabs. The decade under study was the beginning of a great intellectual Arab stirring, when the translated works of Aristotle, the Neoplatonists, Galen, and Euclid began to be absorbed into Arabian scholarship along with Persian and Indian thought. Coded *absent* as there was no direct exchange of culture bearers (such as teachers) or of contemporary literature.

Trade. Not enough information is available regarding this variable. Coded *no data*.

General Exchange. Coded *absent*. See "Cultural Exchange" and "Trade," above.

Administrative Variables

Experience of Ruler. Mahdi began his rule in 775. Hadi became ruler in 785 at the end of the decade and ruled only one year. Coded *absent* because neither ruler had ruled for ten years before the decade.

Youth of Ruler. Mahdi was born in 743, and was thirty-two years old in 775, when he became ruler. Hadi was born in 760 or 761 and was twenty-five years old at his accession. Coded *present.*

Unbridled Ruler. The succession was hereditary; both Mahdi and Hadi were between twenty and forty-six years old, and they ruled a centralized monarchy. Coded *present.*

Hereditary Monarchy. The succession to the Caliphate was commonly accompanied by struggle and even murder within the ruling family. Shortly before his death Mansur is said to have killed his nephew in order to prevent his claiming the Caliphate from Mahdi. When Mahdi became caliph it had been decreed that the successor would be Isa, and the population had sworn to it— usually the previous ruler had the population swear to accept his son or sons as the next in line. But in the second year of his reign Mahdi, after repeatedly asking Isa to come Baghdad, and then bribing him to do so, finally had him brought there. He forced Isa to resign all his claims and free the population from its promise. Then Mahdi's son Hadi was declared heir apparent. Six years later Mahdi appointed his other son, Harun, to be his second successor; he even tried to make him his immediate heir, not only because Harun showed greater abilities, but also because he was his mother's favorite. Mahdi recalled Hadi from Jorjan, but Hadi refused to come and furthermore mistreated his father's messengers. Mahdi, incensed, assembled an army, and went after his son but died on the way, presumably from poison. Harun, who accompanied his father, sent the troops home, buried his father secretly, and acknowledged his brother as caliph. Hadi, not yet twenty-five years old, then attempted to have his little son accepted as heir apparent instead of his brother; Harun was so mistreated at the court that he fled from Baghdad. Hadi then turned his attention to his mother. He felt that she had too great an influence and confined her to the harem. His mother, enraged, had her slaves kill him, whereupon Harun became caliph. Thus within the space of a little more than ten years there were five acts of violence accompanying the succession to the Caliphate. Coded *present.*

Civil War. For the Greeks, the issue of the icons was to divide the Empire. When the Empress Irene became regent in 780, iconoclasts attempted a rebellion against her which she was able to suppress. She transferred the iconoclastic troops to Asia Minor and brought iconodule troops from Thrace to defend the capital, thus reversing a fifty-year policy and bringing about the gradual restoration of the icons. In addition to the issue of the icons, Byzantium was bothered by a pretender to the throne (Nicocephorus) and by dissension in the outlying parts of the empire: the Bulgars rebelled, the Slavs who had been brought to Greece in the middle of the eighth century rebelled, northern and central Italy broke away completely from Greek control.

The caliphs lived in constant fear of uprisings. Although in 777 and 778 there occurred unsuccessful rebellions in Tabaristan and Jorjan, some rebellions were successful. In 756, six years after the establishment of the Abbasid Caliphate, the Umayyad heir was able to establish a new dynasty in Cordova, thus putting an end to more than twenty years of disturbance there. In 785 a dissident Moslem group established a new kingdom in Morocco. The Arab conflicts, in part political and in part religious, were particularly strong between the northern and southern Arabs. (The empire of the Caliphate was beginning to break up, starting in northern Africa and continuing in Iran; the break-up was not particularly notable in the decade under question, but occurred during the first century of the Abbasid dynasty.) It was probably the series of internal conflicts which had induced the caliphs to move their capital nearer to the centers of population, commerce, and military forces which were now in Iraq and Khurasan. These were the areas which had supplied troops to the Abbasid revolution. Coded *present*.

Centralization. At this time the Caliphate was theoretically centralized. But according to Hitti the tremendous distances coupled with the poor communication facilities made each governor supreme in his province, and in actuality his office became hereditary. In the Byzantine Empire during the seventh and eighth centuries, the former immense territories were reorganized into smaller military zones. The military governors were thus brought more closely under the control of the central government, and their powers greatly reduced. It would appear that these reforms in the military zones made the Byzantine Empire more highly centralized than the Caliphate. Coded *absent*.

PART 3: DATA QUALITY CONTROL

We used only one contemporary primary source, that of the Greek historian Theophanes, whose *Chronicle* was followed by many later historians. He was alive (758–817) during the decade, and was eighteen years old when it began. For this study the translation by Leopold Breyer, *Bilderstreit und Arabersturm. Byzantinische Geschichtsschreiber*, vol. 6, ed. Endre v. Ivanka (Graz: Verlag Styria, 1957) was used.

The earliest Arab source we used is Tabari. He was not alive during the decade but could have spoken to people who had themselves witnessed the events of the decade. He was born in 838 and wrote his *Annals* approximately one hundred years after the events of the decade. The abridged translation by Hermann Zotenberg, *Chronique de Abou-Djafar-Mo'hammed-Ben-Djarir-Ben-Yezid Tabari* (Nogent-Le-Retrou: Imprimerie de A. Gouverneur, 1874) was used.

The most recent detailed histories used are Gustav Weil, *Geschichte der Chalifen* (Mannheim: Verlag Wassermann, 1848); and *Geschichte der Islamischen Völker* (Stuttgart: Reiger, 1866). Weil's works are based on those of Ibn Athir, Ibn Khaldun, and some unpublished Arab sources which he has translated. Other recent histories include A.A. Vasiliev, *History of the Byzantine Empire* (Madison: University of Wisconsin Press, 1952); George Ostrogorsky, *History of the Byzantine State*, trans. Joan Hussey (Oxford: Blackwell, 1956); Carl Brockelmann, *Geschichte der Islamischen Völker* (München und Berlin: Verlag Oldenborg, 1939); Philip K. Hitti, *History of the Arabs* (London: Macmillan, 1960). The sources that were coded were Theophanes and Weil.

Publication Year. Theophanes must have written some time between 776 and 817. Weil wrote in 1848 and 1866. Coded *no data* because the sources were written partly before and partly after 1850.

Primary Sources. Coded *no data* because the situation was ambiguous. We relied about half and half on primary and secondary sources.

Authors' Associations. Of the two sources coded, Theophanes was in the service of Emperor Constantine V for some time, and Weil was a professor of oriental languages and a librarian of the University of Heidelberg who translated Arab histories.

The following sources were used but not coded because they were not leading sources. Tabari was a tutor to Ubaidallah Ibn Yahya, the son of the vizier. Vasiliev was a professor of history in Russia and subsequently at the University of Wisconsin. Ostrogorsky was a professor of history at the University of Belgrade. Brockelmann was a professor of Semitic and Turkish languages in German universities. Hitti is Professor Emeritus of Semitic literature at Princeton University.

Coded *no data*; Theophanes was associated with the Conspicuous Rival, and Weil had no association with either the Conspicuous State or the Rival.

Authors' Sympathies. Theophanes displays such objectivity in his work that he even records Michael Lachanodracon's acceptance of bribes from the Arabs; however, he does show his antipathy toward Emperor Leo IV and everyone else who was an iconoclast. Although the Arab authors in general do not display their feelings, if they wrote anything which displeased the caliph their lives were in danger. Weil tells us that the historian Al-Wakidi, the main source of events during the first years of Islam, had to praise Ali and condemn the caliph Mu'awaiyah.

The following sources were not coded. Tabari, like the other Arab writers, extolled the virtues of Mahdi. Brockelmann is a supporter of current Arab nationalism, but his comments on the time of the Caliphate reveal neither pro-Arab nor pro-Greek sympathy. Hitti was educated in Beirut and served as advisor to the Arab states delegation to the U.N. He, Vasiliev, and Ostrogorsky similarly reveal neither pro-Arab nor pro-Greek feelings. Coded *absent*.

Authors' Proximity. Only Theophanes was a contemporary of the event. Tabari wrote about one hundred years after the events. All the others wrote eleven or twelve hundred years after the events. Coded *no data* because Theophanes was contemporary, but Weil wrote during the second half of the nineteenth century.

CHAPTER 9

★ ★ ★

CONFUSION IN NOVGOROD

1476-1485: Conspicuous State, Muscovy ; Conspicuous Rival, Novgorod.

PART 1: SKETCH OF HISTORICAL SETTING (CHIEFLY AFTER VER-NADSKY)

FOR THE DUCHY OF MUSCOVY in the randomly chosen decade 1476–1485, the leading foreign conflict was with the Republic of Novgorod. This period was to mark the outcome of a struggle between the formerly independent Republic of Novgorod and its elective prince, Ivan III, Grand Duke of Muscovy. Novgorodians traditionally had elected the Grand Duke Muscovy as their prince by independent choice. They received greater protection from him than they could have expected from any other Russian prince. However, voluntary choice was of paramount importance to the Novgorodians, and the stage was set for the conflict twenty-four years before our decade began, when the then Grand Duke of Muscovy tried to increase his power. The struggle came to a climax at the time Ivan III of Muscovy imposed himself as Prince by force of arms, thus depriving Novgorod of its right of choice. Because the Novgorodians were militarily weaker than Muscovy, were unable to get effective military aid from their allies, and were torn by internal dissensions, they were to lose their independence.

The struggle between Muscovy and Novgorod began in 1452, with the realization by the Novgorodians that Vasili II, father of Ivan III, was becoming a menace to their independence. When Dimitri Shamiaka, Vasili's cousin and rival for the Grand Duchy of Moscow, sought and obtained refuge in Novgorod after his defeat by Vasili's generals, Vasili viewed this act as a breach of faith on Novgorod's part, and it gave him a reason to move against the Novgorodians. And when, in addition, Vasili did not receive his regular court fees from Novgorod, he led an army against the Novgorodians and defeated them. In the peace treaty of 1456 he made the Novgorodians promise not to let Dimitri Shamiaka's son, nor any other enemies of Vasili II, into the city. He thus deprived Novgorod of freedom in her dealings with those Russian princes who were independent of the Grand Duke of Muscovy and made relations with them treason. Vasili made the peace treaty with Novgorod both in his name and in his son's (Ivan III); by inserting Ivan's name the ground was laid for a later claim to Novgorod as his patrimony.

In 1471, after defeating Novgorod in an armed confrontation, Ivan III compelled the reluctant Novgorodians to concede his house the hereditary right to fill this office. The Novgorodians, however, had no sooner made this concession when they began to think about how they could renounce it and rid themselves of Muscovite domination. By Novgorod law, the Prince could exert his authority only in person and not through deputies. Since Ivan resided 300 miles away in Moscow, effective control of Novgorod in fact, if not in theory, was still retained by the Novgorodians. The Novgorod assembly was dominated by the boyars, or merchant class, who shared their power with the churchmen and the lower class.

The boyars would have difficulty ridding the city of Muscovite domination. Ivan commanded larger and better disciplined forces than they could raise and he had firm control over his people. The boyars had to find a rival prince who could field an army comparable to Ivan's. They had to establish alliances and rally the populace to their side. They were faced with severe problems which they failed to solve. They could not get effective help from abroad, they could not establish effective alliances, and they could not rally their own people. Consequently, their revolt against Ivan's princely authority would prove a miserable fiasco, their power would be broken forever, and Novgorod effectively would be incorporated into the dominions of the Grand Duke of Moscow.

When the decade from 1476 to 1485 began, Muscovy was the ecclesiastical center of Russia, and Ivan III was already a strong ruler of the Duchy. The army had become centralized under him, as had the governmental administration. Collection of tribute for the Mongol overlords, formerly handled by the Mongol Khans, was taken over by Ivan. An organized conscription system was in operation and there were special departments to administer the grand-ducal estates. Novgorod, on the other hand, had at its head an elected prince with limited authority who could be replaced if he did not satisfy the citizens. Novgorod had never been a strong military power and depended customarily upon the elected prince and other service princes to supply additional troops to protect the city. The elected prince thus had an important military function, but the Novgorod popular assembly made the laws. The prince was in effect the employee of a republic whose authority lay in the assembly, and Novgorod lacked the centralization of Moscow.

The city of Novgorod ruled a huge but thinly inhabited domain, covering much of what is now northern Russia. Within this domain the burghers of the city of Novgorod formed an oligarchic republic in which the merchant class possessed a preponderance of power and influence. Thus, important municipal affairs were managed by a small clique of wealthy merchants, or boyars; the numerous clergy and the free commoners looked at these boyars with suspicion and resentment. The citizenry of Novgorod was comprised of five classes, two of noncitizens and three of citizens: a class of rich landed gentry and merchant boyars; a strong church group headed by the Archbishop of Novgorod; and a lower class of artisans and manual workers. Then there were the noncitizens: peasants who lived on state lands, as well as all the inhabitants of Novgorod's north Russian empire which stretched to the Ural Mountains. Even though these people in the provinces had a small voice in Novgorod's policies, their attitude in the struggle with Moscow became important, and where they refused to support Novgorod they in effect became supporters of Moscow. Finally, there were the many slaves in Novgorod.

Malcontents were used as informers by Moscow, as were those boyars who left Novgorod and entered Ivan's service, and commoners who felt mistreated by the Novgorod courts. In spite of established procedure to ensure equality before the law, most of the judges came from the wealthy class, and the poor people therefore often felt deprived of a fair trial. The system of courts acted to increase class strife in Novgorod society. Ivan was quick to seize judicial prerogatives in this struggle between Novgorodian rich and poor and thereby further weaken the unity of the city.

Since the Novgorod merchants had no taste for warfare, they had traditionally entrusted the defense of their state to an elected prince. For many years the election had usually been bestowed on the Grand Duke of Muscovy. Under the Novgorod constitution the elected prince was obligated to follow Novgorodian custom, and if he did not, he could be deposed. He served two main functions, military and judicial. He was to supply troops as protection against Novgorod's enemies, and he was to act as an impartial arbiter in court cases. He could participate in governmental affairs, but only with the mayor's approval. And he was to perform his princely function only while he was in Novgorod. The city assembly, however, was free to act without him. For his services the prince received an annual gift from the provinces, a share in court fees and hunting and fishing rights.

Politically the city was divided into an assembly controlled by the commoners, and the council of lords controlled by the rich boyars. There were five districts in the city, each governed by a *mir* who was in turn governed by the mayor. The mayor was elected by the assembly. The council of lords submitted proposals to the assembly, which then could vote upon them. The boyars were often able to bribe commoners and thus exert control over the assembly.

In 1471 when Novgorod had to decide whether to side with Lithuania or Moscow, the class dissensions intensified. Two groups formed: a pro-Moscow faction composed of the church group and commoners, and a pro-Lithuanian faction, composed of the boyars. Since commerce between Moscow and Novgorod provided bread for the commoners, Moscow was able to get their support. And since the commoners were already dissatisfied with the courts, they were in favor of giving Ivan III more judicial authority. The Russian Orthodox church opposed a union with Roman Catholic Lithuania. But there remained many citizens who were undecided. Having no experienced military leader among their numbers, and taking for granted that effective military leadership was to be found only among someone of princely rank, the Novgorodians looked abroad for a Russian prince in 1471, someone who might replace Ivan III. Russian princes had lately been in short supply, since by 1450 the Grand Duchies of Muscovy and Lithuania had absorbed most of the principalities, such as Tver, which were formerly independent. The Novgorodians were left with only two candidates whom they considered at all eligible—Mikhail and Casimir—both of them Lithuanian.

Lithuania in 1471 was a constitutional monarchy which covered a vast territory extending from Poland in the west to Moscow in the east, and Livonia and Novgorod in the north to the Crimea in the south. Lithuania and Poland were joined in a union, and Casimir, the king of Poland, was also the Grand Duke of Lithuania, as was often the case. Mikhail Olelkovich of the Lithuanian house of Gedymin was the first cousin of Ivan III; his father and grand-father had each been Prince of Kiev. When Mikhail's older brother died in 1470 Casimir did not appoint Mikhail Prince of Kiev. Mikhail, therefore, was attempting to conquer Kiev, and Ivan feared that the Novgorodians would help Mikhail to do so. The Novgorodians in 1470 invited Prince Mikhail Olelkovich to become their service prince and the boyars of Novgorod made a treaty with Casimir. The Lithuanian army promised to support Novgorod against Moscow, but the Novgorodians omitted any promise to help Mikhail obtain Kiev. Ivan III was concerned to learn of Mikhail's invitation. Mikhail was offended by the omission of the promise to help obtain Kiev and departed from Novgorod in 1471, leaving the city without a leader.

The Novgorodians felt they had the right under old law and custom to choose whichever prince they wanted. Ivan III, however, viewed the treaty between Lithuania and Novgorod as treason, and the fact that Casimir was a Roman Catholic made it doubly offensive. Not only was Ivan III able to get the support of the cities of Tver and Viatka, but also the support of the Pskovians, on whom the Novgorodians had counted. Ivan moved against Novgorod in 1471. Casimir, who had an alliance with Pskov, refused to help Novgorod. Novgorod thus was left alone, and at the time when unity was most needed, dissension broke out between the boyars and the commoners. Although the Novgorodians suffered many casualties, the boyars continued to resist; finally they too had to give up the fight. In the treaty of peace which was signed in 1471, the Novgorodians had to promise never again to get help from the Grand Duke of Lithuania nor to invite a service prince from Lithuania. Further, they had to recognize that Novgorod was the patrimony of the Grand Duke of Moscovy and dependent on him, which in effect made Ivan the hereditary prince of Novgorod instead of the elected prince.

Novgorod, although dependent on the Grand Duke, still retained some autonomy. Had the dissident elements been able to unite and defend what autonomy was left, the Novgorodians might have been able to hold off Ivan III. With their city torn by internal strife, and class differences often affecting political interests, the Novgorodians were unable to unite.

In addition, coalitions prior to 1471 became a key factor in the deterrence situation. Earlier Novgorod had counted on the city of Pskov, which at the last moment decided to ally with Moscow. The Novgorodians had also relied on the support of Lithuania, both from king Casimir of Poland and from the houses of Gedymin and Rurik, and hoped' that Casimir and the Lithuanian lords would protect them against Ivan III. This protection never came. The alliance between Casimir and Novgorod was only a small part of Casimir's strategy against Moscow and involved another alliance on his part, one with Khan Ahmad of the Golden Horde. With Ahmad, Casimir contemplated an invasion of Moscow; he never came to Novgorod's aid. Thus, the Novgorodians were left without allies.

The failure of the boyars' coalition policies in 1470 and 1471 lowered their prestige in the assembly. They tried to get control of some of the districts of the city by bribery and when that did not work they tried force. In 1475 some of the residents of the districts were beaten and their homes looted by boyars who were attempting to still opposition. These residents asked Ivan III to arbitrate, and he promptly did in October of 1475. In 1477 a group of citizens became so discontented that they broke ancient precedent and went to Moscow to ask Ivan III to hold court—according to custom Ivan could arbitrate only when he was in residence in Novgorod. After a second group of discontented citizens came to Moscow, Ivan III sent an embassy to Novgorod and demanded full judicial control and at the same time demanded that Novgorod accept him as a sovereign rather than a mere prince. His demand created an uproar in the city. When the Novgorodians refused to grant Ivan such

MAP No. 7

TERRITORIAL EXPANSION OF MUSCOVY

1476 – 1485

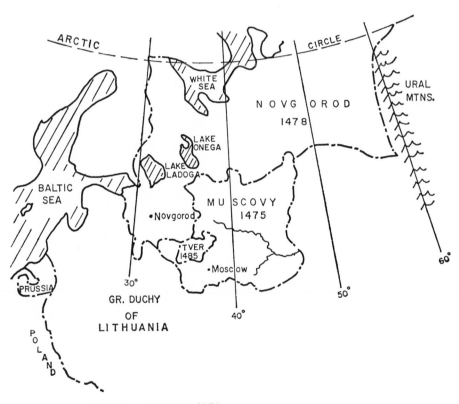

SOURCE: Vernadsky 1959

power, he declared war and marched on the city. Although the boyars defended the city, the commoners and the church group were confused and disorganized. The Novgorodians could not hold out against Ivan's forces. In 1480, after a last attempt, the Novgorodians finally gave up their struggle for autonomy. Ivan was recognized as sovereign.

Ivan had to fight Novgorod twice during the decade but he gained for his expanding Duchy of Muscovy all the eastern part of the Novgorod dominions as well as much of the surrounding rural area. He killed or exiled the boyars, reduced the lower classes to submission, and ended Novgorod's self-government.

PART 2: SURVEY OF VARIABLES (CODED FOR CONSPICUOUS STATE, MUSCOVY)

Dependent Variables

Months of War. There were six months of fighting during the decade, and one hundred fourteen months of peace. The raw score of 6 yields a standard score of 42. For method of transformation, see p. 11.

Territorial Change. Novgorod's eastern dominions extended to the Urals. Ivan III took all of these, as well as the rural districts of Torzhok province and ten of the rural districts in the archbishop's see. In addition, he took the tribute from the remainder of the Novgorodian provinces, although he allowed the collection to remain under Novgorod's jurisdiction. Thus, by the end of the decade under study, Ivan III had greatly enlarged his realm at the expense of Novgorod. The raw score of 252% yields two standard scores: territorial gain 63 and territorial stability 68. For method of transformation see p. 13f.

Military Variables

Defensive Stance. Both the long-term and short-term stance of the Moscovites was offensive; that of the Novgorodians was defensive. Coded *absent*.

Strength of Armed Forces. The Muscovite army was stronger. Novgorod could mobilize a large infantry army in an emergency, and could also call upon the church for a cavalry detachment. But the Novgorodians were not a strong military power and depended on their elected prince and other service princes to supply additional troops to protect the city. The fact that Ivan III was their prince meant, of course, that his forces were being used against Novgorod in this struggle, and this greatly hindered the Novgorodians.

Ivan III had on call a boyar militia, the retinues of his brothers, and auxiliary Tatar troops of various towns and of the vassal Khan of Kasimov, as well as all mounted troops. He could also mobilize infantry from merchants and burghers of various small towns, as well as Cossack troops. Although Ivan started out with only 1,000 warriors in his campaign against Novgorod in 1479, he had given orders that more troops were to follow. The total forces on each side are not given, but Ivan was able to raise many more troops than were the Novgorodians, especially since Novgorod had no service princes to provide additional support for the city. Coded *present*.

Mobility of Armed Forces. Although Novgorod had only a single cavalry detachment, Ivan III had mounted forces consisting of a boyar militia, the retinues of his brothers, and auxiliary Tatar troops—a tremendous advantage in mobility over Novogorod. Coded *present*.

Quality of Armed Forces. Ivan III had a well-organized, well-trained army. His boyar militia was under his personal command. His brothers had their own personal retinues which were obligated to give him assistance when he called for it; in campaigns they expected ranks commensurate with their seniority and with the status of their units. Ivan III also had at his disposal the Cossacks, who fought under their own elected chiefs. Both Ivan's officers and soldiers had a share in the planning of campaigns and displayed initiative, courage, and dedication in battle. In contrast, Novgorod, although able to call up its citizenry in large numbers, had an army poorly trained and armed, with no united command. Against the formidable opposition of Muscovy, Novgorod was powerless. Coded *present*.

Fortifications. The Novgorodians had fortified their city during the siege of 1477 and were successful in holding off Ivan's forces for a time, but they could resist him for only several months, and finally had to surrender. Mucsovy was not fighting a defensive war; hence this variable is coded *absent*.

Prestige. By 1476 the city of Novgorod had lost much of the prestige that it had enjoyed earlier, and Ivan III had already become the most powerful ruler in Russia, with the greatest international prestige of any of the Russian princes. Coded *absent*, because although in fact Ivan was far more powerful than Novgorod he did not enjoy military prestige in a class by itself.

Geographical Variables

Propinquity. In 1476 the Grand Duchy of Moscow and the Novgorod Dominions shared a common border. Moscow was to the southeast of the Novgorod Dominions, with Viatka to the east, Kazan and Riazan to the southeast, Lithuania to the west. The Novgorod Dominions were east of Pskov and extended to the Urals. Coded *present*.

Natural Barriers. There were no significant natural barriers. The Valdai Hills, which rise to about 1000 feet in elevation, are between the cities of Moscow and Novgorod, and many lakes, rivers and swamps are found in the area of Novgorod. Coded *absent*.

Capital City. In 1476 Moscow was fifty miles farther away from their common border than Novgorod—Moscow was one hundred and fifty miles from the border, while Novgorod was only one hundred miles from it. Since the Moscovites, who were farther from the border, invaded the city of Novgorod and defeated it, this difference does not seem to be an important one. Coded *present*, as Moscow was within three hundred miles of common border with Novgorod.

Diplomatic Variables

Announcements. Ivan III made clear his warlike intentions. When the mission from Novgorod arrived in Moscow to ask Ivan to arbitrate, he replied by sending an embassy to Novgorod with a demand for full control of the judiciary in Novgorod. Novgorod answered by recognizing Ivan as a lord but not as overeign; Ivan's response was a declaration of war. Two years later, when the boyars began a conspiracy in Novgorod in 1479, Ivan III acted quietly, without declaring his intention to make war. The Novgorodians, however, learned of approaching troops, and the boyars responded by restoring the old government. Whether Ivan III announced or witheld his intention seems unimportant — for he defeated the Novgorodians both times. Coded *present*.

Surprise Attack. There were no successful surprise attacks. In 1479 Ivan mobilized 1,000 warriors against Novgorod to suppress a boyar conspiracy; he did not declare war. The conspirators, however, may have been warned, as they were not taken unawares. Coded *absent* because there was no strategic surprise.

Alliances. Because Muscovy, the conspicuous state, did not maintain a defensive stance, the alliances mentioned below will be coded *absent*. Coalitions, however, proved vital to the outcome of the struggle between Ivan III and Novgorod. The Novgorodians were left without any of the allies they had counted on, whereas Ivan III had the support of Pskov, Tver, Viatka, and the Kasimov Tatars. His position was further strengthened by his alliance with the Khans of the Crimea, who were leagued with him against Casimir, the Novgorodians' strongest ally. If Casimir *had* come to the aid of Novgorod, Ivan could have counted on the Crimean Khans to support him against Casimir. Coded *absent*.

Active Diplomacy. There was actually no negotiation during the decade, only the presentation and rejection of an ultimatum. When Ivan's ultimatum was rejected by Novgorod, he declared war. Coded *absent*.

Intense Diplomacy. In the treaty of 1478, Novgorod was deprived of her dominions to the east. The provinces still had to pay tribute (collected by Novgorod) to Ivan III. The annual gifts had been traditional. This treaty was an outcome of the war. Coded *present*.

Previous Conflict. The conflict between Moscow and Novgorod began in 1453, when Vasili II, father of Ivan III, led an army against the Novgorodians and defeated them after they had given refuge to his rival. The peace treaty Vasili made with Novgorod proclaimed as treason any dealings between Novgorod and the Russian princes who were independent of Moscow. Consequently, in 1470 when Novgorod signed a treaty with Casimir, Grand Duke of Lithuania, for his support against Moscow, Ivan III viewed this as a traitorous act, and marched against Novgorod. He was able to defeat the Novgorodians and he exacted from them a promise never again to ask for help from Lithuania. During the decade 1476 to 1485, when Ivan III successfully absorbed Novgorod, he put an end to the Novgorodians' struggle for autonomy. Coded *present*.

Cultural Variables

Benefits. On Ivan III's trip to Novgorod in 1475 to arbitrate court cases he was greeted en route by the Archbishop's envoy, who brought gifts. When he arrived at the city he was again presented with gifts. After the judicial hearing the offenders were required to pay court fees to Ivan (but this was traditional, in any case). Ivan was entertained by many prominent Novgorodians and again presented with gifts. On his return to Moscow however, he did not demand gifts from the localities that he passed through, nor after the treaty of 1478, except for the annual traditional gifts from the provinces. Coded *present*.

Cultural Exchange. There was constant cultural exchange between Moscow and Novgorod. The two shared a common language. Not only did they share a common religion, but the metropolitan of Moscow was the head of the Greek Orthodox Church and ordained the archbishops of Novgorod. There was a political connection; for a long time the Grand Duke of Moscow was the favorite choice to the office of elected prince of Novgorod, and after 1471 Ivan III claimed as his patrimony the right to serve as Novgorod's prince. There were commercial contacts, especially on the Volga River, which was controlled by Moscow and constituted the main trade route for goods going from the Orient to Novgorod. There was also the intangible factor that both the Muscovites and Novgorodians considered themselves Russians and shared the concept of the unity of all Russians and all Russian land. Coded *present*.

Trade. Novgorod had to buy grain from Moscow, and conflict meant shortage of bread, and famine. The main road down the Volga River was controlled by Moscow, and it was mainly through Muscovy that the Novgorodian merchants could obtain Oriental goods that constituted a valuable item in their trade with the west. Coded *present*.

General Exchange. Coded *present* because "Cultural Exchange" and "trade", were both coded *present*.

Administrative Variables

Experience of Ruler. Ivan III acceded to the throne in 1462, at the age of twenty-two. When the decade began he had been ruling for fourteen years. Coded *present*.

Youth of Ruler. Ivan III was born in 1440. He was thirty-six years old when the decade under study began. Coded *present* because Ivan was under forty-five years old at the beginning of the decade.

Unbridled Ruler. Ivan III was under forty-five years of age and a hereditary ruler of Muscovy, which was a centralized state. Coded *present*.

Hereditary Ruler. Muscovy was a monarchical duchy with hereditary succession. Coded *present*.

Civil War. There was no evidence of civil war in Muscovy. This was not the case in Novgorod, where there were strong class divisions. In the struggle for autonomy there emerged two factions: the pro-Moscow one, composed of the church group and the commoners, and the pro-Lithuanian one, composed of the rich merchants and the landed gentry, or boyars. The issue between Novgorod and Moscow eventually focused on judicial control; the commoners felt that they were often not given a fair trial by a court made up of people from the boyar class. It was thus easy for Ivan III to get support from the commoners, especially since the commoners gained economically from good relations with Moscow. When the commoners sided with Ivan III, the boyars were not strong enough to withstand Ivan alone and finally had to give up the fight for autonomy. Civil war was not a vital factor in Muscovy. Coded *no data*.

Centralization. Novgorod lacked the centralization of Moscow. The city of Novgorod customarily had at its head an elected prince with limited authority who could be replaced if he did not satisfy the citizens. He had an important military function, but the assembly made the laws. Thus the prince of Novgorod was the employee of a republic whose authority lay in the assembly. But Ivan claimed the right to serve as Novgorod's prince.

Moscow, located in the ecclesiastical center of Russia, was under the control of a strong ruler. The army and government were centralized, as was the collection of tribute. There was an organized conscription system in operation, and special departments to administer the grand-ducal estates. Centralization clearly was a factor contributing to Ivan's success in his struggle with Novgorod. Coded *present*.

PART 3: DATA QUALITY CONTROL

This chapter is based primarily on a secondary work, *Russia at the Dawn of the Modern Age*, which is the fourth of a four-volume exhaustive study on ancient and medieval Russia published in 1959.

The author is George Vernadsky, Professor Emeritus of Russian History at Yale University. His sources are largely contemporary chronicles.

Publication Year. Vernadsky published in 1959. Coded *absent* because this source was published after 1850.

Primary Source. Vernadsky is a secondary source. Coded *absent*.

Author's Association. George Vernadsky is a Russian-born professional historian. He attended the University of Moscow from 1905 to 1910 and took a degree in Russian history from the University of Petersburg in 1917. He taught at the University of Perm from 1917 to 1918, as well as at the University of Taurida in the Crimea from 1918 to 1920. From 1922 to 1927 he taught at the School of Law in Prague and in 1927 he came to the United States. Coded *present*.

Author's Sympathies. He displays no partiality toward either Muscovy or Novgorod. Coded *absent*.

Author's Proximity. He is writing about events which took place more than five hundred years ago. Coded *absent*.

CHAPTER 10

★ ★ ★

THE INEVITABLE WAR

225-216 BC.: Conspicuous State, Rome; Conspicuous Rival, Carthage.

PART I: SKETCH OF HISTORICAL SETTING (CHIEFLY AFTER POLYBIUS AND LIVY)

THE SECOND PUNIC WAR (218–201 B.C.) between Rome and Carthage was the decisive factor in determining whether Rome would confine its borders to Italy and the surrounding islands or extend farther. Although this determination took a few years, the ultimate decision was to expand. The Romans justified the war to themselves as necessary on the grounds that Hannibal had broken the Ebro Treaty and was expanding against Roman interests.

Ancient writers regarded the war as the most significant in the history of Rome, and few modern historians will dispute this verdict. With victory, Rome became the leading power of the ancient Mediterranean world, and it remained the central political unit in Western history until the Empire was split and the medieval period had begun. Romans remembered and discussed the war as long as the Empire existed; it was a traumatic experience from which Italy never quite recovered. Captured towns were sacked and the inhabitants sold into slavery; refugees fled from the area into Greece and elsewhere to escape the results of the war. In the country districts the small farmers were compelled to serve in the armies, and while they were gone their fields were laid waste either by the foraging of the conquerors or by the rear guard of retreating armies determined to diminish the food supplies of their opponents. In the process of repopulating the south after the war, large estates were established and the small farm disappeared. The growth of these estates (*latifundia*) had important implications in the domestic politics of Rome and helped to lay the foundation for the class struggles which were a major factor in the destruction of the Roman republic.

The nominal cause of the war was the attack on Saguntum by Hannibal, the Carthaginian general in Spain; but the basic reasons go much deeper. After a long period of uneasy friendship Rome and Carthage had become involved in the First Punic War (264–241 B.C.) over conflicting policies in Sicily. This war concluded with the Carthaginians evacuating Sicily and agreeing to pay a rather large indemnity in some twenty annual installments. Neither side had fought particularly brilliantly, and the Roman victory was chiefly due to greater Roman reserves of manpower. Upon the conclusion of the war the mercenaries, whom Carthage had utilized in great numbers, demanded their pay. When it was not forthcoming the mercenaries attacked Carthage. The Romans seized this opportunity to take over the islands of Sardinia and Corsica which had remained in Carthaginian hands. Carthage, in no condition to fight another war with Rome, not only was forced to agree to this seizure, but had to pay Rome an additional indemnity. This action served to further increase the enmity between the two rivals.

Once the Carthaginians put down their internal revolt, they turned to Spain to recoup their losses. Spain had rich copper and silver mines, resources which Carthage previously had exploited only superficially. Effective Carthaginian occupation and expansion in Spain would more than compensate for the territory lost to the Romans. Occupation, however, required an army, and the Carthaginian general Hamilcar was consequently given command in Spain. His policies, continued by his son-in-law Hasdrubal and his son Hannibal, succeeded in extending the power of Carthage to the Ebro River and the Sierra de Toledo. In the process of this expansion the Carthaginians not only built up their treasury but, by incorporating Spanish soldiers into their army, built a larger and better land force than Carthage previously had. Hamilcar had convinced himself, and probably most of the other citizens of Carthage, that the only way Carthage could be safe from further Roman aggression was to have a strong army. The navy, which had previously been the chief arm of Punic military power, was severely limited by the treaties with Rome. Moreover, the Carthaginians made no real effort to rebuild it to a large size, perhaps because they did not want to antagonize Rome too directly.

As early as 231 or 230 B.C., the Romans had sent an embassy to Hamilcar in Spain, probably at the insistence of Massilia (present-day Marseilles), a Roman ally with extensive interests in Spain. Hamilcar told the embassy that Carthage had to expand in Spain in order to pay the indemnity which was still owed to Rome. The Romans accepted Hamilcar's explanation but their mission effectively indicated that they were interested in Carthaginian activities in Spain.

In 226 B.C. the Romans sent a second embassy, this time demanding that Hasdrubal (Hamilcar had died by this time) not expand north of the Ebro River. The result of this demand was the Ebro Treaty in which Carthage agreed to remain in territory south of the Ebro River. Rome at the time of the treaty was engaged in fighting the Gallic tribes of northern Italy and was not in a position to intervene further; Carthage was apparently willing to accept the Roman offer which gave the Carthaginians clear title to most of Spain, including several colonies belonging to Massilia.

The treaty broke down over the question of Saguntum. Saguntum was south of the Ebro, but was an ally of Rome as well as of Massilia. At what time Saguntum became a Roman ally is a subject upon which historians are not agreed. Polybius, the chief source for the period, says only that Saguntum had been an ally for several years before the time of Hannibal(221 B.C.). As a result, the determination of the year is dependent upon the historian's interpretations of Roman motives, although such an alliance was probably concluded either during the first Roman embassy to Spain (231 B.C.) or the second (226 B.C.). If it was concluded before the Ebro Treaty the Carthaginians might have understood that Saguntum was specifically exempted from the treaty; if the alliance was concluded after the treaty, then the Romans were clearly violating their own understanding with Carthage. It is apparent, however, that the status of Saguntum was not clearly agreed upon by either side; this uncertainty led directly to the Second Punic War, although if this pretext had not been found perhaps another one would have been.

In 219 B.C. Hannibal (Hasdrubal by this time had also died)

moved against Saguntum. His reasons for the attack came from a frontier quarrel between the inhabitants of Saguntum and the Turdetani. Since the Turdetani were subject to Carthage, Hannibal agreed that it was his duty to intervene. When the Roman envoys visited Hannibal and protested his move against Saguntum, Hannibal said that he was within his treaty rights and Rome had no right to interfere; when the envoys then went on to Carthage itself, the Punic government upheld the action of its general. The citizens of Carthage were by no means united in their stand, and a pro-Roman party under Hanno wanted to concentrate on Africa rather than Spain; the successes in Spain had, however, weakened his party.

Despite the refusal of Carthage to heed the requests of the Roman envoys, Rome did little until after the fall of Saguntum. Some modern historians think that Roman leaders hesitated to act because they were not sure how far their protection of Saguntum should go. Even after the fall of Saguntum there apparently was considerable debate in Rome, with many Roman senators opposed to engaging in a war against Carthage, particularly at a time when it was felt that Rome might also become involved in a conflict with Macedon. On the other hand, it was argued that unless the Romans took action in Spain, their prestige would be damaged and they would find it difficult to hinder the consolidation of Punic power south of the Ebro afterwards.

Whatever the reasons for delay, it was not until March of 218 B.C. that envoys were sent to Carthage to demand the surrender of Hannibal and others who had collaborated in the attack on Saguntum. This was clearly an ultimatum that meant war. Even though the attack on Saguntum might have been deplored by some segments of the population, no patriotic citizen could agree to turn any other citizen over to Rome. When Carthage denied its obligation not to attack Saguntum and refused to surrender Hannibal, the Roman envoys indicated that a state of war now existed between the two countries.

While the Roman-Punic clash was not necessarily inevitable, and could have been avoided if each side had been willing to respect the other's sphere of influence, neither side really sought to avoid the war. Hannibal's attack on Saguntum set it off; but the Romans had been increasingly worried about the growth of Carthage and once they had decided to intervene in Spain they made the ultimatum to Carthage so strong that it was certain to result in war.

The Romans had apparently assumed that Carthage was not as well prepared for war as they were, and that the Second Punic War would be fought along the same lines as the First. The Romans had made plans for one army to strike directly at Carthage while a lesser force was to march against Hannibal in Spain. Hannibal upset their plans, however, by marching directly into Italy, attempting to carry the attack to Rome. He felt that Carthage had little hope of defeating the Romans in any long-term war unless the numerous allies of Rome could be induced to defect. Only by carrying the war directly to Italy was there any hope that the outnumbered and outmanned Carthaginians could encourage others to join with them. During Hannibal's march to Italy, some of the Gauls allied with him; but it was not until after the Battle of Cannae in 216 B.C. that the southern Italian cities, encouraged by the example of Capua (or Naples, the second largest city in Italy), began to defect. Nevertheless, the solid core of Roman strength in central Italy remained firm, and even though some of the cities in the south came over to Hannibal, they did so under terms which were not very helpful to his cause. Few of them gave him many troops or supplies. Although Hannibal was able to win land battles, the Roman fleet controlled the seas and their forces were more mobile. Thus Hannibal was gradually worn down by the numerically superior Roman forces.

After the Romans had learned that they could not defeat Hannibal on the open battlefield, they remained in their fortified cities and moved to carry the war directly to Spain in order to cut off Hannibal's base of operation. Since Hannibal did not have enough troops to occupy very much of Italy, the Romans retook the areas he evacuated as soon as he moved on. Eventually the Romans took Carthage itself, forcing the recall of Hannibal. When the undefeated Hannibal returned, all of Carthage rose in rebellion to greet him; but the Romans were on the scene, armed and prepared, and the Carthaginians were ill-equipped to fight. Hannibal, defeated at the Battle of Zama in 202 B.C., was forced to flee to save his life.

In defeating Carthage, the Romans all but destroyed it; the city

MAP No. 8

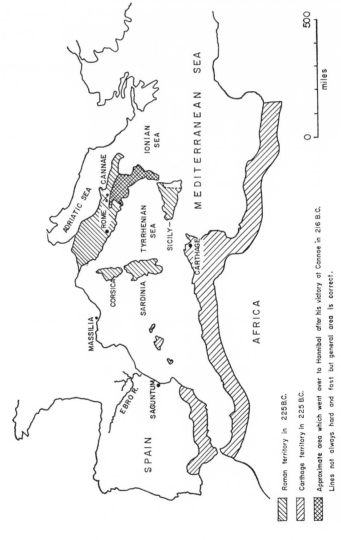

ROME   VS   CARTHAGE   225 – 216 BC.

Roman territory in 225 B.C.

Carthage territory in 225 B.C.

Approximate area which went over to Hannibal after his victory at Cannae in 216 B.C.

Lines not always hard and fast but general area is correct.

SOURCE: Stier 1965

itself was allowed to exist, but all of its colonies were taken over by Rome, and rival puppet states were established around it. Rome was still fearful, however, and Cato is said to have ended every Senate speech with the statement that Carthage must be destroyed, as it finally was in the Third Punic War (149–146 B.C.).

PART 2: SURVEY OF VARIABLES (CODED FOR CONSPICUOUS STATE, ROME)

Dependent Variables

Months of War. War broke out in March, 218 B.C., and lasted throught the rest of the decade under study. Thus there was a total of thirty-four months of war and eighty-six months of peace. The raw score of 34 yields a standard score of 49. For method of transformation, see p. 11.

Territorial Change. After the Battle of Cannae there were mass defections from the Roman side in southern Italy. Unfortunately for Hannibal, while these cities became his allies, they only became allies on terms which allowed them to pursue a more or less independent course, and they did not have to furnish him with either a large number of troops or a great amount of supplies. Hannibal tried to make the alliance attractive enough to encouarge others; if he had demanded too much, the cities probably would have remained Roman. As it was, as soon as Hannibal moved on, the Romans moved in again. The raw score of -19.9% yields two standard scores: territorial gain 34, and territorial stability 60. For method of transformation see p. 13f.

Military Variables

Defensive Stance. Rome must be classed as an aggressive power. Carthage, while hesitant, was only slightly less aggressive than Rome. Neither side tried to avoid a renewal of hostilities. Coded *absent.*

Strength of Armed Forces. The Romans had a larger army and greater resources with a potential of seven hundred thousand foot soldiers and seventy thousand mounted troops; in 218 B.C. there were at least fifty thousand Romans under arms. Hannibal entered Italy with about twenty-six thousand men. Coded *present*.

Mobility of Armed Forces. Rome and Carthage were about equal. The Carthaginians, however, made much better use of their cavalry than did the Romans. Coded *absent*.

Quality of Armed Forces. Man for man, Hannibal had superior forces when he entered Italy, since all of his soldiers were veterans of the campaigns in Spain. Furthermore, in a period when generalship counted for so much, the army of Carthage was clearly superior. Coded *absent*.

Fortifications. The borders were not fortified nor did the armies spend most of their time engaged in siege warfare. Coded *absent*.

Prestige. Although it is clear now that Rome was the greatest power at this time, it probably was not so clear to its contemporaries, — Rome shared power with Macedonia, Syria, and Egypt. Coded *absent*.

Geographical Variables

Propinquity. The Second Punic War started over conflicts concerning common land boundaries in Spain. Coded *present*.

Natural Barriers. The Mediterranean was obviously a barrier and so were the Alps. The inability of Carthage to supply Hannibal either by sea or by the long overland route from Spain resulted in his defeat. Coded *present*.

Capital City. Although Rome, the largest city in the growing Roman Empire, was separated from Carthage by the Mediterranean Sea, it was considered to be close to the frontier, as Carthage was a naval power. Coded *present*.

Diplomatic Variables

Announcements. The Romans made no secret of their intentions. They had clearly showed an interest in Punic expansion in Spain by sending various delegations to the area. The Ebro Treaty indicated that Rome was unwilling to have Carthage move any farther north, but the alliance (whether concluded before or after the treaty) indicated that Rome still regarded Carthage somewhat warily, and these feelings could not have been unknown to Carthage. When the Romans gave Hannibal an ultimatum to withdraw from Saguntum or go to war, their intentions were unmistakably clear. Coded *present*.

Suprise Attack. Neither side was surprised by the other. Coded *absent*.

Alliances. Since Rome was a federation whose diplomatic and military activities were controlled by the Roman Senate, this federation is not considered to be an alliance. Coded *absent*.

Active Diplomacy There were diplomatic missions during the decade under study, but no negotiations. Coded *present*.

Intense Diplomacy The Romans issued an ultimatum which the Carthaginians refused to accept. And while there had been an attempt to outline spheres of influence in the Ebro Treaty of 226 B.C., Rome, by allying with Saguntum, had not observed the treaty. No new treaties were concluded during this period. Coded *absent*.

Previous Conflict. Carthage and Rome were the two chief contenders for power in the Western Mediterranean. They had become involved in the First Punic War (264–241 B.C.) over the conflicting ambitions of both of them in Sicily; when the Romans won the war they still remained suspicious and wary of Carthage, especially as Carthage had recouped and expanded so rapidly in Spain. Rome was apparently willing to provoke the war in order to prevent Carthaginian consolidation of Spain. Coded *present*.

Cultural Variables

Benefits. Carthage was paying an annual tribute to Rome as a result of the First Punic War. Coded *present*.

Cultural Exchange. Cultural exchanges were infrequent. After the First Punic War there was an attempt to draw up certain spheres of influence. Carthage, of course, had to pay an annual tribute to Rome and there were various delegations of Romans to Carthage, but cultural exchanges were not encouraged. Coded *present*.

Trade. There was not enough information available. Coded *no date*.

General Exchange. "Cultural Exchange," above, is coded absent, and "Trade," above, is coded *no data*, hence this variable is coded *absent*.

Administrative Variables

Experience of Ruler. Not pertinent; coded *no data*.

Youth of Ruler. Not pertinent. Rome was ruled by the Senate, an oligarchic aristocratic body, and the people. Coded *no data*.

Unbridled Ruler. Since the previous variable is coded no data, and hereditary monarch, below, is coded absent; this variable is also coded *absent*.

Hereditary Monarchy. There was no hereditary monarchy. The Senate was made up of ex-magistrates, that is, officials elected by the assemblies of the people. These officials were primarily from the upper classes, and the Senate was composed mostly of old families. Coded *absent*.

Civil War. While there was no civil strife in Rome, the Romans had been involved in an exhausting struggle with the Gauls during the first part of the decade. Coded *absent*.

Centralization. There was little significant difference in centralization between Rome and Carthage. Both these states had similar governments, oligarchic republics. The Roman Senate, however, had somewhat more control over its military officials than did the government of Carthage. Hannibal, for example, had almost independent authority and this gave him a more effective chain of command in the field than the Roman leaders enjoyed. In fact the Romans had to delegate more and more freedom in decision making to the generals as the war went on. Coded *absent*.

PART 3: DATA QUALITY CONTROL

The two chief primary sources for the period are the Greek historian Polybius, *The Histories of Polybius*, edited and translated by W. R. Paton (London: Wᵐ Heinemann, 1922-27); and the Roman annalist Livy, book 21, edited and translated by B. O. Foster (London: Wᵐ Heinemann, 1949-61). Polybius was a leading Greek politician who incurred the suspicions of the Romans and was taken as a hostage to Rome in 167 B.C. Despite this, Polybius became an admirer of Rome and came to the conclusion that Roman power was going to grow and to exist for a long time. He wrote a general history of the Mediterranean lands from 264 B.C. to his own time, showing the growth of Roman power. This work, of which considerable portions have been preserved, is the principal authority for the middle period of the Republic. Polybius was writing the history of the generations which immediately preceded his own and he was able to converse with contemporaries, especially with the members of the Scipio family, about some of the events he described. He utilized an account by Fabius Pictor, a senator who took an active part in the Second Punic War, and probably also an account by Cato. To balance these Roman sources he had the work of Syslus, a Greek who accompanied Hannibal, and that of Silenus, another Greek who was with Hannibal. He also utilized other accounts, but there is no indication in his works that he had any inner knowledge of Carthaginian designs or policies. Livy, the second source, relied primarily on Polybius for the period under discussion, although he supplemented him with other sources. While Polybius attempted to explain how Rome rose to such power, Livy considered his task to be that of providing living and inspiring examples of Roman courage, constancy, and fair dealing. Thus Livy is somewhat more slanted than Polybius.

B. L. Hallward's article, "Hannibal's Invasion of Italy," in *The Cambridge Ancient History* (Cambridge: University Press, 1930) vol. 8, has been used to supplement the ancient writers. This work was not coded.

The works of Polybius and Livy are coded jointly.

Publication Year. Polybius wrote in the second century B.C.; Livy much later (he died in A.D. 17). Coded *absent.*

Primary Source. Coded *present.* See "Publication Year," above, and "Author's Proximity," below.

Authors' Associations. Polybius was a Greek; Livy was a patriotic Roman. Coded *present.*

Authors' Sympathies. Polybius was pro-Roman, although he tried to be neutral. Livy was also pro-Roman. Coded *present*.

Authors' Proximity. Polybius wrote at least fifty years after the events, but he had contact with some of the people engaged in them. Livy relied primarily on Polybius. Coded *present*.

CHAPTER 11

★ ★ ★

THE UNEASY TRUCE

25-16 B.C. : Conspicuous State, Rome ; Conspicuous Rival, Parthia.

PART 1: SKETCH OF HISTORICAL SETTING (CHIEFLY AFTER THE *Cambridge Ancient History*, VOL. 10)

THE PERIOD FROM 133 TO 31 B.C. in Roman history is known in most textbooks as the *century* of *revolution*. It was a period of civil and slave wars, of class against class; but at the same time it was a period of imperialistic expansion throughout the Mediterranean. The terminal date of 31 B.C. is set by the Battle of Actium, the battle in which Octavian (later, known as Augustus) defeated Antony and Cleopatra. After Actium the civil strife in the Roman state gradually subsided, and at the same time there was an attempt to come to terms with the enemies outside of the Empire.

The decade under study, 25 to 16 B.C., followed the battle of Actium. Octavian was still in the process of establishing his position as the most powerful political figure in the Roman state, a dictator in fact if not in name albeit a benevolent one. There was still a great deal of unrest and both potential and actual revolts against Octavian's rule; but gradually the opposition died down. Internally Octavian did a patchwork job on the republic so that it still seemed to function, although in fact the republic was a partnership between Octavian and the Senate with Octavian holding all real power.

Externally Octavian adopted a moderate, defensive stance. During the previous century Roman power had rapidly expanded and in the process had come to irritate, anger, and even threaten new border peoples and countries. In general, Octavian attempted to establish frontiers along natural barriers but at the same time shorten the lines of communication; it was in his reign that the

Rhine-Danube frontier came to be established in the north after attempts to shorten it by extending Roman territory to the Elbe had failed. During much of the Roman expansion the chief organized opposition had come in the east from Macedonia, from Egypt, and from Seleucia, mainly because it was in the east that the larger organized states existed. By the first century B.C. the chief eastern power was Parthia, although some of the states in Asia Minor, such as Pontus, had to be reckoned with also. Most of these eastern states had grown to power after the defeat of the Seleucid Empire by the Romans.

Rome and Parthia had first come into official contact in 92 B.C. when the Roman general Sulla was campaigning on the Euphrates River, the boundary of the Parthian territory. Mithridates II, the king of the Parthians, sent an envoy to Sulla requesting Roman friendship and alliance. Such an agreement was made, with Rome recognizing the Euphrates as Parthia's border, in part because both Rome and Parthia feared the growing power of Pontus. But while the two powers had started off on a friendly basis, Armenia soon became a center of contention between them. Armenia was a country beyond the river boundary, and while culturally it was closer to Parthia than to Rome, geographically it could belong either to the Roman sphere or to the Parthian sphere of influence. Rome had become embroiled with Armenia as a result of wars with Pontus, the so-called Mithridatic Wars, which had ended with the conquest of Pontus in 70 B.C. When Pontus had been defeated, its king Mithridates (not the same one as the Parthian king) fled to Armenia to seek aid from his son-in-law Tigranes, king of Armenia. Tigranes was unwilling to march against Rome, but at the same time he refused to turn his father-in-law over to the Romans; as a result the Romans invaded Armenia in 69 B.C. Though badly outnumbered, the Romans, in part through bold military tactics and in part through mismanagement and poor planning by the Armenians, won a great military victory. In desperation Tigranes, fearing for his kingdom, sought help from all the surrounding powers, including Parthia. In order to win Parthian assistance he offered to return territory which Armenia had occupied many years previously. Parthia temporarily hesitated and then refused to act when the Roman general Pompey again assured the Parthians that he respected the Euphrates frontier. At the same time he promised, in case of victory, to restore the lost Armenian areas to Parthia. With this understanding the Parthians allied with Rome.

While the offer of alliance, as far as it can be determined, required little more of Parthia than neutrality in the Roman invasion of Armenia, Parthia did invade Armenia. After attacking Artaxata, the capital, and failing to take it, the Parthians retired from the battle. When the Romans defeated the Armenians, however, Phraates, the Parthian king, proceeded to occupy the western Mesopotamian area promised to him by Rome. Pompey, now that he had defeated the Armenians, and perhaps wanting to establish some sort of friendship with them, ordered the Parthians out of the disputed territory. Without waiting for a Parthian reply to his demand, Pompey began marching his army into the territory. Although the Parthians evacuated the territory, they accused the Romans of double dealing. Phraates at first sent an official protest to Pompey, but upon receiving from him an insolent reply, he attacked Armenia. The Romans immediately appeared on the scene, and Armenia and Parthia came to terms, with Armenia keeping most of the disputed territory.

It is possible that Pompey thought of invading Parthia and pushing the Roman frontier even further east, but for various reasons postponed his action. About 57 B.C. Phraates was murdered by his sons Orodes and Mithridates (not the king of Pontus), and Orodes became king. The young Mithridates, however, revolted, drove out Orodes, and started a full-scale civil war in Parthia, a not uncommon occurrence in that country. Orodes, with the help of a loyal general, Surenas, managed to regain his throne, after which his younger brother Mithridates fled to Roman territory and requested Roman assistance in reinstating him. The Roman general in that area, Gabinius, was preparing to move into Parthia when the exiled Ptolemy XI of Egypt promised him ten thousand talents if he would help him regain the Egyptian throne instead. Mithridates invaded without Roman military support but lost and was put to death.

During this period three men, Pompey, Crassus, and Caesar, were ruling Rome in what is known as the period of the triumvirate. Both Pompey and Caesar were well-known military conquerors, but

Crassus, the third member, was not. He was therefore ambitious to gain military renown. With the consent of both Pompey and Caesar, Crassus began in 55 B.C. to raise an army for his eastern campaign but ran into considerable opposition from the Roman populace. Most of the Romans felt that Parthia had done nothing to warrant an attack from Rome. Because of the public unwillingness to support Crassus's Parthian campaign, but also in part because both Pompey and Caesar already had a great number of men under arms, Crassus's army was made up of press gangs inferior to the usual Roman army of the time.

When Crassus arrived in Syria in 54 B.C., Parthia was still in the midst of the civil war between Mithridates and Orodes and could give little effective opposition to the Romans. Crassus immediatly began an advance into Parthia, winning everything before him, but retired after a few short victories to winter in Syria. Surprisingly Crassus did not attempt to aid Mithridates, who held out until after Crassus had retired for the winter. It may be that Crassus was determined on a campaign of conquest and did not want to substitute one Parthian for another.

During the civil war, however, the Parthian general Surenas emerged as a first-rate military strategist. While we do not know his first name, we do know that he was extremely wealthy, was second only to the king in the Empire, and had enough money and power to carry through military reforms. He was at the time not yet thirty, fairly tall, dressed rather elaborately, and he painted his face like a girl. However, he feared nothing and was a brilliant military innovator. From his retainers he formed a body of some ten thousand mounted archers; he apparently felt this was the largest force that he could keep continually supplied with the necessary weapons. Every ten men had a camel, forming a corps of one thousand camels which carried supplies, especially arrows, wherever they went. This corps gave the Parthian army a ready supply of arrows, something that it had previously lacked—and provided them with a greater staying power in battle than they had before. (In the earlier history of the Parthian army, the Parthian horse archers had usually won at first but had to retreat when their supply of arrows was exhausted. Surenas overcame this by his supply train).

The Parthians were further strengthened by the defeat of Mithridates in the early part of 53 B.C.; Orodes was then able to send an additional thousand armed knights to Surenas, while he himself conducted an offensive against Armenia. Crassus invaded in 53 B.C. with approximately forty four thousand men, including his garrisons, but Surenas literally slaughtered the Roman army. Only ten thousand of Crassus's men found their way back to Syria, while another ten thousand were made prisoners. The rest, including Crassus, were killed. As a result of their victory the Parthians took over the disputed Armenian territory. They did not carry through an invasion into Roman territory, in part because Orodes, jealous of his successful general Surenas, had him put to death. A small Parthian force did enter Syria but it was soon ambushed and defeated.

Although the Romans had provoked the war, they were extremely bitter over the defeat, not only because the Parthians allegedly mistreated Roman prisoners, but also because the Parthians publicly displayed the captured Roman battle standards. Moreover, in the aftermath of Parthian victory, Armenia again came under the influence of Parthia; a marriage alliance was concluded between Armenia and Parthia to strengthen the new relationship. Rome, involved in a renewed outbreak of civil war, was unable to do very much about its eastern frontier. By 44 B.C., when Caesar had emerged triumphant, Rome was again planning an invasion of Parthia, but it was cut short by his assassination on 15 March. Rome again fell into a civil war, with Octavian (Augustus), Antony, and others struggling for power. Antony, however, certainly meant to carry out Caesar's plan of an attack on Parthia as soon as he was able.

Since the Parthians were aware of the Roman plans, they were willing to move against Rome if an opportunity presented itself. They were encouraged to act when some of the people involved in Caesar's assassination sought Parthian help. During the battle of Philippi in 42 B.C., when Antony, Octavian, and Lepidus emerged triumphant, there were Roman representatives of the conspirators in Parthia. The victory at Philippi cut out the plans for a combined movement, but the Roman conspirators persuaded the Parthians in the winter of 41 to 40 B.C. that they still could move effectively against Rome, especially since Asia Minor was denuded of Roman troops, and the two legions in Syria were loyal to the conspirators. Pacorus, the son of Orodes, agreed to lead the Parthian invasion, and the Parthians with their Roman advisors moved against Syria. The campaign was successful at first, with even Antioch coming over to the Parthian side. Many of the Roman client kings, always distrustful of Rome, began to negotiate with the Parthians. The Jews, who hated the rule of the Roman puppet Idumaeans, joined Parthia, although Herod held out against them. The Parthians put the Hasmonean Antigonus (Mattathias) on the Jewish throne.

Antony, the Roman commander in the east, attempted to meet the Parthian threat himself, but he was troubled by a border invasion of Macedonia, and by his difficulties with Octavian in Rome. Instead he sent a subordinate, Ventidius, with a strong force of cavalry and slingers. Ever since they suffered a defeat at the hands of the Parthians, the Romans had apparently attempted to develop a way of combatting the horse archers, and had come to the conclusion that the sling with leaden bullets or pellets would outrange the Parthian arrows. Surprisingly, however, the invading Parthian troops did not rely on mounted archers, perhaps because the Parthian nobility feared another great victory by the common mounted archer. Instead Pacorus relied on heavy cavalry, the cataphracts. The Romans, however, soon found that their lead bullets penetrated the Parthian armor before the Parthians could get close enough to hurt the Roman forces. As a result they were able to route the Parthians and their allies. Pacorus, who was not with his troops when they suffered defeat, regrouped his army and again invaded, but in 38 b.c. he himself was killed and the Parthian forces driven back. Shortly after the defeat of the Parthians and the death of Pacorus, Phraates IV, a younger son of Orodes, murdered his father and seized the throne. Phraates IV seems to have sided with the commoners in their battle with the nobles. His attitude again caused a shift in Parthian military tactics, and the horse archers once more became prominent.

It was not enough, however, to defeat the Parthians on Roman territory; Antony felt that the only way in which the Parthians could be controlled was by a successful Roman invasion for which he began planning. The first steps in this direction were taken in 37

B.C. when Armenia was again forced to submit and become an ally of Rome. Antony, however, occupied no Armenian towns, took no Armenian hostages, and left no Roman garrisons. This delay was dangerous; even though Armenia's policy was to maintain independence by playing off Parthia against Rome, her basic sympathies, like her civilization, were probably Parthian. Moreover, while Artavasdes, the king of Armenia, submitted to Antony, he apparently maintained an understanding with Parthia. There were also several other territories in Asia Minor which had secretly if not openly sided with Parthia in an attempt to overthrow the growing Roman influence.

In 36 B.C., after forcing Armenia to ally again with Rome, Antony set out for Parthia with an army of over one hundred thousand men, including sixty thousand legionnaires, ten thousand Gallic and Spanish horses, and thirty thousand auxiliaries, some sixteen thousand of which were Armenian cavalry. He also brought enormous seige equipment, apparently planning a long campaign which would result in the ultimate occupation of Parthia. From the results of Antony's expedition, it is clear that the Armenians in his army must have kept in contact with the Parthians, since the Parthians knew where the Romans were, but the Romans had no knowledge of the Parthian positions. Antony divided his forces, leaving his supply train and part of his army, including the Armenians, to go off in another direction. Shortly after his departure, the Parthians attacked his supply train. Just before the battle, the Armenians rode back to Armenia, allowing the Parthians, with an estimated force of fifty thousand men to annihilate the Romans guarding the supply train. They carried off or burnt all the supplies. Antony was forced to rely on forage, but the Parthians cut off any small group of foragers. In desperation Antony retreated, with the Parthians harrying him all the way. Before Antony reached Syria it is estimated that he lost about thirty-seven percent of his army, including some twenty-two thousand of his veteran legionnaires. He was at a tremendous disadvantage in his maneuvering with Octavian, who was building up his forces in the west for an eventual showdown with Antony; and the whole Roman settlement in the east was endangered. The Parthians, however, did not attack Syria, but were forced to turn back because of growing internal troubles.

Octavian and Antony patched up their differences so that Antony could get more troops, but his plans to invade Parthia in 35 B.C. were thwarted by the activities of Sextus Pompeius, the son of the famous Pompey. Parthia was still having internal difficulties and also had broken with some of its allies. (On these points the sources are almost nonexistent, and the coins on which we rely for most of our information were either not minted or are not extant.) Encouraged by the Parthian difficulties, Antony in 34 B.C. finally invaded Armenia, capturing the king Artavasdes and two of his sons; but a third son, Artaxes, managed to flee to Parthia. For some two years Armenia was a Roman province and Roman merchants came in great numbers.

Before Antony could move any further in the east, he was forced to withdraw in order to meet the threat of Octavian in the west. Shortly after the Roman legions were withdrawn from Armenia in November, 33 B.C., the Parthians moved in, restored Artaxes, added some border territory, and sat idly by while Artaxes massacred all the Romans he found in his country. The Parthian king Phraates had also put down a revolt in Parthia, and the leader of the revolt, Tiridates, fled to Rome for help. It was on this confusing scene that Octavian appeared in the east in 30 B.C., after defeating Antony and Cleopatra at Actium.

Popular Roman opinion would probably have sanctioned an all-out war against Parthia at this point, but Octavian was opposed to any such action, perhaps because he was not yet certain that his own position was secure. At any rate he made no attempt to revenge the Armenian massacre of Romans, although he did retain the brothers of Artaxes as hostages for Armenia's future good conduct. King Phraates of Parthia sent envoys to Octavian and they were given a friendly reception (although Octavian allowed the pretender Tiridates to take asylum in Syria). The Romans also put a stronger client king (the fugitive king of Media) in Armenia Minor, who was an implacable foe of Artaxes of Armenia. Octavia then indicated to the Parthian envoys that while he was willing to allow the fugitive Tiridates to remain in Syria, he would not give him any support for an invasion of Parthia. With these cautionary actions Octavian felt he could ignore the eastern frontier temporarily, especially since he had left a large number of legionnaires and auxiliary troops in Syria to handle any possible Parthian threat.

Octavian then had to work out a more permanent settlement. His task was complicated not only by the question of Armenia, but also the strong Roman sentiment against Parthia (the Parthians still held Roman prisoners and standards), and the Parthian resentment of Rome for giving haven to Tiridates. Tiridates had fled to Rome again in 26 to 25 B.C. after a second failure to overthrow Phraates and this time was accompanied by Phraates' youngest son, also named Phraates, whom he had kidnapped. Sometime in 23 B.C. Parthian envoys arrived in Rome with a demand for the surrender of Tiridates and the restoration of the young Phraates. It has been conjectured that this Parthian delegation had secretly been encouraged by the Romans in order to negotiate a settlement between the two powers, but the evidence is not sufficient to end scholarly debate on the subject. Octavian immediately returned the young prince, Phraates, but insisted that the Parthians give back the Roman standards and prisoners of war. Though he refused to surrender Tiridates, Octavian again promised he would not lend support to any of the schemes which Tiridates might have for seizing power in Parthia.

A year after the Parthian envoys had returned home, the Parthians had still not fulfilled what Octavian and the Romans felt was part of their agreement, the return of the standards and prisoners. Since there was considerable clamor in Rome for vengeance against Parthia, Octavian, utilizing this public support to increase pressure on Parthia, left late in 22 B.C. for the east. When Parthia still did not react, he ordered the dispatch of a large number of men to the Armenian area in the winter of 21 to 20 B.C. Armenia was nearing the brink of civil war; a small section of the nobility favored Rome and a larger section favored Parthia. The Pro-Roman section had sent an embassy to Octavian requesting that he depose Artaxes, who was anti-Roman, in favor of his younger brother, Tigranes, who had lived in Rome for the last ten years. Using this as an excuse, Octavian slowly, and with increasing tension, moved eastward. Parthia, unwilling to risk war over Armenia, began to negotiate with Rome for a settlement as Octavian came closer. The Parthian king, feeling that a Roman invasion would cost him his throne, agreed to surrender the Roman standards and the prisoners who still survived or who could be found. About 12 May 20 B.C., they were handed over by Parthian representatives to the Romans.

With Parthian interference in Armenia removed, Octavian began moving into Armenia, whereupon the Armenians killed their pro-Parthian king, Artaxes, and made Tigranes king. Octavian did not annex Armenia but instead maintained it as an independent kingdom under Roman supervision. Peace was to be maintained with Parthia on condition that the Parthians recognize Roman suzerainty over Armenia. Octavian himself, perhaps in order to quiet the people who might have called him an appeaser, declared to the Senate that he regarded any further extension of the Empire as undesirable.

The agreement to these Roman terms by Phraates, the Parthian king, made his position more difficult in Parthia, and it has been argued by some scholars that he was once more driven from the throne. But the evidence does not permit an accurate reconstruction of what happened. If he was driven from the throne, he soon recovered it. In 9 or 10 B.C. he took the unusual step of sending his four legitimate sons into Roman territory. They were moved to Rome, where, after being shown to the public, they were supported at public expense. Motives for this are not clear. Official Roman explanations of the time indicate that the four boys were sent as pledges of friendship, hostages. One Roman historian says that Phraates was afraid of revolution and felt that no rebel could prevail unless he was allied with one of his sons; if they were absent he was safe. Still another explanation was offered by the contemporary historian Josephus, who said that Octavian had sent Phraates an Italian slave girl whom he afterwards made his legitimate queen under the name of Thea Urania Musa. She persuaded him to remove his legitimate offspring in order to secure the succession of her own son, who in fact did succeed. The sons were evidently content to go to Rome—they made no attempt to resist or to escape. Octavian however, had a weapon which at any time could be used to undermine the security of a hostile Parthian king.

Rome and Parthia had come to some sort of understanding. Neither really wanted to get too deeply involved with the other since

MAP No. 9

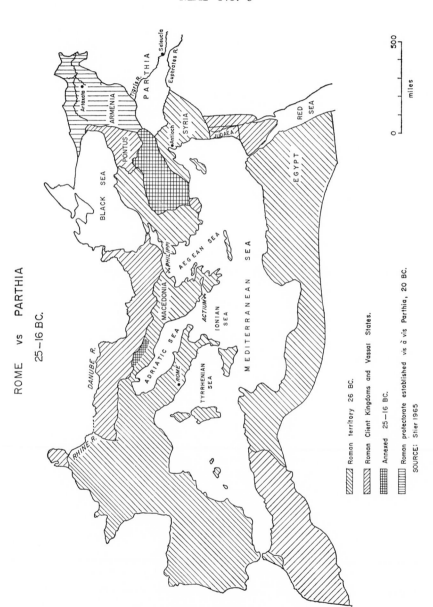

ROME vs PARTHIA
25–16 BC.

Roman territory 26 BC.

Roman Client Kingdoms and Vassal States.

Annexed 25–16 BC.

Roman protectorate established vis à vis Parthia, 20 BC.

SOURCE: Stier 1965

in order to be successful one would have to conquer the other, an almost impossible task. There were still difficulties between the two, chiefly Armenia, which periodically caused trouble; but perhaps the relationship between Rome and Parthia is best signified by the meeting in 6 B.C. on an island in the Euphrates, a neutral spot between the two powers on the river which both recognized as a boundary. Here the king of Parthia met with an adopted son of Octavian, and an exchange of banquets was given. In effect Rome recognized Parthia as an independent state existing side by side with Rome, although not quite of equal power.

PART 2: SURVEY OF VARIABLES (CODED FOR CONSPICUOUS STATE, ROME)

Dependent Variables

Months of War. There was no actual war during the period under study although it was threatened several times. There were 120 months of peace. The raw score of o yield a standard score of 37. For method of transformation see p. 11.

Territorial Change. Armenia is recognized as a Roman protectorate during the period under study. The raw score of 1.5% yields two standard scores; territorial gain 57, and territorial stability 49. For method of transformation see p. 13f.

Military Variables

Defensive Stance. Rome, under Octavian, was clearly passing from an offensive stance to a defensive stance in the east. Parthia had never been in an aggressive stance as far as Rome itself was concerned, and the attitude of the two powers gradually became hostile and defensive towards each other. Coded *present.*

Strength of Armed Forces. The Roman armies outnumbered the Parthian. Coded *present.*

Mobility of Armed Forces. In short-term mobility, the Parthians were much better than the Romans, in part because they relied more on cavalry while the Romans had primarily an infantry army. Coded *absent.*

Quality of Armed Forces. The Romans would have to be called the better soldiers. The Parthian nobles often went off on tangents, neglected supplies, and made brave but foolhardy attacks. Occasionally, however, when the Parthians had an able general such as Surenas, they would fight the Romans on almost equal terms. Usually, though, this was not the case. Coded *present.*

Fortifications. Rome relied primarily on vassal states to oppose any immediate entry of Parthians into the empire. Octavian, however, did leave a large garrison in Syria to forestall any Parthian attempts in that direction. Serious fortifications on the frontier did not come until a later date. Coded *absent.*

Prestige. Rome was the great power at this time and had no immediate rival in its class. Despite the fact that Parthia had defeated a Roman army, it was only a poor second. Coded *present.*

Geographical Variables

Propinquity. Rome and Parthia shared the common boundary of the Euphrates River. Coded *present.*

Natural Barriers. For the most part these were clearly present. The Euphrates itself was a barrier, and it was reinforced to the south by the Syrian desert. To the north Armenia separated the two powers; but while Armenia is a mountainuous area, it was accessible both from Roman and Parthian territory and it was here that the geographical border broke down. Coded *present.*

Capital City. Rome was not within 300 miles of the border, nor were any really large cities. Coded *absent.*

Diplomatic Variables

Announcements. In one action taken by Octavian in the decade under study, his intentions were clear and publicly announced. His aim was to force Parthia to hand over the captured Roman standards and to come to some sort of agreement with Parthia on Armenia. As a result he was successful without actually going to war with Parthia, in part because he had already negotiated for the return of the standards by giving back the king's kidnapped young son. It seems that Octavian pretended he would use force, but actually he was only too willing to come to terms with Parthia without going to war. This variable is coded *no data* as there was no actual war.

Surprise Attack. Coded *no data* for the above reasons. See "Announcements" above.

Alliances. Rome took care to have some sort of agreement with exiled pretenders to the Parthian throne, and also gave subsidies to some of the semi-independent kingdoms, but actually had no coalition or alliance against Parthia during the decade under study, simply because there was no state to ally with. Everything except Armenia was either under Roman or Parthian control. Coded *absent*.

Active Diplomacy. Diplomatic negotiations played an important part in settling some of the disputed points between Rome and Parthia, and eventually resulted in Roman recognition of Parthia as an independent state existing side by side with Rome even if not at the same power level. Coded *present*.

Intense Diplomacy. The treaty concerning the return of the Roman standards was concluded in 20 B.C. Coded *present*.

Previous Conflict. Rome and Parthia had been at sword's point for the previous forty years. The chief issue between them had been the status of Armenia, although even without the existence of the Armenian question an expanding Rome and a growing Parthia would probably have come into conflict. Coded *present*.

Cultural Variables

Benefits. No honors were exchanged during the decade under study unless the return of the Roman battle standards by the Parthians can be regarded as such. Later there were formal honors given in 6 B.C. when representatives of Rome and Parthia met at a neutral spot in the Euphrates. No subsidies were given directly to Parthia, although Octavian gave subsidies to several vassal states in order to strengthen their opposition to Parthia Coded *absent*.

Cultural Exchange. Rome had a hostage system which included a number of Parthians and also provided refuge for some of them. Tiridates, the defeated pretender to the Parthian throne, lived in Syria after Octavian took over in 30 B.C. Octavian also held as hostages the brothers of the Armenian king Artaxes. Between 26 and 25 B.C., Tiridates fled to Rome again after another unsuccessful attempt to obtain the Parthian throne. He brought with him the youngest son of Phraates, also named Phraates, whom he is said to have kidnapped. This son was exchanged for Roman prisoners and standards held by Parthia. Later on in 10 or 9 B.C. Phraates's sons either fled to Rome or were sent there. Coded *present*.

Trade. There was considerable trade between the two powers although there are indications that the Romans attempted to avoid enriching Parthia with their trade and preferred a more difficult and northern route to send and receive goods from China and India. Coded *present*.

General Exchange. Cultural exchange and trade are coded present; thus this variable is also coded *present*.

Administrative Variables

Experience of Ruler. Octavian ruled as Triumvir in the west from the date of the second Triumvirate, 27 November 43 B.C. He became sole ruler after he defeated Antony at the battle of Actium in September of 31 B.C., (after which time he was called Augustus). Thus he had been in power for seventeen years at the opening of the decade studied. Coded *present*.

Youth of Ruler. Octavian was born 23 September 63 B.C. He was thirty-one years old at the opening of the decade under study. Coded *present*.

Unbridled Ruler. There was no hereditary monarchy, hence this variable is coded *absent*.

Hereditary Monarchy. Octavian's succession was based in part on inheritance (he was the adopted son of Caesar) but chiefly on the loyalty of the army and his military victories. Coded *absent*.

Civil War. Although civil war as such was supposedly over with the defeat of Antony by Octavian in 31 B.C., there were a number of significant uprisings during the decade studied. Spain was in revolt, particularly the Cantabrians, and this was not quelled completely until 19 B.C. There were riots and bloodshed in Rome itself concerning the candidacy for consulship of Egnatius, who was later involved in a plot to kill Octavian and was executed. Coded *present*.

Centralization. The Roman state was far more centralized than Parthia. The Parthian king was dependent on the support of other feudal lords, and in fact Parthia was a decentralized empire. Coded *present*.

PART 3: DATA QUALITY CONTROL

The foregoing sketch of the decade is based chiefly on *The Cambridge Ancient History* vol. 10, chapters 4, 8, 9, 13 and 18. This period in Roman history has more primary sources than most other periods, but very little is known about Parthia. *The Cambridge Ancient History* is based primarily on the standard Roman primary sources (contemporary documents, letters, speeches and writings, coins, and other aids to classical scholarship) listed by chapters in its bibliography.

Publication Year. Twentieth century. Coded *present*.

Primary Source. This is a secondary source. Coded *absent*.

Authors' Associations. From the nature of the evidence, even the Parthian accounts have to be based upon Latin or Greek literary evidence. About the only independent Parthian sources are coins. Thus any account is probably told from a Roman point of view. Coded *present*.

Authors' Sympathies. Because of the nature of the sources, it would seem that the authors tend to lean toward Rome, even though in most cases no obvious bias can be detected. The whole history of this period is usually centered around Rome and this in itself tends to inculcate certain attitudes towards Rome and Parthia and their relationships with each other. If there are any signs of sympathy, they tend to give Rome the benefit of the doubt. Coded *present*.

Authors' Proximity. They are writing over nineteen hundred years later. Coded *absent*.

CHAPTER 12

★ ★ ★

THE FIRST CHALLENGE

176-185 A.D.: Conspicuous State, Rome; Conspicuous Rival, Marcomanni-Quadi.

Part 1: Sketch of Historical Setting (Chiefly after Cassius Dio, Herodian, and the *Scriptores Historiae Augustae*)

The Roman Empire was clearly the dominant European political entity during the first few centuries of the Christian era.During the second century it had reached its maximum in territorial extent, in population, and in material prosperity. Edward Gibbon stated, in *The Decline and Fall of the Roman Empire*:

> If a man were called to fix the period in the history of the world during which the condition of the human race was most happy and prosperous, he would, without hesitation, name that which elapsed from the death of Domitian A.D. 96 to the accession of Commodus [A.D. 180]. The vast extent of the Roman empire was governed by absolute power, under the guidance of virtue and wisdom. The armies were restrained by the firm but gentle hand of four successive emperors whose character and authority commanded involuntary respect. The forms of the civil administration were carefully preserved by Nerva, Trajan, Hadrian, and the Antonines, as the accountable ministers of the laws. [p. 78]

Even during its period of greatest power, however, the Romans were not without enemies, and it was during the randomly selected decade from 176 to 185 that the Germanic tribes to the north of the imperial borders began their first effective challenge to Roman dominance. The problems the Romans had in meeting this challenge were repeated with ever-increasing severity in the third century, and even though temporarily halted for a period in the fourth century, eventually brought about the dissolution of the Empire.

The Roman Empire in the second century was in what can best be called a defensive stance. The last notable extension of the Roman boundaries beyond the limits fixed by Augustus took place during the reign of Trajan at the beginning of the second century. Under Trajan's successors, Hadrian, Antonius Pius, and Marcus Aurelius, the frontiers underwent rectifications here and there, but further additions to the territory were insignificant. When Aurelius came to power the Empire probably included about 1,700,000 square miles within its boundaries. Marcus Aurelius was a peace-loving man although he had to spend a good part of his reign fighting off threats to the Empire on the eastern and northern frontiers. The Germanic tribes to the north of the Empire had long ago left the nomadic phase and had entered into a period of intensive agriculture and permanent settlements. The process of settlement was probably the most advanced among the Germans in the area generally known as Bohemia; here Roman customs had been deliberately cultivated and the settlers were on friendly terms with Rome. It was from this area, however, that the greatest trouble appeared.

After the year 150, disturbances on the eastern borders of what is now Germany drove the tribes along the Danube border to seek a more secure abode, preferably on the southern or Roman bank of the Danube. In 167 two of the chief peoples of southern Germany, the Marcomanni and the Quadi, together with some of the lesser tribes (among whom the Vandals come into notice for the first time) broke across the Roman frontier on the middle Danube. These invaders drove the Roman garrisons away from the river line except at the more heavily fortified points between Raetia and Moesia. At the same time the invading action set in motion the Iazyges, a nomadic tribe which overran Dacia and kept the garrisons in the towns beleaguered. Gathering momentum the Marcomanni and their allies passed through the Roman border provinces to Italy itself.

The invasion was not unexpected, but the Romans were at first unable to meet the threat because of the skeletal nature of their forces along the frontier. Earlier, Marcus Aurelius had been forced to transfer many of his Danubian troops to the eastern front where, from 163 to 164, the Romans met and defeated the threatening moves of Parthia. The relocation of troops was regarded as only a temporary expedient, but unfortunately the returning troops brought back the "plague" (probably Bubonic) with them. The disease swept Europe, and while it hit the troops the hardest, it also left many civilian districts almost depopulated. So severe were the after effects that some historians have regarded it as perhaps the most important factor in the decline of the Empire. Even though the Romans knew of the impending German action, they were unable to head it off. Two special legions were enlisted in Italy and sent to the frontier but despite this the Germans invaded in A.D 166 and perhaps by the spring of 167 had crossed the Alps and laid seige to Aquileia. Here the Romans were able to stop the invasion, and by late autumn the Germans withdrew and asked for a truce.

The combination of the Parthian War, the plague, a famine, and the German invasion put a severe strain upon the Roman resources. The state faced not only a military crisis, but a severe financial one as well. Rather than impose fresh taxes upon the harassed provincials, Marcus Aurelius raised money by auctioning the imperial crown jewels, gold and crystal vessels from the palace, and even his wife's gold and silk dresses.

Roman sources for the period are not plentiful enough to allow the modern historian to follow the Marcomannic war in detail, but it seems that there were at least three phases. The first phase ended in 167 with the truce mentioned above, but this was only temporary. As soon as the Romans were able, they determined to punish the Germanic groups. This war began in 170 and lasted until 175, although the majority of the Germanic groups made peace in 174. The settlement of 175 was not quite what the Romans wanted, but the revolt in that year led by Avidius Cassius, commander in chief in the east, persuaded Marcus Aurelius to agree to peace without annexing the territory of the Germanic peoples. Instead he merely demanded the return of Roman prisoners and hostages (perhaps as many as 160,000 people had been taken), and the establishment of a neutral zone of some five miles on the left bank or German side of the Danube. No German settlements were allowed in this strip of territory and German trading rights were sharply defined. To replenish the depleted Roman populations, Marcus Aurelius settled certain German tribes on the Roman side of the frontier and required them to give military service. This was the beginning of the Roman policy which gradually changed the composition of the army. Eventually it was not Romans fighting the Germans but Germans under the Roman banner fighting other Germans.

After making peace Marcus Aurelius begun to move eastward to Syria in order to put down the revolt of Cassius. Before he reached Syria Cassius was murdered by forces loyal to Marcus Aurelius. There were still troops which held out, however, and Marcus Aurelius spent most of the spring and summer of 176 in reestablishing the loyalty of Syria and Egypt. By the end of 176 he had reached Rome, where he celebrated a triumph for his victories over the Germans and for bringing an end to the civil war. The Marcomanni, perhaps encouraged by the absence of Marcus Aurelius, driven by pressures upon them from the east, and fearful of further extension of Roman power, resumed the war in mid-summer of 177. The Roman governors and commanders in the area were unable to put an end to the war and Marcus Aurelius again took to the field with his son, Commodus, whom he had just established as co-Emperor with him. Once on the frontier Marcus Aurelius apparently decided that the only way to stop the German inroads was to annex their territory. He was well on his way to accomplishing this objective when he became seriously ill and died in his sleep on 17 March 180.

Marcus Aurelius had made careful preparations for the succession by elevating his teen-age son, Commodus, to a position of co-ruler. Within a few weeks of his father's death and contrary to the counsel of his father's advisers, Commodus concluded peace with the Germanic tribes on more or less the same terms given by Marcus Aurelius himself in 175. Roman deserters and prisoners were returned, and the Germans accepted regulations limiting the time and place of public assemblies, promised to supply contingents of mercenaries, and agreed not to engage in intertribal warfare. In return Commodus pledged to pay a subsidy to the Germans and to evacuate the Roman forces from Marcomanni territory. While historians, both ancient and modern, have been somewhat condemnatory of Commodus's peace, there was no further trouble on the frontier for the next generation. This was in part owing to the fact that the frontier generals devoted their energies to strengthening

MAP No. 10

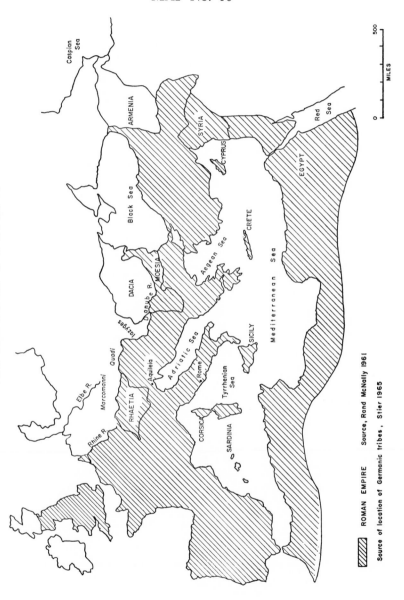

Rome vs. Marcomanni – Quadi 176-185 A.D.

ROMAN EMPIRE   Source, Rand McNally 1961

Source of location of Germanic tribes, Stier 1965

the Roman defenses and to pacifying the border inhabitants. Since it probably would have been difficult for the Romans permanently to have occupied the German territory, it can be argued that Commodus's policy was a wise one dictated both by the needs of the national economy and the concessions which Rome had gained. The Romans had demonstrated that they could meet the German threat; by their withdrawal perhaps they allayed German suspicion of Roman expansion northward.

Thus in the decade under study, Rome, the dominant power, wanted to maintain the status quo. The Roman position had been seriously weakened by troop withdrawals, necessitated at first by the war with Parthia and then by pressures on the Germans themselves from the east. The returning Roman army had brought back a plague which had decimated a good part of the army, effectively weakening both its quantity and quality. Still, through rather drastic financial measures, the Romans had been able to turn back the threat of the Marcomanni. Each time that a total victory was in sight, however, something caused the Romans to be willing to accept either a temporary truce or a negotiated peace. The result was that Commodus concluded the war with the same territorial limits which had existed before the war began, although the Germans did have to give the Romans more military services and there were greater restrictions on commercial interchange between the two. After the peace the Romans continued to build up their defenses but at the same time they also attempted to establish closer friendship with the Germans; that they were at least partially successful is indicated by the fact that the frontier remained quiet for the next several decades despite internal and external difficulties for Rome.

PART 2: SURVEY OF VARIABLES (CODED FOR THE CONSPICUOUS STATE, ROME)

Dependent Variables

Months of War. The actual dates are almost impossible to determine, but the Marcomannic War began in the midsummer of A.D. 177 (about six and a half months of war, rounded to seven, in that year) and ended by the end of March 180. This is counted as thirty-four months of war and eighty-six of peace. The raw score of 34 yields a standard score of 49. For method of transformation see p. 11.

Territorial Change. There was no territorial change. The wars served to maintain the status quo. The raw score of 0% yields two standard scores; territorial gain 49 and territorial stability 36, For method of transformation see p. 13f.

Military Variables

Defensive Stance. Rome was clearly in a defensive stance, while the Germanic groups were in an aggressive one. Coded *present.*

Strength of Armed Forces. The Germans greatly outnumbered the Romans, at least in the area in question. In total forces the Romans outnumbered the Germans. Estimates place the Roman army at about four hundred twenty thousand men before the plague broke out. Immediately adjacent to the Danubian frontier were some sixteen thousand five hundred troops. During the difficulties with the Marcomanni the number was probably increased to about twenty thousand men and other nearby areas were strengthened, but the Romans were still outnumbered by the Germans. The only way the Romans could outnumber the Germans was to deplete the whole Empire of troops, something that they could not afford to do. Coded *absent.*

Mobility of Armed Forces. Roman mobility had been handicapped by the plague, but it was clearly the more mobile of the two armies. The Romans controlled the Danube, which allowed them to transport troops; their whole system of frontier fortification was based upon the existence of highly mobile troops, and while the plague weakened their mobility, the fact that the Romans had enough forces to bring the Germans at least to the negotiating stage indicates that they were still superior. Coded *present.*

Quality of Armed Forces. The Romans, despite the plague, were still superior. Coded *present.*

Fortifications. The Roman frontier was heavily fortified. The first line of defense was the Danube, with a neutral zone on the non-Roman side of the river. The Roman side of the Danube was also guarded by a continuous line of forts and watch towers. Behind these were ditches and other barriers, and key centralized barracks from which troops could be rushed to trouble spots. There were no similar fortifications erected by the Germans. Coded *present*.

Prestige. Rome was without peer. The only challenge had to come internally by revolt or plague, or externally by war on several fronts. Coded *present*.

Geographical Variables

Propinquity. The Marcomanni bordered on Roman territory. Coded *present*.

Natural Barriers. The Danube served as a natural frontier between the Romans and the Marcomanni. Coded *present*.

Capital City. Rome is more than three hundred miles from the Danube River, which served as the frontier. Coded *absent*.

Diplomatic Variables

Announcements. The existence of the league which attacked and for a long time broke through the Danubian frontier was certainly known to the imperial government long before the breakthrough happened; however, there is no record of any formal announcement of intention on the part of the Germans. Coded *absent*.

Surprise Attack. The Romans were expecting trouble on this frontier; in fact, there is considerable evidence that the Roman frontier officials actually succeeded in delaying the crisis until the return of troops which had been sent to the eastern frontier. Roman efforts to counter the crisis were negated by the fact that the returning troops carried the plague which decimated the Roman forces. It seems clear, however, that the Romans had excellent information about what was going on in the German territories. Coded *absent*.

Alliances. Throughout their history the Romans followed a policy of making different types of alliances. That is, they tended to treat their possible enemies in different ways, concluding different types of alliances with neighboring groups. In 170, after Marcus Aurelius had first defeated the Germans, he made an alliance with one group and subsidized it to help restrain another group. Other German groups were formally admitted into Roman territory as allies on condition that they serve in the army or perform other necessary services for the Roman state. Since Rome was such a great power, no single group on her borders could match her. This prestige made it necessary for possible enemies to make alliances to proceed against her. The Marcomanni and the Quadi and perhaps the Iazyges allied against Rome, but these alliances usually were only temporary ones. Coded *present*.

Active Diplomacy. The means which the Romans used to delay the attack of the Marcomanni are not clear from the sources, but the peace was a negotiated one. The contemporary Roman historian, Cassius Dio, indicated that in his opinion the Romans could have destroyed the Marcomanni, yet when the Marcomanni sent a four-man team of negotiators, the Romans were willing to listen to the proposals. Each of the peace treaties the Romans made with the Marcomanni was concluded only after negotiation. Coded *present*.

Intense Diplomacy. The treaties between the Romans and the Marcomanni provided for a neutral strip between Roman territory and the Germans on the German side of the Danube frontier, a regulation of commercial trade, a return of hostages and prisoners, a contribution of troops, and some control over foreign policy. Coded *present*.

Previous Conflict. The Marcomanni had given trouble to the Romans previously. At least as early as A.D. 6 the Romans had entered into military contact with them while another outbreak took place during the reign of Domitian (81-96). Even though none of the previous conflicts were as serious as the one under study, the fact that the Romans had erected a series of fortifications against the Marcomanni would seemingly indicate that they were expecting trouble from them. Coded *present*.

Cultural Variables

Benefits. The sources are somewhat ambiguous on this, but since one of the privileges most desired was closer association with the Romans, the Roman permission to allow Marcomanni to serve in the Roman army or to trade in Roman towns or to have other special privileges can be regarded as honors. Also, the Romans tried to keep their enemies as friendly as possible and when they were unwilling or unable to annex the territory, as was the case with the Marcomanni, they often gave subsidies to ensure close ties. Coded *present*.

Cultural Exchange. Roman culture was widely admired and imitated by the Germans, and many of the Marcomanni had settled close to the Roman settlements. After the Marcomannic wars the Roman policy of utilizing German troops increased the ties between the two groups. Coded *present*.

Trade. There were strong commercial ties between the Empire and the German tribes on its borders. This is evident from the rise of the border cities and the inclusion of commercial rights and privileges in the various treaties made between the Marcomanni and the Romans. Coded *present*.

General Exchange. Both cultural exchange and trade are coded *present*; thus this variable is coded *present* also.

Administrative Variables

Experience of Ruler. Marcus Aurelius was closely associated in the duties of government from a fairly early age, although he did not technically become sole emperor until 161. He had been in office approximately fifteen years in 176. Commodus was joint ruler from 177 and succeeded to sole rule in 180. Coded *absent*.

Youth of Ruler. Marcus Aurelius, the Emperor during the first half of the decade under study, was born in 121; he was about fifty-five at the opening of the decade. Commodus was born in 161 and was fifteen years old when he became co-ruler and nineteen years old when he became sole ruler. Coded *present* because Commodus ruled alone for more than half of the decade and was less than forty-five years old when he acceded to sole rule.

Unbridled Ruler. Coded *absent* because hereditary dynasty depended upon the acquiescence of military forces. See hereditary monarchy below.

Hereditary Monarchy. The dynastic situation during this period was ambiguous. Successors were chosen by inheritance through adoption. The ultimate decision was in the hands of the armed forces: the most successful military leader became the Emperor. Usually, however, the army was not given a chance to intervene. The reigning emperor usually adopted the most successful general or pushed his real or adopted sons into positions of military authority. Coded *no data.*

Civil War. The most serious internal struggle was the revolt of Avidius Cassius while the Emperor Marcus Aurelius was fighting the Marcomanni and Sarmatians. After the death of Marcus Aurelius, the policies of Commodus led to even more internal dissension, although the paucity of the sources makes it difficult to date them exactly. There was a plot to assassinate Commodus towards the end of the year 182; the plot failed, but it did result in an internal reign of terror. There was another suspected revolt in 185. In effect the Roman state was losing some of the stability which had marked the previous half century. Coded *present.*

Centralization. Rome was clearly more centralized. In theory all power came from the Emperor, and while in practice various areas had considerable independence, the German tribes lacked even the theory of centralization. Coded *present.*

PART 3: DATA QUALITY CONTROL

This period in Roman history is one in which the primary sources are sparse. The sources which do exist are often silent on what we want to know. Consulted but not coded because it was not a leading source was H.M.D. Parker, *A History of the Roman World from A.D. 138 to 337* (London: Methuen, 1963).

This sketch is based primarily on the following works, which were coded: Cassius Dio Cocceianus, *Dio's Roman History*, edited and translated by J. W. Cahoon (London: Wm Heinemann, 1949-1956), Epitomes 72, 73; Herodian, *History of the Roman Empire from the Death of Marcus Aurelius to the Accession of Gordian III*, trans. Edward C. Echols (Berkeley: University of California Press, 1961); and

David Magie, trans., *Scriptores Historiae Augustae* (London: Wm Heinemann, 1922-1932).

Publication Year. Early third century except for the *Scriptores*, which was probably fourth century. Coded *absent*.

Primary Source. Coded *present*. See "Publication Year" and "Author's Proximity."

Authors' Associations. All were Roman citizens, and both Dio and Herodian were imperial officials. Coded *present*.

Authors' Sympathies. Pro Roman, even though they might be against some of the personalities involved. Coded *present*.

Authors' Proximity. Dio was alive at the time and might even have participated to some extent in the events recorded, since he was governor in the general area where the events took place. The others were further removed either in time or space. Coded *present*.

CHAPTER 13

★ ★ ★

THE INTERNAL INVASION

376-385: Conspicuous State, Rome; Conspicuous Rival, Visigoths.

PART I : SKETCH OF HISTORICAL SETTING (CHIEFLY AFTER AMMIANUS MARCELLINUS AND ZOSIMUS)

EUROPEAN AFFAIRS during the period under study and for a century or so afterwards were dominated by the various incursions of the Germans and Huns into the Roman Empire. These invasions led ultimately to the disintegration of the Empire, although the eastern portion of it continued to exist in a somewhat different form. Impetus for the Germanic migration is usually attributed to the westward thrust of the Huns. This thrust upset the status quo relationships established by Rome with the Germanic tribes north of the Danube and east of the Rhine. At the beginning of the year A.D. 376 one of the most important among the Germanic tribes were the Visigoths, who were being ferried across the Danubian border by the Roman frontier fleet. The Visigoths came not as invaders but as refugees who had sought entrance into the Empire in order to protect themselves from the threat of the Huns. Even though the Roman officials for various reasons had granted the Goths asylum, Roman subordinates mistreated the Visigoths. Sometime in the year 377 the refugee Goths revolted and much to their surprsie, were able to challenge the Roman army success-fully. By 378 they had inflicted the worst slaughter and defeat that the Roman army had suffered since the time of Hannibal. The Visigoths, however, did not know what to do with their success. Unable to capture any of the fortified Roman cities, they turned to devastation of the countryside rather than to conquest. It was not until October 382 that peace was restored. In the peace treaty which followed, the Goths became allies of Rome and settled within the Empire itself. The damage had been done, however, and the Roman army was so weakened that the only way it could offer effective resistance against future invaders was to incorporate masses of Germans and aliens under their own commanders. In fact, at times the Empire was being defended by relatives of the same groups which were attacking it.

For one hundred years before the decade under study there had been an uneasy peace along the frontier, with Rome clearly in a defensive stance. Since the time of the Emperor Aurelian (A.D. 220–275), the frontier of the Roman Empire had been set at the Danube. Because of trouble with the Goths, Aurelian had withdrawn from Dacia (present-day Rumania); further pacification of the Goths had been carried out by the Emperor Probus (276–282). There had been frontier activity in the years 301, 314, 323, 337 to 40, 364 and 365, but it was not until 367 that a Roman army mounted an offensive, crossed the Danube, and attempted to come to grips with the Goths. The expedition lasted some two years but there was little fighting, largely because the Goths refused to meet the Romans and instead retreated or used guerilla tactics. Eventually the Romans concluded a favorable treaty of peace with the Goths that again recognized the Danube as a frontier.

Rome not only depended on the geographical barrier of the Danube to prevent Gothic incursions but also erected a string of forts close to the frontier. The job of the resident farmers in the camps was to protect the frontier from small bands of invaders. Behind these camps were larger fortified cities where greater troop concentrations were located. From an extant document, the *Notitia dignitatum*, we have an idea of the size of the Roman forces at the end of the fourth century. The Danubian frontier was divided into an eastern and western one: the eastern area, the one with which this study is mainly concerned, had, besides the men in the border camps, some sixty-four corps of infantry and thirty-one of cavalry in forts behind the frontier—about fourty-seven thousand footsoldiers and nearly five thousand mounted ones. Behind these were some forty-one thousand supporting footsoldiers and fifty-five thousand mounted, plus the legions stationed at Constantinople. These forces were more than enough to meet any localized large-scale break through, although a full invasion could only be stopped by massing all the troops in one area and thus weakening other sectors of the frontier. The Roman forces therefore were more than enough to meet the threats which existed on any one frontier, but not sufficient to meet several simultaneous assaults of different frontiers.

The Empire had two capitals, Rome in the west and Constantinople in the east, with the latter serving as the chief capital. Although both of these were large cities, it is nearly impossible to determine which was larger and whether either of them was larger than Antioch, Alexandria, or other large cities. The Empire had much greater resources of manpower than any of the Germanic tribes. Even though the imperial armies were splintered into various factions, they were larger and better trained. Almost every able-bodied male German, however, was part of a citizen army, whereas Rome had come to be dependent upon a professional army.

Since the civil wars of the third century, if not earlier, the Roman emperors had been dependent upon the army for their right of succession. Nominally the position of emperor was an inherited one, but in all cases the inheritance was dependent upon acceptance by the troops. Many emperors tried to assure a peaceful succession by presenting their heirs to the troops during their own lifetimes, or by adopting co-emperors. Neither practice always insured peace on the death of the reigning emperor. Often when news of the death of an emperor reached troops in far-off sections of the Empire they would proclaim their own general as emperor and a struggle for supremacy would ensue. In effect the legal emperor was the man who either succeeded to the throne without opposition or who made good his pretensions by the sword. On the other hand a general who was defeated in battle after having been "acclaimed" by his troops was a usurper. During the fourth century there was not too much difficulty in the succession itself but there were still many usurpers. In the decade under study one such usurping general ruled in the west where he had defeated and killed the legitimate Emperor Gratian.

Internal dissension was further encouraged by the religious disputes within the Empire. Christianity had been made a legal religion by Constantine in 313 and thus had become the religion of the emperors.Even though paganism was still strong, the real difficulty was the numbers and varieties of Christianity, most of which regarded their rivals as agents of the devil. Actual pitched battles took place between the various groups. It appears that the mass of the people adhered to the orthodox trinitarian creed which had been adopted at the Council of Nicea in 325. Some of the early Church historians who blamed the Emperor Valens for allowing the Visigoths to enter the empire said that he did so because they were Arian Christians like himself and could thus counter the growing force of the trinitarian or Athanasian Christians. The Empire before, during, and after the decade under study was subject to a great deal of internal dissension which had probably handicapped it in meeting the various external threats.

The Goths were also divided, and their division was between a pro-Roman Christian party and an anti-Roman pagan party. It was largely the former group which had entered the Empire in 376. All the Germanic tribes had had considerable contact with the Romans, the Visigoths perhaps more than any of the groups outside of the empire. One of the most important contacts was made by Ulfilas, who as a young man had been sent by the Goths to Constantinople, either as a hostage or an ambassador. Although he had probably been a Christian before he entered the Empire, his contacts with the Christians in Constantinople and elsewhere imbued him with a mission of Christianizing the Goths. It was largely due to him that the Germans were concerted. Many of his early converts had been driven out of Gothic territory and sought security within the Empire itself, further strengthening the bonds between the Romans and the Germans. Many other Germans had served in the Roman army, had worked as domestics in Roman households, or had been held as hostages in Romans cities. There were many commercial contacts, at least along the frontier; the Goths were cognizant of Roman ways, Roman ideas, and were perhaps in the position of being swallowed up by a society whose cultural level was more advanced than theirs. The Gothic language itself had begun to include an increasing number of Latin and Greek words.

When the Goths applied for admission into the Roman state they did so because it was the great power which would protect them from the onrushing Huns. They were a pastoral people, recently formed into tribal kingdoms, who were overwhelmed by things Roman and wanted to participate in them. The more pagan elements of the Visigoths had already retreated deeper into the mountains in order to protect themselves. Those petitioning for admission were led by Fritigern, a pro-Roman, who with a large group of followers had earlier been granted asylum in the Empire because of his religious beliefs. He later returned to the Goths but had remained on good terms with the Romans.

In 375 the Visigoths under Fritigern petitioned the emperor to enter Roman territory. The emperor was willing to allow them in, perhaps because he felt that he could utilize them as troops for his army and thus save money. Almost nothing is known about the agreement which allowed Germans into the Empire other than the fact that they were probably to be military allies of Rome. Whatever the reason or whatever the agreement, the Roman navy ferried the Germans across the river at the beginning of 376. Numbers are hard to come by but there were perhaps as many as two hundred thousand men of fighting age plus women and children. Other estimates are considerably lower but could be challenged.

Little is recorded about the preparations the Romans had made for this mass migration. It is known that the Goths were supposed to be disarmed before they entered; it is also known that the frontier troops became much more interested in the German girls than in the German weapons and apparently had let many men slip in with their fighting equipment. Whatever provisions had been made for feeding the emigrants soon broke down and the Visigoths became desperate for food. Part of this breakdown might be attributed to the incompetence of the Roman officials on the scene, and reflects on the abilities of the emperors.

In the year 376 the Empire was ruled by a triumvirate of rulers. Valens, the emperor in the east, had been appointed to the honor by his brother Valentinian in 364, when he was thirty-six years old. In 376 he was therefore approximately forty-eight, but age had not made him the decisive figure that his brother had been. Valens was described by Hodgkin, a nineteenth-century English historian, as being torpid and procrastinating, with muddy complexion, lack-luster eyes, bent legs, and protuberant belly. While Valentinian practiced universal religious tolerance, Valens was an inflexible Arian (a creed which held that the Son of God was a created being). This may account for the somewhat harsh judgments of Valens made by later Christian and pagan writers.

The Emperor Valentinian had died in 375 leaving two minor sons as co-rulers with his brother Valens: Gratian, who in 376 was about seventeen; and Valentinian II, who was only a boy of five. The latter was under the regency of his mother, Justina, the second wife of Valentinian, who probably resented her stepson Gratian. In addition to the tensions between Gratian and Justina, Valens was also jealous of Gratian because of some military successes the boy had won on his own. Nominally Gratian had been associated with his father in his rule since 367, but neither he nor his brother nor his uncle Valens had really been tested in a crisis. To further complicate the difficulties, Valentinian's death had accentuated religious divisions within the Empire. Even though the succession had taken place peacefully, there was still the possibility of revolt.

During the year 376 tensions continued to build up between the Visigoths and the Romans, largely over the steadily worsening conditions of the Germans. If food had been provided by the Empire, the Roman provincial officials had profited from it; there are tales of the Visigoths selling their children for food on the grounds that it would be better for the children to live as Roman slaves than die of hunger. Still the Visigoths did not break out into open revolt, perhaps because a number of their teen-age children had been taken as hostages when they had entered the Empire. At the beginning of the year 377 some of the Visigoth leaders had been invited to attend a banquet given by the Roman official Lupicinus at Marcianople. Only the leaders were allowed to enter the walls of the city—the Visigoths' escorts were kept outside. Either ill feeling between the Visigoths and the townspeople resulted in a pitched battle, or Lupicinus ordered the assassination of the escort. Lupicinus is then said to have ordered the murder of his guests. Fritigern, the Visigoth leader, managed to escape from the banquet, join his forces, and start a full-scale military campaign. The Germans were more than a match for the detachments of Roman troops sent out against them, and soon other Germans crossed the Danube to join them.

Several indecisive campaigns were launched against the Germans in 377, but it was not until 378 that the Emperor Valens was able to join the fray. At the battle of Adrianople in 378, the Roman army was cut to pieces. Valens, his leading officers, and forty thousand troops were killed on the battlefield. The Visigoths had inflicted on the Romans their worst defeat since the Battle of Cannae in 216 B.C. The German cavalry proved superior to the Roman infantry. C.W.C. Oman, the historian of medieval military tactics, has said that Adrianople was a turning point; from this time forward the Romans were forced increasingly to rely on cavalry. Even though the Germans defeated the Roman army, they could not take the Roman cities, and the Gothic army soon degenerated into marauding and looting expeditions in Moesia, Thrace, and elsewhere.

When the provincial officials heard of the German victory many of them slaughtered German hostages, which only served to increase tensions between Roman and German. Gratian, now the chief emperor, was busily occupied in the west; in 378 he appointed Theodosius I as co-emperor and ruler in the east in order to meet the crisis. Theodosius was the son of a famous Roman general who had been executed in 375, apparently on instructions from Valens. Theodosius in a sense is the savior of the Empire in this crisis. Still comparatively young, he avoided meeting the Germans in a large-scale battle, but instead isolated and cut off the small roving bands. At the same time he remained conciliatory towards them, always attempting to regain them as allies. By 382 they had agreed to peace and were settled on wastelands to the south of the Danube where they remained until the end of the decade under study.

The Visigoths, in payment for their acceptance within the borders of the Empire, promised to supply troops for the Romans. They were thus an independent people ruled by their native chieftans who in turn were bound through alliances with Rome. The *foederati*, as they were called, were given both land and other subsidies to maintain their loyalty to Rome. Technically, Rome had not lost any territory from this first Germanic invasion, but Roman control over the Gothic territory was not what it had been. The later mass movement of the Goths indicates how dependent the Romans were upon them for troops.

Theodosius's succession had helped relieve some but not all the internal dissensions within the empire. He was a trinitarian Christian, and this sect now gained favor. Imperial relations with the Germans were complicated by the fact that they were almost all Arians. There was still considerable internal dissatisfaction within the Empire, however, as shown by the sucessful revolt of Maximus in 383. He defeated and killed the Emperor Gratian in the west and became ruler in Gaul, Britain, and Spain. Theodosius ignored the threat of this challenger, and in fact recognized his usurpation as more or less legal until after the decade under study.

The biggest problem Theodosius faced was the need to strengthen and rebuild the Roman army. In order to secure additional manpower Theodosius turned to the very Germans who had defeated the Romans. He began to enlist every Germanic chief who was willing to enter his service. These troops were not incorporated with the national troops, but rather followed their own immediate commanders; these in turn took orders from the Roman generals. In 384, only six years after Adrianople, there were an estimated forty thousand Gothic and other Teutonic horsemen serving under their own chiefs in the army of the east. Within the decade under study the defense of the Empire had come to be dependent upon a group which at its beginning had been considered enemies. The Romans had not actually lost any territory, but Roman authority was certainly weakened in a great many areas, and by 385 the gradual transition of the Roman Empire to a Germanic one is evident to the modern historian.

Thus in the decade under study, Rome, a defensive power in defensive stance, found itself involved in a disastrous war with the Visigoths, a group of people who had been allowed to settle within the boundaries of the Empire. Owing to internal religious, political, and financial difficulties, Rome was unable to offer effective resistance when the Visigoths revolted. The centralized Roman state had broken apart in the hands of some greedy provincial officials. The only way in which the Visigoths could be defeated was by Germanizing the Roman army. As a result at the end of the decade Rome was dependent upon Germans to defend herself from Germans.

MAP No. 11

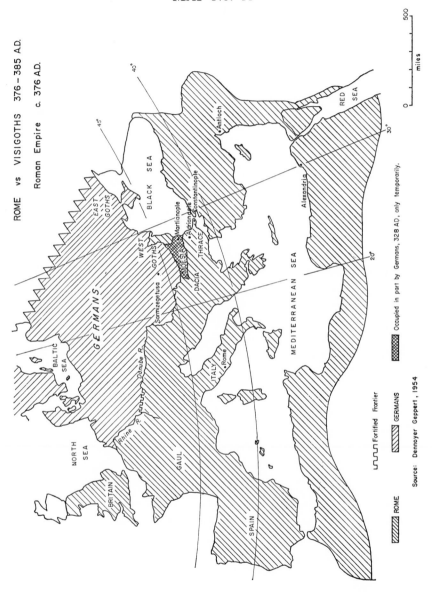

ROME vs VISIGOTHS 376–385 A.D.

Roman Empire c. 376 A.D.

Source: Dennoyer Geppert, 1954

Part 2: Survey of Variables (Coded for the Conspicuous State, Rome)

Dependent Variables

Months of War. During the decade from 376 to 385 there were four and a half years of peace—376 and part of 377, the latter part of 382, and 383 to 385; there were five and a half years of war— most of 377, 378 to 381, and most of 382—or sixty-six months of war. Chronology is very confused, but modern scholarship tends to put the peace in October of 382, although there had been a gradual cessation of activities up to that time rather than a sudden cease fire. The raw score of 66 yields a standard score of 55. For method of tranformation see p. 11.

Territorial Change. Technically there was no real loss of territory, but since the Visigoths were allies and not actual citizens, and since their allied status was entirely dependent upon their own good will towards Rome, it seems clear that Rome had at least lost control of some of its own territory. The raw score of 0% yields two standard scores: territorial gain 49 and territorial stability 36. For method of transformation see p. 13f.

Military Variables

Defensive Stance. Rome was clearly in a defensive stance. Its whole military structure was organized around the concept of defense. The Visigoths entering the Empire were also in a defensive stance, but once they were inside the Empire this condition was changed by what they considered to be unfair treatment. After defeating the Romans, they turned to raiding and looting until the Romans came to terms with them. Coded *present.*

Strength of Armed Forces. On the eastern Danubian frontier there were perhaps one hundred thousand troops readily available to meet any threat, plus the frontier guard and the imperial guard at Constantinople. Demands for other troops could only be met by drawing them from other commands, a highly dangerous procedure. The Roman army was a professional army and made a heavy demand on the resources of the state. The Germans on the other hand had a citizen army in which almost every able-bodied man was a soldier. It has been estimated that although the Visigoths had less than two hundred thousand men of fighting age (probably much less) they undoubtedly outnumbered the troops the Romans could immediately throw against them. Coded *absent*.

Mobility of Armed Forces. Militarily Rome had a well-organized and comparatively efficient army. It was, however, a defensive army and any big breakthrough taxed its resources to the utmost. Any realignment of troops forced the neglect of another area of the frontier and could result in another breakthrough. Within the limits of an infantry army it was fairly mobile, but its progress was slowed by the amount of equipment that it had to carry. For any such mass battle as they had to fight with the Visigoths the Romans were probably not much more mobile than their rivals, and the German cavalry and numbers further weakened their theoretical superiority in mobility. Coded *absent*.

Quality of Armed Forces. Man for man, the Roman soldier was probably superior to the German, since he was better organized, better disciplined, and was more or less professional. This was offset somewhat by German numerical superiority, and by the German reliance upon cavalry as opposed to the Roman concentration upon infantry in the large battles. The Goth's lack of organization, however, kept them from launching long-term sieges. Coded *present*.

Fortifications. The Romans had a whole series of frontier fortifications. The border against the Visigoths was also guarded by the Danube. The Romans, however, had voluntarily ferried the Visigoths across and inside the Empire, where the battles took place. The only real fortifications were the ones around the important cities. Since the Visigoths did not become hostile until some time after peacefully passing through the frontier defenses this variable is coded *no data*.

Prestige. Rome had tremendous prestige. The fact that the Visigoths sought protection within the Roman borders indicates the feelings the Germans had about their neighboring state. Coded *present*.

Geographical Barriers

Propinquity. The Romans and the Goths shared a common

boundary and, in fact, the Goths had been allowed to enter the empire itself. Coded *present*.

Natural Barriers. These were clearly present originally, but since the Goths were inside the Empire at the time of the outbreak, the natural barriers were not helpful. Between the Goths and the Romans was the Danube, a natural barrier to invasion, and this barrier had been strengthened by a series of Roman fortifications. The effectiveness of this barrier was weakened by the Gothic victory inside the Roman territory, enabling the Goths to bring over reinforcements. Coded *present*.

Capital City. Constantinople, the capital and largest city, was less than 300 miles from the border, but by the end of the fourth century it was almost impregnable. Coded *present*.

Diplomatic Variables

Announcements. Coded *absent*. See "Surprise Attack," below.

Surprise Attack. The German revolt came as a surprise to the ruling officials in Constantinople, perhaps because they were ignorant of the treatment the Germans received. One impression is that the Germans revolted as a desperate protest and much to their own surprise found that they had defeated the Romans. Coded *present*.

Alliances. The Visigoths entered the Empire as allies of Rome but outside of this, alliances do not seem to have been an important factor in the war. Coded *absent*.

Active Diplomacy. To the Germans Rome was the great power, as is effectively demonstrated by their desire to enter the Empire and thus protect themselves from the Huns. Negotiations were conducted between the Romans and the Germans in 376 to permit the Germans to enter and in 382 to end the war between the two groups. Coded *present*.

Intense Diplomacy. Little is known of the actual agreements of 376 and 382. The Goths were to serve as allies under their own rulers and probably were to fight under the Roman banner, for which they were given land and a subsidy. The other conditions of this alliance have not come down to us. Coded *present*.

Previous Conflict. The Romans and the Goths had been more or less at peace in the preceding hundred-year period. There had been frontier activity in the years 301, 314, 323, 336 to 340, 364, 365; and the Roman invasion into the Gothic territory from 367 to 369; but none of these incidents can be considered of major importance. With the conversion of the Goths the tensions between Romans and Goths were decreasing .Coded *present.*

Cultural Variables

Benefits. The Romans had utilized various means of recognition to keep the Germans peaceful. Fritigern, one of the Visigoth leaders, had been granted asylum and protection in the Empire prior to the period, and he was considered by the Romans to be extremely friendly to them. Ulfilias, the missionary of the Germans, had served either as hostage or ambassador to Constantinople, but at any rate his treatment had been such that he returned to his people deeply influenced by Roman civilization. Germans were also given commissions in the Roman army and were often paid subsidies by the Romans to keep them quiet or to win their support. Coded *present.*

Cultural Exchange. From the time of Caesar onwards, there was almost continual cultural and commercial exchange between the Romans and the Germans. Although the Germans were probably more imitative of Rome than *vice versa*, it was not all one-sided. In fact by the time of Tacitus in the second century some of the Roman writers attempted to have the Romans adopt the "Spartan" virtues of the Germans. Germans served willingly as domestics and soldiers, but were unwilling slaves, hostages, and refugees in the Empire. The Germans received their religion from Rome and by the time of the entrance of the Visigoths a good portion of them had been converted to Christianity. The Gothic script was based upon the Latin one, and it too was a result of the efforts of Christian missionaries. Coded *present.*

Trade. There was commercial trade between the two groups, especially along the frontier, and Roman products from deep in the interior found their way into German hands. Coded *present.*

General Exchange. Cultural exchange and trade are coded present, hence this trait is coded *present* also.

Administrative Variables

Experience of Ruler. In 376 the only tested ruler of the Empire was the Emperor Valens, and during most of his rule even he had been subject to the control of his brother, Valentinian. Valens had been co-ruler of the Empire since 364, much influenced by his brother until the latter's death in 375. His co-rulers in 376 were the seventeen-year-old Gratian (born in 359) and the five-year-old Valentinian II (born in 371) who was under the regency of his mother, Justina. After the death of Valens in 378, Theodosius was appointed co-ruler and soon became dominant. He was born about 346, and so was about thirty-two when he came to power. Coded *absent*.

Youth of Ruler. During most of the decade the rulers were below the age of forty-five. Valens, forty-eight years old in 376, died in 378. His co-rulers in the west were Gratian, seventeen years old, and Valentinian, five years old. In 378 Theodosius, who replaced Valens in the east was thirty-two. Coded *present*.

Unbridled Ruler. Coded *absent* because hereditary monarchy was coded absent.

Hereditary Monarchy. Succession was dependent upon acceptance by the army; there was no immediate challenge in 375, although Valens had conducted a purge of people he thought might challenge him. With the removal of Valens in 378, Gratian was still able to appoint Theodosius without challenge as his co-ruler in the east. Theodosius, however, was unable to come to the aid of Gratian when he was challenged and defeated by a successful usurper. Valentinian II and his mother managed to rule in Italy to the end of the period. Coded *absent*.

Civil War. The very revolt of the Visigoths certainly constituted civil war. In addition, the Roman Empire during the third century had been more plagued with internal troubles than with the problem of Germans. The civil wars had come to a nominal end by the beginning of the fourth century, but there were still periodic outbreaks, one of which occurred in the decade under study. It was in part to achieve some unifying force that Constantine had supported Christianity but during the fourth century Christianity created as much divison within the Empire as it did harmony. Tensions between the pagans and Christians remained, but even worse were the struggles between the various varieties of Christianity, many of which had become almost regional religions. There were over two hundred different varieties of Christianity, and few of them were willing to live together. Coded *present.*

Centralization. The Roman Empire was what might be called a case of maximum centralization, with all political authority concentrated in an emperor or emperors. Such concentration, while possible in theory, is difficult in practice. There was an imperial civil service which carried on much of the day-to-day work. The emperor's authority was derived from the army, making his continued tenure dependent upon the good will of his fighting men; he hesitated to antagonize them. The Goths on the other hand had a highly decentralized state with a nominal leader but with each individual having a great deal of autonomy, based in part on his fighting ability. Coded *present.*

PART 3: DATA QUALITY CONTROL

The difficulty with any study of the late classical or early medieval period is the comparative lack of literary source material. The best historian of the fourth century, Ammianus Marcellinus, ended his work with the Battle of Adrianople. The only historians who continued his work wrote in Greek, and none of them was contemporary—although the *Epitome Caesarium*, a condensation of imperial history of the time of Theodosius, might be the exception. The best of the later historians is Zosimus, who wrote during the middle of the fifth century. His work was based on historians whose writings are now lost but who were contemporary with the events described here. Both Ammianus and Zosimus were pagan writers and hence critical of the pro-Christian policy of the emperors. Zosimus in fact predated Gibbon in tracing the decline of the Empire and putting the blame on the Christians. In addition to these two secular historians there are ecclesiastical ones, whose main interest was in the affairs of the church rather than of the state. Both

Sozomen and Socrates wrote their ecclesiastical histories about the middle of the fifth century; their orthodox Christian interpretation can be supplemented by the surviving epitome by Photius of the history of Philostorigius, an Arian Christian who wrote a few years earlier; and by Grosius, *Historia contra Paganos*, written in the fifth century. All refer only indirectly to the secular events which were taking place, as they were more concerned with religious events; they occasionally supplement Ammianus or Zosimus.

In addition to these primary sources two monumental works in English deal with the period of the late Empire. Edward Gibbon's *Decline and Fall of the Roman Empire* is perhaps most often read now as a literary classic, but as revised and updated in this century by J.B. Bury, *A History of the Later Roman Empire* (London: Methuen, 1897) vol. 2, it is still valuable. Bury found Gibbon's facts consistent with the literary materials, but occasionally they need modification because of epigraphical and archaeological finds. The second work in English is that of Thomas Hodgkin, *Italy and Her Invaders* (Oxford: Clarendon Press, 1885–1889), which despite its title deals with the general subject of the Germanic invasions into the Empire.

The works coded were Ammianus Marcellinus, *The Roman History of Ammianus Marcellinus*, edited and translated by John C. Rolfe (London: Wm Heinemann, 1956); and Zosimus, *Zosimi Historiae* (Lipsiae, 1794), which are Greek and Latin texts.

Publication Year. Ammianus Marcellinus, about 390 to 400. Zosimus, about the middle of the fifth century. Coded *absent*.

Primary Source. Coded *present*. See "Authors' Proximity."

Authors' Associations. Ammianus Marcellinus and Zosimus were imperial officials and had access to some of the state documents. Coded *present*.

Authors' Sympathies. Both were pro-Roman. Coded *present*.

Authors' Proximity. Ammianus lived during the events described. Zosimus depended upon contemporary accounts, but wrote a hundred years after the events. Coded *present*.

CHAPTER 14

★ ★ ★

THE CONTINUING STRUGGLE

576-585: Conspicuous State, Byzantine Empire; Conspicuous Rival, Persia.

PART 1: SKETCH OF HISTORICAL SETTING (CHIEFLY AFTER SYKES, BURY, BAYNES, OSTROGORSKY, DIEHL, VASILIEV, CHRISTENSEN, AND HIGGINS)

IN THE DECADE from 576 to 585, the Byzantine Empire and Persia were engaged in continuous warfare. Although the Byzantines provoked the war, once they had defeated the Persians they were willing to settle for a negotiated peace. The Byzantine Emperor Tiberius, and Maurice, his successor, felt that peace with Persia would only be possible if both sides could gain it with honor; the death of Chosroes, the Persian king, however, put a stop to negotiations and the war dragged on well past the decade until Chosroes II again negotiated a settlement with the Empire, and in fact regained his throne with Byzantine help. Neither side could totally defeat the other without occupying the country; neither was willing nor able to do so, and peace could only exist through mutual recognition of each other's independence. Since this did not happen, war broke out again in the seventh century. Persia was finally destroyed by a new force, Islam.

With perhaps one exception, from 486 B.C. to A.D. 565 the Roman, now Byzantine, Empire dealt with no nation as an equal and recognized none as peer. To most Romans there was no middle course: peoples either entered Roman territory as allies or vassals or remained outside as enemies. Once Rome had annexed the ancient centers of Greek culture, the distinction between Roman and non-Roman became synonymous with the distinction between civilized and barbarian. The idea became so deep rooted, in part because of long-term dominance, that to the political thinkers of the period the Empire was eternal. The situation which had been created was the eternal order of the universe; the Empire was the world, her Emperor was God, and her law was Providence; it became the Empire's destiny to subdue the outer chaotic wilderness, impose organization, and impart culture. With the advent of Christianity, this ideal did not die, but instead was "baptized" and transformed, and Roman victory came to mean not only the victory of civilization over barbarism, but the triumph of Christianity over paganism as well.

This is not to say that there were no challenges to the Empire's claims. Occasionally it would temporarily recognize an opposing power, but usually only as an expediency; not as a renunciation of sovereignty over territory which it had once ruled. For example, during the fourth and fifth centuries various barbarians swarmed into the Empire and created states which were to some extent independent, but once the Empire felt strong enough to act, as it did under Justinian, then it retook the occupied regions. Through necessity the Empire in effect tolerated the presence of these nations, but never acknowledged their right to independent existence.

The Byzantine Empire, however, was not the only power with such pretensions. Persia had them also. In fact, one reason that Persia became such a formidable enemy of the Empire was because the Persians exercised the same pretensions to world authority that the Byzantines did. The Sassanid monarchs looked upon themselves as the legitimate successors to the ancient Achaemenids and drew their inspiration from Cyrus and Darius. They claimed that the ruler of Persia was the earth's unique king, and that the unchangeable laws of the Medes and the Persians should govern every race and people from the banks of the Indus to the Nubian plateau.

When two such powers meet, they either have to fight for supremacy or come to some sort of agreement. They had in fact reached a sort of *modus vivendi* in the fourth century with the peace of Jovian, and it had lasted until 502. This long peace had helped to change Byzantine attitudes somewhat, although not entirely. In the fourth century, for example, things Roman were equated with civilization, while things non-Roman were considered barbarian, at least in the minds of the Roman philosophers. In the sixth century, however, when Justinian closed the pagan schools at Athens, the professors fled to Persia for refuge, and in fact the intervention of the Persian king enabled them to return home to practice their religion unmolested until their death. In effect the Empire had lost its position as the unique center of culture.

The Byzantine Empire had also ceased by the sixth century to be synonymous with Christianity. This appeared in the writings of the period. The fourth century Roman Syriac writer Aphraates heartened his coreligionists with the conviction that the Roman Emperor Constantius would inevitably conquer the Persians, a conquest which was in accordance with the divine design for the spread of the Gospel and the Empire. In the sixth century, however, the Syriac historian, John of Ephesus, had nothing but praise for the broad and humane tolerance of the Persian monarch. In the fourth century in Persia the Christians suffered severe persecution, but in the sixth century a Persian Christian envoy assured Justin II that the Christians in Persia would fight to the death for their country.

It is the thesis of Martin J. Higgins that one of the reasons for the difficult relations between the Byzantine Empire and Persia in the sixth century was that the Byzantines themselves did not know how to deal with an equal or near-equal power. This difficulty was compounded by Persian willingness to make any Byzantine gesture seem to be the act of an inferior power, with a consequent loss of face for them.

During the first part of the sixth century the two powers had engaged in several wars, but in 561 Justinian, the Byzantine emperor, and Chosroes, the Persian king, agreed on a fifty-year peace. In return for the peace the Byzantines were to pay some four hundred pounds of gold. The nominal reason for the payment, which was to be spread out over the years, was to subsidize Persia for its defense of the Caucasus passes which led into Asia Minor. Persia had controlled the two main passes since the fourth century, and occupation of these spots prevented the inroads of the wild barbarians living beyond them into either Byzantine or Persian territory, and was in fact the most economical method of safeguarding the provinces of Asia Minor from devastating raids. This payment, whatever the nominal reason, proved very difficult for some of the more "nationalistic" Byzantines to accept. In addition to the payment, each country consented to bar all fugitives from the other country and to return such fugitives, if need be forcibly, to their home countries. Perhaps the clause was aimed primarily at the restoration of runaway slaves, serfs, and criminals—political and otherwise, but it also applied to those who fled to the Empire for political reasons. The Byzantine Empire, as the avowed defender of Christianity, found itself in difficulty on this issue, and the requirement was very unpopular with the ordinary citizen, at least to judge from the reaction when it was abrogated. A further difficulty was Armenia, which, while Christian, was otherwise culturally allied with Persia and provided the best entry into Byzantine territory. Many of the points of dispute could perhaps have been settled if both sides had been prepared to make some concessions; but Justin II, successor to Justinian, was unwilling.

Shortly after Justin II succeeded as emperor in 565, the Persian governor of Armenia began to build a Zoroastrian fire temple there. This act could be regarded as a violation of the treaty between the Empire and Persia which guaranteed freedom of worship to Armenia. Armenian Christians objected, but to no avail, and they then negotiated with Justin II, who guaranteed that if they did not succeed in their attempts to prevent the erection of the temple, he would offer them sanctuary. The result was a bloody revolt in Armenia over the temple issue, and the ringleaders, after being defeated by the Persians, fled to Byzantine territory. Not content with merely harboring the fugitives Justin invited them to his capital, received them with much display and honor, and had the whole city of Constantinople acclaim their deeds.

At about the same time (572) another payment of money to Persia fell due and Chosroes, the Persian king, dispatched his envoy to collect it. He gave his envoy strict orders to pretend ignorance of the commotion in Armenia and the Byzantine acceptance of the fugitives. Chosroes, who was growing old, and who was well settled in his position, was apparently unwilling to risk the danger of a disputed succession in a war with the Empire. Justin, however, was unwilling to pass over the matter and in fact flaunted his own violation of the treaty of the Persian envoy. He brusquely terminated the audience with the remark that if Chosroes dared move a finger (the term also means 7/8 of an inch), he would move an arm (twenty-four fingers) and invade Persia. To add insult to injury Justin told the envoy that if Chosroes dared to start a war, he would put Chosroes to death and personally appoint the next king of Persia.

Justin's arrogance made it next to impossible for Chosroes not to accept the challenge; the alternative was to admit that Persia's claims to being a great power were but pretences. This Chosroes was unwilling to do, and so war broke out in 572.

In the first stages of the war Chosroes was clearly the victor, and Justin, who was always on the verge of losing his sanity, had a serious mental breakdown. In this crisis Tiberius, one of the leading generals, was appointed Ceasar, and with Justin's wife, Sophia, co-regent in 574. Tiberius soon reversed the defeats and forced Persia to take the initiative in seeking peace. In 575 a three-year truce was agreed upon, but Armenia was specifically excluded from the area of the truce. Thus while the truce negotiations were going on, war still continued in Armenia. The diplomatic meetings held on the border in 576 were devoted to a futile discussion of who was responsible for the war.

One of the reasons for the long drawn-out negotiations was the Persian hope that other frontiers of the Empire would be attacked, and the superior Byzantine forces would have to be in part withdrawn to meet a threat in another part of the Empire. Despite the Persian delaying tactics, Tiberius was willing to continue negotiations in order to demonstrate that the Empire was not frightened by a war on two fronts and could hold out as long as the Persians. Tiberius was also apparently unwilling to seize any great amount of Persian territory. He seemed to feel that the Byzantines would not be able to hold it for a long period of time without taking almost all of Persia, something that he considered unwise, if not impossible. As the contemporary chronicler Menander says, Tiberius kept insisting on permanent peace on a basis of equal honor. At the same time he indicated that if the two were to preserve equal honor, it would be unsuitable for the Empire to pay subsidies to Persia. Eventually Chosroes was willing to agree to the right of haven for possible refugees from the Persian Empire as well as to the restoration of the Byzantine fortress of Dara, while the Byzantines agreed to evacuate Persian territory and to recognize Persian supremacy

MAP No. 12

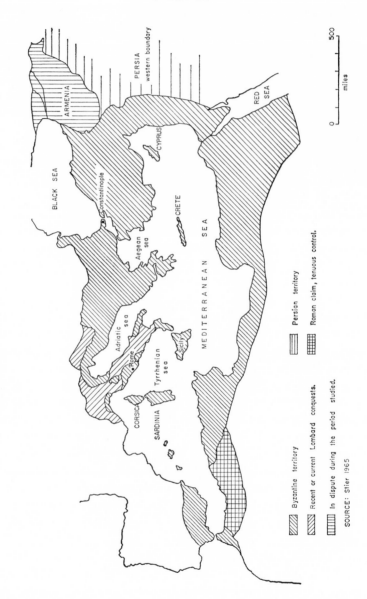

BYZANTINE EMPIRE vs PERSIA   576 – 585

in Armenia. Before the treaty was fully worked out, however, the Persians won a great victory in Armenia and this victory caused Chosroes to change his stand completely. Negotiations were suspended and in the autumn of 577 both sides once more resorted to arms. Again the Byzantines, after first losing, came to dominate the situation and Chosroes in 578 had to flee precipitously from his summer residence. Tiberius then offered peace, and Chosroes was apparently willing to accept, but died before he could act. His son and successor, Ormizod IV, was as arrogant as the Byzantines had been before and refused to negotiate with them at all. Tiberius, who succeeded as emperor in 578, and Maurice, who held the position after the death of Tiberius in 582, continued to fight the Persians.

By 590, after most of the Persian armies had been defeated, the Persian territory subjected to punishing raids, and the Persian people to famine and destruction, a usurper, Bahram VI, rose to challenge Ormizod's position. Ormizod was assassinated and, in order to remove the threat, Chosroes II, his son, was crowned king.

The revolt continued, however, and Chosroes II fled to the Empire for support. Maurice turned down Bahram's offer to restore all the territory lost by the Empire since the fourth century, perhaps because he felt that restoring it would result in a permanent peace. Instead the Byzantines gave Chosroes men and money to defeat the usurper, and when he did so in 591, he made peace with the Byzantines. Unfortunately, the peace served to accentuate Maurice's domestice difficulties; in a revolution in 602 Maurice was assassinated, and Phocas, an army general, seized power. In the ensuing anarchy Chosroes II disregarded the peace treaty and moved against the Empire. At first Chosroes was victorious and for a time reigned supreme in Asia Minor; his reign, however, was only temporary and the Byzantines soon were able to defeat Persia so decisively that Persia fell an easy prey to the new and formidable Arab invaders.

PART 2: SURVEY OF VARIABLES (CODED FOR CONSPICUOUS STATE, BYZANTINE EMPIRE)

Dependent Variables

Months of War. There were no months of peace; the war continued in Armenia even during the armistice; thus there were 120 months of war. The raw score of 120 yields a standard score of 66. For method of transformation see p. 11.

Territorial Change. Despite ten years of war, there was no appreciable gain or loss of territory during the decade. The raw score of 0 yields two standard scores: territorial gain 49 and territorial stability 36. For method of transformation see p. 13f.

Military Variables

Defensive Stance. The evidence for stance during this period is ambiguous. The Byzantines clearly provoked the war, but once it was started the Persians, even suffering defeat, were unwilling to negotiate peace despite Byzantine overtures. Both sides could be considered as being in an offensive stance during part of the decade, and in a defensive stance during the rest—both sides could be classified as reluctantly on the offensive. Coded *no data.*

Strength of Armed Forces. The Byzantine Empire was immeasurably superior in wealth, population, and organization for war, although the actual numbers of soldiers for this period are impossible to come by. The Emperor Maurice was responsible for the reorganization of the Byzantine army. He regrouped it into small, highly mobile bands. These were further divided into heavy cavalry, light cavalry, and infantry; the infantry armed with bows and arrows as well as weapons for hand-to-hand fighting. The Persian army also became a well-organized group, but it could not match the Byzantine army in equipment, tactics, or organization, at least not when the Byzantine army was being effectively led. Coded *no data.*

Mobility of Armed Forces. There were no outstanding differences between the two armies in this respect. Cavalry mobility was about the same; the Byzantines, however, probably had a better infantry and fleet. Coded *absent.*

Quality of Armed Forces. The Byzantine army was superior. Coded *present.*

Fortifications. With the capture of Dara the Persians had the better frontier fortifications; Constantia, the chief Byzantine fortress, was some seventy miles from the frontier. Both sides fortified most of the accessible cities, and it was extremely difficult for one side to take over the fortresses of the other unless aided by subversion from within. This difficulty was indicated by the Byzantine inability to recapture Dara. Coded *present.*

Prestige. In terms of population and resources the Byzantine Empire was the greater power. However, at the time, each side saw itself as the more powerful. Coded *no data.*

Geographical Variables

Propinquity. Persia and the Byzantine Empire bordered each other. Coded *present.*

Natural Barriers. These were present to some extent. There were desert stretches separating the two powers, except in Armenia, which was the most natural entrance into Byzantine or Persian territory. The Chaboras River, which flows into the Euphrates, also served as a boundary—except for the fortress of Nisibis which although on the Byzantine side of the river, had been in Persian hands since the fourth century. Coded *present.*

Capital City. The Byzantine capital of Constantinople was over a thousand miles from the border and was never endangered by Persian attack. At the same time the chief Persian capital was well inside the Persian frontier. Coded *absent.*

Diplomatic Variables

Announcements. Certainly Justin II expected war when he threatened the Persian ambassador. The refusal of the subsidy as provided by treaty was also clearly grounds for war and must be regarded as a clear announcement of intentions. Coded *present.*

Surprise Attack. Coded *absent.* See "Announcement," above.

Alliances. The state of the alliances during this period is ambiguous. Justin had made an alliance shortly before the beginning of the decade with the Turks, a newly emerging power on the border of Persia. The Empire had also allied with the Saracens of Ghassan, at first during the time of Justin and later under Maurice. Justin, however, had not played fair with the Saracens and they viewed with mistrust any long-term alliance with him. Coded *no data.*

Active Diplomacy. The Byzantines and the Persians were negotiating during most of 576, 577, and 578, and periodic negotiations took place at other times as well, but no major agreements were reached. Coded *present.*

Intense Diplomacy. Coded *absent.* See "Active Diplomacy," above.

Previous Conflict. The two countries were more or less at war during most of the sixth century, although Justinian had temporarily purchased a free hand in the west by giving Chosroes I heavy subsidies. Coded *present.*

Cultural Variables

Benefits. There were no honors or subsidies given during this period. However, subsidies previously had played an important part in the peaceful relationships between Persia and the Empire, and it was Justin's refusal to pay these subsidies, as well as the manner in which he refused to do so, which led to this war. Coded *absent.*

Cultural Exchange. Interaction was infrequent. The large Christian population in Persia had some contact with the Empire; the Christians in Persia, however, were primarily Nestorians and they were regarded as heretics by the Byzantines. Even in Armenia, where the more orthodox Christians were dominant, there was suspicion between the two groups, especially after the Byzantine massacre of Christians in Armenia. There were occasional exchanges of personnel, embassies were frequent, and the Byzantines did regard themselves as protectors of Persian Christians while the Persians regarded themselves as protectors of the Zoroastrians in the Empire. Coded *absent.*

Trade. The two countries tried to keep trade at a minimum. The Byzantines even went so far as to develop alternate routes to India and China through the Turks and other peoples. Coded *absent.*

General Exchange. Cultural Exchange and Trade are coded absent hence General Exchange is also coded *absent*.

Administrative Variables

Experience of Ruler. Tiberius was made Caesar and co-regent in 574 but he did not officially become emperor until 26 September 578, when Justin recovered his reason long enough to crown him. Eight days later Justin died. Maurice was crowned emperor on 13 August 582, the day before Tiberius died. Coded *absent*.

Youth of Ruler. Ages of the rulers are unknown. Both Tiberius and Maurice, however, were grown men who had already made their mark in the world before they became rulers. Coded *no data*.

Unbridled Ruler. Since the ages of Tiberius and Maurice are unknown, this is also coded *no data*.

Hereditary Monarchy. Succession was based in part on military prowess. Both Tiberius and Maurice had been effective military commanders before their succession, and in fact both had served as *comes excubitorum*, a sort of commander-in-chief. Each had been selected by the preceding emperor to succeed him. Coded *absent*.

Civil War. No serious riots are recorded during the decade, but certainly the state was widely split on religious questions. Justin favored the orthodox and so did Tiberius. The persecution of the monophysites caused difficulty. Tiberius also moved against the Arians after allowing them to build a church in Constantinople. The church was destroyed in a riot, but the riot was directed against Tiberius. Maurice was somewhat more tolerant, and the religious tension died down until the end of his reign. His forced abdication, however, was caused in part by the religious strife of the period. The danger of civil war is apparent from the efforts of Justinian to make sure that Justin II succeeded him without difficulty, and the fact that Tiberius was crowned by Justin, and Maurice by Tiberius, before they died. Coded *no data*.

Centralization. Although Chosroes had made great efforts to centralize the Persian administration, the Byzantine Empire was much more centralized than Persia. Coded *present*.

PART 3: DATA QUALITY CONTROL

The fragmentary nature of the sources made it necessary to rely on reconstructed secondary accounts for most of the information on the variables.

The chief contemporary sources for the period (which were consulted, but not coded below) are fragments of Menander, *Byzantinische Geschichte*, trans. Ernest Doblhofer (Graz: Verlag Styria, 1955); Evagrius, *Ecclesiastical History*, eds. J. Bidez and L. Parmentier (London: Methuen, 1898); and an account by John of Ephesus, *Ecclesisatical History*, trans. Payne Smith (Oxford: Clarendon, 1860). The *Historia* of Simocatta Theophylactus, ed. C. de Boer (Leipzig: Teubner, 1887) is an account of Maurice's predecessors. Information about the variables very rarely appears in the contemporary literature. These authors wrote in the sixth and seventh centuries, all were Roman, and all, except for John of Ephesus, were pro-orthodox Christian.

Information from the following secondary sources was used in the historical sketch and the survey of variables. They are coded below: Percy M. Sykes, *A History of Persia* (London: Macmillan, 1930); J.B. Bury, *A History of the Later Roman Empire*, (London: Methuen, 1897), vol. 2; Norman H. Baynes, "Rome and Armenia in the Fourth Century," *English Historical Review*, 1910; George Ostrogorsky, *History of the Byzantine State* (Oxford: Basil Blackwell, 1956); Charles Diehl, *Justinien et la civilisation byzantine au VIe siècle* (New York: Burt Franklin, 1960); and *Byzantium: Greatness and Decline*, trans. Naomi Walford (New Brunswick: Rutgers University Press, 1957); A.A. Vasiliev, *History of the Byzantine Empire* (Madison: University of Wisconsin Press, 1964); Arthur Christensen, *L'Iran sous les Sassanides* (Copenhagen: Munksgaard, 1944); Martin J. Higgins, "International Relations at the Close of the Sixth Century," *Catholic Historical Review*, 27 (1941), and *The Persian War of the Emperor Maurice* (Washington, D.C.: Catholic University of America, 1939); *The Cambridge Medieval History*, vol. 2, chapter 9.

Publication Year. These sources were compiled from 1889 to 1964. Coded *present.*

Primary Source. All are secondary sources. Coded *absent.*

Authors' Associations. None of the authors coded were members of either the Persian state or the Byzantine Empire—or their present day successors. Coded *absent.*

Authors' Sympathies. Both Sykes and Christensen were writing on Persia and were sympathetic to Persia, but since much of their source material for this time was dependent on Byzantine writers, the full Persian side of the controversy is difficult to recount. The others have sympathy for the Byzantines, and while attempting to be objective, are influenced by the source material. The sympathies generally tend to favor the Byzantine Empire. Coded *present.*

Authors' Proximity. At least thirteen hundred years removed. Coded *absent.*

CHAPTER 15

★ ★ ★

A DECADE OF NEGOTIATIONS

1276-1285: Conspicuous State, France; Conspicuous Rival, England.

PART 1: SKETCH OF HISTORICAL SETTING (Chiefly after *The Cambridge Medieval History*, vol. 6; T.F. Tout; Powicke; and Langlois)

IN THE DECADE from 1276 to 85, France has to be classed as the dominant political force on the European scene. This position had only recently been achieved, due in part to the personality and actions of Louis IX, the saintly king of France who ruled from 1226 to 1270. External circumstances also played their part. The Holy Roman Empire had been torn to pieces in the struggle of the Hohenstaufens with the papacy. Italy was divided into several segments unable to compete with the developing national monarchs. The Spanish states were just beginning to assert themselves on the European scene. Constantinople had been conquered by the crusaders early in the century and even after it again achieved independence, it would not be classed as a great power. Moreover, Louis also benefitted from the schemes of his brother, Charles of Anjou, who was expanding his power into Italy and the eastern Empire. In effect no European state was able to match the growing might of France. England had been weakened by the internal discontent during the reign of King John and by the minority and difficulties of Henry III. England was still the hereditary enemy, and by the end of the decade under study had once again become the most conspicuous rival. The rivalry between England and France was caused mainly by the English claims to various territories on the continent over which the king of France claimed overlordship. The rival claims made peace difficult between the two, and their relationships ranged from hot to cold wars with intermittent thaws. England and France went to war several times in the thirteenth century, and in the fourteenth they became involved in the Hundred Years War.

From the year 1214, when king John's attempt to recapture his confiscated French territories had been defeated, the foreign relations between the two countries had been regulated by a series of truces. The first of these truces, a six-year one, had been negotiated by king John and the French king, Philip Augustus, in 1214. In spite of the truce, French forces had attempted to invade England in 1216. The invasion arose over John's difficulty with the pope, his nobles, and the English people themselves. The pope had preached a crusade against John, and Philip Augustus had willingly supported the effort. The expedition was led by Philip's son, Louis, who was supported by many of the rebellious English nobles. John managed to come to terms with the pope, and prevented part of the expedition from sailing. Louis himself withdrew in 1217 after the death of John both because of papal opposition and because of his inability to win decisively.

Between 1217 and 1259, there were several periods of official warfare between the two powers owing to failure to renew truces, or in one instance to a denunciation of an existing truce. War broke out between 1224 and 1227; 1229 and 1231; and 1242 and 1243. Fighting, even during the period of open hostilities, was not continuous. Expensive expeditions were mounted but little happened to arrest the growing strength of France. England was also plagued by French-aided rebellions in Gascony, the one continental area which England still controlled.

When all of this has been said, it would appear that neither Henry III (1216–1272) nor Louis IX had any real desire for war. Their wives were sisters, they were personally friendly, and each had a reputation for desiring peace. Louis would have preferred to fight "for the greater glory of God" in a crusade against the Muslims than to fight his fellow king and vassal. As for Henry, he had his troubles at home, on his border with Scotland and his border with Wales; and abroad Gascony was almost continually in rebellion. By 1248 Henry held only a small part of the duchy of Gascony which he claimed. In this extremity, Henry appointed Simon de Monfort as seneschal (or governor) of Gascony with full powers for a term of seven years. Using strong-arm methods, Simon brought the duchy under control; but in spite of his effectiveness he became estranged from Henry who relieved him of his command in 1252. Henry then went to Gascony himself where a new truce with France enabled him to reassert his control. To consolidate his position, he gave the duchy to his son Edward, later Edward I, who had been born in 1239.

In the years from 1258 to 59, many of the points at issue between England and France were seemingly decided at the conference table. Negotiations between Henry and Louis had begun as early as 1257, but were speeded up by the Baron's War in England. Preliminary ratifications were exchanged in the summer of 1259, but the formal acceptance did not take place until Henry went to Paris at the end of the year. Henry abandoned his claims to Normandy, Anjou, Maine, Touraine, and Poitou, and agreed to hold Gascony (also known as Aquitaine) as a fief of the French crown. Louis, for his part, agreed to cede territory which he personally held in three dioceses (Limoges, Cahors, and Perigueux) as a fief of England. The French king also agreed to hand over to Henry certain districts held by Alfonse of Poitiers (Louis's brother) and his wife, Joan of Toulouse, in the event these two died without heirs. These districts included Agen and the Agenais, Saintogne south of the Charente, and possibly the whole of Quercy if it could be shown that Quercy had in fact been given by King Richard of England to his sister Joan, grandmother of the present Joan of Poitiers. Louis in addition promised to pay Henry the sum necessary to maintain five hundred knights for two years.

In actuality Louis had ceded very little: Alfonse and his wife were still alive and likely to live many years. The territory which Louis held in the three dioceses did not amount to very much, and even in Gascony the townspeople had to take an oath to the French king in which they pledged themselves to aid France against England in case the English broke any provisions of the treaty. Henry also remained a vassal of the French king and, as a peer of France, was susceptible to French interference. Henry, however, was in no position to object. In fact he spent the French money to mount an offensive against his own reluctant subjects.

Obviously there was still a great deal of antagonism between the two monarchs, which increased when Louis did not turn over the ceded territory in the dioceses of Limoges, Cahors, and Perigueux.

The strained relationships continued under the successors of Louis and Henry, Phillip III (1270–1285), and Edward I (1272–1307). Though nominal friends, the two cousins actually got along, according to one French chronicler, as well as a dog and a cat. Philip III did nothing to ease the tension when, on the death of Alphonse of Poitiers, he refused to cede the agreed territory to England. Edward in turn, when it came time for him to pay homage (promise loyalty) to Philip for those territories he held from the French crown, did so very ambiguously by giving homage for all the land which he ought to have held. There was even the implication that Edward intended to revive his suppressed claim to Normandy.

After a brief meeting with his cousin Philip, Edward went to Gascony to quiet a rebellion there. No sooner had he moved effectively against Gaston of Bearn, his most troublesome vassal, than Gaston, relying on feudal custom, appealed to the French king for a hearing. Philip accepted the appeal and ordered Edward to desist from further actions against Gaston until the case was decided. Edward formally complied—as both kings fell back on the formalities of feudal law on a very touchy issue. Eventually it was determined that Edward had been in the right, and Philip advised Gaston to make his peace with the English king, which he did. Another decision went against Edward on his interference in a dispute over the ceded territory of Limoges, and as a result Edward withdrew his support of the rebels.

Edward in the meantime was trying to find some way of counterbalancing the growing French power. His activities in this direction have led at least one modern historian to regard him as one of the originators of the balance of power theory. While this judgment is reading too much of modern political theory into Edward's actions, he was certainly attempting to gain allies for any possible future conflict with France. In 1278, Edward betrothed his daughter to Hartman, the son of the Emperor Rudolf, the first of the Hapsburgs; but this alliance was later abandoned. Edward also moved to re-establish close relations with his brother-in-law, Alfonso of Castile, who was at war with France in 1276. Edward also made himself the champion of Blanche of Artois, the widow of Henry III of Navarre and Champagne, even going so far as to arrange for one

of his sons to marry Blanche's only child, Joan. The marriage was
opposed by the French; Edward countered by having his brother,
Edmund, marry Blanche. Though the French king maintained
control in Navarre, Edmund and Blanche ruled Champagne in
Joan's name. Edward's continental possessions were increased in
1279 when his mother-in-law, Joan of Castile, died, and his wife
became ruler of Ponthieu.

These events led to another series of negotiations and resulted in
the Treaty of Amiens, 23 May 1279. Edward gave up his illusory
rights to the three dioceses of Limoges, Perigueux, and Cahors, but
had his wife's claim to Ponthieu recognized and also gained a
portion of Poitiers. Agen and Agenais were finally ceded to him
but his claim to Quercy was subject to further investigation.

Between both kings there still remained an undercurrent of
hostility which periodically came to the surface. Relations began
to deteriorate when Margaret of Provence, the mother of Philip and
aunt of Edward, resorted to force to gain what she considered her
rights to Provence. Philip eventually had to pay his mother a
subsidy to keep her peaceful. Relations further deteriorated when
Edmund, Edward's brother, lost custody of Champagne to his step-
daughter's husband, the son of the king of France. Relations
improved, though, when Charles of Anjou, uncle to the French
king, was removed from the Sicilian throne in 1282 by a revolt of
his subjects. Edward had continually feared a possible attempt by
his uncle Charles and Charles's son to extend their control through
what is today southern France and Italy. Moreover since the
Aragonese had been involved in the Sicilian revolt, French antagonism came to be directed towards them rather than against England.
Philip was killed in 1285 in a campaign against Aragon. At his
death England was still no match for France.

When Edward went to France in May 1286 to perform homage
for Gascony to the new French king, he renounced his claims to
Quercy in return for a money payment. He also finally received
actual possession of Saintonge south of the Charente. In spite of
these agreements, the relationship between England and France
remained strained. Not only was the position of the English kings on
the continent ambiguous, but the peace was also endangered by the
growing rivalry between the two countries over Flanders. On 15

May 1293 an Anglo-Gascon fleet attacked a Norman "pirate" fleet off the coast of Brittany and defeated it. This in effect was the beginning of war, but both Edward and Philip IV at first attempted to confine it. During the negotiations over the incident, the English agreed to allow French garrisons at six Gascon strongholds. To cement the agreement, Edward, whose wife had died, agreed to marry Philip's sister; the offspring of this marriage was to rule the duchy of Gascony, thus separating the area from the English crown. In spite of the agreement, the French king began moving into all of Gascony, justifying his invasion on the grounds that the French parliament had condemned Edward as a defaulter, and the duchy was forfeit. The English parliament, in June 1294, resolved upon war.

The English were handicapped in prosecuting the war by a rebellion in Wales and trouble with Scotland. Moreover most of Gascony was soon in French hands and the monetary burden of the defense of the duchy fell almost entirely upon the English. Edward did manage to gain several allies in his battle against the French, and the war had several truces until it finally ended on 20 May 1303. Gascony was again restored to England; the two kings pledged perpetual peace and friendship. The success of the English was owing in large part to a revolt of the Flemish, who defeated the French heavy cavalry at the Battle of Courtrai (called the Battle of Spurs) in July 1302. In spite of pledges of peace between the monarchs of France and England, the basic issues remained unsettled, and within little more than twenty years the two countries were in the midst of the Hundred Years War.

In the decade between 1276 and 85 France, the dominant power, was interested in weakening the English hold within France by fair means or foul, but hesitated to resort to open war. The English king was reluctant to fight, in part because of difficulties at home. The French King had other war aims on his mind and was unwilling to go to war with the English for something that could possibly be gained without war. The family ties between the two always left an avenue of communication open during times of stress, and the issues were usually settled at the conference table. The decade seemingly indicates that two kings faced with troublesome issues but willing to negotiate can settle many difficult problems.

MAP No. 13

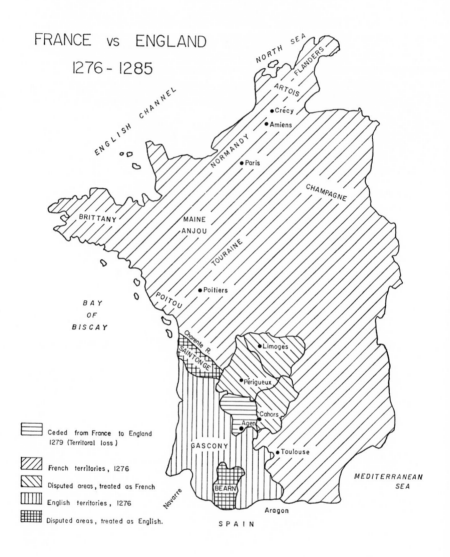

FRANCE vs ENGLAND
1276 - 1285

When Philip III died and was succeeded by his son, Philip IV, the French showed less willingness to negotiate.

PART 2: SURVEY OF VARIABLES (CODED FOR CONSPICUOUS STATE, FRANCE)

Dependent Variables

Months of War. The whole decade was one of peace, uneasy to be sure, but a real attempt was made to settle the issues without resort to arms. The raw score of 0 yields a standard score of 37. For method of transformation see p. 11.

Territorial Change. Both sides gained territory, but it was territory that had been disputed between them, and the territory was gained not by war but by treaty. The raw score of -1.3% yields two standard scores: territorial gain 40, and territorial stability 48. For method of transformation see p. 13f.

Military Variables

Defensive Stance. Both powers were in a partially defensive stance. The fact that the English held land from the French would tend to make France slightly more aggressive. Coded *present.*

Strength of Armed Forces. Probably the French army was larger than the English since the French had a greater population to draw upon. Both sides relied upon feudal levies but by modern terms neither army was very large. Edward led a force against Llywelyn in 1277 which numbered 6,400 men, of whom 1,000 were cavalry. For the second campaign in 1275 there are pay sheets showing that at times Edward had as many as seven thousand to eight thousand foot soldiers, with an average of five thousand. The difference in numbers is caused by the fact that the practice was to take on men for a fortnight or a month at a time, as they were needed or wanted. In 1339 Edward II began the Hundred Years War with about fifteen thousand men, but the English contingent was only about five thousand. Both sides also began to use hired soldiers or mercenaries at this time. Coded *present.*

Mobility of Armed Forces. The relative mobility of the armies was about the same, except that the English had a better fleet than the

French. It was during this decade that the French began an effective building program to match the English fleet. Coded *absent*.

Quality of Armed Forces. Probably the English had a slight edge because of their experience in the Welsh campaigns, and because oj the development of the longbow which appeared in these campaigns. The longbow soon became the dominant weapon and enabled the English to gain military supremacy in the fourteenth century. Coded *absent*.

Fortifications. Here the French had an advantage. Fortifications developed rapidly during this period and since successful warfare consisted primarily of taking and seizing castles, engineers and their seige equipment became an important part of any army. Both sides lacked the organization required to seize castles on any mass scale. Coded *present*.

Prestige. The general consensus is that France was the great power in the arena, at least within the context of the thirteenth-century meaning of that term. Some historians are of the opinion that Philip was the most powerful king in Europe not so much because of his own strength but because of what his father, Louis IX, had built up for him. By the end of the decade England had clearly emerged as the power ranking second to France. Coded *present*.

Geographical Variables

Propinquity. England was separated from France by the English Channel, but the English had territory on the European continent which bordered French territory. Coded *present*.

Natural Barriers. Although these were clearly present as far as the heart of the English or French territory was concerned, there were no natural barriers around the English possessions on the continent, over which most of the disagreements between the two powers took place. The channel, however, made it difficult for France to attack England on home ground without internal help from some of the peoples of Great Britian, especially the Scots. At the same time it was difficult for England to fight on the continent without help from some continental allies. Coded *absent*.

Capital City. Paris, although located in the heart of the French territory and well protected, was less than 300 miles from the frontier. Coded *present.*

Diplomatic Variables

Announcements. Both Edward and Philip, observing the proper rituals of a feudal relationship, attempted to keep the other informed of his desires either by direct communication or through letters or messengers There were almost permanent delegations of the English king at the French court. Each king recognized the other as a powerful and clever potential enemy. The English king was determined to avoid a full-scale conflict with the French. He probably thought it advantageous to avoid a war if in the long run he could get what he wanted without it. This trait is coded *no data* as there was no actual war during this period.

Surprise Attack. This variables is also coded *no data* since there was no war during this decade.

Alliances. During the decade under study the English gradually began working in a series of continental alliances. One such alliance was the so-called League of Macon, 1281, but whatever might have been intended by this league, nothing came of it. Part of the difficulty with an alliance such as this was that the thirteenth-century rulers could form great plans for international intervention but they seldom had sufficient force at their command to realize them. Edward did seek friendly relations with Alfonso of Castile, and he attempted to make a marriage alliance with the Holy Roman Emperor, and later made alliances with various imperial princes. The key French alliance of the period was with Charles of Anjou, king of Sicily; but the aims and ambitions of this coalition are not entirely clear to modern historians. Because of the ambiguous nature of this alliance, this trait is coded *no data* .

Active Diplomacy. There was almost continuous negotiation on the points of dispute. There were embassies in 1276, 1277, 1278, 1279, 1280, 1281, 1282, 1283, and 1285 dealing with the outstanding difficulties between the two powers. Coded *present.*

Intense Diplomacy. The negotiations tended to settle many of the disagreements and led to the treaty of Amiens in 1279, and to the second treaty of Paris in 1286. Coded *present.*

Previous Conflict. The two countries were traditional enemies. During the period 1217 to 1259 there were three outbreaks of war; again from 1294 to 1303 there was another period of intermittent war. Even during the peaceful interludes there were irritating expeditions and counter-expeditions which threatened to erupt more violently. From the French point of view, this animosity was in part owing to the fact that the English kings held territory in France for which they gave nominal allegiance to the French king. From the English point of view, the fact that the English king had to pay homage to the French king was a source of discontent to the various English rulers. Coded *present.*

Cultural Variables

Benefits. Since the English king was a nominal vassal of the French king, some of the knightly obligations had to be performed by both kings and in each other's presence. Although important in 1286, it does not seem to be so important in this particular decade. Subsidies played a minor part in this period. They were occasionally used by both sides, but the practice was not so widespread as it later came to be, in part, owing to the lack of royal funds. Coded *present.*

Cultural Exchange. The best evidence of this were the family ties between the English and French royal houses. Edward's mother and Philip's mother were sisters. Moreover, Edward's brother, Edmund, was the stepfather-in-law to Philip IV, who became king of France in 1285. These marital ties between the two kingdoms were further strengthened by the marriage of the widower, king Edward, to Margaret, the sister of the French king. In fact, the ruling Norman nobility in England at this time, including of course the royal family and court, shared a common culture with the French. French was their language; to the extent that they read at all, the people of both courts would read Latin books; they would hear the same oral literature (in French). Coded *present.*

Trade. There was a good deal of trade between the two powers, especially among their various possessions. At times trade tended to increase, rather than decrease, their traditional rivalry. One example of this is the case of Flanders. Although Flanders was nominally a fief (or possession) of France under French control, the Flanders area was one of the key trading areas of Europe and the English were especially active there. This relationship between England and Flanders probably jeopardized the one between England and France, since the tie between Flanders and France was not too secure and the English were interested in making it even less so. Flanders received much of its raw materials, especially wool, from England, but sold much of the finished product further south; thus the Flemish were dependent upon both England and France. Coded *present*.

General Exchange. As both "Cultural Exchange" and "Trade" are coded present, this variable is also coded *present*.

Administrative Variables

Experience of Ruler. Philip III succeeded to the French throne on 25 August 1270. He had been king for slightly over five years at the opening of the decade. Coded *absent*.

Youth of Ruler. Philip III, nicknamed Philip The Bold, was born 3 April 1245. He was approaching his thirty-first birthday at the opening of the decade. Coded *present*.

Unbridled Ruler. As France could not be called a centralized state at this time, this trait is coded *absent*

Hereditary Monarchy. Succession was by inheritance. Coded *present*.

Civil War. Both countries had internal difficulties, although during the decade under study England was somewhat more troubled than France. The thirteenth century is one of the key periods in the development of the English constitution; included within it are the troubled reigns of John and Henry III. During the decade from 1276 to 1285 there were still difficulties with rebellious subjects; but most of the strife was connected with Wales and its princes Llywelyn and David, nominal vassals to the English king. The Welsh rose in revolt in 1276 and 1285; each time it took about a year to put down the revolt. The French court was full of intrigue. Peter de la Broce was a troublesome subject, and later Flanders rose in revolt; there were also periodic revolts of the French communes, but in general the decade was somewhat quieter in France than in England. Coded *present*.

Centralization. In formal legal structure, the two states did not differ. That is, they were both feudal states in which all power descended from the king. In actual practice England was somewhat more centralized than France because of its smaller size and comparative isolation. The fact that the English king held French territory indicates clearly that France was not highly centralized. Neither state could really be called centralized. Coded *absent.*

PART 3: DATA QUALITY CONTROL

This chapter is based chiefly on standard secondary works. In general the facts are not in dispute, although the events have received several interpretation at the hands of modern historians. Our interpretation is based on the following works: *The Cambridge Medieval History,* vol. 6 chapters 10, 11, 14, and 22; T. F. Tout, *Edward the First,* (London: Macmillan, 1932); Maurice Powicke, *Oxford History of England: The Thirteenth Century* (Oxford: Clarendon Press, 1962); Charles V. Langlois, *Le Règne de Phillippe III le Hardi* (Paris: Hachette, 1887); and Charles V. Langlois, *Histoire de France 1226–1328* (Paris: Hachette, 1901). These works are coded as a group.

Publication Years. 1887 to 1962. Coded *present.*

Primary Source. The sources here are secondary. Coded *absent.*

Authors' Associations. The authors consulted were English and French, with an occasional American. Because of this variety associated with both England and France, this variable is coded *no data.*

Authors' Sympathies. The abovementioned authors attempted to be impartial, but it is felt that *The Cambridge History* usually indicates a sympathy for things English, as do Tout and Powicke. Biographers usually attempt to interpret their subject in the best light and Tout's sympathies are with Edward, as are Langlois's with Philip. Powicke is writing a history of England and so tends to look at things from an English viewpoint, while Langlois maintains a French viewpoint in his French history. The sympathies of the authors are then divided, but they attempt to avoid overt bias. Because of this division of sympathies this variable is coded *no data.*

Authors' Proximity. All these secondary works are at least six hundred years after the events. Coded *absent.*

CHAPTER 16

★ ★ ★

THE HUNDRED YEARS WAR

1376-1385: Conspicuous State, England; Conspicuous Rival, France.

PART I : SKETCH OF HISTORICAL SETTING (Chiefly after *The Cambridge Medieval History*, vol. 7; Burne; and Perry)

FROM 1337 to 1453 England and France were engaged in a long struggle—the Hundred Years War. The war was not continuous, but the reasons for each conflict remained the same. Basic to the difficulty was the fact that since the twelfth century, the English kings controlled territory on the continent for which they had to recognize a king of France as suzerain. From the time of Henry II to Henry V, every English king for over three hundred years was at war at one time or another during his reign with the king of France. The English kings wanted to retain their continental possessions but did not want to go through the ceremony of giving nominal allegiance to the French king; the French kings would have preferred to oust the English kings but, unable to do so, demanded that the feudal obligations be fulfilled. Adding to the antagonisms were at least three minor and predisposing causes: the English wool trade with Flanders, the French alliance with Scotland, and the question of the English king's rights to the French throne.

Flanders was part of the French domain but depended on England to supply wool for its cloth mills. When the Count of Flanders, Louis de Maële, imposed heavy taxes, the artisans of Flanders turned to the English for help. Countering the English influence in Flanders was the French alliance with Scotland, which prevented complete English domination of the Scots. While it probably would have been physically impractical with medieval communications and transport for any one man to have effectively ruled both England and France, Edward III was technically eligible to become king of France in 1328. Edward was the grandson of Philip IV (his mother was Isabella, daughter of Philip IV), and the nephew of Philip's three sons who had successive short reigns, each dying without an heir. In 1328 the French barons passed over Edward's claim to the throne, and selected a son of the brother of Philip IV. Edward was probably ignored because he was born and bred in a foreign country and was already a king, but technically the French refused to recognize descent through the female line. Edward at first accepted the French decision but later, when it was advantageous for him to do so, he advanced his claims to the French throne.

Since France was both richer and more populous than England, the English needed various allies to help in their war against France. The English wool trade ensured that at least part of the Low Countries would be English allies; to cement his alliance Edward III granted subsidies. Transportation of supplies across the channel and the equipment of men added to England's expenses. Although England and her allies probably never had more than twenty thousand men in the field at any one time, the cost of supporting even this number of troops for long periods was beyond the resources of medieval England; the English kings did not have and could not collect the means to keep an army of this size in the field for more than a few months at a time.

While the French at the beginning of the war were more numerous, the English were better soldiers because they had been more accustomed to fighting and were more professional. The crossbow, powerful at short range, as well as the longbow with its greater range and accuracy and its capability of more rapid fire power than the crossbow, were available to the English. Chiefly because of the longbow and better generalship, the English were able to win significant victories over the French at Crecy in 1346 and Poitiers in 1356. But despite such victories the English did not have the resources to garrison the country they raided; even after successful engagements and great victories, they often had to retreat to their bases.

The cost of war was also increasing because of the changing of warfare. The Hundred Years War saw a radical change in military tactics: the day of the feudal horseman was nearly over, effectively neutralized by the longbow. Feudal levies were still important but armed infantry, the key to the English victories, was costly. Warfare had also become heavily weighted in favor of defense; to take offensive action against well-defended cities or castles with well-entrenched archers was to court almost certain disaster. Cannon had begun to be used in seige warfare but firearms had not yet assumed the importance they later had in the fifteenth century. This modified war was carried on in spurts and starts interspersed with truces, armistices, and negotiations.

While there had been several interruptions in the war before 1360, the Treaty of Bretigny brought a longer halt to the war. Through this treaty Edward III, king of England, and his heirs became sovereign over about one-third of the land of France. The abolition of homage due by one king to another was thus calculated to heal the running sore that had sickened the relations of the two neighbors for two centuries. The peace, which was unfavorable to France, had come about through the English victories and through the capture of the French king, John. In return for his freedom and the renunciation by Edward of his rights to the French throne, John gave up French claims to English territory (in France) and agreed to pay a ranson of four hundred thousand pounds. But while peace had been agreed to on paper, the enforcement of the terms was another thing since the treaty involved the actual transference of several provinces of France to England and the withdrawal of French troops from English territory as well as the reverse. These withdrawals proved difficult to accomplish, in part because of mutual suspicion, and in part because John's son and heir, the future Charles V, was unwilling to recognize the loss of his patrimony. Fighting, in effect, never entirely ceased.

There were also other difficulties. In Brittany there was almost a civil war between two rival claimants to the duchy, one sponsored by the English and the other by the French. But it was a struggle over the throne of Castile which led to a renewal of hostilities. King Pedro appealed for help to the English to reestablish himself on the throne which his bastard half-brother, Henry of Trastianare, had seized. Edward, Duke of Aquitaine, better known as the Black Prince, came to his aid. Although the Black Prince defeated the usurper, he gained only trouble from this Spanish campaign; he antagonized the Castilians and received no money from Pedro (who was later murdered by his half-brother). More seriously, Edward's intervention led to trouble in Aquitaine since in order to mount the expedition he had imposed heavy taxes which were granted only over considerable opposition. Some of the discontented nobles appealed over Edward's head to his father, the king of England, against these taxes. Before receiving a reply they also appealed to the king of France, who theoretically no longer had any jurisdiction over the area. Charles V's lawyers, anxious to reassert French authority, convinced the ambitious king that because certain terms in the Treaty of 1360 had not been carried out, he was still nominal king in Aquitaine. Charles willingly heard the appellants, an action tantamount to declaring war on England.

On 30 November 1369, the French king confiscated control of Aquitaine, and the English either had to go to war or accept the decision.

Charles's action was not a sudden decision; he had long waited for an opportunity to assert his authority. He had carefully amassed supplies for war, enrolled allies, and begun a campaign to win over the various nobles in Aquitaine to his banner. Edward III, on the other hand, was almost unprepared for war, and in fact made many conciliatory overtures which Charles ignored. In a move to counter the French success, Edward III resumed his claims to the French throne.

War began again in 1369, with the issues much the same as they had been in the earlier phase. The French armies refused to meet the English armies openly in the field but instead attempted to win over the allies and vassals of the English. As a result no decisive battles were fought in this phase of the war, and even though the English army roamed the countryside at will, they were unable to mount any long sieges and even lost territory. The French alliance with the Castilians, anxious for revenge against the English, enabled the French to control the English Channel, at least to the extent that medieval ships were capable of controlling it. After several setbacks, an internal constitutional crisis at home and protracted negotiations, Edward III concluded a two-year truce at Bruges in 1375, retaining only Calais and a strip of the coast from Bordeaux to Bayonne under his effective control.

Shortly after the two-year truce had expired on 1 April 1377, Edward III, who had ruled England from before the start of the war, died. The ten-year-old Richard II, who succeeded to the throne, found himself involved in a costly overseas war and a bitter constitutional crisis at home. A royal minority was a tribulation for any medieval kingdom, and Richard's was complicated by the pressures of the war with France and the ambitions of his uncles. The war with France was very unpopular with the English people, yet there seemed to be no way to conclude it except by a disastrous loss of face to England and to the young king, something that his reign might not survive. To make matters worse the French had started a deliberate ship-building project which enabled them to raid the English coast and give the English a taste of what they had been doing on the continent. Rye and Hastings were burnt in 1377, and there were assaults on the Isle of Wight and other areas.

Papal politics also complicated the war. During the initial phases of the Hundred Years War, various popes had worked to achieve peace. Though the English were often hostile to papal interference (the popes were then at Avignon and not at Rome) it had often been a real conciliating factor. In 1378, however, the so-called Great Schism began, a period in which there were two popes, one located at Avignon and the other at Rome. Instead of acting as a mediating factor the papacy now tended to encourage the war by aligning one pope on one side and one on another. When France and Scotland declared for the pope at Avignon, England threw her support to the pope at Rome, so that the war between the two contending factions assumed some of the aspects of a crusade. In fact a crusade was even preached in England against the schismatics. When Anglo-French negotiations did begin again in earnest, the question of the schism proved an additional stumbling block, since permanent peace was only possible if one side or the other abandoned its allegiance to a particular pope.

The French also had leadership problems. Charles V's death in 1380 left the French throne in the hands of a minor, Charles VI—he was not quite twelve years old. Both the young kings of England and France were harassed by internal difficulties. The most troublesome event in England was the revolt of 1381 led by Wat Tyler and John Ball. In France there were similar outbreaks but the largest was the *Maillotins* (so-called because the rioters used lead mallets in their massacre of the tax collectors). Flanders was also involved in a revolt and here the difficulties were compounded because one side was backed by the English, while the other was backed by the French.

As the internal crises mounted, both kings made serious efforts to secure peace. A truce with Scotland was negotiated in the summer of 1383, and when Portugal made peace with Castile, the English seized the opportunity to open negotiation with France. As a result, on 26 January 1384, a nine-month truce was agreed upon. It was hoped that a treaty settling all the disputed points would soon follow and that a general disarmament might result. But there were difficulties remaining before a permanent peace could be agreed upon; one of the most obvious was that the truce with Scotland was to expire in February 1384, long before the armistice with France was to end. In order to continue negotiations with France, it was necessary to remain at peace with Scotland. Though the Scottish king was apparently willing to negotiate an extension, he could not control his border lords, who raided into England. It was only after the English had sent a force into Scotland in July 1384 that the two powers again agreed to a peace.

Even with peace in Scotland Richard had difficulty with a parliament somewhat unwilling to give him an open mandate to negotiate a peace with France. However, no sooner had negotiations begun than England's old ally, Portugal, requested help against Castile. Richard, unwilling to irritate France, yet hesitant to abandon a possible ally, refused a formal alliance but allowed the Portuguese to make private levies of English auxiliaries at their own expense. There were also large numbers of people in both England and France who stood to benefit by a continuation of hostilities. Inevitably there was a resumption of hostilities on 1 May 1385, with the expiration of the truce. This time the French carried the war to England by landing some thousand troops and a large amount of supplies in Scotland.

Although there were short truces, the war continued until 1396, when a formal twenty-year truce was concluded. By the terms of the treaty Richard II married Isabelle, daughter of Charles VI.

MAP No. 14

ENGLAND vs FRANCE

1376 - 1385

SCOTLAND

IRELAND

ENGLAND

London
Rye
Hastings
Colais
FLANDERS
Isle
of
Wight
Crecy
Cherbourg
Seine R.
Paris

BRITTANY

FRANCE

Poitiers

BAY
of
BISCAY

AQUITAINE
Bordeaux

Rhone R.

Bayonne

Avignon

MEDITERRANEAN SEA

||||||| English territory 1361

///// French territory 1361

\\\\\ English territory, occupied by France in 1375-85. Battlefronts changing, English losing ground.

English gain 1378

Source: Muir 1964

0   100
      miles

Even though Richard was soon deposed by his cousin Henry, Duke of Lancaster, the truce continued. France was much too distracted by internal dissension to mount an offensive, and the new English king was too preoccupied with consolidating his position to want the war resumed. The suspicions between the two countries continued, none the less, and after Henry IV died in 1413, his eldest son, Henry V, resumed the war. In the renewed struggle England was at first victorious: but it is in this period that Joan of Arc appeared, and the English were finally expelled from their French holdings (except for Calais, which was lost in the sixteenth century).

During this phase of the Hundred Years War both countries were suffering from such internal difficulties as revolts, financial chaos, and the problems of the royal minorities. As a result, even though they were often at war there was no clear decisive action. Unfortunately neither side could make the necessary concessions for a a lasting peace.

PART 2: SURVEY OF VARIABLES (Coded for Conspicuous State, England)

Dependent Variables

Months of War. There was an armistice which had been concluded before 1376 and expired on 1 April 1377; another one was negotiated on 26 January 1384, and expired on 1 May 1385, giving thirty months of peace and ninety months of war. The raw score of 90 yields a standard score of 61. For method of transformation, see p. 11.

Territorial Change. Although the English technically lost the disputed territory in Aquitaine in the two-year armistice concluded at Bruges in 1375, the territory was still in dispute during the decade studied and it was during this time that the French gained effective control of this area. Thus it is counted as territorial loss during this period. The raw score of -25.6% yields two standard scores; territorial gain 34 and territorial stability 61. For method of transformation see p. 13f.

Military Variables

Defensive Stance. The evidence regarding the stance of the two powers is ambiguous. England under Edward III had been the aggressive power. As Edward grew older, however, he was less willing to take the offensive and earnestly tried to avoid a renewal of hostilities. War broke out nevertheless. Coded *no data*.

Strength of Armed Forces. The French army was larger. It seems safe to say, however, that the armies of both sides were small. Medieval chroniclers, like more ancient writers, cannot be trusted on numbers involved in battles unless there is a great deal of supporting evidence. The English army which went to Aquitaine during the period was about twenty-six hundred strong. There were already other troops loyal to the English serving in France, and additional reinforcements were sent over. Most chroniclers estimate that the English had an army of about seven thousand men in France; this is probably fairly close to the actual number. The French had perhaps twice as many, but not all of them were actually engaged in any one battle. Coded *absent*.

Mobility of Armed Forces. The two powers were about the same. If a navy counts towards greater mobility, the English were probably superior at first, but by 1380 the Frency navy could match the English. Coded *absent*.

Quality of Armed Forces. The longbow which was used by the English army had greater range, was more accurate, and could discharge more arrows in a given time than the crossbow, and thus made the English superior to the French. The English infantry was also somewhat more professional than the French army. Coded *present*.

Fortifications. The cities of France were fortified, and France led Europe in the art of scientific fortifications. The more formidable the fortification, the less the possibility of counter attack: a heavily fortified area was almost impregnable to attack. Coded *present*.

Prestige. During most of the Hundred Years War England was clearly the dominant power in western Europe. This supremacy was recognized at the peace concluded in 1360 whereby England was allowed to control a good part of France. When the war resumed in 1369, however, England's position and prestige declined considerably. After the decade studied, England's prestige recovered and remained dominant until near the end of the war. Coded *absent*.

Geographical Variables

Propinquity. France and England are separated by the English Channel. However, Scotland was allied with France and the English held territory directly bordering on France. Coded *present*

Natural Barriers. The English Channel is an obvious barrier. In fact, if the English had controlled the sea during part of the decade they would have been able to carry on the war more successfully. However, there was no such natural barrier between the English territories on the continent and French territory. Coded *absent*.

Capital City. Both London and Paris were well within the territory controlled by their respective countries and were almost invulnerable. However, London was less than three hundred miles from the frontier. Coded *present*.

Diplomatic Variables

Announcements. Both sides were cognizant of the view of the other side, and in the decade under study hostilities were renewed after the lapse of a truce. While each side was suspicious of the other, the ultimate intention of each was clear to the other. Neither side, however, was certain that it had the resources to carry out its intention. Coded *present*.

Surprise Attack. Neither side was surprised by the other. Coded *absent*.

Alliances. Both sides relied on coalitions and alliances. During much of the war France was allied with Scotland and with Castile. The English allies changed frequently, but at various times England was allied with Navarre, Brittany, Flanders, Portugal, the pope (at Rome), and even the Holy Roman Emperor. At other times some of these groups were allied with France. Except when matters of self-interest or defense were involved, as was the case of the alliance between the Scots and the French, most of the allies were willing to change sides. Because of England's ambiguous stance this trait is coded *no data*.

Active Diplomacy. Early in the decade the pope worked consistently to bring about a peace, and even after the Great Schism in

1378 there were many periods of attempted negotiation. Unfortunately neither side could agree on the basic question of the English territories in France and their status *vis-à-vis* France. As a result the issue could only be settled by a military victory. Coded *present*.

Intense Diplomacy. There were several truces during this period. The armistice which had been concluded before 1376 expired on 1 April 1377. Another truce was negotiated on 26 January 1384 and expired 1 May 1385. However, no treaties resulted from these truces and no agreement was reached on major points. Coded *absent*.

Previous Conflict. England and France were traditional enemies, in part because of the nature of the relationship of the English kings with the French; this traditional animosity was increased by the English-French conflict in the low contries, and the French alliance with a hostile Scotland on England's borders. The Hundred Year War had started in 1337 and, while there had been several truces before 1376, the basic issues had not really been settled. Coded *present*.

Cultural Variables

Benefits. The abolition of feudal honors between the two countries temporarily ended benefits. Before this they were regularly exchanged. Subsidies were not involved in the relations between England and France, but they were an important part of gaining allies. Coded *absent*.

Cultural Exchange. Both the English and French royal families were closely related, as the English king's claim to the throne indicates. The fact that the English king was a nominal vassal of the French king kept the avenues of communication open between the two countries, as did the fact that many of the English upper class had interests on the continent and often knew and spoke French. Coded *present*.

Trade. England had strong commercial ties with the English territories on the continent. Flanders, an area politically in the French sphere of influence, was especially important. Coded *present*.

General Exchange. Both "Cultural Exchange" and "trade" are coded present; thus this variable is also coded *present*.

Administrative Variables

Experience of Ruler. Edward had been recognized as king of England on 13 January 1327, and was crowned shortly thereafter. He had been on the throne for forty-nine years in 1376. Richard became king in June 1377. Coded *absent*.

Youth of Ruler. Coded *no data*. During the minority of Richard II (1377–1382) parliament tried ineffectually to govern, partly through a permanent council, partly through itself, naming the chief minister of state. The situation seems to have been unclear at the time, with no one knowing where authority really lay.

Unbridled Ruler. Coded *absent* because "Centralization" was coded absent.

Hereditary Monarchy. Succession was based on inheritance. Coded *present*.

Civil War. Because of the demands put on the emerging states by the strains of continued warfare, there was persistent internal strife. This is evident from the opposition of the nobles on the continent who often switched sides, and from the difficulties of the English kings with parliament; but it is even more evident from the actual revolts which broke out in England and in France. The revolt of 1381 occupies a central part in English history of the period, and both John Ball and Wat Tyler are known to most English schoolboys, as is the slogan of the revolt, "When Adam delved and Eve span, who then was the gentleman?" In France there were many outbreaks, the largest of which, the *Maillotins*, took place in 1382. Similar revolts broke out in the low countries. Complicating some of the internal tension was the fact that both France and England were ruled by minors during part of the period, and minorities in medieval history usually provided an open invitation for dissident elements to express themselves. Coded *present*.

Centralization. In formal legal structure, the two states were very similar. In actual fact, however, England was more unified than France because of her smaller size, relative isolation from the continent, and strong-minded kings. During the minority of Richard II some of this royal control was weakened. Coded *absent*.

PART 3: DATA QUALITY CONTROL

Although the Hundred Years War has been much written about, the phase from 1376 to 1385 has been comparatively neglected. This study relies chiefly upon the various standard secondary works in English and French. The bewildering crosscurrents of the war present the historian with many problems; there is room for wide divergence of opinion on some fundamental questions, but most of the sources would tend to agree on the answers to the questions asked in this study. In attempting to explain motivations, objectives, and personalities there is no agreement either in the sources or the secondary works. Richard II, for example, is still a controversial king of England. Because of the essential agreement in biases, however, the various writers in *the Cambridge Medieval History*, vol. 8 (chapters 12, 13, 15, and 23), Alfred H. Burne, *The Agincourt War* (Fairlawn, N.J.: Essential Books, 1956), and Edouard Perroy, *The Hundred Years War* (London: Eyre and Spottiswood, 1951) can be coded together.

Publication Years. 1930 to 1956. Coded *present.*

Primary Source. These are secondary works. Coded *absent.*

Authors' Associations. The writers of *The Cambridge Medieval History* and Burne are English, while Perroy is French. Coded *no data.*

Authors' Sympathies. They betray no special sympathies for either side and can be considered relatively impartial. Coded *no data.*

Authors' Proximity. They are writing over five hundred fifty years later. Coded *absent.*

CHAPTER 17

★ ★ ★

THE DUTCH REVOLT

1576-1585: Conspicuous State, Spain; Conspicuous Rival, The Netherlands.

Part i : Sketch of Historical Setting (Chiefly after Geyl, Motley, Merriman, and *The Cambridge Modern History*, vol. 3)

During the randomly selected decade from 1576 to 85, Hapsburg Spain was the dominant political power on the European scene, and Philip II, king of Spain, the most powerful of the European rulers. This Hapsburg domination was a continuation, albeit in divided form, of the power established by Charles V, who had not only been king of Spain but the emperor of the Holy Roman Empire as well. Charles came to believe that Hapsburg domains were too extensive for any one man to rule, and had gradually transferred the richest areas to his son Philip, leaving the imperial title to his brother, Ferdinand. By the end of 1556 Philip held the most valuable Hapsburg possessions in the Old and New World, including the various American territories, the Philippines, the Netherlands, Franche Comté, southern Italy, Sicily, and Milan. Ferdinand, who held Austria and Hungary, had been emperor in everything but name since 1552, when Charles had left Germany (although it was not until 3 May 1558 that Charles's abdication became effective).

The extent and wealth of the Spanish possessions made the Spanish ruler a feared rival of almost all the other powers in Europe. The Italian peninsula was almost completely Hispanicized, with only the pope and the Venetians maintaining a precarious independence.

Spanish possessions in the Netherlands (including Luxemburg) and Franche Comté cut deeply into what the French felt to be their area of influence; Spain lay beyond the Pyrenees, forming the Hapsburg Ring—an apparent encirclement of France. The Spanish influence seemed especially threatening during Philip's first years on the throne, for he soon married the queen of England, Mary I, and England had been the traditional enemy of France.

While it may be debatable to identify the power structure of the sixteenth century in national rather than dynastic terms, there was a growing tendency in the period to think in national terms; the revolt of the Netherlands must at least in part be considered a national revolt. Nationalism was complicated, however, by the religious obssessions of the sixteenth century which divided Europe into two armed camps, with Protestants on one side and the Catholic Hapsburgs on the other. There was at least one exception—Catholic France assisted the Protestants; it did so primarily to weaken the power of the Hapsburgs.

When Philip came to the throne of Spain no other country in Western Europe, except perhaps Portugal (which was annexed to Spain in the decade under study), was as free from the taint of the Protestant heresy as the different scattered states of the Spanish Empire. The inevitable result was that the cause of Catholicism and that of Spain came to be synonymous in men's minds. Spain became the champion of the old faith against the new–the leader in upholding the cross against the crescent. The religious divisions made peace difficult; to the average Catholic, Protestantism not only endangered his earthly life but his immortal soul. These feelings were reciprocated by the Protestants.

If religion was the dominant factor on the European political scene, politics still made strange bedfellows. The pope and the king of Spain did not always see eye-to-eye on the religious question; and Philip's father, Charles, had even sacked the Holy City of Rome during a dispute with the papacy, while Philip, the most Catholic of rulers, had gone to war against the pope. The chief rival for Spanish domination was Catholic France, and in order to defeat the Catholic rival, France willingly allied herself with the Protestant heretics. England, which had been a great power a few centuries earlier, was just beginning to reenter the international arena, at first as an ally of Spain against England's hereditary enemy, France.

England and Spain had in fact carried on an undeclared war with France before January, 1557, and a declared war after that. Mary, queen of England, was as devoted as her husband in the attempt to reestablish Catholicism, although Protestantism in England was much too strong to be easily rooted out. The hostilities finally ended in the treaty of Cateau-Cambresis in April 1559, although Mary had died before it was concluded. Philip then married Elizabeth of Valois, the oldest daughter of the king of France. This marriage helped to establish better relations with France. In the long series of wars between the French and the Spaniards which had begun in 1494, Spain clearly had emerged victorious.

Spain had also been engaged in various wars against the Muslims in the Mediterranean, and one of the ambitions of the Spanish rulers had been to mount a gigantic crusade against the infidel Turkish power. When the Venetians, who had always been strong for compromise with the Turks, lost their control of Cyprus in 1570, they called upon the pope for aid. The pope, in turn, appealed to Spain, and Philip was quick to respond. The combined Venetian, papal, and Spanish fleets won a tremendous victory at the Battle of Lepanto towards the end of 1571; but the victory came to little, in part because Venice had no wish to destroy the Turks but rather to gain concessions. The Venetians were also fearful of any increased Spanish power in the Mediterranean and in Italy. After the Venetians concluded peace, Philip himself soon followed suit and the so-called Turkish menace gradually disappeared from the Spanish consciousness.

In western Europe Philip sought to avoid aggressive action and to preserve the status quo after the treaty of Cateau-Cambresis. But there were troubled times during the period; religion, especially, provoked strife and dissension. England under Elizabeth moved gradually into the Protestant camp, tending eventually to match England against Spain in a realignment of forces. However, the disrupted state of France, plagued by religious dissension as well as by continual problems of young kings and the necessary regencies, aided Philip's defensive policy. In rapid succession several kings of France died without heirs. In this time of troubles Catherine de Medici, the regent queen mother, had to be fairly circumspect in her dealings with Spain, since a weakened France was no match for a united Spain. Even in the increasingly Protestant English camp, Elizabeth was playing a waiting game in order to maintain the status quo which was challenged not from without but from within Philip's dominions. It was in the Netherlands that his policy failed, and it was the failure in the Netherlands that led to the involvement first with England in the Great Armada in 1588, then with the other powers, eventually destroying Spanish predominance in Europe.

There are few events in history which are still more hotly debated than the revolt of the Netherlands; the historian who attempts to explain it can do so only with the greatest amount of caution. The revolt had religious overtones which complicated the issue, and it is only in recent years that historians have been able to see both sides of the topic. Most of the nineteenth-century accounts tend to emphasize the Protestant virtues and the Catholic vices, while the few on the other side tend to have an equally black-and-white viewpoint. In the last few decades a number of historians have tended to revise the old versions of history, but no one version is accepted by contemporary historians; the works of Peter Geyl, however, tend to serve as the basis for any future consensus.

In general the revolt began as a national one; that is, the residents of the Netherlands tended to regard Philip and his representatives as outsiders. Philip's father, Charles, had been born in the area and knew the people, but even he had his difficulties there. While the Dutch might have regarded themselves as subjects of the emperor, they saw no reason to give obedience to the king of Spain; from the beginning of his reign, they had indicated to Philip that he would have to treat them with care. In 1558 the States General had given the Spanish king a subsidy on the condition that it be raised only by their own commissioners. Once Philip made peace with France, the States requested that the three thousand Spanish troops in the area leave. Philip had also unintentionally angered the great nobles by redrawing the lines of the bishoprics in the territory and by eliminating many of them as candidates for the episcopal chairs; his reform also struck at the independence of many of the wealthy abbots who joined the opposition to him. Hatred for Spanish policy was further increased by Philip's attempt to introduce into the Netherlands the decisions of the Council of Trent, the Catholic answer to the rising

Protestant movement; these decisions led to a lightening of the organization of the Church and the formulation of a stricter creed.

As a result of these actions by Philip some of the more powerful nobility, under the leadership of the Prince of Orange and the Count of Egmont, organized an incipient revolt. The leaders included both Catholics and Protestants, since the edicts, hated by both sides, threatened the independent power of the nobility. As a first step in their organization the nobility in 1566 drew up a petition to Margaret, Duchess of Parma, half sister of Philip, and the Governess of the Netherlands, requesting that the Edicts be abandoned or modified. Some of the nobility carried the petition directly to the king himself in Spain. But public turmoil increased noticeably and before they received a reply, the more excitable Protestants, especially those in Antwerp, rioted. They invaded the churches and monasteries, seized and smashed images of the saints, and in general wrought havoc. Margaret, frightened by the excesses, formally allowed Protestant worship, but as the rioting action died down, a Catholic reaction enabled her to reassert power.

When Philip first heard the news of the riots, he dispatched his most noted commander, the Duke of Alva, to stamp out the revolt and reestablish royal supremacy. The Duke arrested many of the leaders who had petitioned the king, even though they themselves condemned the violence. In fact, most of those executed by Alva were Catholic. Margaret became so upset by the Duke's actions that she left the Netherlands, and Alva became ruler both in name and in fact. Some of the other nobles, including William of Orange, survived only by leaving the country.

In part because he had survived, and in part because he tended to think of the revolt as an anti-Spanish movement rather than a religious one, William became the leader of the rebellious forces. Although he had been a Lutheran in childhood, he became a Catholic at the age of eleven in order to gain his Netherlands inheritance; now he became a Lutheran again and shortly afterward, a Calvinist. But his conversions, while perhaps sincere, did not divert him from his policy of toleration. At first William's opposition lacked any real effectiveness. Then the Sea Beggars, Dutch national pirates who considered it their patriotic duty to raid the Spanish treasure ships, seized the seaport, The Brill, on 1 April

1572. Once they had the town they justified their attack by claiming to hold it in the name of William of Orange.

Other towns quickly revolted or opened their gates to the forces of the prince so that within a few months all of Holland and Zeeland were under the authority of Orange. Forces allied to William had invaded the Netherlands from Gelderland, and the Duke of Alva, fearing an invasion from France, was unable or unwilling to meet the invasions with force. The French threat, however, vanished on 24 August 1572 with the Massacre of Saint Bartholomew, when most of the French Protestant leaders who had been active in lobbying for French aid to the Netherlands were killed. Alva seized this opportunity to recover the lost territory. Before his campaign was fully successful, however, he was relieved, and a new governor-general, Don Louis de Requesens, was appointed. Requesens attempted to be much more conciliatory than had Alva so that the war lost much of the vigor and ferocity which had previously characterized it. Requesens, however, had to pay his troops from money raised in the Netherlands—a feat that proved to be next to impossible. His unexpected death on 5 March 1576 left a sudden vacancy in the office and the Spanish forces leaderless for several months.

Before a new governor-general arrived, the long-unpaid troops mutinied, turning against the very Netherlanders who had been assisting them and uniting all factions against the Spanish. The Council of State, acting in place of the nonexistent governor, proclaimed the mutineers public enemies and called an assembly. This assembly, consisting of the seventeen provinces of the Netherlands, agreed in November 1576 to unite their forces for the purpose of driving the Spanish soldiers and other foreigners out of the country—the so-called Pacification of Ghent.

The provisions of the Pacification of Ghent were accepted temporarily by Don Juan, the new royal governor-general in February 1577 as a necessary expedient. He soon showed his hand by seizing Namur and requesting additional Spanish troops. Philip sent twenty thousand veteran troops under Alexander Farnese, the duke of Parma, who proved to be an able commander, and, after he became governor general in 1578, a consummate diplomat. The duke of Parma convinced the ten southern and more Catholic provinces that their best chance lay with a return to Spanish rule. The remaining seven northern provinces, determined to gain full independence from foreign control, formed the Union of Utrecht. To this end in July 1581 the northern states solemnly renounced their allegiance to the king of Spain. The duke of Parma retained the initiative in military matters for a while, capturing Antwerp, Bruges, Ghent, and Maastricht and also beating off attempted interference from both France and some of the German states.

Despite the assassination of the prince of Orange in 1584, the northern provinces found it possible to continue the war successfully. While Spanish armies proved ineffective in the swampy and water-logged terrain of the north, the Dutch navy was able to go on the offensive. The Dutch success at sea was aided by the fact that in 1580, when the crown of Portugal fell vacant, Philip became king of that country in spite of some Portuguese objections. Consequently, the sprawling and ill-defended Portuguese empire across the Indian Ocean became a fair target for Dutch attack and plundering. Whatever their losses at home, abroad the Dutch gained unprecedented profits, so much so that it became advantageous to them to keep the war going. Their blockade of the Scheldt River, which diverted the commerce of Antwerp to their own ports and in large measure undermined the prosperity of the provinces still held by Spain, added to Dutch prosperity.

External pressures also distracted Philip, preventing him from throwing the full weight of Spanish power against the Dutch. In 1588 he lost a good portion of his fleet in an ill-advised attack on England (the Spanish Armada). This disaster was followed in the next year by the succession crisis in France—brought on by the assassination of Henry III in 1589—in which Philip intervened to prevent the Protestant contender, Henry IV, from gaining the throne. In sum, Philip was unable to devote his full energies to reducing the Netherlands to subservience. The war continued in an intermittent fashion (with a truce for a time after 1609) until the general peace settlement at Westphalia in 1648, when the independence of the Dutch Republic became an acknowledged fact.

During this period Spain was the dominant power in Europe. Despite the division of the empire, the Spanish Hapsburgs still had much more territory than they could easily control; and while

MAP No. 15

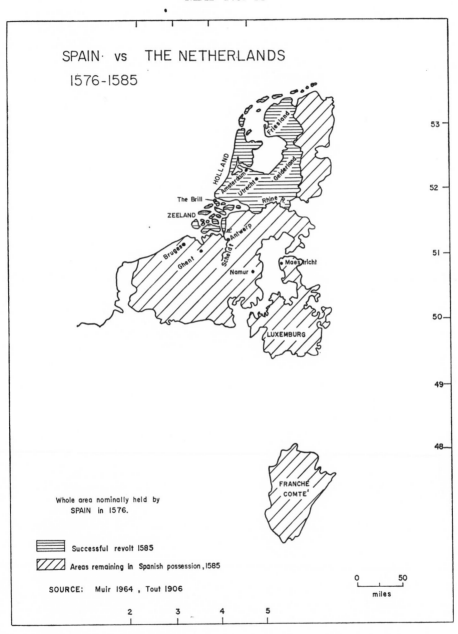

SPAIN· vs   THE NETHERLANDS
1576-1585

Whole area nominally held by
   SPAIN in 1576.

Successful revolt 1585

Areas remaining in Spanish possession, 1585

SOURCE: Muir 1964 , Tout 1906

Philip was certainly ambitious, his ambitions could best be served by the continued preservation of the status quo. Even during the decade under study Spain was able to take over the Portuguese state and possessions with very little difficulty, thus increasing the vast Spanish dominions. Philip's defensive stance was upset by the revolt of the Netherlands and by the religious divisions in Europe—as a good Catholic he could not remain idle or permit the cancerous growth of heresy to spread. Protestantism seemed to Philip an ideology which contradicted all that Europe had stood for. Eventually the two sides learned to live together although, as the history of the period indicates, it is still difficult for either side to look at the other entirely objectively. Unfortunately, it took almost a hundred years of war before each side was willing to admit the continued existence of the other. Even during the height of the quarrel, however, Catholics could be found fighting with Protestants as allies, and vice versa, so that national or dynastic ambitions were perhaps as important as religious ones.

PART 2: SURVEY OF VARIABLES (Coded for Conspicuous State, Spain)

Dependent Variables

Months of War. The revolt of the Netherlands lasted throughout the decade studied; there were 120 months of war. The raw score of 120 yields a standard score of 66. For method of transformation, see p. 11.

Territorial Change. At the end of the decade rebels held a small part of the Netherlands, perhaps as much as ten thousand square miles if all seven northern provinces are counted and an optimum figure is allowed. This must be counted as less than three percent of Spanish territory. The raw score of -2.27% yields two standard scores: territorial gain 38 and territorial stability 51. For method of transformation, see p. 13f.

Military Variables

Defensive Stance. Spain was in a defensive stance—the Netherlands revolted against her dominion. Coded *present.*

Strength of Armed Forces. Spain was the dominant military power in Europe. Spanish infantry enjoyed the highest reputation of the period, and the twenty to thirty thousand troops used in the Netherlands usually outnumbered the Dutch and carried everything before them. Spanish ships were less maneuverable than those of the Dutch or English, however, Coded *present.*

Mobility of Armed Forces. In theory the Spanish and the Dutch were about equal in mobility. However, in practice the Spanish were more mobile because of their superior training and discipline. Coded *present.*

Quality of Armed Forces. When the Spanish armies were able to set up siege equipment and carry on warfare in the traditional pattern they proved their excellence. Their preparation was thorough, their leadership and equipment superior, and they were able to maintain long sieges. Also, the Spanish military units were recruited from a higher social class and were better disciplined than any other contemporary army. Coded *present.*

Fortification. Although the cities were commonly fortified, the boundaries between the northern provinces which revolted and the southern provinces which remained loyal to Spain were not fortified. Coded *absent.*

Prestige. Spain was temporarily without peer, controlling Italy, the Netherlands, the Spanish peninsula, much of the New World, and the Philippines. France was divided by religious questions and the problem of succession. As for England, Elizabeth's position on the throne was still not secure. Coded *present.*

Geographical Variables

Propinquity. Spain was isolated geographically from the Netherlands for the most part by French territory. The easiest route was by sea. The northern and southern provinces of the Netherlands were divided by swamps and other water barriers. The Spanish could not control the north without command of the sea, and this they never achieved. Coded *absent.*

Natural Barriers. The hundreds of miles of territory controlled by France provided natural barriers between Spain and the Netherlands. Coded *present.*

Capital City. Spain and the capital, Madrid, were hundreds of miles from the Netherlands frontier. Coded *absent.*

Diplomatic Variables

Announcements. A petition of protest had been drawn up in 1566 and sporadic fighting had actually begun as early as 1572. However, the seventeen provinces of the Netherlands formally announced their intention to unite and drive out the Spanish in November of 1576 with the Pacification of Ghent. Coded *present.*

Surprise Attack. The intentions of each side were known to the other and neither was surprised. Coded *absent.*

Alliances. Alliances figured prominently in this decade. During part of his rule Philip was closely allied with England through his marriage to Mary. When Mary died he tried to continue the alliance by proposing to Elizabeth, but this plan did not work out. He then married the daughter of the French king, but the marriage did not lead to a full-fledged alliance. Later, however, when France became deeply involved in the religious wars, Philip allied himself with the Catholic faction against the Protestant Bourbons. Since the Bourbons eventually won the struggle, this alliance increased the animosity between France and Spain. Together with the pope, Philip tried to get a Catholic coalition against the various infidels, both Protestant and Moslem. He also had an understanding with the Austrian Hapsburgs.

In the Netherlands, the only hope of the rebels at first was some sort of foreign interference against Spain; William of Orange spent a great part of his time and energy trying to interest the French, the English, or some of the Protestant German princes in coming to his aid. During his lifetime and during the decade under study, aid to the rebels was always too little and too late. At the end of the decade, however, the English, spurred on by the booty of the Spanish empire, began to get more involved in the Netherlanders' revolt. This increasing involvement led to Philip's attempt to punish Elizabeth by sending the invading Armada. Coded *present.*

Active Diplomacy. After the revolt in the Netherlands occurred, Philip was able to negotiate several times with the rebels, but the negotiations always broke down—first on the religious issue (the toleration or establishment of Protestantism), and later because the Dutch were more interested in access to the wealth of the Spanish empire. Coded *present*.

Intense Diplomacy. There were no treaties concluded during this decade. Coded *absent*.

Previous Conflict. The fighting began in earnest when the seaport, The Brill, was seized in 1572 by a small fleet of pirates loyal to the prince of Orange. Because the war continued into the decade studied and beyond, this trait is coded *absent*.

Cultural Variables

Benefits. Although the Spanish king conferred honors and benefits upon those former rebels who came over to his side and lent him their support, he did not confer such honors or benefits upon leaders or other officials of the Netherlands. Therefore this variable is coded *absent*.

Cultural Exchange. Although the Netherlands and Spain were politically joined, there was little cultural exchange between them. The Dutch spoke either a dialect of German or one of French but were unfamiliar with Spanish. Philosophically, they had little in common. Tolerant, worldly-wise Erasmus, who was sympathetic to both sides of the religious struggle but opposed to intransigence, was the hero of the Dutch. Singleminded, Catholic Ignatius Loyola was the Spanish cultural hero. Coded *absent*.

Trade. The Netherlands, the commercial center of northern Europe, traded more with France, England, the Empire, and the Scandinavian countries than with Spain. The unwillingness of Spain to let the Netherlands share in the trade with the Americas prevented any real growth in commercial relationships. Coded *absent*.

General Exchange. "Cultural Exchange" and "Trade" are coded absent, hence this variable is coded *absent* also.

Administrative Variables

Experience of Ruler. Philip II ascended the throne in 1556. He had ruled for twenty years at the opening of the decade. Coded *present*.

Youth of Ruler. Philip was born at Vallodolid on 21 May 1527, the son of Emperor Charles V and Isabella of Portugal. He was forty-eight at the beginning of the decade. Coded *absent*.

Unbridled Ruler. Youth of Ruler is coded absent, thus this trait is coded *absent* too.

Hereditary Monarchy. Philip inherited the crown from his father, Charles V. Coded *present*.

Civil War. The struggle between Spain and the Netherlands was basically a civil war. The Netherlands had been acquired by Spain through marriage and inheritance. The Dutch people, however, had become accustomed to a great deal of independence and the ill-advised efforts of the Spanish to introduce an autocracy simply invited trouble. The only hope of the rebels in the Netherlands for long-term success was to carry the fight outside the Netherlands: the Spanish tried to confine it and prevent outside interference. Even when Spain made concessions, the religious issue complicated the picture; Spanish Catholicism had not yet learned to live with Protestantism and any long-term peace was impossible until the two were able to tolerate each other or until one had eliminated the other. Coded *no data*.

Centralization. Philip was an absolute ruler who had the highest possible sense of his royal prerogatives and duties. While the absolutism was limited by the monarch's inability to be everywhere and do everything, Philip tended not to delegate authority even to the most faithful of his ministers. The inevitable result was that much of his time was occupied with clerical duties and probably not enough with being king. Coded *present*.

PART 3: DATA QUALITY CONTROL

The sixteenth century remains a controversial century as far as historians are concerned because the religious wounds, while healing, are still sore. Only in recent years have Catholic and Protestant historians been able even to approach agreement on some of the outstanding issues. Further complicating the problem of the revolt in the Netherlands is the fact that the southern half of the Netherlands, generally what we now know as Belgium, remained under the control of the Hapsburgs. The interpretation of the period then is overlaid with national justifications on both sides. In English sources there is still another problem: Philip, who controlled the Netherlands, was also the enemy of the English and he had sent the Armada against them. Even the staid *Cambridge Modern History* vol. 3, chapters 7 and 9, tends to interject such terms as "sly" and "tricky" in describing Philip, while Elizabeth, his English enemy, is treated with adulation.

Much of the religious polemic has been eliminated by the recent study of Pieter Geyl, *The Revolt of the Netherlands* (New York: Barnes and Noble, 1958); he attempts to explain the continued independence of the Dutch in geographic terms and thus lessens the need both sides of the religious quarrel seem to feel in justifying their stands taken centuries ago. Geyl's work has achieved a great deal of acceptance in historical circles, but it is not unanimous. The interpretation here has been guided by Geyl, but many of the older histories have been consulted for information. The work of Roger Merriman, *Rise of the Spanish Empire* (New York: Macmillan, 1934), which was somewhat sympathetic to Spain; and John L. Motley's *Rise of the Dutch Republic* (London: George Allen and Unwin, 1929) have been utilized also. Little primary source material was consulted. Fortunately most of the deterrence factors with which this study is concerned are not much in dispute.

Publication Year. All are twentieth-century works with the exception of Motley which originally was published at the end of the nineteenth century. Coded *present*.

Primary Source. Coded *absent*. None were consulted.

Authors' Associations. The majority of works available in English are primarily from a Dutch nationalist and Protestant point of view—in effect pro-revolt. Coded *absent*.

Author's Sympathies. These are usually anti-Philip and pro-Dutch. Even Merriman, who is somewhat sympathetic to Spain, finds it difficult to see the Dutch revolt in an unsympathetic light. Coded *absent*.

Authors' Proximity. Most of them are three hundred or more years removed from the events. Feelings, however, still run strong. Coded *absent*.

CHAPTER 18

★ ★ ★

THE SUN KING THREATENS

1676-1685: Conspicuous State, France; Conspicuous Rival, The Netherlands.

PART I: SKETCH OF HISTORICAL SETTING (Chiefly after *The Cambridge Modern History*, vol. 5)

EUROPEAN INTERNATIONAL AFFAIRS during the latter part of the seventeenth century were dominated by the ambition of Louis XIV to extend the frontiers of France. At the opening of the decade from 1676 to 1685, Louis was engaged in a war in the Netherlands aimed at gaining control of the border fortresses which barred his access to the lower Rhine. Meeting only partial success, Louis made peace and turned his attention to the middle Rhine. Here he utilized a rather novel procedure called the Chambers of Reunion, which contrived legal pretexts for him to claim the jurisdiction he wanted. His success provoked another war.

Opposition to Louis was led by William of Orange, stadholder of the United Provinces and, after 1689, king of England. William was soon joined by Spain, and as the French threat became widely recognized, by Austria and Prussia. By the end of the century Louis was fighting against much of Europe. The deterrence situation is clear. France was aggressively attempting to extend her frontiers. She was opposed by the United Provinces (Holland), by Spain, and by a growing coalition of powers. Louis, however, often caught his opponents off guard; moreover, the French forces were superior, both numerically and qualitatively, to those sent against them. As a result the only counter for his opponents was to attempt to bring sufficient allies into the battle to even the match, whereupon Louis usually negotiated a peace. Occasionally public opinion could be brought to bear, as when Christian Europe was supposedly threatened by a Muslim invasion, but generally Louis recognized only force, or the threat of a coalition against him.

Louis XIV, whose reign (1643-1715) is the longest in European history, gave his name to an age which saw France as the most active and influential country in Europe. From the death of Cardinal Mazarin (the effective ruler during Louis's minority) in 1661, when Louis came into his own, until 1688, he acquired territory of enormous value for France in spite of considerable opposition. After 1688 Louis was opposed by a more effective European alliance, but at the treaty of Ryswick in 1697 France still stood forth as the most powerful of the European states. After yet another war France was much weaker (although Louis was still able to have his grandson recognized as king of Spain in the Peace of Utrecht, 1713). England, in the Peace of Utrecht, acquired Gibraltar, Minorca, Nova Scotia, Newfoundland, and the Hudson Bay region. Continental enemies such as Prussia had been considerably strengthened. Louis had exercised poor judgment. His acts had drained the strength of the French state and laid the foundations for the beginning of the progressive decline which ultimately ended in revolution and the replacement of France by England in the leadership of Europe.

In the period from 1661 to 1668, Louis claimed to be establishing the natural boundaries of France: the Rhine, the Alps, and the Pyrenees, territories which he claimed had either been included in the ancient Roman province of Gaul or in the empire of Charlemagne—whom the French regarded as the founder of their state. Louis in effect said that what once belonged to France continued to be by right the inalienable possession of the French Crown, though it had been sold, exchanged, or given away. He went to war against Spain (1667-1668) in order to acquire the Spanish Netherlands as far as the Rhine and its mouth; he waged his next war against the Dutch (1672-1678) because they had thwarted him in his plans; and the same was true of his excursion against Spain in 1683 to 1684.

In the decade from 1676 to 1685, France was at war from 1676 to 1679 and from 1683 to 1684 and nominally at peace from 1679 to 1683. Louis attempted by numerous diplomatic maneuvers to isolate his proposed victims through bribes, alliances, promises, and threats. He was aided by the aggression of the Turks which prevented the Austrian Hapsburgs from devoting all their energies to his defeat. At the same time Russia was expanding so that the Scandinavian states and Brandenburg-Prussia, as well as Poland, were often more concerned about the eastern than the western front. England's King Charles II, only recently restored, relied in part on subsidies supplied him by France. As the successes of Louis's diplomacy and arms increased, the other European states became at last more interested in stopping him, if only in their own self interest. The result was that many of these states began to make combinations against Louis which became stronger and stronger, eventually matching Louis's strength.

A key to the success of Louis is the number of coalitions and alliances he was able to form against former friends and with former enemies, and vice versa. He managed to isolate Spain from 1667 to 1668, but his quick success led to the weakening of his own alliances and the formation of a triple alliance of the United Provinces, England, and Sweden. Although he negotiated a peace, he remained bitterly resentful of the interference of the United Provinces, the instigator of the coalition.

In order to clear the way for his expected war against the Dutch republic, Louis worked to overthrow the combination which had forced him to make peace. In the case of England this was not too difficult. Charles II had probably joined the Triple Alliance in order to force Louis XIV to raise his subsidies. In fact he had already demanded a higher price from Louis, which Louis had refused. Louis and Charles came to terms on the subsidy on 1 June 1670, and the treaty, known as the Treaty of Dover, was sealed by the personal gift to Charles from Louis of Louise de Keroualle, an especially lovely mistress. Charles was to receive a pension of two million livres and six thousand soldiers in return for aid to France in the event of a war between France and Holland. Charles also agreed to establish Catholicism in England, a promise he had little intention of enforcing even though it probably agreed with his own feelings. Charles in effect accepted Louis's money with a clear conscience, rationalizing that the subsidies enabled him to do what he would have done anyway.

With England apparently settled, Louis now turned his attention to Sweden, tradionally a French pensionary. Sweden's potential enemies were Denmark and the northern German states, especially Brandenburg-Prussia, which aspired to Swedish Pomerania and envied Sweden's primacy in the Baltic. If Swedish Pomerania had been attacked by either Denmark or Brandenburg-Prussia, neither England nor Holland could do much to assist her, but France would have been a valuable ally. It was therefore not surprising that Sweden returned to her normal relationship with France. In return for attempting to close the Baltic to the Dutch fleet and for landing forces in Germany, Charles XI of Sweden received four hundred thousand crowns and a promise of an annual subsidy of forty thousand more.

Additional treaties were made by Louis with Munster, Cologne, Hanover, and Osnabrück which allowed for the unhindered passage of French armies on their way into Holland (since France and Holland did not share a common border) and for some Germans to fight in the French armies. Separate treaties had also been made with Bavaria and Brandenburg-Prussia, although these had not specifically dealt with the question of the United Provinces. The Elector of Brandenburg in addition received a subsidy for promising to support French efforts to conquer the Spanish Netherlands; Ferdinand Maria, Elector of Bavaria, helped Louis through a royal French marriage alliance. Faced with the rumors of some of these alliances and fearing a Hungarian revolt, or a combination of German princes against him, the Emperor Leopold at the end of 1671 promised his neutrality in a war against Holland so long as Louis abstained from attacking Spain or the Empire.

To further add to the isolation of the Dutch, the Turks appeared again in central Europe, invading Poland in 1672 and gaining control of the Ukraine. The Polish hero, and later king of Poland, John Sobieski, defeated the Turks in 1673; the French then promised him monetary support in his struggle against the Turks in return for *stirring* up trouble among the Hungarians, thus effectively diverting the forces of Austria and the emperor from the Dutch war.

Louis, by subsidies, gifts, and by convincing certain states that their own aims coincided with those of France, had drawn away from Holland most of the powers likely to offer aid. However, there were still some loopholes. In 1671 the Dutch and the Elector of

Brandenburg had signed a treaty, to become effective in 1672, whereby the latter would render armed assistance to the Dutch in case they were attacked. Spain had also signed a mutual defence treaty with the Dutch, and the Elector of Mainz was emotionally committed to the Dutch cause even though he maintained friendly relations with France.

The question that has to be asked is why everyone was so willing to go along with Louis XIV. At least part of the answer lies in the fact that most of Europe still regarded Spain or the Hapsburgs as the greatest threat to their growth and security. Even though France was predominant in Europe from 1660, it was France which had enabled the Protestant powers (Brandenburg-Prussia, United Provinces, Scandinavian countries, and even England) to fight successfully against the Catholic Hapsburgs in Spain and in Austria; it was France which had also supported the petty German states against the pretensions of Hapsburg control; and it was France which had helped secure the independence of the Dutch. To most of the powers (except the Hapsburgs) France was not the power to be feared. The Dutch had accepted France as their friend; even while Louis was making his preparations for the attack upon the Dutch, the Grand Pensionary DeWitt apparently could not believe that the French really meant to attack him. As a result the Dutch were unprepared for a land war, although their navy was among the most powerful in Europe and was particularly well adapted to fighting in the shallow water around Holland.

In March 1672 Louis left Paris, and on 6 April of that year he declared war against the United Provinces. The English had preceded him with a similar declaration. The Dutch fleet held its own against the combined navies of England and France, but the Dutch army was unable to offer an effective defense. An estimated French army (including allies) of one hundred thousand to one hundred twenty thousand men marched against the United Provinces from the south while the eastern side was attacked by way of Munster and Cologne. Unable to hold back the French army, the Dutch immediately sued for peace, offering Louis several key cities and a reward of some six million livres, but Louis refused the offer. The French advance was finally stopped in front of Amsterdam by cutting the dikes and flooding the land.

The Dutch then turned to William of Orange, scion of their most august family, making him stadholder, captain, and admiral-general. He immediately began to build the first of his many coalitions which during the ensuing thirty years proved to be the main obstacle to Louis's enterprises. The first coalition included the Dutch, the Emperor Leopold (of Austria) and the Elector Frederick William of Brandenburg-Prussia, but Brandenburg-Prussia was forced to withdraw. A second coalition of the Emperor, Spain, the Duke of Lorraine (whose territory was occupied by France), later joined by Denmark, the Elector Palatine, the Brunswick-Luneberg dukes, and the Elector of Brandenburg-Prussia again, won some successes by encouraging Charles II of England to abandon his alliance with France and make a separate peace with the Dutch on 19 February 1674.

France, however, still continued to win victories, due in part to her brilliant generalship and superior military organization. After the death of the great French general, Marshal Vicomte de Turenne in July 1675, and with the growing cooperation between the allies, the major successes of the French army ended. Louis thereupon made overtures of peace to William of Orange. Although the Dutch had lost their leading admiral, Michiel de Ruyter, and with this the initiative in the Mediterranean Sea, William declined to abandon his allies. In addition, the stadholder strengthened his position through his marriage to his cousin Mary, niece of Charles II of England. This marriage proved popular because English public opinion was turning increasingly against the power of Catholic France—reviving religious fears similar to those long held against Spain. Part of the marriage contract called for Charles to intervene with France to secure peace and, if the peace terms were rejected, for Charles to join the coalition against France.

Louis, aware of the peace sentiment among the Dutch people, appealed over William's head to the States General, with an offer of favorable terms. Six weeks of truce followed, during which there was agreement for a treaty despite the objections of William; he continued to fight the French even after the peace had been concluded on the grounds that he had not been officially notified. His victory at the Battle of Mons saved that territory for Spain.

Peace with Spain, the Empire, and another treaty with the Dutch were concluded in the period from 1678 to 1679 and are known collectively as the Peace of Nijmegen. These were supplemented by treaties between Brandenburg-Prussia and Sweden and between Denmark and Sweden. The war had started as an attempt by Louis to conquer and destroy the United Provinces, but soon developed into a European struggle despite Louis's attempts to localize it. Far from suffering a loss of territory. the United Provinces had gained Maestricht as well as a more favorable commercial treaty with France. Spain had ended up losing the Franche Comté, Valenciennes, Aire, Saint Omer, Cassel, Warenton, Ypres, and several other towns from the Spanish Netherlands. Even though Louis had further expanded France he had done so at the cost of arousing the suspicion of Europe; the attitude of the German princes towards France, for example, was very different in 1678 from what it had been earlier. But Europe was by no means united against France; the so-called concert was very poorly joined together and ready to fall at the slightest push.

Louis in effect was only temporarily frustrated and no permanent coalition had been organized against him. The Mediterranean remained practically a French lake; England under Charles II (and later under James II) demonstrated no real intention of opposing France; central Europe was still badly divided, and the Emperor Leopold soon had to meet a Turkish invasion. Louis quickly changed his plans. Before this time his chief enemy had been Spain, and, taking advantage of her weakness, he had enlarged and strengthened France on the northeastern side. Even his Dutch war had been an attempt to get even with that country for having interfered between France and Spain. But after the Peace of Nijmegen, Louis directed his plans against the Emperor and the Empire. Such a move perhaps resulted from a desire to succeed to the imperial throne, but it was also motivated by Louis's expansionist policies eastward. As soon as peace had been concluded in February 1679, Louis began moving against the Emperor.

Louis utilized the Chambers of Reunion to set the way for expansion. These Chambers were tribunals convened mainly in some of the newly acquired French territory. They assigned to France those areas which at any time in the past had been under French jurisdiction, a continuation of Louis's policy of claiming jurisdiction over any place which had even a tenuous connection with France at any time in the past. The Chamber of Breisach recognized Louis as sovereign of Alsace, and in 1681 he proceeded to annex Strassburg with the help of the threat of an army of some thirty-five thousand men. His attempt to take over Luxemburg in the same way was temporarily thwarted by the Dutch who were so hostile to Luxemburg coming into French hands that they were willing to go to war on the issue. Louis avoided a confrontation with the Dutch, fearing that it would probably have entailed another European coalition against him, and did not take Luxemburg. Rather than give the Dutch the satisfaction that he had been forced by them to withdraw under the threat of war, Louis said instead that he had withdrawn in order not to hamper the Emperor and the German princes who were awaiting an expected Turkish invasion. This allowed him both to save face and gain credit for a sense of moderation which he did not deserve.

William of Orange then acted to prevent Louis XIV from going any further with his acts of reunion. In February of 1683 he organized an Association against Louis which included the Swedes, the Dutch, the Emperor, and the king of Spain; but it was inoperative almost from the beginning. Spain felt that she was losing territory by inaction and attempted to prevent France from taking more Spanish territory through the Chambers: she declared war on France in December 1683. In this war (minor though it was) the English were kept out by a large subsidy, the Dutch by their long-time hatred of Spain and their inability to gain allies, and the Emperor by a Turkish invasion. The war ended with the Truce of Ratisbon in August 1684, where the Emperor agreed for himself and for Spain to a twenty-year truce and the French possession of Luxemburg, Strassburg, and Alsace during that time. Louis hoped that the armistice would be converted into a general peace, and that all the territories made over to him would become permanent possessions of France.

The Truce of Ratisbon marked a turning point; after this time France was opposed by an aroused European coalition brought about in part by the revocation of the Edict of Nantes in 1685, an action which ended the toleration previously granted Protestants in France. This action antagonized Protestants everywhere, most of whom had previously been inclined to be less fearful of "Catholic"

France than of the other Catholic powers. At the same time the action did not endear France to the chief defender of Catholicism, the Emperor, because of Louis's designs on imperial territory. Even the pope had been alienated by Louis's declaration of the independence of the French church from Rome in the so-called Gallican liberties. The revocation had even more serious consequences in England, which under the Stuarts had remained more or less neutral. With the advent of the avowedly Catholic James to the throne in 1685, however, English Protestants, in part because of Louis's action, were increasingly restive towards James's religion and towards France. Even before the revocation, the Elector of Brandenburg had made an alliance with William of Orange which the French action towards the Protestants only served to strengthen. Many of the German princes became even more wary about the actions of the French king, and the formation of the League of Augsburg in 1686 between the Emperor and his subordinate rulers is indicative of this wariness.

The strain of continuous hostilities began showing at home as the French finances suffered from Louis's ambitious plans. With the capture of Buda from the Turks in 1686, and the great victory of Mohacs in 1687, the Hapsburgs became hereditary rulers over Hungary and soon freed themselves from the Turkish threat. Thus, they could turn their attention to the west. The Catholic James was replaced on the English throne by the Protestant William of Orange, thereby changing the whole system of alliances. As a result, when Louis invaded Germany in September of 1688 to begin his seige of Philippsburg, almost all of Europe moved against him, although England did not formally do so until James had fled to France. The year 1689 marked the close of the period of French aggression and the emergence of a united European front against France—even though the French threat was not removed until the death of Louis XIV.

Thus, in the decade under study, France, an aggressive power, was able to move at will against any one power because of her overall superiority. She could only be stopped by a coalition of powers and the threat of a long war of attrition. In a war for a limited objective France was unbeatable. During this decade there emerged a coalition organized against France, but the ability of the French diplomats prevented the coalition's effectiveness until well

MAP No. 16

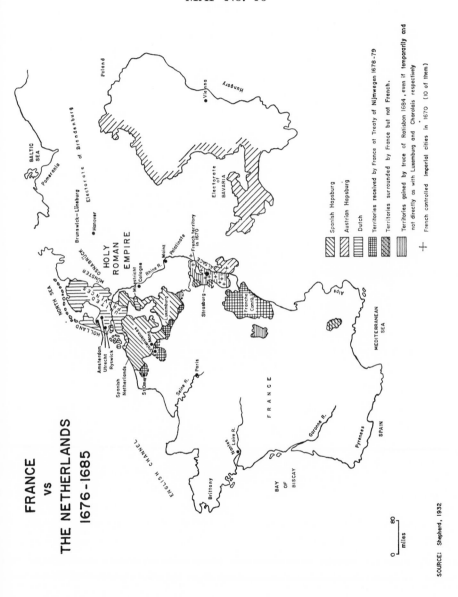

FRANCE
vs
THE NETHERLANDS
1676-1685

SOURCE: Shepherd, 1932

beyond the period. France knew her own superiority and was usually unwilling to forsake going to war unless a real use of force against her appeared to be in the making.

PART 2: SURVEY OF VARIABLES (Coded for Conspicuous State, France)

Dependent Variables

Months of War. The war was under way at the beginning of the decade 1676 to 1685. It lasted until 5 February 1679. There was then an uneasy peace in which France took several aggressive actions, but war did not break out again until 11 December 1683, against Spain. This war was concluded at the Truce of Ratisbon, 15 August 1684—technically an armistice according to our definition—(see p. 9). There were approximately forty-five and a half months of war and seventy four and a half months of peace. The raw score of 46 (rounded to make an even number) yields a standard score of 51. For method of transformation see p. 11.

Territorial Change. The French gained a number of towns and provinces during the period under study, mostly at the expense of Spain. The Dutch gained Maestricht. The raw score of 4% yields two standard scores: territorial gain 60 and territorial stability 53. For method of transformation see p. 13f.

Military Variables

Defensive Stance. France was clearly the aggressive power in an offensive stance. Commercially, however, the United Provinces and England were aggressive. Coded *absent.*

Strength of Armed Forces. The French not only outnumbered the Dutch but the combined armies of a good part of Europe. France had a peacetime army of nearly two hundred thousand men, a huge increase over anything of the sort previously attempted by the states of that time. No other king in Europe had anything to equal this mighty machine, and not even the Emperor could match the French army in numbers unless he had the cooperation of all of his German subordinates, something that rarely happened. Coded *present.*

Mobility of Armed Forces. The French probably enjoyed an advantage because of their large standing army and navy. At times, however, able opponents displayed more mobility, outmaneuvering the French, although in general the French probably had a slight edge over their opponents in this respect. Coded *absent.*

Quality of Armed Forces. The French had the best army. Turenne, the Marshall of France, has been called the ablest soldier in Europe from the time of Gustavus Adolphus to Frederick the Great, and the greatest military name after that of Napoleon (which may be an overstatement). In addition to Turenne, the French generals included Louis de Bourbon and Prince de Condé; there were other outstanding ones. The French infantry was the most formidable in Europe. The best indication of the strength and quality of the army is the fact that from this time on French influence became dominant in military organization, equipment, and terminology. Coded *present.*

Fortifications. The French excelled here also, largely through the work of Vauban, the military engineer whose fortifications retained their importance until the new weapons of the nineteenth century rendered them useless. His forts were held nearly impregnable in his own day, an important factor in a period when the capture of fortresses was considered the key military objective. Vauban was also a master at destroying forts of the French opponents. Coded *present.*

Prestige. France was without an effective challenger. As one modern historian has stated, France built such a tradition of excellence in the diplomatic corps that she gave all the European states a model. Coded *present.*

Geographical Variables

Propinquity. France did not directly border the Netherlands. In order to get to the Dutch the French made treaties with Munster, Cologne, Hanover, and Osnabrück. French borders were, however, contiguous with many of the Dutch allies, including Spain and the Empire. Coded *absent.*

Natural Barriers. These were not significant. France had no real geographical barriers except for the Pyrenees, and by 1676 she had acquired most of the area north of them. To the southeast the Alps served as a partial barrier and probably helped preserve the independence of Savoy and Geneva. The French drive to the Rhine was in part an attempt to secure a natural barrier to the north and to the east. Climate was much the same in the whole area, as was rainfall. Land mass itself was not a problem or a barrier since the largest area—the Empire—was not united. Coded *absent*.

Capital City. The population of both the Dutch and the Spanish Netherlands was compact, vulnerable to any attack, while that of France was much less vulnerable. Hardly any of the chief cities of the Netherlands were more than two hundred miles from the French border. The chief French city, Paris, well-protected by a series of fortifications was, however, less than three hundred miles from the frontier. Coded *present*.

Diplomatic Variables

Announcements. To the outsider the French intentions now seem clear, but there is no suggestion that Louis gave any formal warning. The Dutch in 1672 did not realize what was going to happen to them. The same was true of the Emperor in 1683 and 1684. After that time Louis's intentions, whether announced or not, were clear to all concerned; his treaties of alliance were clear as to his intentions and, while these were secret, many of them leaked to the enemy concerned. Coded *absent*.

Surprise Attack. Although the Dutch were indeed surprised that Louis would attack them, there was no tactical surprise involved here. Coded *absent*.

Alliances. This was an important part of French diplomacy. Louis made all sorts of coalitions, but they stayed together for only so long as it was in the interest of the various members to do so. The success of Louis's war with Spain in 1683 to 1684 was due in part to the fact that no real coalitions could be raised against him. However, France was neither in a defensive stance nor a member of a coalition directed against the Dutch. Coded *absent*.

Active Diplomacy. The Treaty of Nijmegen resulted from the French appeal to the States General; the attempts of the French to isolate the Dutch resulted from negotiation, and so did the various coalitions and alliances. France was the most active diplomatic power in Europe. Coded *present*.

Intense Diplomacy. The Treaty of Nijmegen was concluded in the period from 1678 to 79. Coded *present*.

Previous Conflict. Perhaps the chief reason for the initial French success was the fact that there had been no immediate previous conflict between the Dutch and the French. Most of Europe had regarded the Hapsburgs (either in Spain or in Austria) as the enemy and France as the ally. This situation had changed in 1659 with the Treaty of the Pyrenees, in which France replaced Spain as the dominant power on the continent. The French policy consistently was to consolidate and expand their power. This expansion had been previously thwarted by the Hapsburgs, who had thwarted most of the rest of Europe, also. When the Hapsburg menace had been lessened, France turned to other areas, ones which involved the Hapsburgs only indirectly. The Dutch and their allies felt that the French, in so turning to other areas, had betrayed a long tradition of friendship and support. Coded *absent*.

Cultural Variables

Benefits. Awards of honors were an important part of French diplomacy. While figures on the actual numbers of non-Frenchmen awarded pensions are not easy to determine, most of the secondary authorities tend to agree that Louis XIV utilized his pensions for political purposes. He also utilized subsidies to win over allies, and most of the minor princes of Europe as well as some of the major ones were dependent on French largesse. In addition, the English king was given a mistress as part of his agreement with Louis. Coded *present*.

Cultural Exchange. French ideas and culture were spread throughout Europe. The French language was spoken even in such German areas as the court of Prussia, as well as in much of Europe. French men of letters dominated the continental scene. The French granted pensions to men of science and letters, and of the first sixty names given awards in 1662, fifteen were citizens of foreign countries. German was not in comparable use since the rival court of the Hapsburgs used Latin and Italian as well as German as the standard official languages, probably because of the very diversity of the Hapsburg territories. Coded *present*.

Trade. France used commercial relations to supplement her diplomacy and war-making capabilities, as the commercial treaty with the Netherlands indicates. Coded *present*.

General Exchange. "Cultural Exchange" and "Trade" have been coded present, therefore this variable is coded *present* also.

Administrative Variables

Experience of Ruler. Louis was nominal king from 1643, but his actual personal reign dates from the death of the regent, Mazarin, in 1661. Louis had been king for twenty-three years in 1676, but in actual control for fifteen years. Coded *present*.

Youth of Ruler. Louis XIV was born in 1638, therefore he was thirty-four years old when he launched his attack on the Netherlands, and approaching thirty-eight at the opening of the decade. Coded *present*.

Unbridled Ruler. Louis was a hereditary monarch between twenty and forty-five years of age at the beginning of the decade studied (see "Youth of Ruler," above) and ruled a centralized monarchy. Coded *present*.

Hereditary Monarchy. Coded *present*. (See "Unbridled Ruler," above).

Civil War. Despite the centralizing tendencies of Louis and his predecessors, or perhaps because of them, there were periodic revolts in France. Some of these, especially in Brittany and Bordeaux, were peasant outbreaks. The greatest difficulty, however, was over religion. In 1681 Louis XIV issued an edict declaring that children of Protestant parents might declare themselves converted to Catholicism at the age of seven. In 1682 Protestants were threatened with dire consequences unless they underwent conversion, and at the same time they were excluded from most of the trade unions. The seething unrest of the Protestants periodically led to revolt, but the mass exodus of the Protestants and the revolt of the Camisards did not take place until after 1685.

The Hungarian problem of the Emperor was also an important factor in preventing him from acting promptly against Louis. Coded *present*.

Centralization. France was much more centralized than the Netherlands or for that matter than almost any of her rivals. Louis XIV's occupational role is indicated by the apocryphal saying, "L'état c'est moi." Under this autocrat France grew into an increasingly centralized state (although lack of rapid communication and transportation allowed for more independent action than would be possible in the modern centralized state). While the United Provinces could act in concert, there was much more independence of action allowed among the various provinces. William also had to rule in conjunction with the States General, which had considerable independence from the hereditary stadholder. Coded *present*.

PART 3: DATA QUALITY CONTROL

The chief difficulty with any study of the age of Louis XIV is the abundance of sources. The sketch of this decade has been based for the most part on secondary works by modern historians who, within the limits of historical scholarship, have attempted to be unbiased. Insofar as there is a bias, English historians generally emphasize William of Orange while the Germans give more attention to the Emperor or the elector of Brandenburg. No Spanish works were consulted. All the historians, however, of whatever nationality or religion, agree on the central importance of Louis XIV, and they also agree on the main course of events outlined in this chapter. The published documents of the actual treaties are as close to an unbaised source as one can find. The works which we consulted are: Peter J. Blok, *Life of Admiral de Ruyter*, trans. G. J. Renier (London: E. Benn, 1938); *The Cambridge Modern History* 5:32-63, 137-167, 338-371; J. .F. C. Fuller, *Military History* (New York: Funk and Wagnalls, 1955); Ernest Lavisse, *Histoire de France* (Paris: Hachette, 1911) vol.7; Frederick Nussbaum, *The Triumph of Science and Reason: 1660-1695* (New York: Harper, 1953); David Ogg, *Europe in the Seventeenth Century* (London: Charles Black, 1952); Laurence Bradford Packard,

The Age of Louis XIV (New York: Henry Holt, 1929); and Henri Vast, *Les Grandes Traités du Regne de Louis XIV* (Paris: Alphonse Picard, 1898).

Of these only *The Cambridge Modern History* was coded.

Publication Year. The secondary source coded was published in 1908. Coded *present.*

Primary Source. This study is based primarily upon secondary sources. Coded *absent.*

Authors' Associations. The leading source was English, although French and other national works were consulted. Coded *absent.*

Authors' Sympathies. Most of the writers were pro-Dutch, but almost all respected and perhaps even admired Louis XIV for his attempts. In general the writers in *The Cambridge Modern History* were somewhat biased toward the Dutch (since this became the ultimate English policy) while Ernest Lavisse was more sympathetic to Louis. Coded *absent.*

Authors' Proximity. The authors are writing two hundred and fifty to three hundred years later, except for the treaty documents which were contemporary. Coded *absent.*

CHAPTER 19

* * *

INTERNAL REVOLT AND FOREIGN WAR

1776-1785: Conspicuous State, England; Conspicuous Rival, France.

PART 1: SKETCH OF HISTORICAL SETTING (Chiefly after J. Steven Watson, John J. Meng, Arthur H. Buffington, and Vincent T. Harlow)

DURING THE DECADE from 1776 to 1785, Britain's position as the dominant western power was weakened. An inept government seemingly frittered away its influence in Europe. Thus, when the Americans finally revolted, Britain found herself isolated. France, the conspicuous rival, exacerbated Britain's difficulties by aiding the Americans. The French, however, were very careful to limit the confines of the war. It was a limited war for a limited objective, but even so it confused the French economic scene enough to topple the government into revolution.

At the Peace of Paris in 1763, which brought the Seven Years War to an end, Great Britain emerged as the chief intercontinental power. Although France still remained the major land power on the continent, the British gained maritime and commercial supremacy in both hemispheres and nearly eliminated the French overseas empire. France had ceded Senegal, several West Indian islands, Canada, Nova Scotia, and her claims to territory east of the Mississippi; at the same time the British had recovered Minorca from France and gained dominance in India. France had also agreed to turn over Louisana to Spain in order to compensate the Spanish for their cession of Florida to England. Spain, in addition, granted wood-cutting rights in the Honduras to the British. Frederick the Great of Prussia, the British ally on the continent, was to emerge as a major factor on the European scene.

The British could have demanded even greater concessions from France at the peace treaty in 1763, but as a result of a domestic political struggle for power, the British government was in a hurry to conclude the peace. In the haste to end the war, the British neglected the interests of their ally, Frederick the Great of Prussia. Although fortuitous circumstances enabled Prussia to conclude a face-saving peace, Frederick refused to have much to do with England during the remainder of his lifetime. In the aftermath of the war, the British neglected their navy, while the French, desirous of revenge, rebuilt their military might.

The British also neglected their alliances, with the result that they came to be isolated from the other great powers on the continent. France and Spain, both ruled by the Bourbon kings, had been closely tied together since 1761 by the renewal of a family compact; they were the open and avowed enemies of the country which had become such a great colonial power at their expense. Austria was allied to France, and the ties between these two countries had been strengthened by the marriage of the Archduchess Marie Antoinette to the future Louis XVI. Prussia, somewhat distrustful of France (and Austria), was still alienated from the British. The Swedish king was subsidized by the French. Even Holland, a traditional British ally, was hostile, in part because the increasingly ascendant Republican party looked to France for support in its struggle against the pro-British House of Orange. The Dutch were also angered with British commercial expansion, much of which had been accomplished at their expense. Russia was the only great power with whom an alliance might have been possible, but the Russians demanded subsidies for an alliance, something which the British regarded as an extravagance in time of peace. Also, Russia was expanding against Turkey, and wanted a British guarantee of assistance for further moves in this direction. Great Britain was unwilling to tamper with the status quo in the Levant where she enjoyed a lucrative commerce, therefore she was slow to make a Russian alliance.

France, on the other hand, was carefully rebuilding her navy, revamping her finances, extending her systems of alliances, and seeking an opportunity to weaken the British. War almost broke out several times, but Louis XV hesitated to commit his forces. This situation changed when the new king, Louis XVI, grandson of

Louis XV, was crowned in 1774 and chose the Comte de Vergennes as Minister of Foreign Affairs. All Vergennes wanted was a good opportunity for France to move decisively against the British. Such an opportunity came with the outbreak of the American Revolution.

From the beginning of their struggles with George III, the American colonists aroused the interest of France. Military adventurers as well as sincere friends of freedom hastened to offer their personal services to the Americans. To provide the rebellious colonists with much-needed military stores, the French and Spanish governments subsidized a pseudocommercial company headed by the dramatist Beaumarchais, an ardent friend of America. Vergennes only awaited a favorable moment, as well as the assurance of Spanish support, to actively intervene in the struggle. Unfortunately, no sooner had the Declaration of Independence seemed to imply that the rebellious colonists had gone too far to turn back, when news of the British successes in the campaigns of 1776 made the French cautious once again.

Unless the Americans had some prospects of success, France had no desire to get embroiled in a war with England. Thus both France and Spain attempted to aid the rebels in such a way that aid could not be imputed to them; at least this was the phrase used by the Spanish Prime Minister, Grimaldi. France, however, stretched her neutrality to the limits and proceeded to offer American ships an asylum from adverse conditions as well as the right to equip, arm, and supply themselves and to bring their captured prizes in and sell them—in short, to make the French coast the base of American operations against British shipping and France a partner in privateering.

The French king also had qualms about intervening too directly in the rebellion, simply because it was a rebellion. He feared that the British could then justify aiding the French Protestants, or any other insurgent group in France. Louis XVI had to be convinced that it was in the interests of France to aid the Americans, and that the danger of aiding rebels would be overcome by the advantages which would accrue to France. Vergennes argued that the first power to recognize the United States would have an advantage in the future; moreover, there was always the chance that Great Britain would admit the independence of her former colonies, and cut off any opportunity for France to benefit. With the Declaration of Independence, Vergennes could argue that the colonists were an independent nation, not just rebels, and had become, therefore, a suitable ally of France. Despite such arguments, Louis XVI hesitated until it seemed that the colonists might win in their own right.

When the news of the Battle of Saratoga reached France at the end of November 1777, Louis's reluctance was overcome, and the drafts for a treaty of alliance were begun; this treaty was signed on 6 February 1778. On 7 March 1778, Louis approved the Treaty of Amity and Commerce between France and the independent states of America. This was announced to the British government on 12 March, and on 19 March diplomatic relations between France and Great Britain were broken off, and the American Commissioners were presented at the French court. Great Britain had in the meantime attempted to reconcile the rebellious colonists. By February 1778 a commission of negotiators was authorized to go to America, but by the time the commissioners reached America in May the colonists were secure in the French alliance which had been ratified by the Continental Congress on 4 May. By June, France and Britain were engaged in active hostilities.

The War of 1778 to 1783 was unlike any other Anglo-French war. There were no continental complications; the conflict was purely maritime and colonial. Unlike earlier wars, Great Britain was without a single continental ally. The French system of alliances secured the benevolent neutrality of Austria and kept the peace on the continent. In April 1779 Vergennes was able to induce Charles III of Spain to declare war against Britain in return for French promises of assistance in the recovery of Gibraltar, Florida, Minorca, and the Honduras. Frederick the Great of Prussia, while refusing to receive American diplomatic representatives, remained neutral, thus making it difficult for the British to recruit mercenary soldiers in the German states. Russia in March 1780 issued a Declaration of Neutrality which asserted the most liberal principles concerning contraband, blockade, and the rights of neutrals. The Russian declaration made it impossible for the British to prevent France from securing naval stores in the Baltic. The Dutch entered the war on the French side after the British declared war on them in 1780, in part because of Dutch commercial assistance to the French, but also because the British believed there might be a secret Dutch treaty with the Americans. France and her allies were careful not to attack Hanover, the German kingdom over which George III of England was also ruler, an action which might have disturbed Frederick of Prussia as well as other continental powers.

British military operations in the colonies were handicapped by the unexpected strength of the French fleet in the English channel. Although the French navy was somewhat smaller than the British, it was concentrated, whereas the British fleet was dispersed all over the world. In fact, in the spring of 1778 the French were able to get to sea with a much larger squadron than the British could assemble. By 1779 the Franco-Spanish fleet outnumbered the British Channel fleet three to two, but their efforts to clear the Channel for an invasion of Britain failed, and thereafter France and Spain concentrated upon less spectacular objectives: the Spanish in Gibraltar, and the French in the West Indies and in the American waters. By the close of 1781 all of the British West India possessions except Jamaica, Barbados, and Antigua were in French hands. The French also made a strong attack in India, where they supported an Indian military adventurer Hyder Ali, in the state of Mysore, who was eventually defeated.

The French had intended to avoid employing their own troops in America in the hope that the Americans could hold their own with French aid, but the strains of war proved beyond the capacities of a poorly united colonial government. In 1780 the French government, on the advice of Lafayette, sent over a force of six thousand men which remained more or less inactive at Newport until a supporting fleet arrived the following year. A combined operation then succeeded in capturing an entire British army at Yorktown in 1781. Peace negotiations were soon begun but settlement had to wait upon factors other than the interests of the Americans.

After Yorktown the fighting virtually ceased in America, but continued elsewhere. In the West Indies the Bourbon powers received a severe setback at the hands of Admiral Rodney, who in April of 1782 won a great victory over a French fleet which was intended to attack Jamaica. The British lost Minorca but managed to cling to Gibraltar despite all the Spanish efforts to dislodge them. It soon became apparent to Vergennes that the exchequer at Paris

MAP No. 17

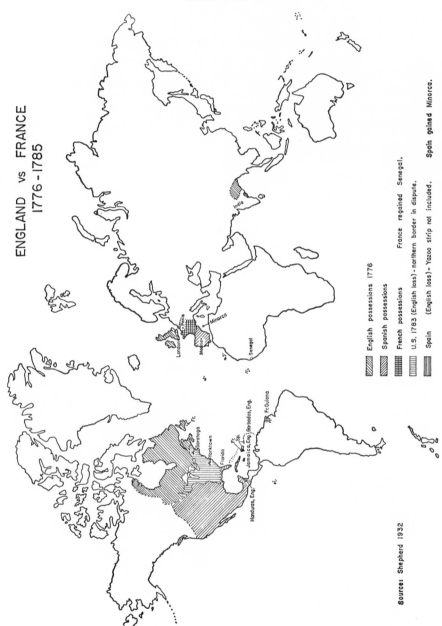

could ill afford further fighting which promised but small dividend. In order to appease Spain for the failure to retake Gibraltar, the French were willing to make some territorial concessions at the expense of the budding United States. The American negotiators, however, heard rumors to this effect just as Lord Shelburne of Britain began to explore the possibility of separating them from their continental allies. In 1783 he offered the Americans all the English holdings east of the Mississippi and south of the Great Lakes, land which Britain could no longer hope to hold, but which the Spanish from their base in New Orleans could aspire to control. This offer forced a settlement, the Treaty of Paris, with the British conceding independence to the rebellious colonies, yielding Minorca and Eastern Florida to Spain, but giving almost nothing to France.

Though the French gained an edge in the contest, Britain had been little hurt, especially since her business transactions with North America continued on an increasingly profitable scale. The war had put an added strain on the already shaky French financial system which was ultimately to prove ruinous. Unable either to raise enough tax revenue or to balance the budget through retrenchments, the government of Louis XVI lived by a series of expedients. The last one consisted of summoning the long defunct Estates General in 1789, thereby bringing on the earth-shaking French Revolution and another series of wars.

PART 2: SURVEY OF VARIABLES (Coded for Conspicuous State, England)

Dependent Variables

Months of War. France signed a treaty of alliance with the Americans on 6 February 1778. Diplomatic relations between Britain and France were broken off on 19 March, although the hostilities did not get under way until June. Preliminaries of peace with France and Spain were signed on 20 January 1783, and George III proclaimed a cessation of arms, as did the Continental Congress, on 24 February 1783. The definitive treaty was concluded on 3 September 1783. For the purposes of this study the beginning of the war has been set at 6 February 1778 with the signing of the alliance between the Americans and France, and the end is counted as the final treaty on 3 September 1783. This makes a total of sixty-seven months of war. The raw score of 67 yields a standard score of 55. For method of transformation see p. 11.

Territorial Change. The greatest territorial loss suffered by Britain was the American colonies. France and Spain gained very little territory. France had to be content with what she felt was to the British an irreparable loss, the newly independent United States; she was in no position to demand territory for herself. The raw score of -39% yields two standard scores: territorial gain 34, and territorial stability 62. For method of transformation, see p. 13f.

Military Variables

Defensive Stance. The British must be regarded as being in a defensive stance; they were defending their empire from rebellion. This in effect put France in an offensive stance. Coded *present.*

Strength of Armed Forces. Traditionally France had the larger army. Size of army, however, was not as important a factor as size of navy, since it was a sea rather than a land war. France had long had a navy second only to the British. In 1778 France had 80 ships of the line in good order and sixty-seven thousand seamen. Spain was also an important naval power and entered the war in 1779 with about 60 ships of the line. In 1778 Britain had a total of 119 first-second-and third-rated ships, but at the beginning of the war only 35 of these were manned and ready for the sea, and an additional 7 were nearly ready. By July 1778 the British had on paper some 45 ships ready for duty, but when these actually put to sea in June it was only with difficulty that 21 British ships could be made ready. Technically the British outnumbered the French navy, but the French navy was in much better condition.

The British army numbered about forty-nine thousand men and officers at the outbreak of the war, of which eight thousand five hundred were in America. During the war the French gave the colonists naval and monetary aid but until the end depended mostly upon American troops. At Yorktown, when the French troops were most in evidence, the combined armies numbered five thousand and seven hundred Continentals, three thousand and one hundred

American militia, and seven thousand French. The British Army that surrendered included over six thousand soldiers. But even after this surrender there were a total of twenty-two thousand British troops (including German mercenaries) in the colonies. In terms of the actual number of troops engaged in the war, the British out-numbered the French. Coded *present*.

Mobility of Armed Forces. The French and British were about equal. Coded *absent*.

Quality of Armed Forces. The French army and navy were probably better than the British, in part because British officers during the period were not a very competent lot. By the end of the war the British navy had begun to assert itself and it was then clearly superior. Coded *absent*.

Fortifications. The British seacoast was not fortified and neither was the French. However, fortifications were particularly important in the Spanish attempts to take Minorca and Gibraltar. Both of these were well fortified and Gibraltar was successfully held, although Minorca was lost. Coded *absent*.

Prestige. Great Britain had emerged in 1763 from the seven Year War as the most powerful European state. Britain gained greater maritime and commercial supremacy than any power hitherto had enjoyed and the very principle of the balance of power which she had done so much to develop and maintain was threatened—which perhaps accounts for the reluctance of many of the continental powers to come to her aid. Coded *present*.

Geographical Variables

Propinquity. France and Britain were separated by the English Channel (except for Hanover in Germany): the British king was also the ruler of Hanover, an area open to French invasion. During most of the eighteenth century whenever Britain fought France, Hanover was involved too. But the French efforts to halt the spread of the war on the continent kept Hanover neutral in this particular war except as a recruiting ground for soldiers. The war was in part a war for empire and both France and Britain held territory in the West Indies and in India where there was considerable fighting.

France and Britain also met in America where France was allied with the rebellious Americans. Coded *absent*.

Natural Barriers. The channel is obviously a barrier. More important in this particular Anglo-French war, however, was the ocean itself. Since Britain was defeated in the United States by the combined French and American army, the problems of fighting a war an ocean away were magnified for both sides. The difficulties of holding the landmass of the United States without a large occupying force also proved to be almost impossible for the British. Coded *present*.

Capital City. London is less than one hundred miles from the nearest point on the coast of France while Paris is over one hundred miles inland, making London within three hundred miles of the frontier. However, neither London nor Paris was particularly vulnerable to a direct attack. The most vulnerable areas in Britain, the villages around Dover, were not very heavily fortified, but neither were they very large. Because of the difficulties of mounting direct attacks on each other, both sides concentrated upon the ocean war in various parts of the world. Coded *present*.

Diplomatic Variables

Announcements. There was no formal announcement of intentions. Undoubtedly the British were conscious of the French enmity against them, since the French archives from 1763 to 1775 abound in memorandums, diaries, letters, and reports which were hostile to them. But the British did little about the hostility; they were perhaps too much involved in internal political maneuverings to take steps to prevent a French attack. The French did notify the British of their treaty with the Americans, but this was far more than an announcement of intention or a warning. It was tantamount to a declaration of war, and in fact led to the severing of diplomatic relations. Coded *absent*.

Surprise Attack. Each side was aware of the other's intentions to attack. Coded *absent*.

Alliances. Coalitions and alliances with continental powers had been the mainstay of British foreign policy *vis-à-vis* France. Because they neglected and treated badly their ally, Prussia, the British found themselves involved in the war with France and without a continental ally. In 1778 the British finally moved to propose an alliance with Russia, and were much surprised when the Empress Catherine rejected their offer. France on the other hand had carefully been building alliances which, if they did not involve direct action against the British, at least promised neutrality. Spain and Holland joined the war as allies of the French; while Prussia, Russia, Sweden, Austria, and others remained neutral or were "belligerent neutrals". Since the Conspicuous State was not a member of an alliance this variable is coded *absent*.

Active Diplomacy. There was little or no negotiation between Great Britain and France before the war started; during the war, however, there was a great deal. Through negotiation Russia and Prussia were kept neutral, and it was through negotiation that the war was ended. Negotiation between the Americans and the British began on 17 April 1782, at Versailles. Coded *present*.

Intense Diplomacy. The negotiations resulted in a preliminary treaty between the British and the Americans signed on 30 November 1782. A preliminary treaty between France, Great Britain, and Spain was negotiated by 10 January 1783, which resulted in an armistice. The final treaty was concluded on 3 September 1783. Coded *present*.

Previous Conflict. France and England were traditional enemies. The period between 1689 and 1815 is often called the Second Hundred Years War, because of the persistent strife between the two powers. In 1763 Britain was the victor over the French in perhaps the most successful war in British and one of the most disastrous in French history, the Seven Years War. In 1770 war had threatened between the two powers, but it was not until the American colonies rebelled that war broke out. Coded *present*.

Cultural Variables

Benefits. There is no evidence of the exchange of honors between the two countries. Subsidies were an important aspect of foreign policy; however, during the decade under study they were not used by the British, but rather by the French. Russia had been reluctant to ally with Britain because of the British refusal to give subsidies. Sweden had been in part won over to France because of the French subsidies. More important, the American revolutionists were subsidized by the French; France gave subsidies to the Americans even before she became involved in the war with Britain, and so did France's ally, Spain; in 1776 the subsidy amounted to a million *livres*. One of the main reasons the Americans were able to carry on so successfully was because of French aid. Since the benefits and subsidies were not given by the Conspicuous State, this variable is coded *absent*.

Cultural Exchange. The end of the Seven Years War had facilitated exchange of ideas and culture between the two countries, and an intellectual collaboration between France and Britain had developed. At Paris Anglomania went so far that plays and books were written making fun of it. The London newspapers, for their part, were justified in saying that London was the general clearinghouse for French merchandise. Even during the midst of the war there were still spokesmen for Britain in Paris. There was considerable exchange and translation of literature, Rousseau and Voltaire into English and Richardson and Locke into French. Most of the upper class British traveled on the continent, although fewer Frenchmen visited Britain. France was still a haven for English and Irish Catholics, although this was not as true as it had been a generation earlier, while Britain gave refuge to various French Protestants. Coded *present*.

Trade. Until the outbreak of war, trade was presumably quite active between England and France, who were both maritime trading nations and near neighbors. In addition to the legitimate trade, there seems to have been extremely active and important smuggling across the channel between the two countries. Coded *present*.

General Exchange. Both "Cultural Exchange" and "Trade" were coded present, hence this variable is also coded *present*.

Administrative Variables

Experience of Ruler. George III ascended the throne 25 October 1760 at the age of twenty-two. He had been king for some sixteen years at the opening of the decade. Coded *present*.

Youth of Ruler. George III was born 4 June 1738. He was thrity-seven years old at the opening of the period studied. Coded *present.*

Unbridled Ruler. George III was a hereditary monarch, between twenty and forty-five years of age at the beginning of the decade (see "Youth of Ruler") and ruled a centralized monarchy. Coded *present.*

Hereditary Monarchy. George III succeeded his grandfather, George II. Coded *present.*

Civil War. The American Revolution was an internal struggle within the British Empire that allowed France a chance for a return match with the British. The Declaration of Independence was adopted in July 1776, but the battle of Bunker Hill (really Breed's Hill) had been fought in June 1775, and Washington had been in command of the rebel forces since July 1775.

Another outbreak of civil violence occurred in the Gordon Riots of London, which resulted from efforts to lessen the political disabilities of the Catholics. The riots lasted from 2 June to 7 June 1780. Earlier there had been riots in Scotland over the same thing. The whole decade was one of unrest within the British area of control. Coded *present.*

Centralization. France in theory was a much more centralized kingdom than Britain, although in actual practice the French state lacked many of the features which we now associate with centralized government. Local government also counted for more in Britain than in France. Coded *absent.*

PART 3: DATA QUALITY CONTROL

The European wars which resulted from the American Revolution have not been much written about, in part because they have been overshadowed by the Seven Years War and the War of the French Revolution. This study has generally utilized secondary sources. There is fairly widespread agreement on most of the variables considered here, although some aspects are still subject to controversy. The reign of George III has, for example, been undergoing a restudy, but for the most part the particular aspect of British foreign policy from 1776 to 1785 has been neglected. The following sources were consulted but not coded. E. Malcolm-Smith, *British Diplomacy in the Eighteenth Century* (London: Williams and Norgate, 1937) and P. E. Roberts, "The French and English in India," *Cambridge Modern History*, vol. 6 (New York: Macmillan, 1909). The following leading sources are coded below: J. Steven Watson, *The Reign of George III* (Oxford: Clarendon Press, 1960); John J. Meng, "The Comte de Vergennes," *Records of the American Catholic Historical Society*, vol. 40, no. 4 (December, 1929); Arthur H. Buffington, *The Second Hundred Years' War*, 1689-1815 (New York: Holt, 1929); and Vincent T. Harlow, *The Founding of the Second British Empire*: 1763-1793 (London: Longmans, 1952). Because of their essential agreement these four writers are coded together.

Publication Years. These works were published between 1929 and 1960. Coded *present*.

Primary Sources. These are secondary sources. Coded *absent* (see "Publication Years", and "Authors'" Proximity").

Authors' Associations. Authors of English, French, and American associations were consulted and found to be in essential agreement on practically all the points at issue in the trait codings. Coded *no data*.

Authors' Sympathies. There was no special sympathy for either side. Coded *no data*.

Authors' Proximity. They were writing one hundred fifty years after the events. Coded *absent*.

CHAPTER 20

★ ★ ★

FIRST STRIKE FAILURE: SWISS VERSUS KIBURG

1376-1385: Conspicuous State, Swiss Confederation; Conspicuous Rival, Kiburg.

PART I: SKETCH OF HISTORICAL SETTING (Chiefly after von Müller and Dierauer)

THIS RANDOMLY SAMPLED DECADE in Swiss history presents us with a model of a deterrence situation which much concerns United States military planners today. Here we have a case of a preemptive surprise attack made by an autocratic state able to commit its forces to a morally disapproved action without notice to its enemies. The surprise attack was made upon a coalition of republics which could not make a similar attack because it would have been morally unacceptable and politically awkward. The republican coalition had to depend upon its second strike capacity, which was great—far greater than that of the autocratic attacker—and which included the introduction of a new weapon, siege cannons using gunpowder.

Here the attacker could not hope to destroy the second strike capacity of the defender. He could only hope to redress the imbalance in forces between them through the advantage of the surprise attack. The attacker, Count Rudolph II of Kiburg-Burgdorf, was the head of a decaying feudal house. The Kiburgs' difficulty was financial. Their income was chiefly feudal dues paid in produce, but to maintain themselves in fourteenth-century aristocratic style they needed to spend heavily; furthermore, to be an effective military power, they needed to supplement feudal levies with hired soldiers, and that cost more money. The Kiburgs had been forced to pawn or sell several valuable properties and were hopelessly in debt.

To get themselves out of their difficulties, Count Rudolph II in the fall of 1383 resolved upon a dangerous stroke. He looked angrily and covetously upon the town of Solothurn, on his northern frontier. For years Solothurn had been his opponent in a lawsuit over the control of two rural districts. Solothurn furthermore was a prospering trading center, and its walls lay within easy reach on his very frontier. He conceived the plan of capturing Solothurn by a surprise night attack. His hope of success lay in the unexpectedness of an attack, there being no public hint of the possibility of war between Solothurn and Kiburg. Since secrecy was essential to success, he took very few people into his confidence. Baron Diebold of Neuenburg was one; the Baron was to furnish him troops in return for 5000 gulden plus half of the booty of the town. Rudolph also gained the support of one of the clergymen of the Saint Ursus foundation inside Solothurn—this cleric it is said was to open a window of his house along the city wall to let the attackers secretly into the town.

Rudolph's need for secrecy prevented him from lining up support among his natural allies, with whom Kiburg had stood against Bern fifty years before: his powerful relative and feudal overlord, the House of Austria, and his numerous fellows in the feudal aristocracy of Swiss Burgundy, all hostile to the rising Swiss power. Solothurn on the other hand was an ally of Bern and Bern in turn was a member of the Swiss Confederation. It was rash indeed for Rudolph to challenge the Swiss power alone; doubtless he hoped that his natural allies would later join him—as it turned out they did not; they abandoned him.

The war began with an atrocity which embittered Swiss memories. The surprise attack on Solothurn failed; the townspeople were warned in time and manned their walls. The Kiburg forces, raging with frustration, took out their anger upon the defenseless peasants of the countryside, many of whom they hanged from the nearest tree. Solothurn now called for help from its ally, Bern. Bern in turn called upon the other members of the Swiss confederation; and a large Swiss army laid siege to Kiburg's chief stronghold, the town of Burgdorf. The Swiss were confident of victory, since they were equipped not only with the conventional catapults but also with the newly introduced gunpowder cannons. These new and terrible weapons did apparently make some impression upon the defenders of Burgdorf, who in any case seemed to be hard pressed. But whatever advantage the Swiss Confederation thus gained they lost through what the Swiss historians describe as the wily faithlessness of their opponents. According to the Swiss, the commander of Burgdorf's garrison asked for a three-week truce, promising to surrender at the end of that time if the siege was not sooner lifted, and agreeing not to strengthen his garrison. The Swiss, confident of victory, agreed; and the contingents from the Forest Cantons and Zürich went home. But the garrison, in violation of the truce, was reinforced and refused to surrender.

The Bernese forces, now alone in the field, could not reduce Burgdorf, so they turned their attention to the large number of castles in the neighborhood held by the vassal nobility of Kiburg. Many of these were captured.

Thus the war dragged on. Although the Kiburg forces had suffered no decisive defeat, they were clearly getting the worst of things. Only a stunning victory could have restored their credit. Their own subordinate leaders, concerned about the pay of their troops, urged them to make peace on good financial terms. Bern was wealthy and Bern wanted the Kiburg lands. At last the new Count (for Rudolph II had died in the early months of the war) realized the hopelessness of his position and agreed to settle. Bern assumed Kiburg's obligation of paying Solothurn an indemnity for the injuries inflicted upon her and gave the new Count thirty-seven thousand eight hundred gulden in cash to boot—thus enabling him to pay off his troops and settle other debts. In return, Bern got control of the Kiburg domain. The key strongholds of Burgdorf and Tun were turned over to Bernese garrisons; and the Counts of Kiburg became in effect Bernese citizens, subject to Bernese courts. Although they retained for a few decades the office of landgrave, they pledged themselves never again to make war without the permission of Bern and Solothurn; and the Swiss Federal Diet was made the arbiter of any future disputes between the parties. Thus the noble house of Kiburg was ruined and its territories absorbed by the Swiss Confederation, which holds them to this day.

As we have seen, this struggle involved the rising Swiss republican peasant and townsfolk against a decaying feudal aristocratic house.

MAP No. 18

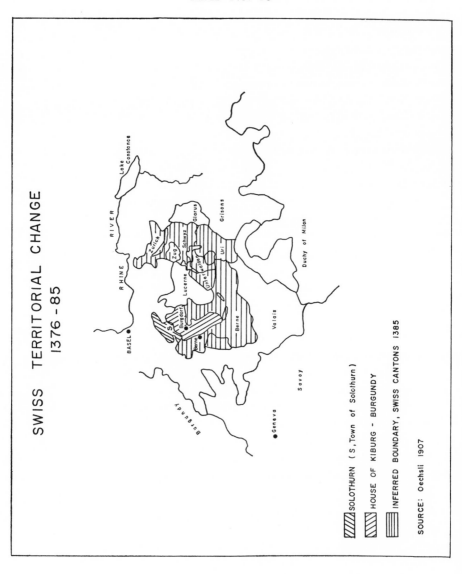

Power politics were complicated by social class antagonisms. There were no other cultural or ideological antagonisms: all parties were southern German Catholics. Several deterrence factors seem clearly relevant to this dispute. The Kiburgs, who began the war, had no subsidies and needed one badly; it seems very likely that if Bern had sought peace and been willing to pay for it, the House of Kiburg would have been open to an offer. The vulnerable proximity of the city of Solothurn to the Kiburg frontier was an essential element in the incident which brought on the war. The Kiburg leaders were *not* acting in accordance with a rational model. Had they made sensible cost-gain calculations, they would have stayed home and there would have been no war. They courted destruction of all they held dear—the fame and power of their noble house. In the event, they sacrificed this dearest of their possessions from their point of view; their decision to attack Solothurn was as huge a blunder as was the decision of the Austrians to attack Serbia in 1914. Consider that they were challenging a power which overmatched them in numbers, equipment (though not mobility), wealth, and military prestige. Their manner of beginning the war provided a comfortable excuse for their own allies to desert them—as indeed happened. They placed themselves in a hopeless position from which only a brilliant military stroke could have rescued them—then they fought the war on the defensive which made such a stroke impossible

In short, *everything depended on the success of the original plot to surprise Solothurn.* If it had succeeded, they might have had a chance to find enough money to hire enough troops to beat off the revengeful Swiss. It failed, and they were lost at the outset.

PART 2: SURVEY OF VARIABLES (Coded for Conspicuous State, Swiss Confederation)

Dependent Variables

Months of War. War between the Swiss and Kiburg began on 10 November 1382 and ended on 7 April 1384 for a total of seventeen months of war. The raw score of 17 yields a standard score of 45. For method of transformation see p. 11.

Territorial Change. Since the result of the war was to make Kiburg a vassal of Bern, we have counted this outcome as a territorial gain by the Swiss of all the Kiburg territory; so it was, de facto and de jure, in that (1) Kiburg committed itself to make no war without permission of Bern, (2) Kiburg placed in Bern's hands the two strongholds of the country, and (3) the counts of Kiburg became in effect Bernese citizens. The raw score of 13% yields two standard scores: territorial gain 61 and territorial stability 58. For method of transformation see p. 13f.

Military Variables

Defensive Stance. While Bern had long entertained designs on the Kiburg territories, the situation at the outbreak of the war presents a clear defensive stance. Neither Bern nor Solothurn was then threatening to attack Kiburg; they had no thought of war at the time; consequently, Kiburg was in an offensive stance, and the Swiss Confederation in a defensive one. Coded *present.*

Strength of Armed Forces. The Swiss apparently had a considerable advantage in numbers. According to Johannes von Müller, the Swiss fielded over fifteen thousand troops, while the Kiburgers evidently were unable to put half that number against them and depended upon their fortifications for refuge; after the first desperate attempt on Solothurn (which according to von Müller involved only 200 men), Kiburg remained permanently on the defensive. A reinforcement of horsemen into their main garrison at Burgdorf seemed to have constituted a substantial gain, and the relief force which finally lifted the siege of Burgdorf numbered only 1300. (According to Dierauer, the Bernese had meanwhile sent most of their armies home to save the cost of their pay, thinking the Kiburgers already beaten—as it turned out, they were). Coded *present.*

Mobility of Armed Forces: The Swiss townsfolk and peasants were largely infantry; the Kiburg forces presumably contained a higher proportion of cavalry and hence were more mobile, one would infer. The opening surprise attack required considerable mobility, since the Kiburg forces had to be mobilized in secret. Therefore, although no specific reports are at hand, it seems reasonable to infer that the Kiburg side had an advantage in mobility. Coded *absent.*

Quality of Armed Forces. The Swiss infantry may not yet have gained the reputation it later enjoyed but already had proved itself in several severe battles in earlier wars. The Swiss had a siege train including not only the old-fashioned catapults, but also the newly introduced gunpowder cannons, Whether the Count of Kiburg knew in advance that the Swiss would be so equipped is, however, doubtful. Nevertheless, the information at hand would indicate that so far as modern observers can judge, the Swiss enjoyed an advantage in the actual quality of their armies. However, it is an open question whether the Kiburg people perceived this or whether instead, despite the repeated demonstrations of Swiss military capacity, they still thought of them as a rabble of peasantry or townsmen, and not really a match for the warlike nobility. Coded *present.*

Fortifications. These played a dominant part in planning and fighting. The war turned out to be entirely a matter of attacks upon fortified places. Its first brief phase was the unsuccessful attempt of Kiburg to surprise the fortified town of Solothurn. Its second phase was the unsuccessful Swiss siege of the Kiburg fortified stronghold of Burgdorf. Its third phase was the successful Bernese campaign to capture a considerable number of small castles of Kiburg's feudal vassals. Since the war opened with a surprise attack upon a fortification, the hypothesis that fortifications tend to discourage the outbreak of war is not supported by this case. Coded *present.*

Prestige. Kiburg had a poor reputation at this time while the Swiss enjoyed a good one. Kiburg was known to be badly in need of money; it had been selling or pawning off its sovereign rights one after another. Money had by now become essential to warfare since without it reliable troops could not be had, and it was clear that Kiburg had neither money nor credit. The Swiss on the other hand included prosperous towns like Zürich and Bern, well able to meet military payrolls, as well as a large, sturdy peasantry in the rural cantons whose worth in battle had been repeatedly demonstrated. Coded *present.*

Geographical Variables

Propinquity. The territories of Bern and Solothurn bordered on those of Habsburg-Kiburg. Coded *present.*

Natural Barriers. There are no mountain or river barriers between Burgdorf, the Kiburg stronghold, and either Solothurn or Bern. Coded *absent*.

Capital City. The distance from Bern to Burgdorf is twenty-three kilometers, from Burgdorf to Solothurn is twenty-two kilometers. Both Bern and Solothurn were then on the frontier of the Kiburg territories. This proximity was a key factor in the outbreak of the war and clearly led to the breakdown of the deterrent position of Bern and Solothurn, at this time in a defensive stance. For the surprise attack by Kiburg on Solothurn depended for its hope of success on this proximity, which theoretically might well enable the Kiburg forces to cross the frontier at night and reach the city walls of Solothurn without any warning being communicated to Solothurn. Coded *present*.

Diplomatic Variables

Announcements. Since the Kiburg plan involved complete surprise, no hint of a danger of war was given. Announcement of intention was clearly absent; there is a good chance that if the Solothurners had let the Kiburgers know that they were ready for them, the war might never have taken place. Coded *absent*.

Surprise Attack. Kiburg gambled heavily on the success of a sudden surprise attack. However, tactical surprise was lost and the people of Solothurn were warned in time to defend their walls. Coded *absent*.

Alliances. Kiburg fought the war without a single ally; none of their many former allies supported them—the Kiburgers were most conspicuously let down by the Duke of Austria. This isolated diplomatic position was a consequence of the secrecy needed if the plot was to achieve success. They could not consult their other allies in advance; the Duke of Austria set the pattern for staying out of the war by announcing that since he had not been consulted about it, he felt no obligation to take part in it. Solothurn, on the other hand, not only had the support of the Swiss Confederation, but also of Duke Amadeus of Savoy, then an important power in south-western Switzerland. Coded *present*.

Active Diplomacy. Kiburg had been conducting a lawsuit against Solothurn. No other diplomatic negotiations are mentioned and the secret nature of the plot strongly indicates that there were none. Dierauer calls this Kiburg enterprise a "mad" one; and so it seems to have been. Had the Kiburgers been diplomatically active, and had they suggested the possibility of a war, their isolated situation would have been made clear to them. They counted upon the effect of a sudden surprise to overcome these handicaps, but this precluded diplomacy. Coded *absent*.

Intense Diplomacy. There was no Intense Diplomacy; coded *absent*.

Previous Conflict. The previous hundred years had been dominated by the conflict between the Swiss and the House of Austria, to whom Habsburg-Kiburg was connected by family relationship. For a time, it is true, the House of Habsburg-Kiburg had had its own conflicts with Habsburg-Austria, in which it was supported by Bern. However, during the Laupen war (1339), Habsburg-Kiburg broke its alliance with Bern to join with Austria and a large confederation of feudal lords against Bern. Later, Kiburg became the vassal of Austria in return for money payments. Coded *present*.

Cultural Variables

Benefits. Discussion of the Kiburg financial problems mentions no subsidies before the war and their absence can safely be presumed. The outcome of the war suggests that a subsidy would have prevented it in the first place. The war was a purely financial enterprise on the part of Kiburg. Coded *absent*.

Cultural Exchange. Probably the Kiburg domains and the possessions of the city of Solothurn were not clearly separated but interlocking. Kiburg had possessions in areas dominated by Solothurn and vice versa. At the subcultural level all the combatants were culturally part of a single system. They were all German speakers who all acknowledged the nominal suzerainty of the Holy Roman Emperor. On the other hand, the Kiburg leaders were keenly conscious of their noble blood and contemptuous of the bourgeoisie of Bern and Solothurn. Coded *present*.

Trade. Without having any direct evidence at hand, we nevertheless would presume active trade between Solothurn, Kiburg and Bern. See "Cultural Exchange" above. Coded *present*.

General Exchange. Coded *present* because Cultural Exchange and "Trade" were both coded present.

Administrative Variables

Experience of Ruler. Not pertinent to the Swiss Confederation. Coded *no data.*

Youth of Ruler. Not pertinent to the Swiss Confederation. Coded *no data.*

Unbridled Ruler. The Swiss Confederation was a loose one with no permanent executive head. Our secondary sources do not even mention the name of the leader of the Swiss forces, although we have some information about the Counts of Kiburg. This case is clearly one of a hereditary monarchy pitted against a confederation of republican states. Coded *absent.*

Hereditary Monarchy. Not pertinent to the Swiss Confederation. See "Unbridled Ruler", above. Coded *absent.*

Civil War. There was no civil war. Coded *absent.*

Centralization. While the Counts of Kiburg-Habsburg had to reckon with feudal underlords whose military and civil obligations were strictly limited, nevertheless they must be considered a more highly centralized organization than the Swiss Confederation. But Bern as a city must have had a more highly centralized government than Habsburg-Kiburg.

The problem at issue here is whether a more highly centralized state is more likely to begin a war than a less highly centralized one. There is clear light shed on this issue by this decade. This particular crisis, which led to a decisive war, depended for its origin and its consummation on the absolute control over war and peace enjoyed by the Count of Kiburg. Had he been required to consult with feudal underlords, he could not have hoped to maintain the secrecy he needed. Coded *absent.*

PART 3: DATA QUALITY CONTROL

The sources consulted were secondary and tell the story from the Swiss viewpoint. The chief works used were Johannes von Müller,

"Die Geschichte der Schweizerischen Eidgenossenschaft," (Leipzig, 1805-1808) and Johannes Dierauer, *Geschichte der schweizerischen Eidgenossenschaft* (Gotha, 1913), vol. 1 and 2. Only these two works describe the events of the war in any detail; several other histories of Switzerland were consulted, including one by a modern German scholar. No disagreement on any essential point was found in these others, but they treated the war very briefly, giving it only a few sentences.

Johannes von Müller (1752-1809) was a poorer scholar than Dierauer, but he was less biased. Dierauer was not only a Swiss patriot, but he was partial towards the Swiss townsfolk and peasantry against the Kiburg aristocrats—so that his work displays a social class orientation as well as a national one. Von Müller, on the other hand, although of Swiss peasant origin and briefly an enthusiastic supporter of the French Revolution, wrote the final version of his history, which we used, as a servant of the House of Hesse-Cassel in Germany; his work displays no social class bias and the temperature of his moral indignation at the Kiburg surprise attack seems considerably cooler than that of Dierauer.

Dierauer (1842-1920) unlike von Müller, was a well-disciplined historian by the standard prevailing today—a professional, trained in the universities of Zürich, Bonn, and Paris, who made his living as a senior librarian in the Swiss city of Saint Gall, his native canton, from 1874 until his death. He had the benefit of much nineteenth century scholarship, which included the collection and publication of many of the contemporary source documents, and his work remains today the standard authority in its field. Nevertheless, as already indicated, he did not attempt to conceal his feelings of hostility and contempt toward the House of Kiburg.

There is agreement on the main facts among all secondary sources consulted; both Dierauer and von Müller cite contemporary documents, including the financial records of the city of Bern covering the expenses of the war. The exact date of the beginning of the war, the night of 10 to 11 November, is given by von Müller in a document which purports to be a version of a contract between von Kiburg and his confederate setting forth the terms of the assault; Dierauer's briefer report of the terms of this agreement is consistent. The war came to an end with the execution of a treaty, whose date is a matter of record. Hence it does not seem likely that the bias of our sources—though the data comes to us entirely from Swiss primary sources or through Swiss editors or compilers—could materially distort the data on the number of months involved. Similarly, the territorial settlement was effected by a formal treaty, a copy of which was deposited in the Austrian Habsburg archives, since their legal rights were affected—and this again could hardly have been distorted. It is not to be doubted that this war resulted in the absorption of the territories of the House of Kiburg by Bern. The actual map is from Wilhelm Oechsli, *Schweizergeschichte für Sekundar-Real-Und Mittelschulen* (Zürich: Verlag der Erziehungsdirektion, 1907), but since this again rests on the treaty, it can hardly have been much distorted through bias.

Publication Year. Von Müller published in 1832, Dierauer in 1913. Coded *no data.*

Primary Source. Both authors are secondary. Coded *absent.*

Authors' Association. Dierauer was a partisan of the Swiss townsfolk and peasantry against the Kiburg aristocrats. Although von Müller was of peasant origin himself, his work displays less bias against Kiburg. Coded *present.*

Authors' Sympathies. Both authors are pro-Swiss Confederation, although von Müller is somewhat less partisan than Dierauer, a democratic republican those theoretical orientation was an additional source of hostility toward Kiburg. Coded *present.*

Authors' Proximity. Both authors wrote five and a half to six centuries after the events recorded. Coded *absent.*

CHAPTER 21

★ ★ ★

THE GOLDEN SWORD

1476-1485: Conspicuous State, Swiss Confederation; Conspicuous Rival, Charles the Bold, Duke of Burgundy.

PART I: SKETCH OF HISTORICAL SETTING (Chiefly after Kirk)

IN THIS REPORT we are concerned with the manner in which Louis XI, king of France, persuaded the Swiss Cantons to fight their ally Charles, the duke of Burgundy, and thereby to destroy the most powerful French adversary. Louis cleverly set these two allies against each other. He paid the Swiss enough gold so that they forgot their old ties of friendship with Burgundy. They destroyed Charles, and with him, the power of Burgundy.

Louis XI has been called the Spider King. Historians are fond of picturing him spinning a web of intrigue so tangled that his victims could not extricate themeslves. The events of the randomly chosen decade from 1476 to 1485 in Europe reveal how Louis caught Charles of Burgundy in his web and entangled him so thoroughly that he perished. Louis XI knew Burgundy well. As the dauphin he had lived at the Burgundian court for several years, enjoying the protection and the lavish hospitality of Duke Charles the Bold's father. But the young Charles was never comfortable while Louis was there. He did not understand Louis and resented his presence. It was a great relief to him when Louis was able to return to France.

If Charles did not understand Louis, Louis understood Charles only too well. He knew Charles's vanities, his weaknessess, and his dislike of facing reality. If it was clear that these ambitious men would clash, it was also clear that Louis would win. He was prepared to maneuver, to bribe, and to deceive to get what he wanted. Louis involved the Holy Roman Emperor, the Swiss Confederates, Sigismund of Austria, and René of Lorraine in his affairs. He secretly bought their support and then he sat back to watch as they did his fighting for him and destroyed his most powerful rival.

In the complicated events that preceded the decade there were four principal actors in the arena (there were also three minor players, René of Lorraine, Yolande of Savoy, and the Holy Roman Emperor, Frederick; but the parts they played are not important enough to describe in detail.) The four principals were Louis XI, king of France; Charles the Bold, duke of Burgundy; Sigismund of Austria; and the Swiss confederates. Louis's aim was to augment his kingdom, and to do so he was willing to buy support wherever he could. Sigismund of Austria was both poor and weak, and he needed rich and powerful friends to help him survive; when Charles did not give him the help he wanted, he turned to Louis. Charles the Bold wanted to restore the old kingdom of Burgundy. He was ambitious and rash, but he played the game according to the only rules he knew, the rules of the age of chivalry.

France, Austria, and Burgundy each had a central head of government and a clear and unified policy. Of the four principals only the Swiss confederates had no single authority and thus no clear policy. Delegates from each canton made up the assembly of the Swiss Diet, and there was no central figure to head it. But there was one thing on which the Swiss could be counted to agree, and that was money. It became the means for Louis to get the Swiss to do what he wanted.

The Swiss confederates had been closer to Burgundy than to any other ruling house. Swiss nobles used to visit the Burgundian court, and commercial dealings between the Swiss and Burgundy were of long standing. The Swiss looked upon Burgundy as a friend; they did not seem to feel menaced by Charles's' ambition to make Burgundy bigger and stronger. But when Charles obtained Upper Alsace from Sigismund of Austria in 1469, he took the first step toward his own destruction; with this purchase he unwittingly gave Louis XI the idea of using the Swiss to destroy Charles. Louis would become the strongest power in Europe if he could absorb Burgundy. If he could get the Swiss to break Charles for him, he would have what he wanted, at no danger to his realm. He put powerful Swiss agents on his payroll and gave them money to use where it would do the most good. Within five years he was able to manipulate the Swiss into starting a war with Charles.

Although the Swiss had long been friendly with the Burgundians, both the Austrians and the French were long-time enemies of the Swiss. Only thirty years before the decade began, the Swiss had fought bitterly against France. However, after 1444 relations between France and the Swiss improved, even though the Austrians remained their enemies. The Swiss made a treaty with France, sent an embassy to the French court, and in 1459 entrusted Louis XI to negotiate a truce between them and Austria. But the trouble with the Austrians was not over, and a year later the Swiss fought them again. When they agreed to another armistice it was to be for fifteen years, but before half the time was up the Swiss once more were fighting Austria. This time the Swiss agreed to stop fighting if Sigismund of Austria would pay them ten thousand guilders within a year, and as a pledge they demanded Waldshut and the whole of the Black Forest from him.

Sigismund was faced with the problem of where to raise the money. He went to Louis, but Louis refused to help him, for he was afraid the Swiss would be offended if he gave money to their long time enemy. Then Sigismund turned to Charles the Bold, duke of Burgundy. Although Charles did not want to offend the Swiss, he did want very much to extend his holdings in Alsace. He therefore agreed to give Sigismund fifty thousand florins as well as letters of protection in return for a mortgage on and custody of the landgraviate of Alsace, the county of Ferette, Brisach, and the four towns of Rheinfelden, Seckingen, Lauffenburg, and Waldshut. Of the fifty thousand florins Sigismund was to keep forty thousand for himself and use the remaining ten thousand to pay the Swiss what they demanded. He was free to redeem the property if he made the payments at one time, in one sum, and at one place—Besançon in Franche Comté.

Charles, by this action, thus substituted himself for Sigismund of Austria as the neighbor of the Swiss, which on the face of it was a satisfactory arrangement for both himself and his friends, the Swiss. However, no sooner was the money paid than Sigismund called upon Charles to furnish the protection he had promised— namely, to send his armies against the Swiss. Charles refused to help the Austrians for he did not see that he had any problem with the Swiss.

But Charles did have a problem with Alsace. Peter von Hagenbach, the administrator whom he had sent to govern the Alsatian towns, had placed a duty on wine, and the inhabitants were objecting violently to it. To further complicate matters for Charles, the city of Muhlhausen, a Swiss ally, owed money to subjects of the duke of Burgundy; when the money was not paid, von Hagenbach cut off trade relations. At the interruption of trade with one of their allies, leaders in Bern became angry. This was the kind of opportunity Louis had been looking for, and he seized it. He began to use Bern in his plan to break Charles. His first move was to put on his payroll a Bernese family, the Diesbachs. They were to build up support for war against Burgundy. The Diesbach family was old, large, and powerful; and by hiring its many members Louis made Bern the focus of his operations against Burgundy and made the Diesbachs the managers of these operations.

By 1470 Louis, with the help of the Diesbachs, had made sufficient inroads into Bernese politics to negotiate a new treaty with the Swiss, whereby neither side was to give aid to the duke of Burgundy in case a war should arise between him and either of the parties. Zug and Glarus were opposed, and the other Swiss cantons apparently gave only a verbal assent. Only Bern signed. Then the Diesbachs were able to get the Council of Bern to forbid Bernese enlistment in the military service of any foreign state, thus cutting off a recruiting resource that Charles had counted on. Although the Swiss for the most part were still anxious to maintain their ties of friendship with Burgundy, it is clear that Louis's attempts to align them with him and against Burgundy were meeting with success. The Swiss confederates had no single policy, and no single leader to act for them. But many Swiss individuals were willing to side with Louis and even fight for him in order to get rich. And for these individuals the Diesbachs had plenty of Louis's money.

As for Sigismund of Austria, when he could not get Charles to help him in his fight with the Swiss, he turned to Louis. Sigismund needed money which Louis would give him on the condition that he would make peace with the Swiss. Thus Charles, working to reconcile the Swiss and Austrians, was unaware that Austria was now secretly aligning with France and that he himself would be their victim.

In Alsace the inhabitants were getting more and more uneasy. Charles went there and attempted to reduce the friction among the townspeople. While he was in Alsace he heard rumors of a new agreement between Louis and the Swiss. Disturbed, he wrote to the Swiss and asked if they had made a treaty with France against him. He received the reassuring reply that friendly relations between Burgundy and the Swiss would continue.

Louis's next step was to engineer a peace treaty between Austria and the Swiss. Sigismund of Austria was anxious to make peace; Louis proposed to give him the amount he needed to pay Charles the mortgage money and redeem the Alsatian towns. But Louis was also anxious to keep up appearances and not reveal the fact that he was bribing the Austrians. He therefore kept secret from most of the Swiss the details of the arrangement. Lucerne and Zürich lent their support to Bern's, and it was agreed that Sigismund would demand the surrender of Alsace from Charles. At the same time Austria and the Swiss made an offensive and defensive alliance with the towns of Basle, Strasbourg, Colmar, and Schlettstadt.

Then suddenly, without any warning, Charles was told that Sigismund of Austria was renouncing their alliance, returning the letters of protection and redeeming the mortgaged territory in Alsace, having deposited the money at Basle. Charles still did not seem to understand that he had been duped. He answered by refusing the money, since it was not being returned in accordance with the terms of the agreement. The news of the refusal caused agitation among the Alsatians, who were chafing under Peter von Hagenbach's rule. Von Hagenbach went immediately to Charles and asked him to send troops to Alsace. But Charles felt this step to be unnecessary, for the Swiss had repeatedly assured him that they had no hostile intentions toward him. Von Hagenbach returned and found the Alsatians more agitated than before. When he ordered the inhabitants to contribute their labor for work on fortifications, they revolted and declared themselves for Austria. Von Hagenbach was imprisoned by the mob and a few days later Sigismund arrived and reestablished Austrian authority over A'sace. So far the Swiss had not come to Sigismund's aid.

The injustices that the Alsatians had suffered under the administration of Peter von Hagenbach became the pretext for the Swiss to help Austria. Swiss school texts and traditional accounts of this episode claim that von Hagenbach's tyranny was the reason the Swiss entered the war against Burgundy. Much is made of the feelings of Swiss loyalty to their Alsatian allies and their rage at von Hagenbach's mistreatment of them. Although von Hagenbach was evidently a harsh and unpleasant administrator, he was also an able one; and under his jurisdiction the Alsatian towns enjoyed a thriving commerce, unmolested by the brigands who had virtually controlled traffic under Austrian rule. The Swiss were in no way harmed by the improvement of trade in Alsace. They may have felt concern for their allies, but their real concern was to get their money on time.

Charles and Louis had previously signed a truce whereby Louis promised not to give aid to the Swiss; this truce was due to run out. Louis waited until after it had been renewed, in order not to alarm Charles; then, in mid-June 1474, he confirmed the treaty which he was to finance between Austria and the Swiss. The Council of Bern tried to persuade the reluctant confederates to join with the French and Austrians against Charles of Burgundy; Diesbach assured the Council that the extension of the truce between Charles and Louis did not mean any improvement of relations between them. He urged the Council to continue its preparations for war. The allied towns in Alsace and agents of Sigismund and of Bern all urged war against Burgundy in order that Alsace might be preserved. In August Louis told the Swiss that his truce with Burgundy formed no obstacle to immediate hostilities. He surreptitiously offered to pay to each of the eight cantons and also Freiburg and Solothurn two thousand francs (at this time Freiburg and Solothurn were independent allies of the Swiss; not until 1481 did they become members of the Swiss Confederation). In addition, if the Swiss were willing to do all the fighting without the assistance of French troops, Louis would pay eighty thousand francs yearly as long as the war continued. In September a secret treaty to this effect was drawn up, but it was not sent to the cantons for ratification for fear they would reject it. In October the Swiss told Sigismund that they would not fight Burgundy alone. They agreed, however, to send forces into Alsace to clear out the Burgundian invaders if Sigismund paid the expenses, which were estimated at eight thousand guilders. The Swiss knew Sigismund would get money from France.

After Sigismund got the money, he had the imperial envoys call upon the Swiss confederates, as members of the Holy Roman Empire, to aid in defending it against the Duke of Burgundy. The next step was for the people of upper Germany to announce themselves enemies of Burgundy and send a messenger to Charles, who was encamped with his army outside of Neuss, fifty kilometers north of Cologne in the Rhine valley. The Swiss responded to the appeal of the Holy Roman Emperor. They announced that their actions were based on their alliance with Austria, and they acknowledged that neither their territory nor their rights had been threatened. But they said privately that they would never have fought Burgundy if it had not been for Louis's inducements. The war which Louis had secretly planned and paid for in order to destroy Charles of Burgundy was soon to begin.

However, not all of the cantons had yet agreed to fight. Unterwalden and Appenzell refused to join Bern. Glarus and Zug waited to see what the rest would do. Without waiting for unanimous consent, three thousand Bernese troops marched toward Alsace at the end of October; they were joined by five hundred more from Freiburg and Solothurn. Burgundian troops commanded by the governor of Franche Comté had assembled at the fortress of Hericourt. The Swiss troops attacked them, the Burgundians fled, the Swiss pursued; when the first skirmish was over the Swiss had not lost a man. Thus, by the end of 1474 the war between Charles of Burgundy and the Swiss had begun.

But weeks went by and the Swiss soldiers did not receive their pay from Sigismund, for he had not received the money Louis XI had promised him. The people of Bern became uneasy; Bern had pledged the other cantons to Louis, had signed the treaty with Louis, and now stood committed. In March of 1475, fourteen hundred men set out for the town of Pontarlier, led by two of the members of the Bern Council. They attacked Pontarlier, but their retreat was cut off. When the Council of Bern heard of their danger the members ordered twenty-five hundred men to help them and alerted the other cantons. Lucerne raised eight thousand men, other cantons promised aid also. The Swiss Diet voted for a general arming. Then came word that the troops at Pontarlier had beaten back the enemy and were on their way home. It was very clear to those who wanted the war to continue that it might end if the men returned from Pontarlier. The Diesbachs emphasized in the Council of Bern that the city's honor was compromised. The Council ordered the forces at Pontarlier to remain there. The Swiss Diet however refused to send help to Pontarlier if the men there were no longer in danger. Bern decided to continue alone, raised two thousand troops, and called upon Solothurn and Bienne to help them. Zürich and all the other cantons except Glarus called Bern's actions arbitrary and a peril to the Confederates. But when the long-expected money from Louis finally arrived, there was a quick change of feelings; and at the end of April troops from Bern, Basle, and Lucerne marched toward Grandson. The castle of Grandson was on their line of march. They captured the castle and killed the entire garrison. Having secured the pass they returned.

Then came news that the Burgundian army was pouring into Lorraine. Diesbach led an army of Swiss to meet them. Without ever actually announcing war, Bern occupied the mountain passes and Grandson, Orbe, and Jougne. But the other cantons still did not feel bound by the treaty with France to continue a war with Burgundy. The treaty provided that if they fought Burgundy, Louis was to join them, and if he were prevented from doing so he was to forfeit 80,000 francs. He had not joined them, and he had not forfeited the money. The other cantons did not benefit from further fighting as Bern did; for there was another clause to the treaty, one which gave a special retainer to Bern; and none of the other cantons received it. Thus, the Bernese, who had been promised the most money, were naturally the most eager to fight for Louis.

But finally the Swiss Diet acceded to the pressures Bern had been applying and issued a general call to arms. Zurich sent troops, and the other cantons let their men volunteer. By November of 1475, after a year of fighting, the Swiss and their allies had captured seventeen towns and twenty-seven castles. At one point the Savoy troops, allies of Charles of Burgundy, almost crushed the Swiss; but three thousand reinforcements from the Oberland joined them, and enabled the Swiss troops to overrun Savoy. The Bernese had long hoped to control the Vaud, and they had accomplished it at last.

In 1476, when the decade began, therefore, the Swiss had been fighting Duke Charles of Burgundy for over a year. Charles, still hopeful of restoring the kingdom of Burgundy, would not yet face the fact that the Swiss had become united. He had been unwilling to believe that Louis would violate the treaty between them and help the Swiss. Now he was unwilling to accept the fact that his old friends the Swiss were his foremost threat.

At the beginning of the year 1476 the Swiss Diet met and resolved to fight with their own forces as well as those of Freiburg and Solothurn. They made a formal request that Louis help them and hinted that they would direct Charles's enmity against France if he declined. They mentioned the dangers that threatened from Charles, and stressed a defensive strategy towards Charles, who was close to their borders. Soon afterwards some Swiss forces met the Burgundian army and were cut off. The cantons rallied to their aid, but it was too late. The defeat of the Swiss provided a new motive for fighting—revenge.

The battle of Grandson was fought in February of 1476. When a voice among Charles's troops called out for the men to save themselves, the Burgundian army fled without ever engaging the Swiss. Charles lost a thousand men to one hundred Swiss. He felt however that nothing had been decided by the battle since his force of twenty thousand had turned their backs on half that many Swiss without exchanging a blow. He therefore determined to meet the Swiss again and defeat them. He tried to raise even more troops but could not get the money to pay for them. He tried to reorganize his forces but the morale of his men was low.

After the battle of Grandson the Swiss once again told Louis that they wanted not only his money but also his help in the war. They threatened to quit the fight unless he joined them. Louis countered with a promise to double the pensions he was paying to them. Then Swiss spies brought back the news that the Burgundian army was bigger than ever, and that Charles was moving towards them. The Swiss stopped arguing with Louis and began to build defenses against the Burgundians at Morat; when they had erected extensive fortifications they summoned all the confederates and

MAP No. 19

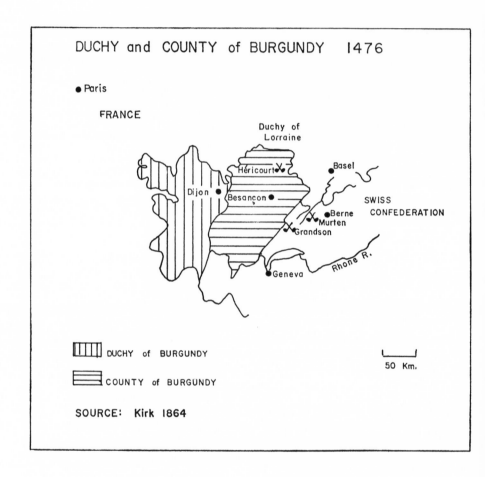

DUCHY and COUNTY of BURGUNDY 1476

● Paris

FRANCE

Duchy of
Lorraine

Héricourt

Basel

Dijon ●

Besançon ●

SWISS
CONFEDERATION

●Berne
Murten
Grandson

Rhone R.

●Geneva

▦ DUCHY of BURGUNDY

☰ COUNTY of BURGUNDY

SOURCE: Kirk 1864

50 Km.

MAP No. 20

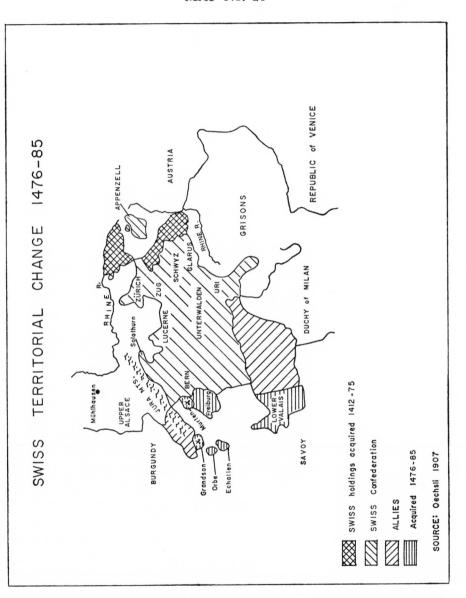

SWISS TERRITORIAL CHANGE 1476-85

SOURCE: Oechsli 1907

allies. Instead of remaining behind his intrenchments at Grandson, Charles moved up to Morat. In June of 1476 the two sides met, with René of Lorraine fighting alongside the Swiss. Although the Swiss suffered heavy losses, they were the victors. They retook the Vaud towns of Morat, Orbe, Grandson, and Eschallens from Savoy, Charles's ally.

When the battle of Morat was over the Swiss resumed their negotiations with Louis. As usual, he was late with his payments and, as usual, he was trying to reduce the amount that the Swiss claimed he owed them. While the Swiss and Louis argued over money, Charles was busy reorganizing his army once more. In September of 1476 he crossed Franche Comté into Lorraine and defeated René. René tried to get the Swiss to help him retake Lorraine from Charles, but the Swiss were uninterested until René promised forty thousand florins if the Swiss would send an expedition. The Burgundian army had now shrunk to less than ten thousand. The Swiss, together with René and their other allies numbered almost twenty thousand. They retook Lorraine, and then in January of 1477, at Nancy, destroyed the Burgundian army and killed Charles.

Louis now had what he wanted. The Swiss had done for him that which he had been unwilling to do himself. He had secretly bribed them to destroy his most powerful enemy, and they had done so. A fitting tribute to the part the Swiss played in Charles of Burgundy's destruction came from a representative of one of the confederates six months later (Kirk 1864:551): "Remember our faithful service to the king in the matter of the duke! Remember our faithful service to the king in running down and killing the duke of Burgundy. Who had never done any harm to us; no, neither he nor his forefathers. Gladly would he have continued our neighbor and our friend. Yet we declared him our enemy and hunted him down!"

PART 2: SURVEY OF VARIABLES (Coded for Conspicuous State, Swiss Confederation)

Dependent Variables

Months of War. There were twelve months of war between the Swiss confederates and Burgundy during the decade, and one hundred and eight months of peace. The raw score of 12 yields a standard score of 44. For method of transformation see p. 11.

Territorial Change. The Swiss gained the Savoy towns of Morat, Grandson, Orbe, and Eschallens, an increase of 11.5%. The raw score of 12% yields two standard scores; territorial gain 61 and territorial stability 58. For method of transformation see p. 13f.

Military Variables

Defensive Stance. The Swiss were in an offensive stance vis-à-vis Charles of Burgundy, and he was on the defensive. However, Charles was in an offensive stance vis-à-vis Sigismund of Austria, an ally of the Swiss. Coded *absent* for the Conspicuous State, the Swiss confederates.

Strength of Armed Forces. The Burgundian army in 1474 had been estimated at between twenty and forty thousand men and three hundred pieces of ordnance; it was probably much closer to twenty thousand than forty thousand. Each time he faced the Swiss confederates Charles lost part of his force. At Grandson the Swiss had a smaller army than Charles—about ten thousand to his more than twenty thousand. At Morat the two sides were equal—almost twenty thousand each. At Nancy the Swiss had twice his number against him—about twenty thousand to his ten thousand. Charles the Bold could not augment his forces from his Flemish holdings, for his subjects there were not at all interested in a war which did not touch their territory. Thus, as the war progressed, the Burgundian treasury became depleted and Burgundian military resources deteriorated. The Swiss, in the pay of France, did not have any financial worries, and with strong allies, they did not have to worry about a dwindling army. Coded *absent* because the Conspicuous State, the Swiss Confederation, did not have larger armies than Charles (except at the end of the war).

Mobility of Armed Forces. The Swiss army customarily did not rely on cavalry, although nobles and citizens of high rank did appear in knight's harness to cover the movements of infantry and to lead the pursuit. Charles, however, had a force of between eight and nine thousand cavalry in his full army. Thus he undoubtedly had the advantage of mobility over the Swiss. Coded *absent*.

Quality of Armed Forces. The Swiss soldiers were both feared and admired throughout Europe. They were considered enthusiastic, zealous, and lacking in cowardice and personal ambition. There were no stragglers, no deserters among them. Their military tactics consisted of marching forward in a phalanx of spears, never faltering. "God fights on the side of the Swiss" was a saying throughout the Rhineland, where they were believed invincible.

Charles the Bold also had a reputation as an excellent warrior; in 1474 he had never been beaten. The Burgundians payed their soldiers even when not on active duty so that they were in a constant state of readiness. However, their concepts of the use of the army in combat were still medieval. It was difficult for such an army to preserve ranks as it moved forward over uneven terrain, and in the face of the rigidly held Swiss phalanx the Burgundians were at a tremendous disadvantage. Coded *present*.

Fortifications. Fortifications appear to have been important in at least one of the battles. For six weeks before the battle of Morat the Swiss had made careful defense preparations. The existing fortifications consisted of a palisade which extended far into the water of the lake, as well as a strong wall, a double ditch, towers, and a castle. The Swiss had strengthened the existing fortifications by adding bastions and outworks. The whole area served as a fortress and apparently many more men than Charles could raise would have been required to assault it successfully. Coded *present*.

Prestige. Under Burgundian rule the Low Countries enjoyed economic prosperity and an artistic flowering. The income that the dukes of Burgundy got from holdings there enabled them to live in luxury. The furnishings, the food, the jewels, the garments of the Burgundian court were on a lavish scale unknown anywhere else in Europe and were the object of comment and envy by neighbors. And their wealth made the Burgundian nobility choice marriage partners—Charles had wed the sister of Louis XI, and he tried to marry his daughter to the heir of the Holy Roman Empire. Thus, the duchy of Burgundy was highly respected.

The Swiss were well regarded for the united front they presented and the excellent armies they could raise, not for their money and amount of territory as in the case of Burgundy. Coded *absent* because the Swiss Confederation's reputation was not as great as that of Burgundy.

Geographical Variables

Propinquity. The duchy and county of Burgundy (now part of France) were on the west of Switzerland. Coded *absent* because the situation was ambiguous in that Burgundy's army occupied Alsace (adjacent to the Swiss Confederation) without effectively incorporating this territory into its political system.

Natural Barriers. The Jura Mountains, with their steep passes, separate Switzerland from Burgundy and Alsace. The Swiss mountain troops have long been agile in getting up and down these mountains, but they provide an almost impenetrable barrier to foreign armies. Coded *present*.

Capital City. Bern, the largest Swiss city, was approximatly sixty-five kilometers from the border; and Dijon, the largest city in the duchy of Burgundy, was approximately one hundred forty kilometers from the border (Charles used both Besançon and Dijon as capitals). Coded *no data* because the Swiss Confederation as such had no capital city.

Diplomatic Variables

Announcements. Until the last minute Charles was unwilling to accept the idea that the Swiss would actually fight him. He had no intention of fighting them and said so repeatedly. The Swiss, allies of the French, and in the pay of the French, tried to make Charles believe that they would not fight him, while at the same time they tried to reassure Louis of France that they would. They kept much of what went on at meetings of the Swiss Diet secret. Charles should have known that Louis was eager to defeat him and was using the Swiss against him. But Louis had given his promise to Charles not to help either the Swiss or Duke René of Lorraine if they went to war with Burgundy. Louis broke his promises about both and gave the Swiss and René a great deal of money, even though he did not himself engage in the fighting. Thus, Charles was duped, and because the Swiss did not announce their intention to fight him, he proceeded as though they would not. When the Swiss finally made the announcement, there was nothing Charles could do except fight, for Swiss troops were by then massing in Alsace. Coded *present* because the Swiss Confederation formally announced its intention before actually attacking.

Surprise Attack. Coded *absent* because Burgundy was given a formal warning before actual fighting began.

Alliances. Leagued against Charles were the Swiss; Louis XI of France; Count Sigismund of Austria; the Holy Roman Emperor Frederick; and Duke René of Lorraine. Leagued with him were only the Duchess Yolande of Savoy; the Count of Romant; and Sforza, the duke of Milan. Charles was completly overpowered. Coded *absent* because the Swiss Confederation was not in a defensive stance.

Active Diplomacy. When Charles refused to accept mortgage money for the four Alsatian towns that he had bought from Sigismund, he immediately sent an embassy to the Swiss confederates to explain his position to them. He received word in return that they did not feel hostile toward him, even though Bern was in fact already calling for aid to the allies in Alsace. The Swiss concealed their true feelings from Charles; they did not want to negotiate with him, and he was thus unable to settle the matter diplomatically. Charles did not seem to realize that Louis XI was negotiating with the Swiss to get them to fight him.

There was more than one diplomatic mission among the principals and their allies; (1) the mission from Charles the Bold to the Swiss where he received a reply in return, and (2) the mission from Louis to the Swiss among others. Coded *present.*

Intense Diplomacy. Coded *absent* because no agreements were concluded between the Swiss confederates and Burgundy.

Previous Conflict. There was none. Until almost the very moment in 1474 when fighting began between the Swiss cantons and Charles the Bold, duke of Burgundy, there had been no previous history of conflict. Quite the opposite. Relations between the Swiss and Charles had been peaceful, as they had been between them and his father, Philip the Good. The Swiss had gone so far as to enter into an agreement with Philip that neither of them should give aid to enemies of the other. Since the Swiss customarily shunned foreign entanglements, this agreement is a testimonial to their trust and confidence in Burgundy. And even after Bern and Lucerne sent forces to Alsace to help their rebellious allies, other Swiss cantons were extremely reluctant to enter the fight and thus break the long ties of friendship that had existed between them and Burgundy. Coded *absent*.

Cultural Variables

Benefits. We can find no evidence that the Swiss or Charles paid any subsidies. But the subsidies paid by Louis to the Swiss were the key factor in the decade. Louis paid the Swiss, the Holy Roman Emperor, Sigismund of Austria, and René of Lorraine to wage war against Charles. Coded *absent* because the Swiss did not confer subsidies upon their rival (Burgundy) nor did Burgundy confer subsidies on the Swiss.

Cultural Exchange. The Swiss had maintained close ties with Burgundy for many years and it was common practice for Swiss nobles to visit the Burgundian court. From ancient times there had been commercial dealings between the two. But despite their long association with Burgundy, Louis XI of France, by use of money payments, convinced the Swiss that it was in their interest to fight Charles the Bold. Coded *present*.

Trade. The Swiss customarily bought their supplies of corn, wine, and salt from Franche Comté and Burgundy and traded in return their surplus dairy products. Coded *present*.

General Exchange. Coded *present* because "Cultural Exchange" and "Trade" were also coded *present*.

Administrative Variables

Experience of Ruler. Not pertinent to the Swiss Confederation. Coded *no data* (Charles of Burgundy acceded to the duchy in 1467).

Youth of Ruler. Not pertinent to the Swiss Confederation. Coded *no data*. (Charles of Burgundy was forty-three years old at the beginning of the decade.)

Unbridled Ruler. The cantons were self-governing. Coded *absent*.

Hereditary Monarchy. Charles of Burgundy inherited the dukedom from his father. The leaders of the Swiss cantons were elected. Therefore this variable is coded *absent*, since the Swiss did not have a hereditary monarchy.

Civil War. The ostensible origin of the conflict between Charles and the Swiss was the rebellion of the Alsatians against the administration of Peter von Hagenbach. Alsace had come under the Burgundian ruler four years previously; the Swiss, who had entered into an alliance with the Alsatian towns of Basle, Strasbourg, Colmar, and Schiettstadt now sided with their allies against von Hagenbach, the Burgundian governor, and aided them in the rebellion. However, the Swiss did not present a united front themselves at this time. Indeed, the policy which dominated the decision to aid the rebels was largely that of Bern, and many of the other cantons were, and continued to be, against the rebels and friendly toward the Burgundian rule in Alsace. However, our sources did not contain sufficient data on actual civil disturbances (i.e., public defiance of the de facto authorities in which someone was killed) within the Swiss cantons over the issue of Alsace for us to make direct inferences regarding civil war. Therefore we have coded this variable *no data*.

Centralization. Charles the Bold's holdings were widely scattered and included the Low Countries. The Duke was count of Flanders, Brabant, and Holland as well as of Burgundy. There was political union among all his principalities, and there was a Great Council in which all the provinces had representation, with a Chamber of the Great Council to handle judicial matters and a congress of all the local estates, the Estates General. In 1471 a standing army was recruited from all the principalities.Thus there was a high degree of association among the component parts of the Burgundian duchy, and at the top was the single ruler, Charles the Bold. As a feudal hereditary duke he could and did act with great authority.

The Swiss confederates were centralized through their diet, but there was no head of government who could act for all the cantons. Consequently the duchy of Burgundy had the higher degree of centralization. Coded *absent*.

PART 3: DATA QUALITY CONTROL

The chief source for this chapter is John Foster Kirk, *History of Charles the Bold* (Philadelphia: Lippincott, 1854) vol. 2 and 3. This secondary source is a definitive work on the relations between the Swiss and Charles the Bold and is based on manuscript sources in Swiss archives. This is the only work which was coded.

Other secondary sources consulted but not coded are: J. Michelet, *Louis XI et Charles le Téméraire* (London: C.J. Clay, 1896); M. de Barante, *Histoire des Ducs de Bourgogne* (Paris: Imprimerie le Normant, 1854); Pierre Champion, *Louis XI* (Paris: Librairie Ancienne Honoré Champion, 1929) vol. 2; Wyndam Lewis, *King Spider* (New York: Coward McCann, 1929); Ruth Putnam, *Charles the Bold, Last Duke of Burgundy* (New York: Putnam, 1903); Hildburg Brauer-Gramm, *Der Lanvogt Peter von Hagenbach* (Göttingen: Musterschmidt-Verlag, 1957); Johannes Dierauer, *Geshichte der Schweizerischen Eidgenossenschaft* (Gotha: F.A. Perthes, 1913) vol. 2; Wilhelm Oechsli, *Schweizergeschichte* (Zürich: Verlag der Erziehungsdirektion, 1907); and *The Cambridge Medieval History* (Cambridge University Press, 1958 and 1959), vol. 1, chapter 7; vol. 8, chapter 10.

The two primary sources consulted but not coded are Philippe de Commynes, *Memoires* (Paris: Librairie Ancienne Honoré Champion, 1925) and Olivier de la Marche, "Memoires, 1435-1489" in *Nouvelle Collection des Memoires Relatifs à l'histoire de France* (Paris: Didier, 1854). Both these primary sources were helpful in following the affairs of the Burgundian cause. De Commynes wrote about the decade under study between 1489 and 1491, and de la Marche wrote at about the same time, approximately five years after the decade had ended. Both men were aides of Charles. Philippe de Commynes was the godson of Charles the Bold's father, and became part of Charles's household. In 1471 Charles sent de Commynes as an envoy to Louis XI of France, who won him over; in 1472 de Commynes left Charles for Louis. De Commynes is cool and critical towards Charles and has been credited with Louis's intrigues against Charles.

In contrast Olivier de la Marche remained with Charles until the battle of Nancy; after Charles was killed he was taken prisoner by the Swiss, then released. De la Marche is a warm and loyal follower of Charles. As members of royal households neither de Commynes nor de la Marche can be considered objective or unbiased.

The following coding applies only to Kirk's *History of Charles the Bold.*

Publication Date. This work was published in 1864. Coded *present.*

Primary Source. Kirk is a secondary source. Coded *absent.*

Author's Association. Kirk was secretary to the historian W.H. Prescott from 1848 to 1858, and traveled in Europe with Prescott during this time, visiting Swiss archives. He was an editor and a lecturer in European history and wrote from the viewpoint of a professional historian. Coded *no data* since Kirk was associated with neither the Conspicuous State, nor its Conspicuous Rival.

Author's Sympathies. Kirk's sympathies were with Charles the Bold and he held Louis XI of France responsible for Charles's involvement in the war with the Swiss. He felt that the Swiss put money first in this affair. Coded *absent,* because, as noted above, Kirk's sympathies were with the conspicuous rival and against the Swiss.

Author's Proximity. Kirk wrote in 1864, almost four hundred years after the events. Coded *absent.*

CHAPTER 22

★ ★ ★

THE SWISS COLD WAR

1576-1585: Conspicuous State, Protestant Cantons; Conspicuous Rival, Catholic Cantons.

Part i: Sketch of Historical Setting (Chiefly after Dierauer)

The main events of the decade from 1576 to 1585 in Switzerland formalized an internal rupture within the Swiss Confederation. The Protestant and Catholic cantons each formed a *Sonderbund*, or supranational alliance—the Protestants with France, the Catholics with Spain and Savoy.* From the deterrence standpoint, on one hand, despite great strain and tension, no war broke out. On the other hand, there was a constant deterioration of relationships which later led to a civil war. This decade thus consisted of a precarious balancing of threats and maneuvers in which each move on one side was counterbalanced by an opposite move on the other. The two sides were more or less approximately matched and, through a balance of power, they exercised mutual deterrence.

During the decade from 1576 to 1585, the Swiss Confederation (and the rest of Europe) was involved in the bitter struggle between Christian ideologies. The Swiss had been fired by Protestantism at the beginning of the century and had played an active part in the movement. Now, near the close of the century, the Counter-Reformation movement had many Swiss supporters; in addition, outsiders—among them strong Jesuit leaders—were attracted there. In the international arena the major European powers were preoccupied with problems of their own and paid the Swiss little

---

* In this chapter, we are treating the allied Protestant cantons as the Conspicuous State, and the allied Catholic cantons as the Conspicuous Rival. See p. 5.

attention: Spain was engaged in a struggle to win the Netherlands; France had religious and political dissension at home; England was concerned with Spain; and Austria was between wars with the Turks. But, although otherwise employed, both Spain and France were interested in obtaining Swiss support. Thus, the beginning of the decade found the Swiss Catholics and Spain sympathetic, which was not the case with the Swiss Protestants and France. Savoy, to the southwest of Switzerland, had long coveted the area around Lake Geneva; and Geneva—under Calvin and even for many years after his death a center of Protestantism—looked to the Swiss Protestant cantons to curb the ambitions of the Duke of Savoy.

The decade from 1576 to 1585 in Switzerland was a decade of uneasy peace. Twice there was threat of war; twice war was averted. In the clash of ideologies and in the bitter partisan feeling there is much which suggests our present-day cold war. Then, as now, there was a constant fear that the other side would become stronger and a constant jockeying for power. Alliance followed alliance and counter alliance followed counter alliance in an intricate series of internal and external diplomatic negotiations. When the decade was over there was still peace, but the alignments which emerged during the decade actually split the confederation; and although the cold war remained cold during the decade, it later became hot—again and again—three times in the three centuries that followed. The religious dissension that was finally resolved politically in 1848 did not dissipate culturally even then, but remains alive though much weakened in Switzerland to the present day.

The decade opens then in 1576 with two religious camps: the Catholics, consisting of the five forest cantons of Schwyz, Uri, Unterwalden, Zug, and Lucerne, as well as Appenzel (Inner Rhoden), the abbey of Saint Gall, and the bishopric of Basel; and the Protestants, consisting of Zürich, Bern, Schaffhausen, Appenzel (Outer Rhoden), Glarus, and the towns of Saint Gall, Basel, and Bienne (or Biel). The Catholics had already begun to take the offensive, and the Duke of Savoy, with Catholic support, had recovered the districts south of Lake Geneva which Bern had seized from him earlier. Threatened by this recovery of lands, Geneva had renewed an alliance with Bern.

The Protestants at this time did not have any outstanding leaders, but the Catholics had three: Charles Borromeo, Jacob Blarer von Wartensee, and Ludwing Pfyffer. Borromeo was the archbishop of Milan and nephew of Pius IV. Von Wartensee was the bishop of Basel and one of the most prominent clerics of his time. Pfyffer was the mayor of Lucerne and had been the chief of the Swiss mercenaries in the French Wars of Religion. These men had done much to restore the Catholic faith in the cantons (Pfyffer so much that he was called the Swiss King); they were key figures during the decade.

The first event of significance in the decade took place in 1577. The Catholic cantons changed their treaty with the duke of Savoy into an auxiliary and protective alliance which now put foot soldiers at the Duke'ș disposition. The Catholic cantons agreed to support the Duke in case of attack and agreed not to protect Geneva against him. The alliance was formally sworn to in 1578.

As a counter move to the alliance with Savoy, the mayor of Bern in the same year asked at the annual meeting of the Diet that Valais be taken into the Confederation on the same terms as the old Bernese areas. The five Catholic cantons refused. In 1579 Bern, under pressure from France to make an alliance against Savoy, now together with Solothurn signed an Eternal Compact with France to protect Geneva; under its terms Henry III took over the protection of Geneva and Valais, and Geneva guaranteed to the king's subjects free trade and passage while denying these to the king's enemies.*

This Eternal Compact aroused the Catholics' worst fears and they immediately took vigorous action on every front: a Papal Nuncio arrived in Lucerne; the five Catholic cantons, joined by Solothurn, made an alliance with the bishop of Basel in an attempt to stop Biel, Bern, and Basel from absorbing the Basel bishopric; and Borromeo, archbishop of Milan, founded a college to educate forty-two Swiss.

---

* Solothurn had associated closely with Bern since 1295. In the Burgundian war Solothurn had allied with Bern. Shortly after signing the Eternal Compact Solothurn switched its allegiance to the Catholic cantons.

In 1580 the alliance with the bishop of Basel was sealed but the Catholics refused to show it to the Diet. Under its secret terms they pledged to assist each other in bringing back recalcitrants and to unite in offensive war and in the guarantee of free markets. But there was inserted a proviso that the bishop was not to use force upon recalcitrants without the canton's consent. And in the same year Freiburg and Solothurn entered into an alliance, thus further broadening the Catholic sphere of influence.

In 1581 the cantons turned their attention again to affairs in Savoy. The Catholics renewed their alliance with the new duke of Savoy, Prince Karl, son of Philibert. Much to Bern's concern, the prince wanted to regain Burgundy and Geneva. War almost broke out, but the other Protestant cities which were allied with France were able to restrain Bern from fighting over Geneva. Bern now agreed to give her previously withheld consent and go along with the rest of the Protestant cantons; in 1582 she gave her support to an alliance with France. This alliance gave Bern French protection for her entire territory, including what had been Savoy's. Now Bern began to promote an alliance with Geneva.

But an alliance between Bern and Geneva was not in Savoy's interest and Savoy opposed it. Bern and Zürich countered by trying to make an alliance between Strassbourg and the Confederation so that Strassbourg could be admitted as an associate. Strassbourg felt that she was one of the key cities in control of the Rhine and should therefore be protected by the Swiss. The Catholic cantons refused to admit Strassbourg on the grounds that she was not a Catholic city and that the pope and the emperor were against it.

As to the alliance with Geneva, only Zürich finally signed. The Catholic cantons refused and continued their friendship with Savoy. Further, they intimidated Basel and Schaffhausen to such an extent that these cities were afraid to join. Thus, in 1584 Geneva was guaranteed the protection of two Swiss cities: Zürich and Bern. Under the terms of the agreement Geneva was to be almost equal to Zürich and Bern, but Bern was not to make a separate alliance with Geneva for twenty-eight years. The Catholic cantons were so opposed to this agreement that they tried to take Geneva before the Diet.

TABLE 22.1
ALLIANCES

Protestants	Catholics
Zürich, Bern, Schauffhausen, Appenzel (Outer Rhoden), Glarus, town of Saint Gall, town of Basel, Biel (Bienne)	Schwyz, Uri, Unterwalden, Zug, Lucerne, Appenzel (Inner Rhoden), abbey of Saint Gall, bishopric of Basel

1. Alliance with Duke of Savoy, 1578

2. Eternal Compact: Bern and Solothurn with France to protect Geneva and Valais, 1579

3. First five Catholic cantons ally with bishop of Basel. Secret alliance, 1580. Freiburg and Solothurn ally.

4. Bern joins alliance with France in which France agrees to protect territories of Bern, 1582

   Zürich and Bern agree to protect Geneva, 1584.

5. Civil war in France; Henry III solicits soldiers to fight. Most cantons agree, 1585.

6. Pfyffer leads Uri and Lucerne to pledge 8,000 soldiers to fight with the Holy League in France ,1585.

7. Bern and Schaffhausen consolidate their forces, 1585

8. Catholics agree to protect Rapperswil, Baden, Kaiserstuhl, Bremgarten and Millingen. Send delegate to Spanish governor in Milan for help in case of war, 1585

9. Protestants send embassy to Catholic cantons to ask them to give up outside alliances and to admit Geneva, 1585

10. Golden (Borromean) League 1586

In this same year the city of Mulhausen in Upper Alsace, pro-French following her conversion to Protestantism, was now involved in a legal problem called the "Finniger Affair." The Catholic cantons insisted that Mulhausen submit the affair to the Diet for arbitration. Mulhausen refused, for such a step would deprive her of her judicial sovereignty. The Catholic cantons thereupon demanded that Mulhausen be ousted from the Confederation.

To make matters even more strained, the heir to the French throne had died in 1584 and the succession involved France in a civil war. In 1585 Henry III solicited a corps of six thousand Swiss soldiers before the Diet in Solothurn, and a majority of cantons consented. But Lucerne and Uri refused, and soon the others, led by Pfyffer, joined in the refusal. Then Pfyffer made a countermove and called up between seven and eight thousand men to fight with the Holy League in France. And despite the remonstrances of the French ambassador he started out for France with his troops.

This action of Pfyffer's gave the Protestants grave cause for alarm, and Zürich, Basel, Bern, and Schaffhausen began to consolidate their forces, fearing an attack by the Catholics. When the Catholics learned of this Protestant consolidation *they* feared an attack by the Protestants, and they too took action. They made a secret agreement to protect the key passes of Rapperswil, Baden, Kaiserstuhl, Bremgarten, and Millingen and to arrange for a messenger service with Freiburg and Solothurn. Then they sent a delegate to remind the Spanish governor in Milan of the help Spain had promised them. War seemed imminent.

The Protestants felt the time had come to take a step which they had long considered. In an attempt to resolve the differences between themselves and the Catholics, the Protestants now sent an embassy to the Catholics, asking them to renounce all other separate alliances, to restore confidence in the Confederation, and further, to admit Geneva, a key to their defense, into the Confederation. They urged the Catholics with great persuasiveness to practice religious tolerance.

But the Catholics were not persuaded. They were unable to view Geneva as a key to the defense of the Confederation, as the Protestants did. They felt it was up to the Protestants to begin the practice of religious tolerance. And they refused to accept any blame

MAP No. 21

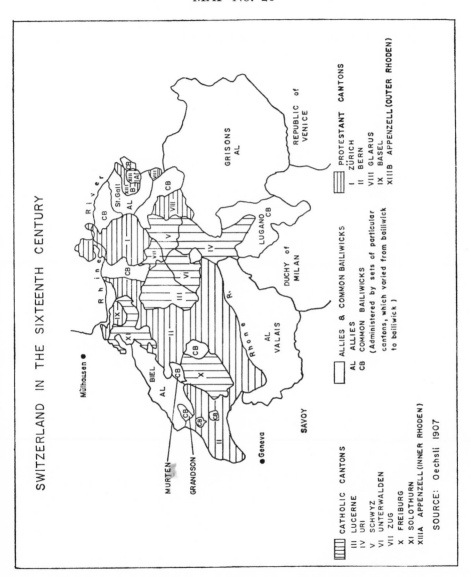

SWITZERLAND IN THE SIXTEENTH CENTURY

CATHOLIC CANTONS
III LUCERNE
IV URI
V SCHWYZ
VI UNTERWALDEN
VII ZUG
X FREIBURG
XI SOLOTHURN
XIIIA APPENZELL (INNER RHODEN)

PROTESTANT CANTONS
I ZÜRICH
II BERN
VIII GLARUS
IX BASEL
XIIIB APPENZELL (OUTER RHODEN)

ALLIES & COMMON BAILIWICKS
AL ALLIES
CB COMMON BAILIWICKS
    (Administered by sets of particular
    cantons, which varied from bailiwick
    to bailiwick)

SOURCE: Oechsli 1907

for the separation. Their minds had in fact already been made up. They were even then in the act of forming an alliance to preserve the Catholic faith. This alliance, The Golden, or Borromean, League, was concluded the following year (1586) and it replaced all other alliances in matters of religion. Since it could be applied to Geneva, it thus erected an intercantonal alliance with repressive force above the Confederation. This action of the Catholics was the final split in the Confederation; and when they made an alliance with Spain they further widened the break between themselves and the Protestants.

In addition to this series of moves and countermoves in the political arena there was another event, the *calendar quarrel*, which further heightened the religious tensions of the decade. The quarrel began in 1582, when the Catholics introduced the new-style Gregorian calendar. The Protestants wanted nothing to do with the new calender because it came from the papacy. The fight dragged on for three years. Although the new-style calendar won, the Protestants determinedly retained the old-style Julian calendar for another one hundred and fifteen years.

PART 2: SURVEY OF VARIABLES (Coded for Conspicuous State, Protestant Cantons)

Dependent Variables

Months of War. There was peace during the entire decade and no months of war. The raw score of 0 yields a standard score of 37. For method of transformation see p. 11.

Territorial Change. There was no territory lost or gained through military maneuvers. There were juridical adjustments which gave the appearance of territorial change in the Vaud and in the domains of the titular bishop of Basel. These adjustments did not, however, appear to involve any actual change in the military control of these territories but only in their nominal legal status. As to Vaud, the changes involved formal recognition by a majority of the Confederation of a conquest which had actually taken place fifty years before. In the Jura mountains between Porruntry and Bienne, the titular bishop of Basel strengthened his legal position against outsiders, but in fact he seems at the same time to have lost effective control of the eastern parts of his domain. We are not certain that no effective territorial change took place here; but it does seem clear that if there was any at all, it was slight indeed, and to unravel the tangled situation in these obscure mountain valleys during this decade would require more extensive study than we were able to give it.

The raw score of 0% yields two standard scores: territorial gain 49 and territorial stability 36. For method of transformation see p. 13f.

Military Variables

Defensive Stance. The Counter-Reformation took a vigorous offensive stance in the Catholic cantons through the Jesuits and through individuals like Borromeo; the archbishop of Milan; von Wartensee; the bishop of Basel; and Pfyffer, the mayor of Lucerne. Although the Protestants actively promoted an alliance with Geneva and were interested in the spiritual conquest of the bishopric of Basel, their stance seems to have been somewhat more defensive than the Catholics. Their attempt to reconcile the differences between the two faiths in 1585 was a conciliatory gesture which was rebuffed by the Catholics. The Catholics not only rebuffed the Protestants but, in a strong offensive action, entered into the Golden or Borromean, League, thus creating the final split in the Confederation. The Protestants, the conspicuous cantons, were on the defensive. Coded *present.*

Strength of Armed Forces. We are concerned here not merely with the Swiss armies, but also with the armies of their allies. The Catholics could count on the strength of Spain, Austria, and Savoy, whereas the Protestants could count on France alone, and France at this time was involved in an internal struggle. It would seem that the Catholics would have had more strength than the Protestants if war had broken out. Coded *absent*

Mobility of Armed Forces. There is no evidence of any differences in mobility between Catholics and Protestants. Coded *absent.*

Quality of Armed Forces. The Swiss prior to 1525 had a reputation as outstanding soldiers and were used as mercenaries by the major European powers. Their reputation as mercenaries declined somewhat after 1525. There is no indication that the Catholic and Protestant cantons differed markedly during our decade. Ludwig Pfyffer had been the chief of the Swiss mercenaries in the French wars of religion (1562–1570), and since he was the leader of the Catholic bloc and known as the Swiss king it may have been that the Catholic cantons enjoyed the greater military reputation. Coded *absent*.

Fortifications. The Catholics felt the need to protect the passes to Rapperswil, Baden, Kaiserstuhl, and Millingen; but there is no indication that they actually took steps to fortify them during the decade. We know that Geneva was fortified, but there is no indication that any attention was given to its further fortification during this decade. Coded *no data*.

Prestige. The two largest, presumably most prosperous cities— Zürich and Bern—were Protestant. But their chief ally, France, had financial troubles at this time. The Catholic cantons, though perhaps smaller and less prosperous, had the support of rich and powerful Spain, Austria, and Savoy. On balance, their relative prestige was probably not significantly different. Coded *absent*.

Geographical Variables

Propinquity. The Protestant and Catholic factions were geographically intermingled; the Catholic forest cantons separated Protestant Bern from Protestant Glarus; Protestant Bern separated Catholic Freiburg from the Catholic Forest cantons (see map 21). The informal headquarters of the Catholic faction was at Lucerne, that of the Protestants at Aarau. Coded *present*.

Natural Barriers. Lake Geneva formed a barrier between Savoy and Switzerland to the north. The Alps formed a barrier between the Spanish-held Milan and Switzerland to the north. The Catholics felt a need to protect Rapperswil, Baden, Kaiserstuhl, Bremgarten, and Millingen; and considered asking Spain to help protect them. Coded *present*.

Capital City. The largest Protestant cities were Zürich in the north of Switzerland and Bern in the south of Switzerland. The Catholic cantons were in the main rural and had no large cities. The location of these two large Protestant cities seems to have had nothing much to do with the intense feeling between the Catholic and Protestant cantons. Coded *no data.*

Diplomatic Variables

Announcements. The intentions of both parties were usually revealed in announcements and at meetings of the Diet. But the Catholic cantons did take secret action, first in 1579 against Biel, Bern, and Basel in an agreement with the bishop of Basel; and again in 1585 in an attempt to protect Rapperswil, Baden, Kaiserstuhl, Bremgarten and Millingen and to arrange for a messenger service with Freiburg and Solothurn. This latter arrangement was at a critical moment, for the Catholic cantons had sent an envoy to Milan to tell the Spanish governor that they were in danger of attack by the Protestants, and might call on him for the help Spain had promised them. The fact that these actions were taken in secret could only have heightened the anxiety that the Protestants already felt. In the main however, the intentions of the Catholics toward the Protestants and vice versa were clear—feeling was too intense to conceal. Coded *no data* because no war actually took place during the decade.

Surprise Attack. Coded *no data,* because no war took place.

Alliances. During the entire decade there were constant attempts by both the Protestants and the Catholics to get foreign support, as well as attempts by each side to win cantons away from the opposing ideology. Freiburg and Solothurn, in particular, sometimes were pulled toward the Protestant bloc, sometimes toward the Catholic (they finally joined with the Catholics). The Catholics made alliances with Savoy, Spain, the Holy Roman League, the bishop of Basel, and with each other. The Protestants made alliances with France, with Geneva, and with each other. Of all the deterrence variables in the decade under study, alliances were the most used. At the end of the decade, when the Protestant cantons in 1585 tried to restore confidence in the Confederation by an appeal to the Catholics to renounce all other separate alliances, the Catholics refused. They countered with an alliance to uphold the Catholic faith in their territories, each one promising to punish backsliding members and to help each other if attacked by external enemies, notwithstanding any other leagues, old or new. This League, the Golden, or Borromean League, which was concluded in 1586, marked the final breaking up of the Confederation into two parties and was followed by the Villemergen Wars of the seventeenth and eighteenth centuries; it culminated in the War of 1849, more than two hundred and fifty years later. Coded *present*.

Active Diplomacy. There was constant negotiating going on: among the cantons, between the blocs—Protestant and Catholic—and among each bloc and its foreign allies. Because war did not actually break out in this decade, the negotiations can be called successful in part. But had they been more effective, perhaps the Borromean League would not have been formed, and the intense feeling between the two ideologies might then have simmered down instead of leading to future wars, as it did. There is of course a striking parallel between the conflicting ideologies of Protestantism and Catholicism and our own situation today between the free world and the Communist powers. Coded *present*.

Intense Diplomacy. The following treaties were concluded during the decade by the Catholic cantons:

1578—The Catholic cantons changed their treaty with Savoy into an auxiliary and protective alliance, with the cantons agreeing to support the Duke of Savoy in case of an attack and supply him with foot soldiers. The Catholic Cantons also agreed not to protect Geneva against Savoy.

1580—The cantons of Schwyz, Uri, Unterwalden, Zug and Lucerne, joined by Solothurn (which was allied secretly with the bishop of Basel) pledged to assist each other in war and to guarantee free markets.

1581—The Catholic cantons renewed their treaty with the new duke of Savoy, Prince Karl (son of Philibert).

1586—The Golden (or Borromean) League concluded an alliance between the Catholic cantons to preserve the Catholic faith.

The Protestant cantons signed these treaties:

1579—Bern and Solothurn signed the Eternal Compact with France to protect Geneva. Geneva, for its part, guaranteed free trade and free passage to the subjects of King Henry III of France and promised to deny them to his enemies.

1584—Zürich and Bern agreed to protect Geneva. Coded *present*.

Previous Conflict. During the second half of the sixteenth century, Switzerland was involved in a bitter internal struggle between Catholicism and Protestantism, a struggle which would eventually lead to wars. Although the Confederation was neutral in the international arena, the Protestant cantons aligned themselves with the French, and the Catholic cantons with the Austrians and Spanish, thus following a policy of conflicting foreign interests which culminated in 1584 in the alliance of Protestant Bern, Geneva, and Zürich against Savoy and the Catholic cantons. At this time Spain was the leading supporter in Europe of the Catholic Counter-Reformation. Although the Spanish king had promised help to the Catholics against the Protestants, they had not called upon him; the cantons were never actually at war with one another, neither during the decade nor for many years afterward. Coded *present*.

Cultural Variables

Benefits. None are mentioned. Coded *absent*.

Cultural Exchange. No information on cultural exchanges between Protestant and Catholic Swiss came to hand. But since the two denominations tended to be concentrated in many particular geographical clusters, scattered among one another, and since with respect to everything but religion the German-speaking Swiss on one hand and the French-speaking Swiss on the other hand would have to be classed as taking part along with other German (French) speakers in a common German (French) culture, this variable is coded *present*.

Trade. Not enough data available to permit coding. Coded *no data*.

General Exchange. Coded *present* because "Cultural Exchange" was coded present.

Administrative Variables

Experience of Ruler. This variable is not pertinent to the Protestant cantons. Coded *no data.*

Youth of Ruler. This variable is not pertinent to the Protestant cantons. Coded *no data.*

Unbridled Ruler. The cantons were a Confederation of republican states. Coded *absent.*

Hereditary Monarchy. Except for Ludwig Pfyffer, the leaders of the Swiss cantons are not mentioned by name. This case is one of a Confederation of republican states split on the religious issue and allied with the major European powers—Catholics with Spain and Austria, Protestants with France. Coded *absent.*

Civil War. There was no serious internal dissension among the Protestant cantons. Coded *absent.*

Centralization. The Swiss Confederation was composed of self-ruling republican states and no centralization was possible. The Protestants had no outstanding leaders during this period, but the Catholics had three—von Wartensee, Borromeo, and Pfyffer. Other than having conspicuous leaders, there is no evidence of any other significant difference concerning centralization between Catholics and Protestants. Coded *absent.*

PART 3: DATA QUALITY CONTROL

This chapter is based on Johannes Dierauer, *Geschichte der schweizerischen Eidgenossenschaft* (Gotha: Perthes, 1913), vol. 3. Dierauer was a well-disciplined professional historian and was trained in the universities of Zürich, Bonn, and Paris. He was a senior librarian in the Swiss city of Saint Gall from 1874 until his death. Nineteenth-century scholars had collected and published many of the contemporary source documents and they were thus available to Dierauer.

Publication Year. Dierauer was published in 1913. Coded *present.*

Primary Source. None were used. (Primary sources, however, were available to Dierauer.) Coded *absent.*

Author's Association. Dierauer was born in an area (Bernegg in Saint Gall) approximately half Catholic and half Protestant. Certainly his higher education at the University of Zürich must have been tinged by the Protestant point of view, for the University is a center of Protestantism in Switzerland. Coded *present.*

Author's Sympathies. Dierauer does not conceal his suspicion of the Counter-Reformation and its zealous proponents. He shows a consistent bias in favor of the Protestants and against the Catholics. Protestant motives are always praiseworthy, Catholic motives always suspect. Protestant leaders are not singled out for praise, but political or opportunistic ambitions are consistently attributed to Catholic leaders like von Wartensee or Ludwig Pfyffer. This bias is understandable in the light of the antagonism in Switzerland between Catholics and Protestants which exists even today. The feeling is a much more intense one than is found in our own country and may be hard for an American to appreciate. Coded *present.*

Proximity. Dierauer wrote in the twentieth century, more than four hundred years after the events occurred. Coded *absent.*

CHAPTER 23

★ ★ ★

FINDINGS

WE HAVE LOOKED at Conspicuous States in twenty historical periods widely scattered in time and space among preindustrial societies. We have asked of each period: How peaceful was it for that Conspicuous State? And did that State gain or lose territory? Then we looked at twenty-nine other factors and hoped that their correlations might help explain the success of that state in avoiding war when it wished to. We also hoped that correlations with these factors might help explain the success or failure of that state in the land-grabbing game of power politics during each of these twenty decades.

Seventeen of the twenty states we chose to study were those whose rivalries were given most attention in encyclopedic world histories. These states were invariably among the largest and most powerful states of their civilizations. The other three studies were of decades in three successive centuries of the Swiss Confederation— chosen because of its republican constitution. (Nearly all the other seventeen were monarchies, and nearly all the monarchies were hereditary.)

If we look at our world today, it seems to be clear that since 1945 the two most Conspicuous States have been the United States and the Soviet Union. Our findings do not support the view that deterrence armament by the United States or the Soviet Union would makes World War III less likely, but they do support the view that attention to the quality and mobility of armed forces now could make territorial loss less likely should such a catastrophe take place.

WAR FREQUENCY

Deterrence and War Frequency

This study embodied four specific tests of the deterrence hypothesis. (1) It contrasted those periods in which the Conspicuous State was in a defensive stance and had larger armed forces than did its Conspicuous Rival with those periods when it did not. (2) It contrasted those periods in which the Conspicuous State while in a defensive stance had more mobile, armed forces than did its Conspicuous Rival with those periods when it did not. (3) It contrasted those periods in which the Conspicuous State, while in a defensive stance, had better quality armed forces than those of its Conspicuous Rival with those periods when it did not. (4) It contrasted those periods in which the Conspicuous State, while in a defensive stance, had extensive fortifications with those periods in which it did not. In all four of these tests, it was predicted, in accordance with the deterrence hypothesis, that wars would be less frequent during the periods when the Conspicuous State, while in a defensive stance, enjoyed the specified military advantages, than during other periods.

None of these predictions was strongly supported by our correlations (see table 23.1). Stance taken by itself seems to be clearly

TABLE 23.1

MILITARY DETERRENCE AND WAR FREQUENCY

Military Deterrence Factors	Relationship to War Frequency (Months of War A732)			
	Point Biserial Correlation	t	Degrees of Freedom	Individual Significance Level (one-tailed)*
Defensive Stance (718)	.00	.00	16	.50
Strength of Armed Forces (B701)	-.0090	-.30	17	.50
Mobility of Armed Forces (B702)	.26	1.1	18	.14
Quality of Armed Forces (B703)	.14	.56	15	.31
Border Fortifications (B704)	-.19	-.70	13	.25
Prestige of Armed Forces (713)	-.11	-.46	17	.35

*From the tables of Hartley and Pearson (1950)

unrelated to Frequency of Warfare; hence one must conclude that among leading rival states it does not take two nations to make a war but only one—a conclusion offering no comfort whatever to advocates of unilateral disarmament in the United States today. When Conspicuous States in a defensive stance assembled larger armies than their rivals, war seemed to have been almost as likely to take place as when they did not. Armed forces of high reputation, and especially armed forces of relatively high mobility, usually were to be found among Conspicuous States more often engaged in war, even though in a defensive stance. This finding is not encouraging to those who suppose that military preparations are likely to lead to peace. It is well to remember that a cause-effect theory is certainly not shown to be true when the correlations it calls for are present, but it is generally held to be disproved when they are absent. The merit of the deterrence theory should have been proved if powerful states, which wish to keep the peace, should tend to succeed in this wish when they take care to have large and mobile armed forces, which arouse the respect of later historians. We find instead that among the historical periods we studied, more mobile and better quality armed forces were raised by these states which *failed* in their aim to keep the peace. It is true that our correlations are not high or significant enough to show this clear tendency beyond doubt, but they are high enough to discredit the notion that a Conspicuous State which seeks peace lessens the likelihood of war by strengthening and improving its armed forces. The only comfort our findings offer to the advocates of deterrence theory is to be found in our results about purely defensive armament—border fortifications. States enjoying strongly fortified borders may well turn out to have a slightly better chance of enjoying peace than those without. But this tendency is not strong enough to produce a high or statistically significant correlation in our sample. Contemporary prestige of armed forces likewise leans in the deterrence direction but so slightly as to support rather the conclusion that it hardly matters at all.

Thus it seems unlikely that military preparations help Conspicuous States very much to keep peace. This conclusion is less surprising when the sampling design of the present study is considered. We selected that state in a given paideia (major civilization) which for a predesignated period was most conspicuously involved in conflicts with other states, and we called it the Conspicuous State. Next, we selected the other state which, in or near the paideia in question, seemed most often to be involved in either diplomatic or military rivalry with the Conspicuous State and we called this other state the Conspicuous Rival.

Consequently, it can be said that with respect to apparent need for armed forces, this study involved little variance: nearly all the Conspicuous States had obvious need for armed forces to protect themselves against possible attack by their Conspicuous Rivals. That is to say, our survey of history indicates that leading civilized societies have usually lived in danger of war, and few statesmen of such societies have ever been in a position to neglect their nation's armed forces in good conscience. The most striking exception seems to be China during the last few decades of the first century B.C., when the great Hun enemy seemed thoroughly pacified and no other serious rivals were in sight.

In a parallel study, a cross-cultural survey of primitive tribes (Naroll 1964a:26; Naroll et al. 1971) similar results were found. In that study, a low positive correlation was found between War Frequency on one hand and Military Obstacles and Military Readiness on the other.

TABLE 23.2

GEOGRAPHICAL FACTORS AND WAR FREQUENCY

Geographical Factors	Relationship to War Frequency (Months of War A732)			
	Point Biserial Correlation	t	Degrees of Freedom	Individual Significance Level (one-tailed)*
Propinquity (712)	-.22	-.97	18	.19
Natural Barriers	.07	.32	18	.38
Capital City Location (716)	-.10	-.41	16	.35

*From the tables of Hartley and Pearson (1950)

Geography and War Frequency

As table 23.2 shows, the geographical factors we studied have had little if any relationship to war frequency among the Conspicuous States we studied. In our sample, war tended to be slightly less frequent when the Conspicuous States shared a common land boundary with their Conspicuous Rivals. The importance of the distance from the capital cities of the Conspicuous States to their boundaries seemed negligible. And oddly enough, when Conspicuous State and Conspicuous Rival were separated by natural barriers they tended to be involved in warfare a little *more* often with each other. But none of these tendencies were large or statistically significant. Thus from our study it seems most unlikely that these geographical factors mattered, which suggests that time-and-space factors, however tactically important to the military staff officer, do not seem to affect the likelihood of war among leading states.

Diplomacy and War Frequency

Similarly, as table 23.3 shows, diplomatic policies of the sort here studied have had little if any effect on War Frequency among the

TABLE 23.3

DIPLOMATIC FACTORS AND WAR FREQUENCY

Diplomatic Factors	Relationship to War Frequency (Months of War A732)			
	Point Biserial Correlation	t	Degrees of Freedom	Individual Significance Level (one-tailed)*
Announcements of Intention (A705)	.29	1.06	12	.17
Surprise Attack (705)	.09	.31	12	.38
Alliances, D.S. (A706)	.05	.20	14	.42
Active Diplomacy (A707)	.22	.96	18	.19
Intense Diplomacy (B702)	-.26	-1.1	18	.14
Previous History of Conflict (714)	-.01	-.07	18	.50

* From the tables of Hartley and Pearson (1950)

conflicts we studied. Announcements of Intention—warnings by aggressor states—were, if anything, associated with longer or more frequent rather than shorter or less frequent wars.

If no war at all began during the period studied, Announcements of Intention was coded *no data* and the period was omitted from the calculation of correlations. So we are measuring whether such announcements tend to be associated with shorter wars. If they prevented a war altogether, then our correlations would not consider that fact. This seemingly odd and self-defeating policy has a simple explanation: we did not find in our sample even one case where such an announcement was credited with such an effect. We concluded that either such an effect must be rare indeed or that an announcement by way of a warning which in fact staved off war did not seem sufficiently important to be mentioned by the historians we consulted.

Likewise, in the conflict situations we studied, diplomacy was if anything the more active if the warfare was more frequent. In other words, more diplomatic missions were sent during periods of more frequent warfare than during periods of less frequent warfare.

Not surprisingly, there were more treaties concluded between the rivals during periods of less frequent warfare than during periods of more frequent warfare. The only surprising thing about this measure of intensity of diplomacy was the fact that it correlated so modestly with frequency of warfare after all.

Other diplomatic factors proved even less relevant to the Frequency of Warfare. We found no relationship worth mentioning between frequency of warfare and a previous history of conflict among the rivals; the use of surprise attack to begin a war; or, most important of all, the organization of a web of defensive alliances. This last point is one which statesmen and the public would do well to note carefully indeed. Collective security as a diplomatic policy did not seem to succeed in making war less likely among the conflict situations we studied.

Cultural Factors and War Frequency

Table 23.4 is the first instance in this chapter where we have anything to do with meaningful correlations. We found trade to

TABLE 23.4

CULTURAL FACTORS AND WAR FREQUENCY

Cultural Factors	Relationship to War Frequency (*Months of War A732*)			
	Point Biserial Correlation	t	Degrees of Freedom	Individual Significance Level (*one-tailed*)*
One-sided Benefits (A709)	.13	.56	17	.31
Cultural Exchange (A708)	-.44	-2.1	18	.03
Trade (B708)	-.35	-1.2	12	.13

* From tha tables of Hartley and Pearson (1950)

be more frequent in more peaceful decades than in less peaceful ones. So too we found the exchanges of culturally influential elites such as visiting teachers, students, missionaries, royal brides, entertainers, or hostages to be more frequent in peaceful decades. These results are not quite so trivial as they might seem. They flatly contradict the findings from a similar test in a cross-cultural survey which covered mostly primitive tribes (Naroll 1964a; Naroll et al. 1971). Perhaps this contrast may arise from the fact that many primitive people tend more often than civilized ones to fight most frequently with nearby neighbors who have a common culture—that is, speak mutually intelligible dialects of the same language and share a common value system and a common set of manners and customs.

Hence, these results may be sufficiently interesting to call for further study. Cultural exchanges are widely praised today. For decades if not centuries cultural exchange has figured prominently in after-dinner speeches welcoming distinguished visitors from abroad. The proponents of cultural exchange dislike war and seem to think that mutual cultural understanding between nations makes war between them less likely. Apparently the proponents of cultural exchange see war as an outgrowth of ethnocentric prejudice and suppose that the dispelling of prejudice by first-hand contact would make for peace.

A skeptic might point out that among civilized societies cultural differences are considerable and these differences include important inconsistencies in value systems. Consequently he might think that peaceful intercourse would actually stregthen ethnocentric feelings instead of weakening them, by reinforcing certain cultural stereotypes.

Needless to say, our results are very far from demonstrating the success of cultural exchange policies in reducing the likelihood of war. In the first place, most of our codings (A708, B708, C708) were subjective, and the coders had the War Frequency data in mind. True, in general, as must already be clear from our discussion of military deterrence and geographical and diplomatic factors, our coders have not tended to be much influenced by our hypotheses; nevertheless it would be well to have their work confirmed by naive coders. More importantly, cross-lagged correlations to establish time sequence are urgently needed. Perhaps cultural factors do indeed promote peace. But perhaps it is only that cultural factors are more common in time of peace than in time of war. Obviously, when two nations are at war, trade is discouraged between them. Presumably, when two nations are at war, influential elites are not so likely to visit back and forth, either.

TABLE 23.5

ADMINISTRATIVE FACTORS AND WAR FREQUENCY

Administrative Factors	Relationship to War Frequency (Months of War A732)			
	Point Biserial Correlation	t	Degrees of Freedom	Individual Significance Level (one-tailed)*
Experience of Ruler (A710)	-.04	-.18	14	.46
Youth of Ruler (B710	-.13	-.46	12	.35
Unbridled Ruler (C710)	.20	.85	17	.22
Hereditary Monarch (D710)	.27	1.1	17	.14
Civil war (711)	.24	.93	14	.19
Centralization (717)	.22	.99	18	.19

* From the tables of Hartlev and Pearson (1950)

Administrative Factors and War Frequency

As table 23-5 shows, none of the administrative situations we examined proved to have any clear relationship with War Frequency. If our findings suggest any relationship at all, they suggest that perhaps older, hereditary monarchs ruling centralized states are slightly more likely to be at war than other sorts of rulers.

TERRITORIAL GAIN

The analysis of Territorial Gain is important for two reasons. First, Territorial Gain is a major goal of statesmen playing the game of power politics. That game seems to have been actively played in most paideias most of the time, and it seems to be going on actively today between the United States and the Soviet Union in places like Cuba, Vietnam, and the Middle East. It would be interesting to know what factors indeed make for success in the power politics game.

A second and more profound reason for studying territorial gain is the role that such gain plays in cultural evolution. The game of power politics is often played by states, nations, and empires with differing cultures. A state loses the game entirely when it loses all of its territory. Its people are then absorbed and administered by rivals. True, conquered peoples often exert strong cultural influences upon their conquerors. Conquered Greece gave her philosophy and science to conquering Rome, conquered Judea her monotheistic moral code to conquering Rome; and conquered China gave nearly her entire culture to the conquering Manchus. Nevertheless, such instances as these are probably exceptions rather than rules. Most of the people Rome conquered largely gave up their native cultures and took up Latin speech and Roman ideas; in Italy, France, and Iberia this change was permanent. It would be useful indeed to study the frequency with which Territorial Gain brings with it adoption of the culture of the conquerors by the conquered (time did not permit us to investigate this question in our study). To the extent that territorial expansion is associated with culture spread, then culture traits—ways of life—functionally associated with Territorial Gain tend to be selected for survival. Territorial Gain is thus presumably at least in some part a selection factor in cultural evolution.

Deterrence and Territorial Gain

From our study, it looks as though attention to military preparations helps in the game of power politics. (See Table 23.6) Thus while we do *not* support the commonly-held notion that military preparations of peacefully minded nations help avoid war, we *do* find a little support for the commonly held notion that military preparations help win wars. We do not find that size, nor mobility nor border fortifications of military forces is particularly helpful.

TABLE 23.6

MILITARY DETERRENCE AND TERRITORIAL GAIN

Military Deterrence Factors	Relationship to Territorial Gain (A730)			
	Point Biserial Correlation	t	Degrees of Freedom	Individual Significance Level (one-tailed)*
Defensive Stance (718)	-.35	-1.5	16	.08
Strength of Armed Forces (A701)	.07	.33	17	.38**
Mobility of Armed Forces (A702)	.01	.05	16	.50
Quality of Armed Forces	.37	1.6	17	.06
Border Fortifications (A704)	.15	.60	16	.28
Prestige of Armed Forces (713)	-.01	-.05	17	.50

   * From the tables of Hartley and Pearson (1950)

   ** By linear interpretation

It is often said that God is on the side of the largest battalions. If God takes sides, it is not the side of the largest battalions, nor that of the best fortified battalions, nor that of the most renowned. Rather God, if he takes sides at all, seems to stand at the side of the well-trained battalions. If we must spend billions of treasure on armies, perhaps we should be wise to spend generously on a fewer number of highly trained airborn divisions, rather than on a greater number of less well-trained, less mobile ones.

Geography and Territorial Gain

Our findings (See table 23-7) offer no support for the soldier's traditional concern with terrain. Tactically—in planning individual

TABLE 23.7

GEOGRAPHICAL FACTORS AND TERRITORIAL GAIN

Geographical Factors	Relationship to Territorial Gain (A730)			
	Point Biserial Correlation	t	Degrees of Freedom	Individual Significance Level (one-tailed)*
Propinquity (712)	.07	.31	18	.38
Natural Barriers (715)	-.10	-.45	18	.35
Capital City Location (716)	-.20	-.83	16	.22

* From the tables of Hartley and Pearson (1950)

battles no doubt, terrain is often of crucial importance. But here we are not considering tactics, but strategy. We are considering the winning of entire wars rather than the winning of particular battles. We find that there may be a slightly greater tendency for Conspicuous States to expand their territories when they are fighting neighbors than when they are fighting more distant rivals. But we find that, if anything, natural barriers tend to be associated with territorial loss. It is as though states enjoying the protection of natural barriers tended to rely too much upon them and thus were vulnerable to determined enemies.

Diplomacy and Territorial Gain

Just as the diplomatic policies studied here had little if any effect upon War Frequency, so we find no evidence that Diplomacy helps much in its other chief ostensible purpose, the furthering of the state's interest in the game of power politics (see table 23-8).

TABLE 23.8

DIPLOMATIC FACTORS AND TERRITORIAL GAIN

	Relationship to Territorial Gain (A730)			
	Point Biserial	t	Degrees of Freedom	Individual Level (one-tailed)*
Announcements of Intention (A705)	-.23	-.82	12	.22
Surprise Attack (B705)	-.01	-.04	12	.50
Alliances, D.S. (A706)	-.10	-.38	14	.38
Active Diplomacy (A707)	-.50	-2.4	18	.01
Intense Diplomacy (B707)	.02	.11	18	.46
Previous History of Conflict	-.27	-1.19	18	.14

* From the tables of Hartley and Pearson (1950)

The only substantial relationship we have uncovered is one which would seem to offer no comfort whatever to the relationship between the activity of diplomats and the success of their states in gaining territory. The more territory a state is *losing*, the more *active* its diplomats. (Needless to say, we presume territorial loss to be the cause and not the effect of diplomatic activity. The data supports either interpretation equally well.)

Cultural Factors and Territorial Gain

Not surprisingly, territorial gain proved unrelated to either one-sided benefits or trade (see table 23.9). However, our results do

TABLE 23.9

CULTURAL FACTORS AND TERRITORIAL GAIN

Cultural Factors	Relationship to Territorial Gain (A730)			
	Point Biserial Correlation	t	Degrees of Freedom	Individual Significance Level (one-tailed)*
One-sided Benefits (A709)	-.13	-.57	17	.31
Cultural Exchange (A708)	.22	1.00	18	.17
Trade (B708)	.08	.28	12	.42

* From the tables of Hartley and Pearson (1950)

suggest the possibility that there may be a relationship between Cultural Exchange and Territorial Gain. If it is confirmed by a restudy, as its low significance level demands, this finding might suggest that such Cultural Exchanges are more likely in times of uncertain boundaries.

Administrative Factors and Territorial Gain

Our findings suggest that centralized states or those led by experienced rulers tend to do well in the game of power politics, while hereditary monarchies tend to do less than well, as do states internally divided by civil war. Please remember that our centralization codings looked to the ostensible, publicly announced system of government rather than to the way the state was actually run behind the scenes. As we said in chapter I, we coded a Conspicuous State as more highly centralized than its Conspicuous Rival if its ostensible plan of government afforded the central government more control over provinces, other things being equal. We also coded Conspicuous State as more highly centralized if, other things being equal, within the central government power was concentrated into relatively fewer hands than in the central government of the Conspicuous Rival. This finding suggests that throughout the period of recorded history, among preindustrial societies, there may have been a tendency for more highly centralized states to spread their territories at the expense of less highly centralized ones.

TABLE 23.10

ADMINISTRATIVE FACTORS AND TERRITORIAL GAIN

	Relationship to Territorial Gain (A730)			
Administrative Factors	Point Biserial Correlation	t	Degrees of Freedom	Individual Significance Level (one-tailed)*
Experience of Ruler (A710)	.36	1.4	14	.09
Youth of Ruler (B710)	.06	.22	12	.42
Unbridled Ruler (C710)	.16	.67	17	.28
Hereditary Monarchy (D710)	-.24	-1.06	17	.17
Civil War (711)	-.26	-1.02	14	.17
Centralization (717)	.28	1.23	18	.12

* From the tables of Hartley and Pearson (1950)

OTHER FINDINGS

As part of our study, we correlated each independent variable with every other. (See table C-2 of Appendix C for the complete correlation matrix.) Of these 406 correlations, we think about two dozen may tell us something. (See table 23-11). (Of course, we have allowed for the group significance problem here; see pages 377-378 below).

TABLE 23.11

CORRELATION MATRIX — COMMUNICATION CLUSTER

	Defensive Stance 718	Intense Diplomacy B707	Absence*** of Natural Barriers (715)	Capital City Near Frontier (716)	Cultural Exchange (A708)	Trade (B708)	Civil War (711)
Defensive Stance 718	—	.44	.12	.25	.47	.29	.46
Intense Diplomacy B707	.44	—	.21	.33	.52	.63	.74**
*Absence*** of Natural Barriers (715	.12	.21	—	.70**	.48	.54	.32
Capital City Near Frontier (716)	.25	.33	.70**	—	.56*	.72*	.32
Cultural Exchange (A708)	.47	.52	.48	.56*	—	.82**	.49
Trade (B708)	.29	.63	.54	.72*	.82**	—	.76
Civil War (711)	.46	.74**	.32	.32	.49	.76	—

    * Significant at the 5% level both individually and as a group member (See pages 377-387).

    ** Significant at the 2% level both individually and as a group member (See pages 377-387).

    *** Variable 715 was originally coded for the *presence* of natural barriers on the frontier. Its coefficients here all were negative in sign.

Communications Cluster

While time has not permitted us to perform any formal factor or cluster analysis, it is apparent from inspection that seven traits are loosely associated in a group. Five of the seven traits in the group have to do with communications and travels. Hence we are calling the group the Communications Cluster.

There seem to us to be two interesting things about this cluster. First, capital cities tend to be closer to frontiers when natural barriers are absent. This tendency suggests the inference that considerations of defense are less important in determining the location of capital cities than considerations of ease of communications abroad.

Secondly, we are intrigued and puzzled by the presence of Civil War in this cluster. Why should Civil Wars be more frequent in states with more lively communications abroad? No doubt Civil Wars might well turn out to encourage not only Defensive Stance but also Intense Diplomacy. But would Civil Wars also tend to encourage foreign trade and cultural exchanges? It seems rather more attractive to suspect that in some way Civil Wars might tend to be more frequent in the presence of easier and more active foreign travel. Needless to say, our study is very far from having demonstrated any such thing, but it does raise an interesting question here.

Military Factors

Inspection discloses a second cluster of interrelated traits. This cluster, however, seems to be a trite and trivial one. It seems to say no more than that more military minded states and rulers pay more attention to mobility and quality of armies. The four traits involved here are Defensive Stance, Quality of Armies, Mobility of Armies and Unbridled Ruler.

SUMMARY OF MAIN FINDINGS

The chief object of our search in this study was for factors correlated with peace. We found none of any consequence. Our study indicated there is no real support for the belief that either military or diplomatic efforts have tended in the long run to make peace much more likely among the defensively oriented Conspicuous States we studied. We also looked for factors which made for success in the land-grabbing game of power politics. We sought correlations between Territorial Gain and other factors. We do not assume that it is good for people to be consistent winners at that game, but we do assume that it is bad for people to be consistent losers.

Here we found a little support for the view that centralized states or those led by experienced rulers tend to do well at the game of power politics. But again, to our considerable surprise, we did not find that attention to military preparations seemed to make much of a difference.

The main point of this pilot study is clear. If its findings can be trusted, they tell us that for Conspicuous States, at least, the search for peace and security through armed force is in vain. Those who live by the sword may indeed expect to perish by the sword. The world arena of power politics has been a bloody one. Prominent states cannot escape involvement in war. World peace perhaps may be found through world law—through a world federation or a global conquest empire—who knows? But if this pilot study faithfully reflects the state of affairs in the world of power politics, and if that state of affairs continues unchanged, there is little hope for either peace or security in arms. In the absence of a world order, we must continue to live with the waste and slaughter of war.

How much confidence can we place in these findings? In our final chapter, one of us offers an answer.

CHAPTER 24

★ ★ ★

CAN WE TRUST OUR FINDINGS?

by Raoul Naroll

DETERRENCE CORRELATIONS IN GENERAL

THE MAIN OBJECT of this pilot study has been to test the feasibility of a cross-historical survey of factors attending War Frequency and Territorial Gain. Our chief focus has been on military deterrence. Here we found no reason to believe that military preparations tended to make wars less likely. How confident can we be of this finding? In effect, what is the lower limit we can reasonably expect to find in the universe of the correlations between War Frequency (Months of War) on one hand, and our seven deterrence variables (Defensive Stance, Strength of Armed Forces, Mobility of Armed Forces, Quality of Armed Forces, Prestige of Armed Forces, Defensive Fortifications and Defensive Alliances) on the other hand?

For this purpose we can use the method of confidence intervals (Blalock 1960:305–9). The user of this method states the risk of error he is willing to assume. Given such a level of confidence, the method designates the limits or boundaries wherein the true correlation can be expected to lie. The mathematics of the method assumes random sampling; when samples depart from randomness they must also reckon with the possibility that sampling bias alters these limits.

We are content for our present purpose to accept a risk of five percent. Table 24-1 shows the lower limits of the seven deterrence correlations. Column C shows these limits as computed from the present sample. But the length of the confidence interval between the observed correlation and the limits is a simple function of the sample size. Column D shows the lower limits at the 95% level of confidence which the correlations we observed would enjoy

TABLE 24.1

LOWER CONFIDENCE LIMITS, POINT BISERIAL CORRELATIONS

Months of War (730), 5% one-tailed

A	B	C	D	E	F
Predicate Trait	Point Biserial Correlation	Lower Confidence Limits			
		N= 20 P=.05	N=403 P= .05	N=403 P= .01	N=403 P=.001
Defensive Stance (718)	.00	-.40	-.08	-.12	-.15
Strength of Armed Forces (B701)	-.009	-.39	-.09	-.13	-.16
Mobility of Armed Forces (B702)	.26	-.13	.18	.15	.11
Quality of Armed Forces (B703)	.14	-.29	.06	.03	-.01
Border Fortifications (B704)	-.19	-.58	-.27	-.30	-.34
Prestige of Armed Forces (713)	-.11	-.48	-.19	-.22	-.26
Alliances, Defensive Stance (A706)	.05	-.38	-.03	-.07	-.11

if the sample size had been 403 instead of 20. Column E shows the lower limits for a sample size of 403 at the 99% level of confidence; Column F at the 99.9% level.

From Table 24-1, Column C, it is clear that now we can have confidence in only one of our deterrence findings. Even considering our small sample, it seems unlikely that Mobility of Armed Forces, as measured by us, has a strong negative association with War Frequency. Our lower limit of -.13 is a weak negative association. But let us suppose that a random sample of 403 historical periods were to find the same correlations we found on our sample of 20 historical periods. Then we would be confident indeed of five of our findings that there was at best no more than a weak negative correlation between War Frequency on one hand and Defensive Stance, Strength of Armed Forces, Quality of Armed Forces, and Defensive Alliances. The only mode of deterrence which we might then expect to enjoy any measure of consistent success would be Border Fortifications.

Thus our findings tend to discredit the deterrence hypothesis. But only in the case of one deterrence variable, mobility of Armed Forces, can we feel any measure of confidence in our findings.

As to the others, our study encourages us to hope that from a restudy of a much larger sample (say about 400 historical periods) we could expect to discredit confidently four other supposed military or diplomatic deterrents.

MOBILITY OF ARMED FORCES AS A DETERRENT

Our confidence in our findings does not however depend only upon sample size; upon that depends errors arising from chance alone. But we need to worry about other possible sources of misplaced confidence than chance.

Causal Sequence

In our sample, we found a *positive* correlation between Mobility of Armed Forces and War Frequency. From this, we have inferred that in the universe as a whole there is in fact no strong *negative* correlation. And hence, we infer that if a nation increases the mobility of its armed forces while on the defensive, it does not much reduce the likelihood that it will nevertheless be attacked. But might our results not merely reflect another sequence of relationships altogether? Suppose that a nation is in fact attacked. Might it not then wish to strengthen its defenses by increasing the mobility of its armed forces? We do not believe that in fact this latter explanation holds good. In none of the decades that we studied did we notice a tendency of the Conspicuous States which we studied to increase the mobility of their armed forces. In none of these periods did we notice any change in the relative naval strength of the Conspicuous States. In none did we notice any increase in the proportion of cavalry to infantry of the Conspicuous State. In all twenty periods, the measure of the relative mobility of armed forces of the Conspicuous State and its Conspicuous Rival reflected the preexisting situation—the situation at the beginning of the decade in question—as far as we could tell.

Sampling Bias

Has sampling bias misled us? After all, our sample was not strictly random. True, the particular decade we studied was randomly chosen; but the century and civilization (paideia) were chosen rather for our convenience than from any rigorous representative sampling plan.

Did we somehow tend to favor civilizations and periods in which Mobility of Armed Forces tended for some reason to be less effective a deterrent than in the universe at large?

If so, we should expect to find some substantial association between both variables on one hand and the disfavored regions and time periods on the other. The most disfavored region was the Middle East and the most disfavored time period was the ancient period. As table 24-2 shows, all associations are slight and plausibly attributable to mere chance.

TABLE 24.2

CONTROLS

Months of war (730 / Mobility of Armed Forces (B702)

		Months of War (730)		Mobility of Armed Forces (B702)	
		Correlation	two-tailed significance	Correlation	two-tailed significance
	Sampling				
566	Mideast Region	.22	.36	-.21	1.00
567	Ancient Period	-.05	1.00	.15	1.00
	Unit Definition				
565	Swiss Group	-.33	.16	-.14	1.00
	Data Quality Controls				
A424	Publication Year	.00	1.00	-.04	1.00
B424	Primary Sources	.14	1.00	.14	1.00
A425	Authors' Associations	-.58	.05	-.29	.74
B425	Authors' Associations	-.39	.10	-.09	1.00
A426	Author's Sympathies	-.18	1.00	-.27	.85
B426	Authors' Sympathies	-.01	1.00	-.02	.74
427	Authors' Proximity	.26	.29	.23	.41
	Galton's Problem				
560	Area-Time	.02	1.00	-.12	1.00
561	Time-Area	-.02	1.00	-.12	1.00
	Regional Associations				
562	Greek Paidea	.09	1.00	.19	.89
563	Western Paidea	-.01	1.00	.07	1.00
564	Chinese Paidea	.06	1.00	-.19	1.00
	Temporal Associations				
568	Medieval	-.05	1.00	-.33	.47
569	Modern	.13	1.00	.25	.72

So, it does not seem likely on the face of it that sampling bias is causing a substantial negative correlation in the universe to disappear from our sample. However, it would be better to use a stratified random sample of periods and civilizations and thus to eliminate this possibility altogether.

However, our sample has a strong bias of another sort. That bias is the bias in favor of conspicuousness. We have studied Conspicuous States and their Conspicuous Rivals. These states have been the leading powers of their time and place. Our results apply only to them. We do not know if they apply at all to second or third-line powers. Thus we can use this study to generalize about the chances of a policy of deterrence succeeding today when followed by leading powers like the Soviet Union or the United States. But we must be more careful about applying it to smaller, less conspicuous powers like Yugoslavia, Turkey, or Sweden.

Finally, our sampling universe is a universe of preindustrial states. None of the states we studied had steam, oil, or electric motors. None had steamships, railways, motor trucks, or airplanes. The soldiers we studied moved ashore on foot or on horseback, afloat on galleys or sailing ships. We cannot presume that these changes in technology have not changed the deterrence situation.

Let us take a quick look at the actual course of events in the nineteenth and twentieth centuries. Did the deterrence measures of Britain's naval armaments from 1900 to 1904 avoid World War I? Did the border fortifications of France's Maginot Line avoid World War II? Were the defensive alliances of the collective security period of the 1930's an effective deterrent against the Axis powers? Did the overwhelming atomic superiority of the United States in 1950 deter the North Koreans from attacking the South Koreans? Did the immense sea and air transport capacity of the United States deter the North Vietnamese from invading South Vietnam? Has the high quality of Israel's armed forces deterred the Arabs from attacking her?

The preceding forensic paragraph is no substitute for a proper objective cross-national survey. The applicability of our findings to present day conditions must be tested by a formal study and until then we can only guess. But on the face of it, certainly one could not say that deterrence prospects today seem manifestly to have improved in any marked way or to any marked extent.

We did *not* however focus on the success of deterrence policies in avoiding catastrophic wars. The opinion of a man like Winston Churchill that the atomic balance of terror had preserved the world from World War III is not to be lightly dismissed. Indeed, the whole subject of escalation is of pressing relevance here. But we have not studied either catastrophic wars as such or escalation as such, so we can draw no conclusions about them.

Unit Inconsistency

In this pilot study, for our special purposes, in seventeen of our sampling periods, our units were paideas; but in the other three, our sampling unit was the Swiss Confederation. As table 24-2 shows, the Swiss did seem to be relatively more peaceful than the rest of our sample. But with respect to mobility, they differed hardly at all. So our unit inconsistency does not seem to have mattered here.

Coding Reliability

We did not run formal reliability tests on our codings. However, we do have two types of reliability checks. Each of our chapters was read by a professional historian who was an expert on the civilization in question. These readers found much fault in our interpretations of events; but none of them disagreed with either our War Frequency or Mobility ratings. The original ratings on all variables were made by one of the three authors. Each of these ratings was checked by a research assistant. One of the twenty Months of War ratings was thus corrected; but all the original ratings on Mobility were confirmed.

Data Bias

Have historians consistently misled us about War Frequency or about Mobility of Armed Forces? Should we be concerned here about the undoubted tendency of the historical record to be biased? There is no doubt that record is biased in the direction of oversimplifying a complex and confusing mass of events, or that it is biased in favor of the wish of the political authorities to present their affairs to their public and to posterity in the best possible light. Still, the occurrence of wars as we have defined them is not a matter easily concealed or misrepresented. A ruler or a historian need not be a genius at propaganda or at public relations to perceive that his interest lies in a three-point policy. (1) The ruler should confirm the occurrence of wars (the public is sure to know about them anyway). If the very existence of an unhappy war is denied, that denial of so notorious a fact only discredits him who denies it. (2) The ruler should select for wide publicity those events of the war which reflect the greatest credit upon his regime. (3) The ruler should ignore those events of the war which reflect discredit upon his regime.

The possibility of bias in reports on Mobility of Armed Forces appears to be small, for like reasons. Here, too the general proportion of cavalry to infantry is not likely to be a state secret. Similarly, the existence and approximate size of fleets of warships is also hard to conceal.

So, on the face of it, we would not seem to be especially vulnerable to propaganda bias in either of these measures. But let us look at our measure of bias. We expect primary sources and secondary historians nearer in time to events, to display greater familiarity with them. But we expect later secondary sources to be more objective. Especially, we expect historians writing in the last two centuries to be skeptical of self-serving claims within the historical record. For nearly two hundred years now, a critical appraisal of historical sources has been the hallmark of the well-trained professional historian. Finally, we would expect historians not associated with the states being studied to be more objective than those who are associated. But we would expect historians who express sympathy for the viewpoint of the states being studied to be less objective. Table 24-2 (p. 347 above) does indicate that authors associated with the states studied do tend to report shorter wars than those not so associated. And they may also, to a lesser extent, tend to report a relatively less mobile armed force.

We can measure the extent to which this association may be misleading us. Our measure is the coefficient of first-order partial correlation (Blalock 1960:333–36). This measure makes several assumptions. (1) It assumes that the variables concerned are linearly related; but then so do our coefficients of correlations themselves; these measure only linear association. Of course, by linear association I mean the tendency for the two variables to be so related that their path of regression tends to form a straight line (see Blalock 1960:276–77). (2) This measure of partial correlation assumes that any corrrelation between the control variable (A 425—Authors' Associations) and each of the controlled variables (730—Months of War and B702—Mobility of Armed Forces) results from the control variable as the cause tending to produce variations in the controlled variables as effects. This assumption is however a conservative one. Our partial correlation will tell us how much association remains between the two controlled variables after allowing for the influence upon them of the control variable. What would happen if the correlation between control and the controlled is due to some other relationship than control as cause and controlled as effects? Then we should *under*estimate the partial correlation. (3) This measure of partial correlation assumes that the control variable (Authors' Associations) is accurately measured, without random error or bias. The reader will remember (p. 32 above) that the control variable, Authors' Associations, is a measure of the nationality of the historian. This measure seems to be one about which we would seldom be mistaken. The first-order partial correlation among the three variables comes to 0.12. This correlation is still positive in sign; it is however less than half as great as the raw (zero order) correlation between Months of War and Mobility of Armed Forces of .26. Thus if in fact there is a tendency for Authors' Associations to bias their reports on both War Frequency and Mobility of Armed Forces, and if we have measured this tendency accurately, we still have reason to believe that increasing Mobility of Armed Forces does *not* tend to reduce War Frequency. But we are not so confident as we were before.

The remaining tests for data quality—tests of historical record bias—do not give any cause for concern.

Cultural Diffusion (Galton's Problem)

Are we being misled by cultural diffusion? Is there a tendency for neighbors in time or space to copy one another with respect to patterns of War Frequency or Armed Forces Mobility? Evidently not at all, as Table 24-2 (p. 347, above) shows. The linked pair correlations are very small or negative in sign. Only high positive correlations would give us grounds for concern.

Regional Associations

Are we perhaps generalizing to the world at large the special characteristics of particular civilizations? Is any one region unduly contributing to our result? This question is the reverse of the question asked about sampling bias. There we looked at neglected or underrepresented regions. Here we look at the heavily represented ones. As table 24-2 (p. 347 above) shows, there is little or no special tendency for either variable to be associated with the civilizations from which most of our periods were drawn. Both would need to have had high correlations of like sign to give us grounds for concern.

Temporal Associations

We may ask the same question about particular periods of time. As Table 24-2 shows, we have much the same reassuring answer. There was little if any tendency for War Frequency to be associated with either the medieval or the modern time period (or for that matter, with the ancient period, as we have already remarked in our discussion on sampling).

Deviant Cases

Are there any particular cases in our sample when high relative mobility of armed forces of a state in a defensive stance *was* in fact associated with a long period of peace? and if so, is there any reason to suspect that the preponderance of cavalry over infantry, or of naval transport, had anything to do with that peace? Not one such case occurs in our sample, not one!

Summary

Our examination of all but one rival hypothesis leaves us as confident as ever in our finding that an increase in Mobility of Armed Forces does not tend to decrease War Frequency. Our analysis of causal sequence has been reassuring. Our analysis of sampling bias has been reassuring, although we would have been better off with a strictly random sample of centuries for study. But our results apply only to leading states in nonindustrial civilizations. Our analysis of unit inconsistency has been reassuring, although we would have been better off if we had used consistent units throughout. Our informal checks of data reliability were reassuring, although we would have been better off with formal reliability measures. Our analysis of Galton's problem was entirely reassuring. So was our analysis of Regional Associations and of Temporal Associations. There were no deviant cases in our sample at all which is itself a reassuring finding.

We remain concerned about the possibility that our correlation may have been somewhat exaggerated by bias arising out of Authors' Associations. This concern suggests that a future restudy might perhaps seek data on the variables concerned from historians of varying associations, to compare their findings, and—with respect to the dependent variable at least—to use only periods in which historians with rival associations agree.

And we ought to take care to document and test for reliability our classification of historians' associations. These associations usually seem patently obvious. Very well then: our coefficient of reliability will be all the higher.

Despite these doubts arising from possible bias associated with historians' associations, our results still create a modest presumption against the deterrence hypothesis that an increase in the mobility of armed forces by a Conspicuous State in a Defensive Stance will tend to make war frequency smaller.

COMMUNICATIONS CLUSTER

The other main finding of our study has been the existence of what we have called the Communications Cluster (p. 342 above). Two of these interrelationships proved particularly strong. There was the finding that Trade tends to be found together with Cultural Exchange. We would have been surprised to find it not so. Then there was the second finding that capital cities tend to be located near frontiers which lack natural barriers. From the military

point of view this is both interesting and a little surprising. If
capital cities tended to be located with an eye to relative military
safety, we would have expected the relationship to be the other
way around. Let us examine this finding to see if perhaps we might
be misled by our work. Since the entire Communications Cluster
is a collection of interrelated correlations, our confidence or lack of
confidence about this finding can be more or less extended to the
cluster as a whole.

Chance

Since our sample is so small, may we have been misled by mere
sampling accident? Through a streak of luck, could we have just
happened to pick twenty historical periods in which capital cities
just happened to be located near the frontier when natural barriers
were absent? That question is the question of individual statistical
significance. Or, since we ran so many correlations, and since we
did not in advance make any predictions about the relationship
between location of capital cities and natural barriers along the
frontier, would we not expect one or two correlations as seemingly
high and strong as this one to turn up by chance alone among so
many trials? That question is the question of group significance.

The individual significance level of this correlation, by Fisher's
Exact Test, two-tailed, is .00904. We would expect to get a result
this high only nine times in a thousand by chance alone.

The group significance level of this correlation, as set forth and
explained in Appendix D below (pp. 377–387) is even stronger—
only .002. We would expect a group to contain as many nominally
significant correlations as this group contained by chance alone in
only two such groups in a thousand—and this particular correlation was the most highly significant in the whole group.

Despite the small size of the sample and the large number of
correlations run, then, it is not very likely that mere chance or
luck produced the correlation we found between location of capital
cities and natural barriers along the frontier. Nevertheless, since
these relationships were not predicted in advance, some doubt must
remain until they are found again in a new sample.

Causal Sequence

Since the natural barriers existed before the cities were built, or were made into capital cities, the direction of causality is clear. Manifestly, it is the absence of natural barriers which has attracted the cities near to the frontiers. It would seem reasonable to explain this attraction from the role of trade in city development. Where natural barries are absent, trade tends to become easier. As trade flourishes, cities grow. Large cities tend to be chosen as convenient capitals.

TABLE 24.3

CONTROLS

Natural Barriers (715) / Capital Cities (716)

		Natural Barriers (715)		Capital Cities (716)	
		Correlations	two-tailed significance	Correlations	two-tailed significance
	Sampling				
566	Mideast Region	-.03	1.00	-.15	1.00
567	Ancient Period	.19	.77	-.24	1.00
	Unit Definition				
565	Swiss Group	-.03	1.00	.24	1.00
	Data Quality Controls				
A424	Publication Year	-.31	.45	.25	.62
B424	Primary Sources	.22	.69	-.04	1.00
A425	Authors' Associations	.08	1.00	.10	1.00
B425	Author's Associations	.19	.75	-.04	1.00
A426	Authors' Sympathies	.13	1.00	-.04	1.00
B426	Authors' Sympathies	.26	.52	-.06	1.00
427	Authors' Proximity	.09	1.00	-.07	1.00
	Galton's Problem				
560	Area-Time	-.22	.69	-.06	1.00
561	Time-Area	.03	1.00	-.18	.79
	Regional Associations				
562	Greek Paidea	.13	1.00	-.12	1.00
563	Western Paidea	-.36	.27	.47	.13
564	Chinese Paidea	.38	.26	-.37	.29
	Temporal Associations				
568	Medieval	-.22	.63	.11	1.00
569	Modern	.05	1.00	.15	1.00

Another possible explanation. Perhaps another tendency working alongside the first: cities located near frontiers free of natural barriers tend to grow and flourish, and the states to which they belong likewise tend to grow and flourish, causing them to become conspicuous to historians in later times and thus to come into our sample.

Sampling Bias

Table 24.3 shows the application of all our control tests to the correlation between location of capital cities and absence of natural barriers along the frontier. Our measures of sampling bias are entirely reassuring. The correlations with Middle Eastern paideias are so small as to be meaningless, and the correlations with ancient time periods are opposite in sign. Our selection bias does not seem then to have affected the correlation we are controlling.

Unit Definition Inconsistency

Again, there is no tendency for our Swiss cases to produce a spurious correlation between location of capital cities and location of natural barriers along the frontier. (Those readers who think of Switzerland as sheltered by the immense natural barriers of the Alps should take a look at a relief map of Europe. The Alps lie in the center of Switzerland, not along its frontiers.)

Coding Reliability

Again, no formal reliability tests were run on the codings of these variables. But again we had two reliability checks. None of our professional historian readers objected to any of our codings on either of these variables, although they found many other faults with our work (see p. xli above). In the check of the ratings of the three authors by research assistants, no fault was found with any of the codings on natural barriers, and only one coding on capital city location was challenged (and changed).

Data Bias

We would hardly expect historians to be biased in their reports on the location of capital cities. We would hardly expect historians to be biased in their reports on the location of bodies of water or of mountain barriers along the frontiers. Not surprisingly, none of our data quality controls gives us any grounds for concern. All but one are low; the correlations of the exception (A424 Year of Publication) are opposite in sign; thus if there is a reporting bias there—which seems unlikely—it is a bias which has tended to lower our correlation, not one which has tended to raise it.

Cultural Diffusion (Galton's Problem)

While natural barriers do not diffuse from culture to culture, fashions in the location of state capitals might. However, both our correlations with interdependence controls are negative in sign. Only a positive correlation would arouse our concern.

Regional Associations

Can we have been misled into generalizing about all history from the special characteristics of one or two particular regions? Table 24.3 (p. 355 above) reassures us that such is not the case. All three regional tests (Greek, Western, Chinese) show opposite signs for the associations of the two variables. Hence if anything, regional association has tended to lower the absolute value of the correlation between natural barriers and location of capital cities.

Temporal Associations

Can we have been misled into generalizing about all history from the special characteristics of one or two particular time periods? Again Table 24.3 is reassuring. Of the two favored time periods, the medieval period has correlations opposite in sign. The modern period has correlations so small as to be meaningless.

Deviant Cases

The correlation we seek to explain is that which affects the location of capital cities. We find that capital cities tend to be located near frontiers in the absence of natural barriers there. What exceptions to that rule do we find and how might we explain them? We have three exceptions in our sample (1) Rome vs. Carthage, 225–216 B.C. Rome is located near the sea, a natural barrier. But the sea facilitates rather than blocks trade (our concept of natural barriers was devised with military rather than commercial aspects in mind). (2) England vs. France, 1776–1785. Exactly the same case. London, like Rome, is located near the sea. The sea is a natural barrier—one that long protected England from invasion, as every Englishman learns in childhood. But the sea facilitates rather than hinders trade, and never has any sea helped a nation to acquire a greater trade than the sea that lies at the mouth of London's Thames. (3) T'ang China vs. Tibet, 776–785. Ch'ang-an, the T'ang capital, was located near the great mountain barrier of Tibet. But to the north of that barrier runs the great Silk Road to Turkestan and the west. The location of Ch'ang-an, near the eastern end of the Silk Road, on the Wei River near the confluence of the Huang Ho, was a location which facilitated trade along other routes than the route blocked by the mountain barrier (for an illustrative map showing trade routes, see Pankala 1966:36).

Summary

This finding is interesting. None of our control tests raised any doubts in our minds. We are confident about causal sequence. We are confident about the statistical significance of our findings, both individually and as a member of a group. Though our sample is biased, and our units inconsistent, neither of these departures from the best survey design seem to have affected our findings about capital cities and natural frontiers. Our coding reliability seems to have been high, and there is no reason to believe that bias in the historians we studied has influenced this finding. Our confidence in our tests for bias of historians—our data quality control tests—is heightened since these tests did find some suggestion of possible bias in some of the other variables studied (see Appendix B below). Cultural diffusion clearly cannot explain the finding. Nor is it a product of any particular civilization or time period. It apparently applies to all the history of the major old world civilizations for the last twenty-five hundred years. Finally, none of the three deviant cases in our sample really constitute clear exceptions to the hypothesis that capital city location tends to depend upon trade and communications rather than upon defense.

GENERAL CONCLUSIONS

Most of our findings about the futility of military deterrence by leading states are inconclusive and untrustworthy. They need to be checked out on a larger sample. Their applicability to industrialized societies also needs to be tested by a cross-national survey. One of these findings, that relating Mobility of Armed Forces to Frequency of Warfare, is fairly well supported by the present study, but even that one is somewhat weakened by the apparent presence of parallel reporting bias related to the associations of the reporting historians.

A restudy of military deterrence to verify or correct these findings ought to improve the research design of the present study in these ways: (1) it ought to study a strictly random sample of centuries and civilizations (paideias); (2) it ought to use consistent sampling units throughout; (3) it ought to study the status of armed forces and other deterrence variables *explicitly* at the beginning of the decade in question, in order to fix causal sequence firmly; and (4) whenever possible, it ought to take its data (on the dependent variable at least and, even better, on both variables) from two historians with opposing associations: one associated with the conspicuous state and the other with its conspicuous rival.

A parallel cross-national survey of deterrence among modern industrial states is also needed.

Our unexpected discovery of a Communications Cluster of intercorrelated traits has as its most significant theoretical finding that capital city location tends to follow considerations of trade rather than considerations of defense. Despite the smallness of sample size, we can have considerable confidence in this finding.

As a pilot study, I submit, this research may be deemed entirely successful. It has demonstrated the feasibility of applying the cross-cultural survey method of anthropology to the comparative study of history. It has defined its working concepts rigorously, and in such a way as to be suitable for use in any historical context. It has applied these concepts in fact to events in a wide variety of historical contexts. It has demonstrated a practical method of sampling, of unit definition, of interdependence control, of data quality control, and of temporal and regional controls. It has shown the special strength of cross-historical surveys in enabling causal sequence to be observed directly by lagging the observations of the supposed cause and the supposed effect.

APPENDIX A

SAMPLING PROTOCOL

PRESENTED in the following pages are a body of definitions, corollaries and rules which when carried out will yield two comparative historical samples, a *general* sample and a *special* sample.

Each of these samples considers a number of specified historical traditions or paideias. In each paideia, the sampling procedure seeks a decade from each century on which peace data or territorial change data is available concerning the largest state of the tradition and its principal rival at the time.

The *general sample* defines paideias culturally in terms of the societies making use of bodies of writing whose importance is evidenced by wide translation. In fact, such historical traditions involve the higher civilizations of the old world and by focusing on two Conspicuous Rivals at each given period we focus on the power politics of the leading military powers of the world. While the definition is silent on the relative military and economic importance of states belonging to the defined traditions and states not so belonging, in fact it will almost always be the case that the defined traditions include the states with the largest populations, the largest cities, the greatest collection of experts of all kinds, the greatest wealth, and the greatest military power. These are the great cultural traditions, the people who have created modern civilization collectively—the Europeans and the people of the Middle East, India, Southeast Asia, and the Far East.

For many purposes such a sample would of course be far too restrictive: these great cultural traditions have had no monopoly on important inventions; they do not include representative samplings of art styles, value systems, kinship systems, religious systems, and so on. But in a study of power politics they are indicated for two reasons: first, they have been or include almost all the great powers or almost all the great states; and second, they have kept all the records of power politics of any importance which survive for study.

The *special sample* follows the fortunes of two European powers of special interest to this study, the Great Russian state and the Swiss Confederation. The importance of Russia today is obvious. (China would have been designated a third special study were it not already included in the general sample.) The Swiss Confederation gives us the longest tradition of a European republic engaged in power politics. No other comparable record of republican affairs exists, except for ancient Greece and republican Rome, whose affairs are already included in the general sample.

Rules and Definitions

DEFINITION 1.0. *Paideia*. A paideia is defined as a body of writings in a single script including works on philosophy, art, fiction, folk traditions, ethics, science, or mathematics (but excluding historical records as such) which have been extensively translated for the sake of their contents as such, not merely as ethnological specimens or sources of historical data.

DEFINITION 2.0. *Script*. A script is a unique collection of graphemes by means of which a spoken language as used by speakers in the home can be substantially reproduced.

COROLLARY 2.1. A script may be ideographic, phonetic, or some combination of the two.

COROLLARY 2.2. The arrangement of morphemes and their choice in script may customarily differ widely from that used in domestic speech; the test is not whether the script *does* substantially reproduce domestic speech but whether it *can*.

DEFINITION 2.3. *Grapheme*. A named set of allographs with a constant set of referrents (morphemes, phonemes, or some combination of the two). (Example: the first letter of the Latin alphabet.)

DEFINITION 2.4. *Allograph*. A graphic pattern which is distinguishable at sight from all the other patterns in the writing system and which forms one of a grapheme set. (Example: A, a, *a*.)

DEFINITION 2.5. *Unique*. A script is unique if at least seventy-five percent of its graphemes lack any allograph which is interchangeable with the allograph of another script.

DEFINITION 2.6. *Interchangeable*. Allographs of two scripts are interchangeable if a reader of one script is likely to equate the allograph of another with an allograph of his own; and if the two sometimes have a common referrent. (Example: the combination MAK would be recognizable to readers of Greek, Latin, and Cyrillic scripts and might be taken by many readers of each to refer to the same series of allophones.)

DEFINITION 3.0. *Extensively Translated.* A body of writings has been extensively translated when text equivalent to ten million English words originally written in it has been translated into a language written in another script.

DEFINITION 4.0. *Major Civilization.* A major civilization consists of those societies which keep records in the script of a paideia.

DEFINITION 4.1. *Society.* Domestic speakers of a mutually intelligible dialect who belong to the same state if they belong to any state at all.

DEFINITION 4.2. *State.* A group of people defined by themselves as the occupants of a stated territory encompassing at least 10,000 square kilometers whose leaders assert and wield exclusive control over warfare.

DEFINITION 4.3. *Warfare.* Public, lethal, licit group combat between members of territorially defined groups.

DEFINITION 4.4. *Special Tradition.* A special tradition is the historical record of a particular state of special interest and thus arbitrarily selected for the special sample. This study has two special traditions so designated: the Great Russian and the Swiss.

> DEFINITION 4.41. *The Great Russian Tradition.* The Great Russian Tradition is defined as the history of the state to which the city of Moscow belongs, from the expulsion of the Mongols to the present day.

> DEFINITION 4.42 *The Swiss Tradition.* The Swiss tradition is defined as the history of the Swiss Confederation from its founding by Uri, Schwyz, and Unterwalden in 1291 to the present day.

DEFINITION 5.0. *Base Decade.* The following decades are designated base decades (the digits 76 having been selected by blindfold finger stab on a table of random numbers): for the Christian era: A.D. 76 to A.D. 85, A.D. 176 to A.D. 185, A.D. 276 to A.D. 285, A.D. 1876 to A.D. 1885 (all years inclusive). For earlier times: 25 B.C. to 16 B.C., 125 B.C. to 116 B.C., 225 B.C. to 216 B.C. (all years inclusive).

DEFINITION 5.1. *Sampling Period.* The sampling period for each base decade shall consist of that decade and the five following decades.

DEFINITION 5.2. *Sampling Guide.* For each paideia or special tradition studied, a secondary history (or histories) shall be designated the sampling guide. (Examples: for the Hellenic tradition, including users of the Greek, Latin and Cyrillic alphabets, *the Cambridge Ancient History, the Cambridge Medieval History,* and *the Cambridge Modern History* might well be designated sampling guides; for the Chinese tradition, J. M. de Mailla's *Histoire de la Chine* might well be so designated.)

DEFINITION 5.3. *Encyclopedic Histories.* Specific works are designated as encyclopedic histories for specific traditions, as follows:

DESIGNATION 5.31. *Steiger.* G. Nye Steiger, *A History of the Far East* (Boston: Ginn, 1944) is designated the encyclopedic history for the Far East, Turkestan, Tibet, India, and Southeast Asia.

DESIGNATION 5.32. *Langer.* William L. Langer, *An Encyclopedia of World History* (Boston: Houghton Mifflin, 1948) is designated the encyclopedic history for the Middle East, North Africa, and Europe, except as stated in Designation 5.33 below.

DESIGNATION 5.33. *Encyclopedia Britannica.* The section "History," of the article "Europe" in the *Encyclopedia Britannica*, 1946 Edition (8: 844–91) is designated the encyclopedic history for the European major civilization after A.D. 476 (although not for the Swiss or Russian special traditions).

Sampling Procedure—General Sample

RULE 6.0 For each sampling period in each Major Civilization a Conspicuous State and its Conspicuous Rival shall be designated by a formal content analysis of the appropriate Encyclopedic History.

6.1 Protocol for designation of Conspicuous State (CS)

6.11 References in Encyclopedic History to states in conflict situations are counted. References to battles, treaties which settle disputes, ultimata or warnings, are examples of references to conflict situations. Each state involved and referred to is counted separately. References to groups of states by distinct name are counted separately from references to individual states. Thus most references to conflict situations will involve at least two states, one on each side of the conflict.

6.12 That state or group of states most frequently mentioned thus by name in the encyclopedic source during the sampling period is designated the Conspicuous State for that period. (No implication is thereby made that this state was actually the *most* conspicuous state, or the leading or most important state, but only that it was one of the most active states in international affairs during the period in question.)

6.13 States not mentioned by name but only by implication (e.g., mention of one state fighting a battle with an unnamed opponent) are ignored in this counting.

6.14 For the Russian study, this step is omitted, since Russia itself is treated as the most conspicuous state (The Grand Duchy of Moscovy and its successor states).

6.15 For the Swiss study, the Swiss Confederation itself is treated as the most conspicuous state for those sampling periods in which there is no evidence in the encyclopedic source of conflicting foreign policies being followed by the Swiss cantons.

6.16 Where the Swiss cantons are pursuing conflicting foreign policies so that the confederation as such is not an effective member of the international arena, the canton referred to most often concerning foreign affairs (in Langer) is sought.

6.161 References (in Langer) to Swiss cantons, either individual cantons or groups, *e.g.*, "Bern and Zürich," "the Catholic Cantons" are counted.

6.162 Only references which mention a canton or group of cantons in a context implying rivalry with a non-Swiss power (whether or not the non-Swiss power is allied with rival Swiss cantons) are counted.

6.163 References in a context implying rivalry include mentions of war or of negotiation of opposing interests.

6.164 That canton or group of cantons most often referred to becomes the Conspicuous State (that is, is treated as such) for the sampling period in question. If there is a tie, it is broken by using a table of random numbers.

6.2 Protocol for designation of Conspicuous Rival of C. S.

6.21 List every reference to another power or territory in a context implying rivalry with the Conspicuous State (CS), including mention of war or of negotiation of opposing interests.

6.22 If a reference which is unidentified occurs to a rival (*e.g.*, a battle is mentioned but the opponent not named; a conquest is mentioned but the other power involved is not named) then the identification of this unidentified reference is to be sought in the Secondary History; if it is not identifiable there either, it is to be ignored.

6.23 Tally the references to each rival mentioned at the bottom of the list.

6.3 Rules governing count of statements of conflict in Conspicuous State or Conspicuous Rival designation:

RULE 6.31 Each distinct assertion of rivalry constitutes a distinct statement for counting purposes regardless of length. On one hand, a single statement might sometimes occupy several sentences; on the other hand, a single sentence might sometimes make several statements.

RULE 6.32 Each mention of a distinct state either by name of the state, name of its official, or name of its location constitutes a distinct statement for counting purposes.

RULE 6.33 Each mention of a distinct activity involving conflict constitutes a distinct statement for counting purposes.

RULE 6.34 Each mention of a distinct geographical place of activity constitutes a distinct statement for counting purposes.

RULE 6.35 Each mention of a distinct year in which an activity took place constitutes a distinct statement for counting purposes.

RULE 6.351 A single incident is counted only once even if mentioned more than once. By a single incident is meant the same parties engaged in the same activities in the same place at the same time in the same way.

RULE 6.36 Where the membership of an alliance, association, or coalition of states is identified in the encyclopedic history section concerned, each reference to the alliance, association, or coalition shall be counted as a reference to each of the members; but where it is not there identified, then the alliance, association, or coalition shall be considered as a unit for counting purposes.

DEFINITION 6.37 The phrase "encyclopedic history section concerned" means that portion of the encyclopedic history being used to conduct the Conspicuous State or Conspicuous Rival designation.
(Example: "Louis XIV's further progress was arrested by a coalition of the United Provinces, the Emperor, the German princes, and Spain." This counts as four statements: France vs. the United Provinces [the Netherlands], France vs. Austria [the Emperor], France vs. Spain, France vs. the German Princes.)

RULE 6.38 Where a single sentence is used as the basis of more than one statement, the basis of breakdown shall be noted in the designation form.

RULE 6.39 A peace treaty is a reference to a conflict event. All parties to the treaty are considered mentioned by implication; so we check to see who were the parties if this is not already clear.

7.0 Designation of a Decade for Study.

7.1 Beginning with the period C 476 to C 485 (where C is the century concerned), evidence is sought for the war or peace condition during the decade. This evidence is sought in the Designated Sampling Guide. (Example: for Switzerland, the sampling guide is Johannes Dierauer, *Geschichte der Schweizerischen Eidgenossenschaft*, 5 vols. Gotha: Perthes, 1915.) For modern Europe, the sampling guide is *The New Cambridge Modern History*.

7.2 Decade designation definitions.

DEFINITION 7.21 Condition change report: a report in the sampling guide which signals change from war to peace or from peace to war.

7.211 A change from war to peace is signaled by the report of the conclusion of a peace treaty or agreement, including an armistice whose term is indefinite or longer than one year; the provision that an armistice may be ended at any time by giving notice is not considered in determining the length of the armistice.

7.212 A change from peace to war is signaled by a declaration of war or by an open, public, deliberate group invasion by an armed body which makes known its readiness to impose its will by force. If the highest authorities of the attacking society recall the armed invaders, apologize for their invasion, deny that it was authorized and offer compensation for any harm done, then the invasion is presumed not to be deliberate. (N.B., a collection of words which signal such a change needs to be made.)

DEFINITION 7.22 Condition status report: a report in the sampling guide which refers to an incident which indicates the war-peace status in force at the time it took place:

> 7.221 Reports of battles or of peace negotiations or of damage by foreign armies indicate a war status is in force.
>
> 7.222 Reports of commerce, alliances, or of diplomatic visits other than peace negotiations indicate a peace status is in force.
>
> 7.223 Each battle is counted separately.
>
> 7.224 Mercenaries are counted as members of employing state, not as members of state of origin.

7.3 Decade designation rules

Rule 7.31 For the decade in question, the sampling guide must contain at least one condition status report or condition change report.

RULE 7.32 Condition status reports must not be inconsistent with previous condition status reports or condition change reports, unless the two inconsistent reports occur in the same calendar year and further unless the first such report is preceded by another report consistent with it while the second such report is followed by another report consistent with it: W W P P or P P W W.

RULE 7.33 Condition change reports should be sought to document the preceding change establishing the opening situation, although they are not strictly necessary.

RULE 7.34 Change and status reports are sought first through the use of the index to the sampling guide. References there to the Conspicuous Rival are checked in the text of the sampling guide.

RULE 7.35 If no selection is made in the entire sampling period then the task is repeated, using the full text of the sampling guide.

Sampling Procedure—Special Sample

RULE 8.1. For each special sample the state or confederation embodying the special tradition concerned shall be taken in place of the Conspicuous State of the major civilization for each sampling period.

RULE 8.2. Otherwise, the sampling procedure for the General Sample shall be followed as given above (items 6.0 through 6.5).

COROLLARY 8.3. If and when the Great Russian tradition qualifies as the largest state in the European civilization, for each such sampling period, the Great Russian special sample will coincide with the general sample for the European civilization.

```
      PROGRAM FITTER (INPUT, OUTPUT, TAPE5 = INPUT, TAPE6 = OUTPUT,      0100
     1 TAPE1, TAPE2, TAPE3 )
CFITTER PROGRAM TO FIT NORMAL DISTRIBUTION WITH WDPC LIBRARY FUNCTIONS   0110
      DIMENSION X(058,085),P(100),RECIP(100),Q(100),Y(100),ITEM(10)      0120
  140 FORMAT(16I3)                                                       0130
  150 FORMAT(10E8.3)                                                     0140
      FISH(Q000FL)=0.5*ALOG(ABS((1.0+Q000FL)/(1.0-Q000FL)))             0150
      AT3R(Q001FL) =ATAN(Q001FL) ** 0.33333333                          0160
      AT4R(Q002FL) =ATAN(Q002FL) ** 0.25                                0170
      AT5R(Q003FL) =ATAN(Q003FL) ** 0.2                                 0180
      READ   (5,140)N,  L,K1,K2, (ITEM (I), I = 1,10) ,KEDGE , LINEUP    0190
C N = NUMBER OF TRIBES OR OTHER OBSERVATIONS PER TRAIT (VARIABLE)        0200
C L = NUMBER OF VARIABLES                                               0201
C OPTION I -- SET K1 AT FIRST TRANSFORM NO,K2 AT LAST TRANSFORM NUMBER,  0202
C             LEAVE ITEM BLANK                                          0203
C OPTION II -- SET K1 AT 1,K2 AT NUMBER OF TRANSFORMS, AND SPECIFY       0204
C             TRANSFORMS DESIRED IN ITEM. K2 .LE. 10.                   0205
C KEDGE -- FOR EDGEWORTH CORRELTION, SET KEDGE = 1.SEE STA 2130          0206
C LINEUP -- FOR FULL PAGE OF COMPUTATION TABLE FOR EACH TRANSFORM,       0207
C             SET LINEUP AT 1.                                          0208
  210 FORMAT(1H0,4H N= ,I5,4H L= ,I5)                                    0209
      CONST=9.0*10.**30                                                 0210
      WRITE (6, 210)N,     L                                            0216
      DO 3000J = 1,L                                                    0220
      IF(LINEUP.GT.0) GO TO 280                                         0230
      WRITE (6, 260)                                                    0240
  260 FORMAT (1H1, 5X, 20HVARIABLE  TRANSFORM , 3X, 4HMEAN, 10X, 5HSIGMA 0250
     1 , 10X, 5HGAMMA, 13X, 2HAA, 10X, 7HCHECK 1, 10X, 7HCHECK 2  )     0260
  280 READ   (5,150)(Q(I), I=1,N)                                       0270
      DUMMY = 0                                                         0280
      DO 2120 I = 1, N                                                  0290
      Q (I)  = Q(I)  + 1.0000001                                       0300
      IF(Q(I).LT.CONST) GO TO 360                                      0305
C DUMMY VALUES OF P AND RECIP, GEARY READS Q AND SKIPS THIS VALUE  OF I  0310
  330 P (I) = 1.0                                                       0320
      RECIP (I) = 1.0                                                   0330
      GO TO 2120                                                        0340
  360 P (I) =  Q(I) + 1.001                                             0350
      RECIP (I)  = 1.0 / P(I)                                           0360
      DO 2119 INDEX = 1,85                                              0370
      GO TO(1,2,3,4,5,6,7,8,9,10,11,12,13,14,15,16,17,18,19,20,21,22,   0371
     1 23,24,25,26,27,28,29,30,31,32,33,34,35,36,37,38,39,40,41,42,     0372
     1 43,44,45,46,47,48,49,50,51,52,53,54,55,56,57,58,59,              0373
     1 60,61,62,63,64,65,66,67,68,69,70, 71,72,73,74,75,76,77,78,79,    0374
     1 80,81,82,83,84,85      ) INDEX                                   0375
    1 X (I,1) =  Q(I)                                                   0376
      GO TO 2118                                                        0380
    2 X(I,2) = ALOG(P(I) )                                              0400
      GO TO 2118
    3 X(I,3) =  ALOG( SQRT( P(I) ) )                                    0420
      GO TO 2118
    4 X(I,4) = X(I,2) ** 0.333                                          0440
      GO TO 2118
    5 X(I,5) = SQRT(X(I,2) )                                            0460
      GO TO 2118
```

```
    6   X (I,6) = ATAN(X (I,2) )                                          0480
        GO TO 2118
    7   X(I,7) = SQRT( Q(I) )                                             0500
        GO TO 2118
    8   X (I,8) =  ATAN( X(I,7) )                                         0520
        GO TO 2118
    9   X(I,9) = Q (I) ** 0.333                                           0540
        GO TO 2118
   10   X(I,10) =  Q(I) ** 0.25                                           0560
        GO TO 2118
   11   X (I , 11) =  ATAN( Q (I) )                                       0580
        GO TO 2118
   12   X (I,12) = RECIP (I)                                              0600
        GO TO 2118
   13   RADIAN = SQRT(Q (I) / 100.0)                                      0620
C       ALL VALUES GREATER THAN 100 ARE TREATED AS 100                    0630
        X (I,13) = 2.0 * ARCSIN (RADIAN)                                  0640
        GO TO 2118
   14   X(I,14) = ATAN(X (I,9))                                           0660
        GO TO 2118
   15   X (I,15) = ATAN(X (I,10))                                         0680
        GO TO 2118
   16   X (I,16) =  SQRT(X (I, 11))                                       0700
        GO TO 2118
   17   X(I,17) = X (I,11)   ** 0.333                                     0720
        GO TO 2118
   18   X(I,18) = X (I, 11) ** 0.25                                       0740
        GO TO 2118
   19   X (I,19) = X (I,11) ** 0.9                                        0760
        GO TO 2118
   20   X ( I,20) = X (I,11) ** 0.8                                       0780
        GO TO 2118
   21    X (I,21) = X (I,11) ** 0.7                                       0800
        GO TO 2118
   22   RADIAN = SQRT( Q (I) / 1000.0 )                                   0820
C       ALL VALUES GREATER THAN 1000 ARE TREATED AS 1000                  0830
        X (I , 22) = 2.0 * ARCSIN ( RADIAN)                               0840
        GO TO 2118
   23   X(I,23)=ALOG(ABS(P(I)/(1.0-P(I))))                                0860
        GO TO 2118
   24   X(I, 24) = ALOG( P(I) + SQRT( P(I) ** 2 + 1.0 )  )               0880
        GO TO 2118
   25   X(I, 25) = ALOG( P(I) + 5.0)                                      0900
        GO TO 2118
   26   X(I, 26) = ALOG( P(I) + 10.0)                                     0920
        GO TO 2118
   27   X(I, 27) = ALOG( P(I) + 20.0 )                                    0940
        GO TO 2118
   28   X(I, 28) = ALOG( P(I) + 40.0 )                                    0960
        GO TO 2118
   29   X(I, 29) = ALOG(P(I) + 80.0)                                      0980
        GO TO 2118
   30   X(I, 30) = ALOG(P(I) + 160.0)                                     1000
        GO TO 2118
   31   X(I,31) = FISH( P (I) )                                           1020
```

```
         GO TO 2118
  32  X (I, 32) = TANH( Q (I)  )                                        1040
         GO TO 2118
  33  X (I, 33) = ATAN( X (I, 25)  )                                    1060
         GO TO 2118
  34  X (I , 34) =  ATAN( X (I,  26)  )                                 1080
         GO TO 2118
  35  X  (I , 35)  =  ATAN( X  (I, 27)  )                               1100
         GO TO 2118
  36  X (I, 36) = ATAN( X  ( I , 28)  )                                 1120
         GO TO 2118
  37  X (I, 37) =  ATAN( X (I, 29)  )                                   1140
         GO TO 2118
  38  X (I, 38) =  ATAN( X ( I, 30)  )                                  1160
         GO TO 2118
  39  X (I, 39) =  SQRT( X(I, 25)  )                                    1180
         GO TO 2118
  40  X (I, 40) = SQRT( X (I, 26)  )                                    1200
         GO TO 2118
  41  X (I, 41) =  SQRT( X  ( I , 27)  )                                1220
         GO TO 2118
  42  X (I, 42) = SQRT( X ( I, 28)  )                                   1240
         GO TO 2118
43   X (I, 43)  = SQRT( X  (I, 29)  )                                   1260
         GO TO 2118
  44  X (I, 44)  = SQRT( X  ( I , 30)  )                                1280
         GO TO 2118
  45  X (I, 45)  =  1.0  +  RECIP (I)                                   1300
         GO TO 2118
  46  X  (I, 46) =  SQRT( X ( I, 45)                                    1320
         GO TO 2118
  47  X( I, 47)  =  ALOG( X(I, 45)  )                                   1340
         GO TO 2118
  48  X (I, 48) =  ATAN( X (I, 45)  )                                   1360
         GO TO 2118
  49  X (I, 49)  =  SQRT( X  (I, 47)  )                                 1380
         GO TO 2118
  50  X (I , 50)  =  ATAN(  X (I, 46)  )                                1400
         GO TO 2118
  51  X (I, 51)  = ATAN( X  (I, 47)  )                                  1420
         GO TO 2118
  52   X (I , 52)  =  X (I, 45) ** 0.33333333                           1440
         GO TO 2118
  53   X ( I , 53)  =  ATAN( X(I, 52)  )                                1460
         GO TO 2118
  54  X (I,54) = FISH( X (I,11)  )                                      1480
         GO TO 2118
  55  X (I,55) =  FISH( X (I,2)  )                                      1500
         GO TO 2118
  56  X (I,56) = FISH(P (I) ** 0.33333333)                             1520
         GO TO 2118
  57 X (I, 57)  = FISH( X (I,33)  )                                     1540
         GO TO 2118
  58  X (I , 58) = FISH( X (I, 5)  )                                    1560
         GO TO 2118
```

```
 59    X (I, 59)  = FISH( X (I, 17) )                              1580
          GO TO 2118
 60    X (I, 60)  =  FISH( X (I , 18) )                            1600
          GO TO 2118
   61 X (I,61) = FISH(RECIP (I) )                                  1620
          GO TO 2118
 62    X(I, 62) = AT3R(X(I, 23 ))                                  1640
          GO TO 2118
 63    X(I, 63) = AT3R(X(I, 36 ))                                  1660
          GO TO 2118
 64    X(I, 64) = AT3R(X(I, 31 ))                                  1680
          GO TO 2118
 65    X(I, 65) = AT3R(X(I, 40 ))                                  1700
          GO TO 2118
 66    X(I, 66) = AT3R(X(I, 25 ))
          GO TO 2118
 67    X(I, 67) = AT3R(X(I, 41 ))                                  1740
          GO TO 2118
68     X(I, 68) = AT3R(X(I, 37 ))                                  1760
          GO TO 2118
 69    X(I, 69) = AT3R(X (I,26 ))                                  1780
          GO TO 2118
 70    X(I, 70) = AT4R(X (I,23 ))                                  1800
          GO TO 2118
 71    X(I, 71) = AT4R(X (I,36 ))                                  1820
          GO TO 2118
 72    X(I, 72) = AT4R(X (I,31 ))                                  1840
          GO TO 2118
 73    X(I, 73) = AT4R(X (I,40 ))                                  1860
          GO TO 2118
 74    X(I, 74) = AT4R(X (I,25 ))                                  1880
          GO TO 2118
 75    X(I, 75) = AT4R(X (I,41 ))                                  1900
          GO TO 2118
 76    X(I, 76) = AT4R(X (I,37 ))                                  1920
          GO TO 2118
 77    X(I, 77) = AT4R(X (I,26 ))                                  1940
          GO TO 2118
 78    X(I, 78) = AT5R(X (I,23 ))                                  1960
          GO TO 2118
 79    X(I, 79) = AT5R(X (I,36 ))                                  1980
          GO TO 2118
 80    X(I, 80) = AT5R(X (I,31 ))                                  2000
          GO TO 2118
 81    X(I, 81) = AT5R(X (I,40 ))                                  2020
          GO TO 2118
 82    X(I, 82) = AT5R(X (I,25 ))                                  2040
          GO TO 2118
 83    X(I, 83) = AT5R(X (I,41 ))                                  2060
          GO TO 2118
 84    X(I, 84) = AT5R(X (I,37 ))                                  2080
          GO TO 2118
 85    X(I, 85) = AT5R(X (I,26 ))                                  2100
2118   CALL FLOW (1,J,I,INDEX)                                     2118
2119   CONTINUE                                                    2119
```

```
2120 CONTINUE                                                            2120
     IF(KEDGE.NE.0) GO TO 2270                                           2130
C FOR EDGEWORTH CORRECTION, INPUT KEDGE = 1 ON PROBLEM CARD              2140
     DO 2250 KK =  K1,K2                                                 2150
     IF(ITEM(1).GT.0) GO TO 2190                                         2160
     ICE = KK                                                            2170
     GO TO 2200                                                          2180
2190 ICE = ITEM (KK)                                                     2190
2200 DO 2210 I = 1, N                                                    2200
2210 Y (I) = X (I,ICE)                                                   2210
     IF(LINEUP.LE.0) GO TO 2250                                          2220
     WRITE (6,2240)J, ICE                                                2230
2240 FORMAT (1H1, 12HVARIABLE NO.,I2, 18HTRANSFORMATION NO.,I2)          2240
2250 CALL GEARY (N,Q,Y,J,LINEUP,ICE)                                     2250
     GO TO 3000                                                          2260
2270 DO 2900 KK = K1, K2                                                 2270
     ICE = ITEM (KK)                                                     2280
     ZNI = 0                                                             2290
     SUMY = 0                                                            2300
     SUMY2 = 0                                                           2310
     SUMY3 = 0                                                           2320
     DO 2400 I = 1, N                                                    2330
     IF(9.0*10.0**30.0.LE.Q(I)) GO TO 2400                              2340
     ZNI = ZNI + 1.0                                                     2360
     SUMY = SUMY + X (I,ICE)                                             2370
     SUMY2 = SUMY2 + X (I,ICE) ** 2                                      2380
     SUMY3 = SUMY3 + X(I,ICE)**3                                         2390
2400 CONTINUE                                                            2400
     XBAR = SUMY / ZNI                                                   2410
     SIGMA = SQRT(SUMY2/ZNI - XBAR **2)                                  2420
     GAMMA = (SUMY3/ZNI - 3.0*(SUMY2/ZNI) * (SUMY/ZNI) + 2.0 * ((SUMY/   2430
    1ZNI)**3)) / SIGMA ** 3                                              2440
     DO 2480 I = 1, N                                                    2450
     T=(Q(I)-XBAR)/SIGMA                                                 2460
     T22=-(T**2/2.0)                                                     2470
2480 Y(I)=X(I,ICE)+GAMMA*(T**3-3.0*T)*(EXP(T22))/6.0*.39894228           2480
     WRITE (6,2510)ICE , J                                               2500
2510 FORMAT (1H1, 40HEDGEWORTH CORRECTION, TRANSFORMATION NO.,I5,        2510
    112H,VARIABLE NO, I5)                                                2520
2900  CALL GEARY (N,Q,Y,J,LINEUP,ICE)                                    2530
3000   CONTINUE                                                          2540
     STOP
     END
     SUBROUTINE GEARY(N,Q,Y,J,LINEUP,ICE)                                STA0010
C  R C GEARY AND E S PEARSON, TESTS OF NORMALITY  - BIOMETRIKA OFFICE    STA0015
C    LONDON NEW STATISTICAL TABLE , NO. 1, N.D.     SEE ALSO BIOMETRIKA  STA0016
C    VOL 28, 1936, PP 295-305.                                          STA0017
     DIMENSION Y(200),Q(200)                                            STA0020
     DOUBLE PRECISION ZM2,SSSTD,SSTD,CHECK1,AA,SIGMA,GAMMA,V1,V2,V3      STA0030
40 FORMAT(1H ,F5.0,2F20.5,2E20.5,2F15.5)                                STA0040
50 FORMAT(1H0,5H ZNI= F5.1,6H SUMY= F15.5,7H SUMY2= E15.5,10H     SUMY  STA0050
   13= E15.5)                                                           STA0060
70 FORMAT(1H0,4H V1= D25.18,4H V2= D25.18,8H     V3= D25.18/ 1H         STA0070
   1 10H  SIGMA=D25.18, 10H    GAMMA=D25.18,10H    ZM2=  D25.18)         STA0080
90 FORMAT(1H04HAA= D25.16,11H,CHECK SUMS,D25.16,10X,D25.16)             STA0090
```

```
100 FORMAT(1H ,10H LINE NO.    ,                                    STA0100
   120H    RAW VARIABLE    ,20HTRANSFORMED VARIABLE              STA0110
  2 20H TRANS, VARIABLE**2  ,20H TRANS.VARIABLE**3              STA0120
  3 29HCUM. PERCENT   STANDARD SCORE       )                   STA0130
      SUMY=0.0                                                  STA0140
      SUMY2=0.0                                                 STA0150
      ZNI=0.0                                                   STA0160
      ZNP=0.0                                                   STA0165
      DO 230 I=1,N                                              STA0170
      IF(9.0*10.0**30.LE.Q(I)) GO TO 230                        STA0180
      SUMY=SUMY+Y(I)                                            STA0200
      SUMY2=SUMY2+Y(I)**2                                       STA0210
      ZNI=ZNI+1.0                                               STA0220
230   CONTINUE                                                  STA0230
      ZZ=SUMY                                                   STA0240
      V1=SUMY/ZNI                                               STA0250
      V2=SUMY2/ZNI                                              STA0260
      ZM2=V2-V1**2                                              STA0270
      SIGMA=DSQRT(ZM2)                                          STA0280
      ZNI=0.0                                                   STA0290
      SSSTD=0.0                                                 STA0300
      SUMY=0.0                                                  STA0310
      SUMY2=0.0                                                 STA0320
      SUMY3=0.0                                                 STA0330
      SUMY4=0.0                                                 STA0340
      IF(LINEUP.LE.0) GO TO 370                                 STA0350
      WRITE(6,100)                                              STA0360
370   DO 530 I=1,N                                              STA0370
      ZNP=ZNP+1.0                                               STA0375
      IF(9.0*10.0**30.LE.Q(I)) GO TO 530                        STA0380
      ZNI=ZNI+1.0                                               STA0410
      SUMY=SUMY+Y(I)                                            STA0420
      Y2=Y(I)**2                                                STA0430
      SUMY2=SUMY2+Y2                                            STA0440
      Y3=Y(I)**3                                                STA0450
      SUMY3=SUMY3+Y3                                            STA0460
      SUMY4=SUMY4+(Y(I)+1.0)**3                                 STA0470
      PRCNT=(SUMY/ZZ)*100.0                                     STA0480
      STRD=(Y(I)-V1)/SIGMA+5.0                                  STA0490
      SSSTD=SSSTD+STRD-5.0                                      STA0500
      IF(LINEUP.LE.0)  GO TO 530                                STA0510
      WRITE(6,40)ZNP,Q(I),Y(I),Y2,Y3,PRCNT,STRD                STA0520
530   CALL FLOW(2,J,ICE,I)                                      STA0530
      CHECK1=SUMY3+3.0*SUMY2+3.0*SUMY+ZNI-SUMY4                 STA0540
      V3=SUMY3/ZNI                                              STA0550
      GAMMA=(V3-3.0*V2*V1+2.0*V1**3)/SIGMA**3                   STA0560
      SUMWA=0.0                                                 STA0570
      CALL FLOW(3,J,ICE,0)                                      STA0580
      DO 650 I=1,N                                              STA0590
      IF(9.0*10.0**30.LE.Q(I)) GO TO 650                        STA0600
      WRE=V1-Y(I)                                               STA0610
      WAB=ABS(WRE)                                              STA0620
      SUMWA=SUMWA+WAB                                           STA0630
650   CALL FLOW(4,J,ICE,I)                                      STA0650
      AA=(SUMWA/ZNI)/SIGMA                                      STA0660
```

```
C   AA TAKEN FROM FORMULA 4 P.2, TESTS OF NORMALITY              STA0661
C   GAMMA TAKEN FROM SQRT(B SUB 1), FORMULA 2 P.2, TESTS OF NORMALITY  STA0662
C   THE VALUE OF M SUB 3, THE THIRD MOMENT, IS TAKEN FROM KENNEY AND  STA0663
C   KEEPING, MATHEMATICS OF STATISTICS, PART TWO, 2ND ED., NEW YORK, VAN  STA0664
C   NOSTRAND, 1951, P. 27.                                       STA0665
C   PROOF OF THE FORMULA IS GIVEN IN CROXTON AND COWDEN PP 832 AND FOLLOW.  STA0666
C   CROXTON AND COWDEN  APPLIED GENERAL STATISTICS, 2ND ED., NEW YORK,  STA0667
C   PRENTICE HALL,1955, P 832 AND FOLLOWING                      STA0668
        CALL FLOW(5,J,ICE,0)                                     STA0669
        IF(LINEUP.GT.0) GO TO 710                                STA0670
        WRITE(6,690)J,ICE,V1,SIGMA,GAMMA,AA,CHECK1,SSSTD         STA0680
  690 FORMAT(1H ,2I10, 6D15.5)                                   STA0690
        RETURN                                                   STA0700
  710 WRITE(6,50)ZNI,SUMY,SUMY2,SUMY3                            STA0710
        WRITE(6,70)V1,V2,V3,SIGMA,GAMMA,ZM2                      STA0720
        WRITE(6,90)AA,CHECK1,SSSTD                               STA0730
        RETURN                                                   STA0740
        END                                                      STA0750
        FUNCTION ARCSIN (RADIAN)                                 0010
        TRIAL = 0.785398                                         0020
        DO  110  II = 1, 30                                      0030
C       TABLE SEARCH LOOP                                        0040
        TRY = SIN(TRIAL)                                         0050
        IF( RADIAN-TRY)70,90,100                                 0060
   70   TRIAL = TRIAL - 0.785398 / (2.0 **II)                    0070
        GO TO  110                                               0080
   90 GO TO 120                                                  0090
  100   TRIAL = TRIAL + 0.785398 / (2.0 **II)                    0100
  110     CONTINUE                                               0110
C       TABLE SEARCH LOOP TERMINUS                               0120
  120   ARCSIN=TRIAL                                             0130
        RETURN                                                   0140
        END
        SUBROUTINE FLOW (I,J,K,L)                                0010
        CALL OVERFL(N)                                           0015
        IF(N.GE.2) GO TO 60                                      0016
   50 FORMAT (1H , 11HAC OVERFLOW,4I5)                           0050
   40 WRITE (6,   50)I, J, K, L                                  0040
   60 IF DIVIDE CHECK 80,100
   80 WRITE (6,   90)I, J, K, L                                  0080
   90 FORMAT (1H ,  9HDIVIDE **,4I5)                             0090
  100 RETURN                                                     0100
        END
```

APPENDIX C

★ ★ ★

CODINGS, CORRELATIONS, AND SIGNIFICANCE LEVELS

This appendix consists of five tables as follows:

C.1   TRAIT DATA. Contains codings of independent and dependent variables, both raw scores and transformations.

C.2   CORRELATIONS AND SIGNIFICANCE LEVELS. Contains point biserial and phi correlation coefficients and significance levels (where no less significant than 10 % one-tailed) for correlations between independent and dependent variables and for correlations among dependent variables.

C.3   CONTROLS: DATA. Contains codings for data quality controls, interdependence controls, regional controls and time period controls.

C.4   CONTROLS: CORRELATIONS. Contains point biserial and phi correlations between dependent and independent variables as subject traits on one hand and controls as predicate traits on the other hand.

C.5   CONTROLS: SIGNIFICANCE LEVELS. Contains significance levels for the correlations in Table C.4, where no less significant than 10 % one-tailed.

	GEOGRAPHICAL VARIABLES				DIPLOMATIC VARIABLES						CULTURAL VARIABLES				ADMINISTRATIVE VARIABLES					
B 704	Prestige 713	Propinquity 712	Natural Barriers 715	Capital City 716	Announcements A 705	Surprise Attack B 705	Alliances A 706	Active Diplomacy A 707	Intense Diplomacy B 707	Previous Conflict 714	Benefits A 709	Cultural Exchange A 708	Trade B 708	General Exchange C 708	Experience of Ruler A 710	Youth of Ruler B 710	Unbridled Ruler C 710	Hereditary Monarchy D 710	Civil War 711	Centralization 717
19	-.11	-.22	.07	-.10	.29	.09	.05	.22	-.26	-.01	.13	-.44	-.35	-.44	-.04	-.13	.20	.27	.24	.22
01	-.01	.07	-.10	-.20	-.23	-.01	-.10	-.50	.02	-.27	-.13	.22	.08	.22	.36	.06	.16	-.24	-.26	.28
26	-.30	-.35	-.34	.48	.39	-.65	-.25	-.16	-.20	-.27	-.30	.28	.36	.28	.59	-.24	-.10	.02	-.06	-.14
64	.23	.00	-.12	.25	-.23	-.09	.67	.47	.44	.26	-.20	.47	.29	.47	-.28	.00	-.44	-.16	.46	.00
44	.28	-.01	.10	-.12	-.15	-.03	-.36	-.40	-.08	-.01	.26	-.40	-.36	-.40	.53	-.16	.50	.39	-.21	.02
43	.28	-.20	-.02	.20	-.05	-.30	.41	.21	.19	.07	-.16	.21	.05	.21	.09	-.12	-.12	.08	.32	-.12
03	.07	-.11	.00	-.22	.19	-.17	.33	-.05	.14	-.11	.43	-.05	-.13	-.05	.17	-.25	-.01	.34	.24	.44
20	.26	-.25	.21	-.35	.05	-.21	.56	.21	.00	-.25	.29	-.10	-.19	-.10	.00	-.41	-.29	.20	.22	.36
18	.16	-.07	-.21	-.34	.14	.23	-.10	-.14	-.19	-.07	.07	-.21	.13	-.21	-.04	.17	.08	.07	.16	.64
31	.41	-03	-.15	-.13	-.03	-.03	.41	.20	.01	-.03	-.12	.20	.14	.20	-.09	-.19	-.60	-.44	.26	.4
56	-.11	.12	-.24	.07	-.21	.33	.31	.16	.02	.12	.02	.06	.15	.06	-.49	.46	.07	.13	.25	-.2
--	.02	.30	-.31	.34	-.32	-.25	.82	.18	.26	.30	.05	.49	.42	.49	-.69	.23	-.34	-.05	.28	-.2
---	---	-.12	-.04	-.34	-.84	.36	-.12	-.04	.14	-.12	.06	-.04	-.30	-.04	.04	-.21	-.01	.06	.22	.2
		---	-.05	-.14	-.09	.33	-.02	-.32	.00	.68	.21	-.10	-.05	-.10	-.48	-.08	-.17	-.33	-.0
			---	-.70	.04	.02	.07	.04	-.21	.33	-.02	-.48	-.54	-.48	.13	-.25	.12	-.12	-.32	-.0
			.005	---	.09	-.22	.04	.23	.33	.14	-.04	.56	.72	.56	-.12	.35	-.05	.04	.32	-.33
.007					---	-.45	.08	.22	-.45	-.09	-.07	-.25	-.11	-.25	-.06	-.35	-.30	-.07	-.10	.12
						---	-.37	-.05	.25	.33	.50	-.33	-.15	-.33	-.26	.37	.31	.14	.08	-.10
							---	.24	.05	-.02	-.10	.24	-.04	.24	-.31	-.27	-.40	-.12	.00	-.13
								---		43	-.05	-.12	.20	.30	.20	-.40	.12	-.33	-.12	.76	-.0
.01									.07	---	.25	.16	.52	.63	.52	-.12	.54	.16	.16	.74	.1
												.21	-.10	.30	-.10	-.48	.78	.17	.08	.04	-.0
923			.04	.02				.03			---	-.43	-.05	-.43	-.18	.27	.40	.55	.05	.2
923)			.07	.02				.03			.08	---	.01	.82	1.00	.00	.12	-.33	-.20	.49	-.1
.03			(.04)	(.02)				(.03)				(.08)	(.000012)	(.01)		-.23	.76	-.03	.05	.76	.0
														.07		.00	.12	-.33	-.20	.49	-.1
																---	-.35	.19	.04	-.38	.1
																	---	.47	.27	.42	.0
																		---	.71	.01	.1
											.03								---	.32	.0
					.005	.006						.08	.07	(.08)						---	.1

L); the remaining columns and lines are of qualitative variables. The coefficients of correlation between two quantitative variables are product-moment coefficients.

relationship in one direction (plus or minus) only. Each of these then gives the probability of obtaining the particular result actually obtained, or one even... probabilities of product moment coefficients were computed by using the standard error of these coefficients and entering a normal distribution... exact test). Two kinds of probabilities were omitted: (L) those greater than 0.10; (2) those between two variables whose relationship was an... General Exchange (C 708) are set off in parenthesis because these always agree with those of Cultural Exchange (A 708) and so were not cou...

TABLE C-I: TRA...

Chapter No.	Decade Beginning	Conspicuous State	Conspicuous Rival	MONTHS OF WAR		TERRITORIAL GAIN		TERRITORIAL INSTABILITY		MILITARY VARI...				
				Raw Score	Transformed Score	Raw Score	Transformed Score	Raw Score	Transformed Score	Defensive Stance 718	Strength S.I. A 701	Strength D.S. B 701	Mobility S.I. A 702	Mobility D.S. B 702
3.	CHINESE 125 B.C.	Former Han Dynasty	Huns	105	66	3.6%	59	3.6%	53	A	P	A	A	A
4.	25 B.C.	Former Han Dynasty	Huns	0	37	0%	49	0%	36	A	P	A	A	A
5.	776 A.D.	T'ang Dynasty	Tibetans	51	52	0%	49	0%	36	P	P	P	A	A
6.	1076	Sung Dynasty	Tanguts	34	49	0%	49	0%	36	A	P	A	O	A
7.	1376	Ming Dynasty	Yunnanese	1	39	6%	60	6%	55	A	P	A	A	A
8.	ISLAMIC 776	Abbasids	Byzantines	72	56	.01%	49	.01%	36	A	P	A	O	A
9.	RUSSIA 1476	Muscovy	Novgorod	6	42	252%	63	252%	68	A	P	A	P	A
10.	GRAECO-ROMAN 225 B.C.	Rome	Carthage	34	49	-19.9%	34	19.9%	60	A	P	A	A	A
11.	25 B.C.	Rome	Parthia	0	37	1.5%	57	1.5%	49	P	P	P	A	A
12.	176 A.D.	Rome	Marcomanni-Quadi	34	49	0%	49	0%	36	P	A	A	P	P
13.	376	Rome	Visigoths	66	55	0%	49	0%	36	P	A	A	A	A
14.	576	Byzantines	Persia	120	66	0%	49	0%	36	O	O	O	A	A
15.	WESTERN 1276	France	England	0	37	-1.3%	40	1.3%	48	P	P	P	A	A
16.	1376	England	France	90	61	-25.6%	34	25.6%	61	O	A	A	A	A
17.	1576	Spain	Netherlands	120	66	-2.27%	38	2.27%	51	P	P	P	P	P
18.	1676	France	Netherlands	46	51	4%	60	4%	53	A	P	A	A	A
19.	1776	England	France	67	55	-39%	34	39%	62	P	P	P	A	A
20.	SWISS 1376	Swiss Confederation	Kiburg	17	45	13%	61	13%	58	P	P	P	A	A
21.	1476	Swiss Confederation	Burgundy	12	44	11.5%	61	11.5%	58	A	A	A	A	A
22.	1576	Swiss Protestant	Swiss Catholic	0	37	0%	49	0%	36	P	A	A	A	A

MONTHS OF WAR TRANSFORMED SCORES (T.S.)
Entry is value of Z where:
X = Number of months of war in the decade
$Y = 2 \text{ Arcsine } \sqrt{(X/100)}$ (i.e., twice the arcsine of the square root of one one-hundreth.)
S = Standard deviation of the Y scores
$\bar{Y}$ = Mean of the Y scores
$Z = 50 + 10 \ [(Y - \bar{Y})/S]$

TERRITORIAL GAIN T.S.
Entry is value of Z, computed as in Transformed Scores in Months of War, where:
X = Percentage of territorial gain or loss enjoyed or suffered by the Conspicuous State from or to its Conspicuous Rival or its allies during the decade studied, considering gain as a plus score and loss as a minus score.

$Y = \text{Arctangent } \sqrt{X}$

TERR...
Entry is v...
Transformed
X = Absolute
(i.e., minus

	A 703	Quality D.S. B 703	Fortifications S.I. A 704	Fortifications D.S. B 704	Prestige 713	Propinquity 712	Natural Barriers 715	Capital City 716	Announcements A 705	Surprise Attack B 705	Alliances A 706	Active Diplomacy A 707	Intense Diplomacy B 707	Previous Conflict 714	Benefits A 709	Cultural Exchange A 708	Trade B 708	General Exchange C 708	Experience of Ruler A 710	Youth of Ruler B 710	Unbridled Ruler C 710	Hereditary Monarchy D 710	Civil War 711	Centralization 717
P	A	P	A	A	P	P	A		O	O	A	A	A	P	P	A	O	A	P	P	P	P	A	P
P	A	A	A	P	P	P	A		O	O	A	A	A	P	P	A	O	A	A	P	P	P	A	P
A	A	P	P	A	P	P	P		O	O	P	P	P	P	P	P	O	P	A	P	P	P	P	A
O	A	P	A	P	P	P	A		A	P	A	A	A	P	P	A	A	A	P	P	P	P	A	A
A	A	A	A	P	P	P	A		A	A	A	A	A	A	A	P	A	P	P	A	A	A	A	A
P	A	P	A	P	P	P	A		A	P	A	P	P	P	P	A	O	A	A	P	P	P	P	A
P	A	A	A	A	P	A	P		P	A	A	A	P	P	P	P	P	P	P	P	P	P	O	P
A	A	A	A	A	P	P	P		P	A	A	P	A	P	P	A	O	A	O	O	A	A	A	A
P	P	A	A	P	P	P	A		O	O	A	P	P	P	A	P	P	P	P	P	A	A	P	P
P	P	P	P	P	P	P	A		A	A	P	P	P	P	P	P	P	P	A	P	A	O	P	P
P	P	O	O	P	P	A	P		A	P	A	P	P	P	P	P	P	P	A	P	A	A	P	P
P	O	P	O	O	P	P	A		P	A	O	P	A	P	A	A	A	A	A	O	O	A	O	P
A	A	P	P	P	P	A	P		O	O	O	P	P	P	P	P	P	P	A	P	A	P	P	A
A	O	P	O	A	P	A	P		P	A	O	P	A	P	A	P	P	P	A	O	A	P	P	A
P	P	A	A	P	A	P	A		P	A	P	P	A	A	A	A	A	A	P	A	A	P	O	P
P	A	P	A	P	A	A	P		A	A	A	P	P	A	P	P	P	P	P	P	P	P	P	P
A	A	A	A	P	A	P	P		A	A	A	P	P	P	A	P	P	P	P	P	P	P	P	A
P	P	P	P	P	P	A	P		A	A	P	A	A	P	A	P	P	P	O	O	A	A	A	A
P	O	P	O	A	A	P	O		P	A	O	P	A	A	A	P	P	P	O	O	A	A	O	A
A	A	O	O	A	P	P	O		O	O	P	P	P	P	A	P	O	P	O	O	A	A	A	A

TORIAL INSTABILITY T.S.
ue of Z, computed as in
Scores in Months of War where
alue of territorial gain
igns are dropped).

' = √ ln X

N.B. The foregoing transformations were selected heuristically because they produced quasi–normal distributions, which satisfactorialy resembled the normal distribution in skewness and kurtosis, according to the Geary—Pearson tests of normality (Geary and Pearson, n.d.)

OTHER COLUMNS:
P = Trait present
A = Trait absent
O = No data on trait

TABLE C-2

CORRELATIONS AND
SIGNIFICANCE LEVELS

Category	Variable	Code	DEPENDENT VARIABLES — Months of War A732	Territorial Gain A730	Territorial Instability A731	MILITARY VARIABLES — Defensive Stance 718	Strength, S.I. A701	Strength, D.S. B701	Mobility, S.I. A702	Mobility, D.S. B702	Quality, S.I. A703	Quality, D.S. B703	Fortifications, S.I. A704
Dependent Variables	Months of War	A732	---	---	---	.00	-.02	-00	.13	.26	.32	.14	.29
	Territorial Gain	A730	---	---	---	-.35	.07	-.22	.01	-.21	.37	.06	.15
	Territorial Instability	A731	---	---	---	-.22	.19	.11	.08	-.14	-.04	-.09	-.36
Military Variables	Defensive Stance	718			.08	---	-.26	.70	.10	.35	-.20	.60	.01
	Strength, S.I.	A701					---	.40	-.03	-.18	-.17	-.37	-.38
	Strength, D.S.	B701						---	-.01	.13	-.25	.33	-.13
	Mobility, S.I.	A702							---	.79	.31	.35	-.22
	Mobility, D.S.	B702								---	.23	.56	-.08
	Quality, S.I.	A703	.09	.06							---	.52	.24
	Quality, D.S.	B703									.06	---	-.04
	Fortifications, S.I.	A704			.08								---
	Fortifications, D.S.	B704											.05
	Prestige	713											
Geographical Variables	Propinquity	712			08								
	Natural Barriers	715			.08								
	Capital City	716			.03								
Diplomatic Variables	Announcements	A705			.0934								
	Surprise Attack	B705			.0045								
	Alliances	A706											
	Active Diplomacy	A707		.01		.07							
	Intense Diplomacy	B707				.08							
	Previous Conflict	714											
Cultural Variables	Benefits	A709											
	Cultural Exchange	A708	.03			.07							
	Trade	B708											
	(General Exchange)	C708	(.03)			(.07)							
Administrative Variables	Experience of Ruler	A710		.0916	.008		.08						.08
	Youth of Ruler	B710											
	Unbridled Ruler	C710				.08	.04					.02	
	Hereditary Monarchy	D710											
	Civil War	711											
	Centralization	717									.008		

The upper right half of this table shows coefficients of correlations. The first three columns and lines are of quantitative variables (see Tabl... coefficients; between one quantitative and one qualitative variable are point biserial coefficients; between two qualitative variables are phi c...

The lower left half of this table shows one—tailed probabilities. That is to say, the table shows the probability of obtaining this unlikely a... less likely if in fact the two variables are not related, and the result is a mere chance freak of sampling or other random factor. The pr... table; of point biserial coefficients by using Student's t distribution; and of phi coefficients by obtaining the exact probabilities (Fisher's... artifact of coding definitons, e.g., between Strength, Defensive Stance (B701) and Defensive Stance (718) in general. Probabilities of... in the group probability calculations.

I	II	III	IV	V	VI	VII	VIII	IX	X	XI	XII	XIII
Chapter No.	Decade Beginning	Conspicuous State	Leading Source	Interdependence Area–Time 560	Interdependence Time–Area 561	Publication Year A 424	Primary Source B 424	Author's Associations "A" A 425	Author's Associations "B" B 425	Author's Sympathies "A" A 426	Author's Sympathies "B" B 426	Author's Proximity 427
3	Chinese 125 B.C.	Former Han Dynasty	Ssu–ma–Chien Pan Ku	16	02	A	P	P	P	P	P	P
4	25 B.C.	Former Han Dynasty	Pan Ku	17	04	A	P	P	P	P	P	O
5	776 A.D.	T'ang Dynasty	Liu Chu Ouyang Hsiu	18	09	A	P	P	P	P	P	A
6	1076	Sung Dynasty	De Mailla	19	10	A	A	P	P	O	A	A
7	1376	Ming Dynasty	De Mailla	20	14	A	A	P	P	O	A	A
8	Islamic 776	Abbasids	Theophanes; Weil	15	08	O	O	O	A	O	A	O
9	Russian 1476	Muscovy	Vernadsky	14	16	P	A	P	P	O	A	A
10	Graeco–Roman 225 B.C.	Rome	Cambridge Modern History	01	01	A	P	P	P	P	P	P
11	25 B.C.	Rome	Cambridge Ancient History	02	03	P	A	P	P	P	P	A
12	176 A.D.	Rome	Cassius Dio, etc.	03	05	A	P	P	P	P	P	P
13	376	Rome	Ammianus Marcelinus, etc.	04	06	A	P	P	P	P	P	P
14	576	Byzantines	Sykes, Christenson, etc.	05	07	P	A	A	A	P	P	A
15	Western 1276	France	Cambridge Medieval History, etc.	06	11	P	A	O	A	O	A	A
16	1376	England	Cambridge Medieval History, etc.	07	12	P	A	O	A	O	A	A
17	1576	Spain	Geyl, Motley, etc.	08	17	P	A	A	A	A	A	A
18	1676	France	Cambridge Modern History	09	19	P	A	A	A	A	A	A
19	1776	England	Watson, Meng, etc.	10	20	P	A	O	O	O	O	A
20	Swiss 1376	Swiss Confederation	von Müller, Dierauer	11	13	O	A	P	P	P	P	A
21	1476	Swiss Confederation	Kirk, History of Charles the Bold.	12	15	P	A	O	A	A	A	A
22	1576	Protestant Swiss	Dierauer	13	18	P	A	P	P	P	P	A

Column IV -- "Leading Source" shows the author or title of the
books chiefly relied on for the data of the studies and whose
characteristics are given on columns VII through XIII. The full
citation of the sources, together with a commentary on their
manner of compilation, is given at the end of the chapter whose
number is shown in Column I. Except for Chapter 17, where more
than one source is listed in Column IV, the other sources referred
to (including the miscellany alluded to by "etc.") all have like
characteristics, all have like entities in columns VIII through XIII.
For example, Chapter 12 has the entry "Cassius Dio, etc." By
consulting the Data Quality Control section of Chapter 12, p. 000,
the reader can see that the sources referred to under "etc." can only
be Herodian and the Scriptores Historiae Augustae. This follows
since Column VIII shows that the sources relied on for this period
are primary sources rather than secondary sources, and Chapter
¹dentifies the group Cassius Dio, Herodian and Scriptores
ꞧe Augustae as primary sources

ꞧngs, VIII - XIII
: present; A -- trait absent; 0 -- no data on trait

CONTROLS			INTER-DEPENDENCE CONTROLS ✱		REGIONAL CONTROLS					TEMPORAL CONTROLS		
SYMPATHY A 426	SYMPATHY B 426	PROXIMITY 427	AREA-TIME 560	TIME-AREA 561	GREEK 562	WESTERN 563	CHINA 564	SWISS 565	MIDEASTERN 566	ANCIENT 567	MEDIEVAL 568	MODERN 569
								.09				
								.09				
.07	.05			.00058		.05						
					.05							
											.09	
.0034	.09					.01						.01
						.07						
							.08					
							.01					
.0034	.03											
		.05				.07		.06				
							.07					
			.03		.09		.07					
	.08		.04		.02			.06				
							.08					
					.0975					.04	.03	

positive signs.

TABLE C-4

CONTROLS: CORRELATIONS

DATA QUALITY

		PUBLICATION YEAR A424	PRIMARY OR SECONDARY B424	ASSOCIATIONS A425	ASSOCIATIONS B425
Dependent Variables	Months of War A732	.00	.13	- .58	- .38
	Territorial Gain A730	-.06	-.10	.16	.27
	Territorial Instability A731	.39	-.37	-.00	-.10
Military Variables	Defensive Stance 718	.25	-.04	.00	.09
	Strength, S.I. A701	-.09	-.08	-.21	.08
	Strength, D.S. B701	.34	-.25	-.19	-.08
	Mobility, S.I. A702	.07	.00	-.15	.01
	Mobility, D.S. B702	-.03	.13	-.29	-.09
	Quality, S.I. A703	.13	.00	-.33	-.24
	Quality, D.S. B703	.04	.03	-.12	.07
	Fortifications, S.I. A704	-.01	.01	-.14	-.36
	Fortifications, D.S. B704	-.14	.18	.25	.05
	Prestige 713	-.07	-.16	-.30	-.08
Geographical Variables	Propinquity 712	-.47	.35	.78	.56
	Natural Barriers 715	-.30	.21	.07	.18
	Capital City 716	.25	-.04	.10	-.04
Diplomatic Variables	Announcements A705	.50	-.14	-.35	-.38
	Surprise Attack B705	-.52	.27	.32	.14
	Alliances A706	.09	.00	-.12	.00
	Active Diplomacy A707	.44	-.02	-.40	-.51
	Intense Diplomacy B707	.22	.03	.13	.06
	Previous Conflict 714	-.20	.35	.58	.40
Cultural Variables	Benefits A709	-.54	.63	.12	.16
	Cultural Exchange A708	.31	-.26	.27	.09
	Trade B708	.27	.25	.35	.05
	General Exchange C708	.31	-.26	.27	.09
Administrative Variables	Experience of Ruler A710	.19	-.47	-.09	.21
	Youth of Ruler B710	-.03	.33	.38	.17
	Unbridled Ruler C710	-.16	.16	-.05	.08
	Hereditary Monarchy D710	.02	.05	-.17	-.25
	Civil War 711	.45	-.05	-.35	-.56
	Centralization 717	.00	.26	-.40	.06

	NTROLS		INTER-DEPENDENCE CONTROLS		REGIONAL CONTROLS					TEMPORAL CONTROLS		
	SYMPATHY B 426	PROXIMITY 427	AREA–TIME 560	TIME–AREA 561	GREEK 562	WESTERN 563	CHINA 564	SWISS 565	MIDEASTERN 566	ANCIENT 567	MEDIEVAL 568	MODERN 569
17	−.00	.26	.02	−.02	.09	−.01	−.06	−.32	.21	−.05	−.05	.13
12	.00	−.10	−.34	.05	−.12	−.21	.21	.32	.17	−.01	.19	−.23
45	−.38	−.16	.09	.68	−.25	.38	−.26	.09	−.05	−.19	.09	.10
29	.41	−.07	.05	−.29	.26	.34	−.37	.14	−.35	.00	−.22	.26
00	−.12	−.25	.16	−.10	−.27	−.21	.35	−.39	.20	−.10	.08	.01
00	.12	−.40	−.25	−.43	−.07	.33	−.14	.01	−.23	−.21	.03	.20
27	−.23	.10	−.21	.19	.05	−.10	−.23	−.20	.31	.00	−.10	.11
27	−.01	.23	−.11	−.11	.19	.06	−.19	−.14	−.14	.14	−.33	.25
30	−.05	.11	−.10	−.10	.14	−.10	−.20	−.01	.29	.21	−.03	−.20
04	.32	.21	.12	−.16	.55	.06	−.41	.16	−.23	.33	−.27	−.05
.03	−.04	.04	−.28	−.03	−.12	.16	−.01	.28	.05	−.26	.43	−.25
37	.31	.03	−.05	−.05	.07	.21	−.10	.44	−.23	−.10	34	−.30
09	−.11	−.09	−.08	−.08	.12	−.01	−.03	−26	−09	.09	−.14	.12
00	45	.28	.36	.13	.28	−.61	.28	−.14	.21	.32	.25	−.68
13	.26	.09	−.21	.02	.12	−35	.37	−.03	−.03	.19	−.21	.05
04	−.05	−.07	−.05	−.18	−.12	47	−37	.24	−.14	−.23	.11	.14
25	−09	−.14	.21	−.09	.09	.12	−35	.05	.25	−.10	.16	−.10
29	−.05	.27	.13	.13	.05	−.45	.28	−.21	.15	.15	.10	−.27
04	.28	−.14	−.20	−.20	−.07	.41	−.16	.56	−.25	−.24	.03	.23
−.30	.03	.03	.10	−.21	37	.31	−.62	−.03	−.03	−.04	−.21	.32
14	.05	.00	−.05	−.15	.11	.00	−34	−.14	.14	.00	−.20	.25
00	54	.28	.13	.05	.28	−35	.00	−.14	.21	.32	.00	−37
07	−.02	52	−.02	.20	.02	−.45	.26	−.50	.07	.35	−.16	−.21
−.05	−.06	−.26	−.04	−.04	−.06	.38	−.30	.30	−.27	−.20	.10	.10
14	.18	.25	.03	−.08	.05	.31	−.64	.25	−.19	.33	−.22	−.05
−.05	−.06	−.26	−.04	−.04	−.06	.38	−.30	.30	−.27	−.20	.10	.10
−59	−.33	−.25	.19	.46	−.28	.13	.13	.00	−.16	−.13	−.25	.48
65	.39	.25	−.12	−.18	.21	−.19	−.12	.00	.16	.30	−.05	−.28
00	−.11	−.11	.55	−.02	−.44	−.29	.45	−.36	.40	−.12	.04	.08
−.29	−.44	−.18	.53	−.02	−.60	.07	.26	−.50	.07	−.21	.04	.17
−.33	−.21	−.09	.16	.05	.21	.16	−.49	−.42	.22	−.09	.01	.10
−.05	.26	.32	.15	.36	.40	−.32	−.05	−.38	.18	.50	−50	.05

TABLE C-5

CONTROLS: SIGNIFICANCE LEVELS

		PUBLICATION YEAR A424	PRIMARY OR SECONDARY B424	ASSOCIATIONS A425	ASSOCIATIONS
Dependent Variables	Months of War A732			.01	
	Territorial Gain A 730				
	Territorial Instability A 731	.05	.06		
Military Variables	Defensive Stance 718				
	Strength S.I. A 701				
	Strength D.S. B 701				
	Mobility S.I. A 702				
	Mobility D.S. B 702				
	Quality S.I. A 703				
	Quality D.S. B 703				
	Fortifications S.I. A 704				
	Fortifications D.S. B 704				
	Prestige 713				
Geographical Variables	Propinquity 712	.07		.03	
	Natural Barriers 715				
	Capital City 716				
Diplomatic Variables	Announcements A 705				
	Surprise Attack B 705				
	Alliances A 706				
	Active Diplomacy A 707	.09			
	Intense Diplomacy B 707				
	Previous Conflict 714			.08	
Cultural Variables	Benefits A 709	.04	.01		
	Cultural Exchange A 708				
	Trade B 708				
	General Exchange C 708				
Administrative Variables	Experience of Ruler A 710				
	Youth of Ruler B 710				
	Unbridled Ruler C 710				
	Hereditary Monarchy D 710				
	Civil War 711				
	Centralization 717				

✳ Significance levels for Interdependence Tests are given only for correlations with

★ ★ ★

GROUP SIGNIFICANCE TESTS

THE PROBLEM we seek to solve in this annex is the problem of group significance, the so-called dredging, combing, or mudsticking problem. "They throw the mud on the wall and see if it sticks," is the way one critic has described this cross-cultural survey method. In this study, the mud that stuck consists of our Communication Cluster. We did not posit these associations in advance. They were a comparatively small number of significant associations gleaned from a much larger number of correlations which did not attain significance. But as common sense tells us, and as Banks and Textor (1963) and Textor (1967) have shown, even if the data are mere nonsense collections of random numbers, if thousands of correlations were run with a computer, dozens of them are bound to turn up statistically significant.

Our solution to this problem is an elaboration of the *Whiskers* solution used by Banks and Textor (1963) and Textor (1967:54). We ourselves ran nonsense correlations and compared these findings as a group with the findings of our real data runs as a group.

The first step in our solution was the preparation of a special computer program to generate Whiskers variables. Banks and Textor (1963) and Textor (1967) had several sets of these variables. In Textor (1967:54) the Whiskers variables differed in the dichotomous cut. Of the 400 societies in his sample: 50% had purple whiskers, 50% did not; 40% had blue whiskers, 60% did not; 30% had green whiskers, 70% did not; 20% had pink whiskers, 80% did not; 10% had yellow whiskers, 90% did not; 5% had white whiskers, 95% did not.

Some Characteristic of Fourfold Contingency Tables

The point of varying the dichotomous cuts lies in their implications on the marginals of fourfold contingency tables and thus on the number of possible arangements of the four cells in the table. Consider the examples in table D.1. Suppose we have a sample of 100 houses. 50 of these have red roofs; the other 50 have black roofs. 40 have red doors; the other 60

TABLE D.1

Houses With

	Red Roofs	Black Roofs	
Red Doors		40	
White Doors		60	
	50	50	100

Houses With

	Elm Trees	Maple Trees	
Tulips		10	
Roses		90	
	5	95	100

have white doors. Further, 10 of them have tulips growing in their gardens; the other 90 have roses. 5 have elm trees; the other 95 have maple trees. We wish to correlate roof color and door color; flower choice and tree choice. In both correlations, the sample size is the same—100. But the number of possible combinations of the traits in question is quite different. In correlating roofs and doors, there are exactly forty-one different cell arrangements possible with the given marginals. In correlating trees and flowers, there are only six! The marginal totals are the row and column totals shown in the tables: 40, 60, 50, 50 in the roof-door; 10, 90, 95, 5 in the tree-flower table. When the marginal totals are given, the table has only one degree of freedom; when you fix any one of the four cells, the other three are thus determined. In the roof-door example, suppose that we have 25 houses with both red roofs and red doors. Then, since 40 houses altogether have red doors, 15 of them must have black roofs and red doors; in the same way, 15 must have red roofs and white doors; and therefore 35 must have black roofs and white doors. Fill any one of the four cells and the other three are determined.

This being so, the maximum number of possible arangements of the whole table is fixed by the smallest marginal, whose value is called M. Then the maximum number of possible arrangements of the fourfold contingency table is $M+1$.

In the roof-door example, the smallest marginal is forty, so the maximum number of possible variations of roof-door arangements is
$40+1=41$.

This is at once obvious if we look at the first cell in the table, that of the count of houses with both red roofs and red doors. There cannot be more than forty such houses, since there are only forty houses with red doors. There can be as few as none at all, since all of the houses with red doors could have black roofs. Thus if the smallest marginal is forty, the maximum number of arrangements is forty-one: there are forty possible counts of one through forty plus one for the count of zero.

Thus we see that in the trees-flowers example, the maximum possible number of arrangements is six. In that example, the most unlikely possible arrangement with a negative sign is that of no houses at all with both elm trees and tulips. Such an arrangement would occur by chance alone more than half the time. With these marginals, then, it is impossible for a negative arrangement to be statistically significant at all.

For these reasons, Banks and Textor (1963) and Textor (1967) varied the dichotomous cuts in an attempt to reflect the vagaries of possible significance levels.

There is another factor at work influencing the results of Whiskers runs and that is the coarseness of the mesh of possible results.

In technical terms, the distribution of probabilities of the various possible arrangements in a contingency table is discrete rather than continuous. Consider for example table D.2.

TABLE D.2

EXACT PROBABILITIES FOR VARIOUS CELL FREQUENCIES

		Present	Absent	Total
Trait A	Present	A	B	15
Trait B	Absent	C	D	5
	Total	4	16	20

Cell A	Cell B	Cell C	Cell D	Fisher's Exact Probability
0	15	0	1	.001032
1	14	3	2	.031992
2	13	2	3	.248710
3	12	1	4	.718226
4	11	0	5	1.000000

Source of Probabilities: Lieberman and Owen 1962:58, for values of $N = 20$, $n = 16$, $k = 5$.

With the marginal total given in that table, there are five possible outcomes of any trial of a hypothesis involving a correlation between two traits. Suppose that we predict a negative correlation between them. The most supportive outcome would be to find no cases at all in which both traits are present, a result significant at the .001032 level. Thus it is not possible for any outcome at all to be significant at the .001 level; it is not possible with these marginals to attain that level of significance no matter how high the true correlation in the universe sampled. The next most favorable outcome would be to find only one case in which both traits were present, a result significant at the .031992 level. After that comes the outcome in which there were two cases where the traits were both present, a result significant at the .24810 level. The key point to grasp firmly in mind is that this test cannot produce a result which just barely attains significance at the .05 level, or just barely misses significance at the .05 level. We cannot expect this particular set of marginals to yield results nominally significant at the 5% level in more than 3.1992% of trials. Either it does somewhat better than 5% or much worse. This state of affairs presumably goes far to explain the discrepancies between the theoretically expectable results of Textor's Whiskers values and the much lower frequencies of nominally significant values which Textor actually obtained.

Randomizing Methods

The Banks-Textor Whiskers variable method has already been described. A proportion varying from 5% to 50% of the cases are randomly assigned to a particular Whiskers category. The user of the tables in any particular case must try to match up his case as well as may be with the results from the appropriate Whiskers variables—that is, from the two Whiskers variables whose dichotomous cut most nearly approximates the two he is interested in. Such a procedure seems exceedingly cumbersome and, so far as I know, has never actually been applied. We are simply given the materials so that we may follow it if we wish (e.g., Textor 1967:56).

The procedure we have followed here is somewhat different. We used a special computer program to provide us with sets of Whiskers variables which exactly matched the marginals of each of the thirty-nine substantive dichotomous variables used. The program (1) reads the coding of a particular variable; (2) tallies the number of cases present, cases absent, and cases with no data; (3) randomly chooses a case; (4) calls that randomly chosen case *absent*; (5) randomly chooses another case, and calls that randomly chosen case *absent*; (6) and so on until as many randomly chosen cases are coded absent as there are *absent* cases in the particular variable being Whiskerized; it (7) then calls the next randomly chosen case *no data*, And so on, until (8) all cases in turn are assigned values of *no data* and *present*.

The program will produce as many sets of Whiskers variables with marginals modeled on a particular variable as are called for by its user. We generated ten Whiskers variables for each of the 44 substantive variables, a total of 440 such variables. (We tested the Whiskers variables for randomness by the Wald-Wolfowitz run test. Of the 43 such variables tested, none at all proved to have too few runs at the 5% level of significance, and only two proved to have too many.)

Correction Factors

We ran our three dependent variables against these 440 Whiskers variables for a total of 1320 point-biserial correlations. Theoretically we would have expected to find 66 of these to be significant at the 5% level, two-tailed. In fact, we only found 53, or 80% to be so. Therefore, in our group significance work we take 80% as our correction factor on point-biserial correlations. (The statistically trained reader will notice that the standard error of that proportion is only .011, or 1.1%.)

We ran our twenty-nine substantive societal characteristics (those shown in table C.1) against the 440 Whiskers variables; thus we generated 12,760 fourfold contingency tables. We would expect theoretically that 2,552 of these would have attained the 20% level of significance, two-tailed. In fact, however, only 602 did attain that level. Our computer checked the marginals on each of the contingency tables to see if it was possible for such an arrangement to occur with such marginals attaining the 20% level of significance, two-tailed. On no less than 6,276 of these—nearly half the total—it reported that even so modest a level of significance as 20% was unattainable with the given marginals.

Our correction factor for substantive correlations among the independent variables then was

602/2552 = .2359 or 23.59%.

(The standard error of that proportion is only .0026 or 0.26%.)

Similarly, we expected 1320 correlations significant at the 20% level of the 6600 correlations run between our fifteen control variables (those on table C.4) and the 440 Whiskers variables; in fact we found only 246; thus our correction factor on control variables is 246/1320 or .1863 or 18.63%. (The standard error of that proportion is .0107 or 1.07%.)

Advance Predictions

Table D.3 tests the significance of the advance predictions as a group. In all, thirty-one advance predictions were made. All these were tested by point

TABLE D.3

GROUP SIGNIFICANCE OF ADVANCE PREDICTIONS

N	R	One-tailed individual probability	Group probability	Subject Trait	Predicate Trait
31	5	.03	.098	Months of War (A732)	Cultural Exchange (A708)
30	4	.06	.22	Territorial Gain (A730)	Quality of Armed Forces (A704)
29	3	.08	.41	Territorial Instability (A731)	Border Fortifications (A704)
28	2	.08	.67	Territorial Instability (A731)	Natural Barriers (715)
27	1	.09	.89	Territorial Gain (A730)	Experience of Ruler (A710)

Point biserial correlations

One-tailed individual significance tests

Correction factor .803

Advance predictions set forth in Table 1.1, pp. 6-7 above.

Group probabilities are cumulative binomial probabilities from Weintraub (1963).

biseral correlations; since the direction of the relationship was predicted in advance, the test is one-tailed. Five of the thirty-one tests were significant at the 10% level, one-tailed. The correction factor for point biserial group tests is .80; therefore we test the probability of getting five successes in thirty-one tries when the probability of success is .08. The tables of Weintraub (1963:168) show a probability of slightly under 10% for such an event.

Of the five successful predictions, the most successful was that which occurred between months of war and cultural exchange. (Our measure of success is the individual significance level. This correlation departed more extremely from chance expectation than any of the other four.) Therefore we assign to this correlation the group probability of .098. If we have only ninety-eight chances in a thousand of getting five successes in thirty-one tries, then the most unlikely of the five at least has only ninety-eight chances in a thousand of belonging to such a group.

But if we presume that this first member is statistically significant, this means we presume it did *not* occur by chance. So under this presumption we must eliminate it from the group in testing further hypotheses about chance likelihood.

We are left then with four nominally significant results out of thirty. The probability of four successes in thirty tries, when each try has an 8% chance of success is given by Weintraub (1963) as slightly less than .22.

And so we continue with the queue, as shown in table 24.6. The group probabilities rise with each line of the queue. In this example only the first line has a group probability sufficiently low to make it even a little interesting.

Other Correlations between Independent and Dependent Variables

There were fifty-six correlations between independent and dependent variables run. Of these, four were significant at the 10% level, one-tailed. We would expect four successes in a group of fifty-six tries, with a likelihood of success of .08 in each try, in 18.5% of such groups. Therefore we cannot consider these results significant as a group.

However, one of the results is so extreme that taken by itself it is most unlikely to have occurred even once by chance in fifty-six tries. The individual significance level of the correlation between Territorial Instability and Experience of Ruler (A710) was .0012. Weintraub (1963:363) gives us a probability of .054 for one success in fifty-six tries when the likelihood of success is .001 per try; and of .106 when the likelihood of success is .002 per try. Interpolating, we estimate the likelihood of getting even one correlation as extreme as this one in fifty-six tries at .064.

Correlations Among Independent Variables

Table D.4 displays the group significance tests for correlations among the independent variables. The procedure followed on table D.4 differs from that followed on table D.3 only with respect to the source of group probablity calculations. In the first such calculation for example, we wish to know what is the likelihood of thirty-one successes in a group of 356 tries with an individual probability of success of .0479 (.20×.2393). We cannot use the Weintraub's tables, because they do not extend to groups larger than 100. We could use the Harvard Computation Laboratory binomial tables (1955); but they would require us to interpolate not only between n = 340 and n = 360 but also between p = .04 and p = .05. We could use the hand computation methods given by Smith (1953), but that would be tedious. It is most convenient, and sufficiently accurate, to use the approximation given by the cumulative Poisson tables of Molina (1942). To use these tables, one computes the expected frequency. In this case, the expected frequency in 356 tries with a probability of .0479 per try is $356 \times .0479 = .1703$.

Then Molina's table (part 2, p. 18, a = 17; c = 31) gives a probability of .001448. (This may be compared for accuracy with the Harvard tables value for

TABLE D.4

GROUP SIGNIFICANCE OF CORRELATIONS AMONG
INDEPENDENT VARIABLES

Expected frequency: $356 \times .2 \times .2393 = 17.03$

N	C	Individual probability two-tailed	Approximate Group Probability*	Subject Trait	Predicate Trait
356	31	.0090	.002	Capital City (715)	Natural Barriers (715)
355	30	.0096	.003	Civil War (711)	Active Diplomacy (A707)
354	29	.011	.005	Civil War (711)	Intense Diplomacy (B707)
352	28	.014	.009	Announcements (A705)	Prestige (713)
351	27	.016	.015	Centralization (717)	Quality of Armed Forces (A703)
350	26	.022	.025	Trade (B708)	Cultural Exchange (A708)
349	25	.027	.041	Propinquity (712)	Previous Conflict (714)
348	24	.040	.063	Unbridled Ruler (C710)	Quality of Armed Forces (B703)
347	23	.042	.095	Trade (B708)	Capital City (716)
346	22	.049	.140	Cultural Exchange (A708)	Capital City (716)

*Molina (1942); II: 19 A; a=17.

$p = .05$, $n = 360$, $r = 31$ of. 000007, and for $p = .05$, $n = 340$, $r = 31$ of .00107. (Evidently our tabled value of .002, rounded upward from .001448, errs on the cautious side.)

We see then from table 24.7 that seven of the thirty-one individually significant correlations must be conceded to have a group significance of 5% or better. We would not expect to get as many as twenty-five correlations as significant as these thirty-one from a group of 356 tries in as many as 5 such groups out of 100.

Data Quality Controls

Of those data quality control tests run against dependent variables, using point biserial correlations, six were nominally significant at the 20% level, two-tailed. The least likely of these six may be assigned a group probability of 11. (The Harvard tables give a probability of .106 for n = 21, p = .16, r = 6.) That least likely relationship is the correlation between Months of War (A732) and Authors' Associations (A425).

We see from table D.5 that of the data quality control tests run against independent variables, two have a group significance of 5% or better.

TABLE D.5

GROUP SIGNIFICANCE OF CORRELATIONS BETWEEN
INDEPENDENT VARIABLES AND DATA QUALITY CONTROLS

Expected frequency: $196 \times .2 \times .1863 = 7.3$

N	C	Individual probability two-tailed	Approximate Group Probability*	Subject Trait	Predicate Trait
196	14	.007	.018	Propinquity (712)	Authors' Sympathy (A426)
195	14	.007	.018	Previous Conflict (714)	Authors' Sympathy (A426)
194	12	.022	.068	Benefits (A709)	Primary/Secondary (B424)

*Molina (1942); II: 8; a=7.3.

Time-and-Space Controls

Twenty-four point biserial correlations were run between dependent variables and regional or temporal controls. Of these, three attained a nominal significance level of 20%, two-tailed. We would expect at least that many through chance alone most of the time. Harvard binomial tables give a probability of .76 and none of these has so high an individual significance level that we would be at all surprised to see it alone occur by chance. This group then must be dismissed as lacking statistical significance.

TABLE D.6

GROUP SIGNIFICANCE OF CORRELATIONS AMONG
TIME-AND-SPACE CONTROLS AND INDEPENDENT VARIABLES

Expected frequency: 208 × .2 × .1863 = 7.75

N	C	Individual probability two-tailed	Approximate Group Probability*	Subject Trait	Predicate Trait
208	18	.027	.001	Modern Period (569)	Propinquity (712)
	17	.028	.003	Chinese Paideia (564)	Active Diplomacy (A707)
	16	.029	.007	Western Paideia (563)	Propinquity (712) (D710)
	15	.031	.014	Greek Paideia	Hereditary Monarchy (D710)
	14	.07	.029	Medieval Period (568)	Centralization (717)
	13	.08	.055	Ancient Period (567)	Centralization (717)
	12	.105	.098	Greek Paideia (562)	Quality of Armed Forces D.S. (B703)

*Molina (1942); II: 8-9; a=7.8.

Table D.6 shows the tests of group significance for correlations between independent variables and regional and temporal controls. Five of these must be
considered to have a group significance of 5% or better, since we would not
expect as many as 15 correlations out of 208 to attain a nominal significance
level of 20% or better.

Interdependence Controls

These tests are all one-tailed tests, since the correlation must be positive in
sign to constitute evidence of cultural diffusion. Of the six run against the
dependent variables, only one is significant, but that one is strikingly so. Its
individual significance level is only .00058. Weintraub tells us we can expect
so unusual a result in less than 4 such groups out of 1000 (n = 6, p = .0006,
R = 1, p = .00359). Clearly then the correlation between Time-Area alignment and Territorial Stability is statistically significant.

Of the fifty-six interdependence tests run on twenty-eight substantive variables,
two were nominally significant. at the 4% level. (Taking a correction factor of
.236, we have N = 28, P = .010, R = 2.) Weintraub gives a probability of .03.
Therefore, we may assign the more significant of the two that group probability:
Unbridled Ruler (C710) /Area-Time Alignment.

Summary

Table D.7 sets forth the more plausible results of this study, considering not only individual but also group significance tests. Even with a sample size of only twenty, thirteen of our correlations proved to be significant at the 2% level, both individually and as group members. That none of these included any of our deterrence hypothesis tests further tends to support our conclusion that military deterrence does not seem likely to prove successful in the long run.

TABLE D.7

PLAUSIBLE FINDINGS

Subject Trait	Predicate Trait	Significance Panels		Correlation Coefficient
		Individual	Group	
Capital City (716)	Natural Barriers (715)	.0045	.0015	-.707
Territorial Instability (A731)	Time-Area Interdependence (561)	.00058	.004	.69
Intense Diplomacy (B707)	Civil War (711)	.0056	.005	.746
Civil War (711)	Active Diplomacy (A707)	.0048	.0027	.765
Cultural Exchange (A708)	Trade (B708)	.011	.025	.826
Quality of Armed Forces, D.S. (B703)	Unbridled Ruler (C710)	.02	.095	-.61
Territorial Instability (A731)	Time-Area Interdependence (561)	.0005	.003	.69
Greek Paideia (562)	Hereditary Monarchy (D710)	.018	.001	-.606
Western Paideia (563)	Propinquity (712)	.014	.003	-.61
Chinese Paideia (564)	Active Diplomacy (A707)	.013	.007	-.63
Modern Period (569)	Propinquity (712)	.013	.014	-.68
Authors' Sympathy (A426)	Propinquity (712)	.0034	.018	1.00
Authors' Sympathy (426)	Previous Conflict (714)	.0034	.018	1.00

GLOSSARY

Alignments. *See* Galton's Problem.

Allograph. In a given script, the variant forms of a single grapheme are called allographs. For example, in the Latin alphabet, A, a, a, and a are four allographs of a single grapheme. While each grapheme differs in meaning from every other, allographs of a single grapheme all have the same meaning.

Bias. *See* sampling bias, coding bias, reporting bias.

Coding Bias. Any consistent circumstance or factor which makes coders who are classifying historical reports for comparative purposes err in a consistent manner or in a consistent direction. Contrasts with random error.

Combing Problems. *See* Group significance.

Conspicuous Rival, cf. Conspicuous State. The Conspicuous Rival is defined as the rival state whose rivalry with the Conspicuous State is given the most attention in Langer's *Encyclopedia of World History*.

Conspicuous State. That state whose conflicts with other states are given the most attention during a given decade in a given civilization (*Paideia*) in Langer's *Encylopedia of World History*.

Contingency Tables. *See* Fourfold contingency tables.

Correlation. A correlation exists between two variables if a knowledge of one permits prediction of the value of the other with a greater likelihood of success than would be expected from chance alone.

Cross-Cultural Survey. A worldwide study of a sample of all human societies (mostly primitive societies), seeking to test hypotheses about functional relationships between variables by means of correlations.

Cross-Historical Survey. A study of a sample of given historical periods representative of all such periods in societies with written historical records sufficiently detailed to permit study. The study seeks to test hypotheses about functional relationships between variables by means of correlations.

Cross-Lagged Correlation. A correlation in which two successive observations of the same variables are made on each subject (historical period) at successive time intervals. The purpose of the cross-lagged correlation is to see whether there is a higher correlation between the supposed cause at the earlier period and the supposed effect at the later period than the other way around.

Deviant Case. An example which departs from the group tendency in a correlation. For example, if in a sample of young children we find a correlation between height and weight, then a heavy short child or a lightweight tall child would be a deviant case.

Diffusion. *See* Galton's Problem.

Dredging Problem. *See* Group Significance.

Encyclopedic History. A work of history, such as Langer's *Encyclopedia of World History*, which seeks to compress a wide sweep of events covering thousands of years into a single volume.

Fourfold Contingency Table. A statistical table displaying the relationship between two dichotomies. For example, consider a school class, with thirty girls and forty boys. Suppose that twenty-five of the students have brown hair and forty-five have hair some other color. Then a fourfold contingency table would show the number of boys and the number of girls with or without brown hair.

Example of a Fourfold Contingency Table

	Boys	*Girls*	*Total*
Brown Hair	10	15	25
Other Color Hair	30	15	45
Total	40	30	70

Fundamentum divisionis, Basis of Classification. A classification scheme has a single *fundamentum divisionis* when one criterion alone is used to make all distinctions between classes. If students in a school are classed by age and only by age regardless of sex or academic achievement, then age constitutes the *fundamentum divisionis* of the classification.

Galton's Problem. The problem of statistical interdependence (lack of independence) arising from cultural diffusion. The statistical mathematics of significance tests assumes that each trial is independent of all others. In fact, because of cultural diffusion, several members of a cross-cultural or cross-historical sample may share common features from a common source and thus be interdependent. The solution to Galton's problem here applied is to arrange the historical periods and states studied geographically and chronologically so as to put neighbors together as well as may be. Such an arrangement is called an alignment or an interdependence alignment.

Goodenough's Rule. The principle in anthropology that the concepts most useful for comparing behavior of a given sort in a number of societies are not necessarily the same as the concepts used to describe the same behavior in any particular single society.

Grapheme. A single symbol in a script. For Example: in the Latin alphabet the letter *A*.

Group Significance. The problem of group significance is the question of the probability of getting at least the observed number of nominally significant correlations from among a group of trials as numerous as that in question. A nominally significant correlation is one which, if run alone, would be statistically significant.

Interdependence. *See* Galton's Problem.

Linked Pair test. A solution to Galton's problem (cf.) The linked pair test consists in arranging sample members into alignments of neighbors, then correlating each member's score on a given variable with its neighbor's score.

Mudsticking Problem. *See* Group Significance.

Normal Distribution. A mathematical distribution defined by the formula

$$Y = \frac{1}{\sqrt{2\pi}} \, e^{\frac{-X^2}{2\sigma^2}}$$

This formula in fact represents the distribution toward which many random distributions are known to take. Many of the most sensitive and powerful tests of statistical significance assume that the data being correlated is normally distributed.

Normalizing Transform. A mathematical transformation of a collection of numbers intended to produce a normal distribution without changing their relative ranks. For example, the square root transformation would consist of substituting for each number in the collection the square root of that number.

One-Tailed. *See* Tail.

Paideia. A higher civilization, defined by the possession of a common body of literature written in a single script, the mastery of which literature is the accepted mark of learning requisite for professional teachers of adults.

Phi Coefficient. A coefficient of correlation used to measure association in fourfold contingency tables (cf.)

Point Biserial Coefficient. A coefficient of correlation used to measure the correlation between a ratio scale (for example, a collection of standard scores) and a dichotomy. In this study for example, we measure War Frequency by standard scores and measure Defensive Stance by a dichotomy. We correlate War Frequency with Defensive Stance by means of a fourfold contingency table.

Post Hoc Ergo Propter Hoc. "After, therefore because of." The name for the fallacy of supposing that what follows is the necessary consequence of what precedes.

Random Error. Any source of reporting or coding error which has no tendency to take any particular direction but is as likely to err in one direction as in another. Certain errors in counting or certain kinds of misunderstanding or certain sorts of manuscript copying errors would be examples of random error.

Reporting Bias. Any consistent circumstance or factor which leads a historical source or historian to make reports which err in a consistent direction. Authors of memoirs consistently tend to represent their own behavior in a favorable light, for example. Contrasts with random error.

Sampling Bias. Any factor or circumstance which favors or disfavors the choice of any particular member of a sampling universe so that its chance of being selected for study differs from other units in the sample.

Script. A system of writing. (Example: the Latin alphabet, the Greek alphabet, the Hebrew alphabet, the Hindu (Devanagari) alphabet, Egyptian hierogly-phics, Mesopotamian cuneiform, Chinese ideographs, Japanese kana.)

Standard Deviation. The root mean square deviation. A standard deviation of a group of numbers is defined as the result of the following series of operations: (1) computing their arithmetic mean (average), (2) subtracting each number in turn from the mean, (3) squaring the difference obtained in step 2, (4) adding the squares obtained in step 3, (5) Dividing the sum obtained in step 4 by the number of numbers, and (6) taking the square root of the quotient obtained in step 5.

Standard Score. The standard score of a number is given by the following operations: (1) computing the arithmetic mean (average) of the group, (2) subtracting that mean from the number concerned, and (3) dividing the difference thus obtained by the standard deviation of the group.

Statistical Significance. The likelihood that a given operation would occur by chance. This significance is usually expressed in terms of percentages or decimal fractions. When a correlation is said to be significant at the 5% or the .05 level, that statement means that according to the calculations of mathematical statistics we would expect a correlation this large or larger through chance alone in only 1 sample in 20, or 5 samples in 100. *See also* Tail.

Systematic Error. A synonym for Bias (cf.).

Tail. The term *tail* in probability theory refers to the two extremes of the normal probability distribution, each of which thins out rather like a kangaroo's tail. When a significance test is called *two-tailed* this means the test measures the likelihood of a result as extreme as the one observed in either direction. Thus if a correlation of $+0.85$ is said to have a two-tailed significance level of .05, that means we would expect in only five tries per hundred from such a sample to get any correlation lying between $+0.85$ and $+1.00$ or between -0.85 and -1.00, all numbers inclusive. Two-tailed significance levels are appropriate if the direction (mathematical sign) is not predicted in advance. A one-tailed significance level deals only with correlations as large or larger with the same sign as the correlation in question.

Transform. *See* Normalizing transform.

Two-Tailed. *See* Tail.

Universe. In sampling theory, a sampling universe is the name given to the collection of units from which the sample is drawn and whose characteristics the sample is intended to represent.

BIBLIOGRAPHIES

General

ADAMS, BROOKS
  1955   *The law of civilization and decay.* New York: Vintage.
AUSUBEL, H.
  1950   *Historians and their craft.* New York: Columbia University Press.
BACKUS, P. H.
  1959   Finite deterrence, controlled retaliation. *U. S. Naval Institute Proceedings.* 85:23-29.
BANKS, ARTHUR S. AND ROBERT B. TEXTOR
  1963   *A cross polity survey.* Cambridge, Mass.: M.I.T. Press.
BEARD, CHARLES
  1928   *Whither mankind.* New York: Longmans, Green.
BERNHEIM, ERNST
  1908   *Lehrbuch der Historischen Methode und der Geschichtsphilosophie.* 6th ed. Leipzig: Dunkker and Humblot.
BLALOCK, HUBERT M., JR.
  1960   Correlational analysis and causal inference. *American Anthropologist* 62:624-53.
BOSSUET, JACQUES B.
  1892   *Discours sur l'histoire universelle.* 4th ed. Paris: C. Poussielgue.
BRODY, RICHARD A.
  1960   Deterrence strategies: An annotated bibliography. *Conflict Resolution* 4:443-57.
BUCKLE, THOMAS HENRY
  1913   *History of civilization in England.* 4 vols. New York: Hearst's International.
BURNS, ARTHUR LEE
  1959   A graphical approach to some problems of the arms race. *Conflict Resolution* 3:326-42.
COLLINGWOOD, R. G.
  1956   *The idea of history.* New York: Oxford University Press.

COULBORN, RUSHTON
1959   *The origin of civilized societies*. Princeton: Princeton University Press.
CROCE, BENEDETTO
1938   *La storia*. Bari: Editori Laterza.
CUMONT, FRANZ
1912   *Astrology and religion among the Greeks and Romans*. New York: Putnam.
DUNCAN, ACHESON J.
1959   *Quality control and industrial statistics*. Rev. ed. Homewood, Ill.: Irwin.
EISENSTADT, S. N.
1963   *The political systems of empire*. New York: Free Press.
ENGELS, FREDERICK
n.d.   *The origin of the family, private property and the state*. Moscow: Foreign
       Language Publication House.
EVANS-PRITCHARD, E. E.
1963   *Essays in social anthropology*. New York: Free Press.
FINKELSTEIN, LAWRENCE S.
1962   Behind the headlines. *Canadian Institute of International Affairs* 22, no. 1.
FLEMING, D. F.
1962   *Does deterrence deter?* Philadelphia: Peace Literature Service, American
       Friends Service Committee.
FREEMAN, LINTON C.
1965   *Elementary applied statistics for students in the behavioral sciences*. New York:
       Wiley.
GEARY, R. C. AND E. S. PEARSON
n.d.   *Tests of normality*. London: Biometrika Office.
GELB, I. I.
1963   *A study of writing*. Rev. ed. Chicago: University of Chicago Press.
GOODENOUGH, WARD H.
1956   Residence rules. *Southwestern Journal of Anthropology* 12:37.
GOODMAN, L. A. AND W. H. KRUSKAL
1963   Measures of association for cross-classification. III. Approximate
       sampling theory. *Journal of the American Statistical Association* 58:310-64.
HADLEY, ARTHUR T.
1961   *The nation's safety and arms control*. New York: Viking.
HARTLEY H. G. AND E. S. PEARSON
1950   Tables of the probability integral of the t distribution. *Biometrika*
       37:168-72.
HAVARD COMPUTATION LABORATORY
1951   *Tables of the cumulative binomial probability distribution*. Cambridge:
       Harvard University.

KAHN, HERMAN

n.d. The arms race and some of its hazards. In *Legal and political problems of world order*, edited by Saul H. Mendlovitz, pp. 22-55. New York: Fund for Education Concerning World Peace through World Law.

KENDALL, MAURICE G.

1962 *Rank correlation methods*. 3d ed. London: Griffin.

KENNEY, J. F. AND E. S. KEEPING

1951 *Mathematics of statistics, Part Two*. Princeton: D. Van Nostrand Company.

KISSINGER, HENRY A.

1957 *Nuclear weapons and foreign policy*. New York: Harper.

KÖBBEN, ANDRE J. F.

1967 Why exceptions? the logic of cross-cultural analysis. *Current Anthropology* 8:3–19.

KROEBER, ALRED L.

1944 *Configurations of culture growth*. Berkeley: University of California Press.

LANGER, WILLIAM L.

1948 *An encyclopedia of world history*. Boston: Houghton Mifflin.

LENS, SIDNEY

n.d. Revolution and cold war. *Beyond Deterrence Pamphlets*. Philadelphia: Peace Literature Service, American Friends Service Committee.

LIEBERMAN, GERALD J. AND DONALD B. OWEN

1961 *Tables of the hypergeometric probability distribution*. Stanford: Stanford University Press.

MARSH, ROBERT

1967 *Comparative sociology*. New York: Harcourt and Brace.

MARX, KARL

1906 *Capital*. New York: Modern Library.

MAURY, L. F. ALFRED

1860 *La magie et l'astrologie dans l'antiquité et au moyen âge*. Paris: Didier.

McCLINTOCK, CHARLES G. AND DALE J. HEKHUIS

1961 European community deterrence: Its organization, utility and political feasibility. *Conflict Resolution* 5:230–53.

MEYER, EDWARD

1924 *Kleine Schriften*. 2d ed. Halle: M. Niemeyer.

MEYERHOFF, HANS

1959 *The philosophy of history in our time*. New York: Doubleday.

MICHAELIS, HERBERT, ed.

1964 *Die Grosse Illustrierte Weltgeschichte*. 2 Vols. Gutersloh: C. Bertelsmann.

MILBURN, THOMAS W.

1959 What constitutes effective deterrence? *Conflict Resolution* 3:138–45.

MOLINA, E. C.

1942   *Poisson's exponential binomial limit.* New York: Van Nostrand.

MURDOCK, GEORGE PETER

1949   *Social structure.* New York: Macmillan.

NAROLL, RAOUL

1961   Two solutions to Galton's problem. *Philosophy of Science* 28:15-39.

1962   *Data quality control.* New York: Free Press.

1964a Warfare, peaceful intercourse and territorial change: A cross-cultural survey. Mimeographed. Evanston, Ill.: Northwestern University.

1964b A fifth solution to Galton's problem. *American Anthropologist* 66:863–67.

1966   Does military deterrence deter? *Transactions* 3:4–20.

1967   Imperial cycles and world order. *Papers, Peace Research Society* (International) 7:83–101.

1969   Cultural determinants and the concept of the sick society. In *Changing perspectives in mental illness*, edited by Robert F. Edgerton and Stanley C. Plog. New York: Holt, Rinehart and Winston. Pp. 128–155.

1970   What have we learned from cross-cultural surveys? *American Anthropologist* 72: 1227–1288.

n.d.   *Mankind: Painful progress.* New York: Columbia University Press, in preparation.

NAROLL, RAOUL AND RONALD COHEN, eds.

1970   *A handbook of method in cultural anthropology.* New York: Natural History Press.

NAROLL, RAOUL AND E. D. BENJAMIN, F. K. FOHL,
M. J. FRIED, R. D. HILDRETH AND J. M. SCHAEFER

1971   Creativity: A cross–historical pilot survey. *Journal of Cross-Cultural Psychology* 2: 181–188.

OTTERBEIN, KEITH

1970   *The evolution of war.* New Haven: HRAF Press.

PANKALA, MARIA

1966   *A correlated history of the Far East.* Rutland, Vt.: Tuttle.

PELZ, DONALD C. AND FRANK M. ANDREWS

1964   Causal priorities in panel study data. *American Sociological Review* 29: 836–847.

PERKINS, DEXTER

1960   Peace and armaments. *Virginia Quarterly Review* 36, no. 4.

PIERCE, ALBERT

1956   On the concepts of role and status. *Sociologus,* n.s. 6: 750–55.

QUIGLEY, CARROLL

1961   *The evolution of civilizations.* New York: Macmillan.

ROZELLE, RICHARD M. AND DONALD T. CAMPBELL

1969   More plausible rival hypotheses in the cross-logged panel correlation technique. *Psychological Bulletin* 71:74–80.

SIBLEY, MULFORD

1962   Unilateral initiatives and disarmament. *Beyond Deterrence Pamphlets*, March. Philadelphia: American Friends Service Committee.

SIEGEL, SIDNEY

1956   *Nonparametric statistics for the behavioral sciences.* New York: McGraw-Hill.

SINGER, J. DAVID

1962   *Deterrence, arms control and disarmament.* Columbus: Ohio State University Press.

SMITH, ED SINCLAIR

1953   *Binomial, normal and Poisson probabilities.* Bel Air, Md.: Ed S. Smith.

SNYDER, GLENN H.

1959   *Deterrence by denial and punishment.* Princeton, N. J. Center of International Studies. Research Monograph no. 1:1–39.

1960   Deterrence and power. *Conflict Resolution* 4:163–78.

1961   *Deterrence and defense.* Princeton: Princeton University Press.

SNYDER, RICHARD C. AND JAMES A. ROBINSON

1961   *National and international decision-making.* New York: Institute for International order.

SOROKIN, PITIRIM A.

1937–   *Social and cultural dynamics.* 4 vols. Reprint. New York: Bedminster
1941   Press.

SPENGLER, OSWALD

1926   *The decline of the West.* Translated by C. F. Atkinson. 2 vols. New York: Knopf.

STEIGER, G. NYE

1944   *A history of the Far East.* Boston: Ginn.

STEWARD, JULIAN H.

1949   Cultural causality and law: A trial formulation of the development of early civilizations. *American Anthropologist* 51:1–27.

SWANSON, GUY E.

1960   *The birth of the gods: The origin of primitive beliefs.* Ann Arbor: University of Michigan Press.

TOYNBEE, ARNOLD

1934   *A study of history.* 12 vols. New York: Oxford University Press.

TURNER, RALPH

1941   *The great cultural traditions.* 2 vols. New York: McGraw-Hill.

TYLOR, EDWARD B.

1889 On a method of investigating the development of institutions: Applied to laws of marriage and descent. *Journal of the Anthropological Institute of Great Britain and Ireland* 18: 245-62. Also in *Readings in Cross-Cultural methodology*, edited by Frank W. Moore, pp. 1-28. New Haven: HRAF Press, 1961.

VICO, GIOVANNI B.

1834- *Opere.* 6 vols. Edited by Guiseppi Ferrari. Milan: Societa tipog.
1835 de'classici italiani.

VOEGELIN, CARL AND F. M. VOEGELIN

1961 Typological classification of systems with included, excluded and self-sufficient alphabets. *Anthropological Linguistics* 3:55-96.

WALKER HELEN M. AND JOSEPH LEV

1953 *Statistical inference.* New York: Holt.

WEBB, E. J., DONALD CAMPBELL, RICHARD SCHWARTZ AND LEE SECHREST

1966 *Unobtrusive measures: Nonreactive research in the social sciences.* Chicago: Rand McNally.

WEINTRAUB, SOL

1963 *Tables of the cumulative binomial probability distribution for small values of p.* New York: Free Press.

WHITING, JOHN W. M. AND IRVIN L. CHILD

1953 *Child training and personality: A cross-cultural study.* New Haven: Yale University Press.

WITTVOGEL, KARL A.

1957 *Oriental despotism.* New Haven: Yale University Press.

WRIGHT, QUINCY

1942 *A study of war.* 2 vols. Chicago: University of Chicago Press.

China

BUSHELL, S. W.

1880 The early history of Tibet. From Chinese sources. *Journal of the Royal Asiatic Society of Great Britain and Ireland*, n. s., 12:435-541.

DE GROOT, J. J. M.

1921 *Chinesische Urkunden zur Geschichte Asiens.* Vol. 1. Berlin: de Gruyter.

DE MAILLA, JOSEPH A. M.

1777 *Histoire générale de la Chine.* 12 vols. Paris: D. Pierres.

EBERHARD, WOLFRAM

1960 *A history of China.* Berkeley: University of California Press.

HSU, FRANCIS L. K.
    1968   *Clan, caste and club*. Princeton, N.J.: Van Nostrand. Pp. 60-78.
OSGOOD, CHARLES E.
    1959   Suggestions for winning the real war with communism. *Journal of Conflict Resolution* 3:295-325.
MC GOVERN, WILLIAM
    1939   *The early empires of central Asia*. Chapel Hill: University of North Carolina Press.
PAN KU
    1938   *History of the former Han dynasty by Pan Ku: a critical translation with annotations*. Translated by Homer Dubs. Baltimore: Waverly Press.
POLO, MARCO
    1961   *Travels of Marco Polo*. Edited by Milton Rugoff. New York: New American Library Signet.
WATSON, BURTON, Trans.
    1961   *Records of the Grand Historian of China, Ssu-ma Ch'ien*. Vol. 2. New York: Columbia University Press.
YÜ YING-SHIH
    1967   *Trade and expansion in Han China*. Berkeley: University of California Press.

Islam

BROCKELMANN, CARL
    1939   *Geschichte der Islamischen Völker*. München und Berlin: Verlag Oldenborg.
HITTI, PHILIP K.
    1960   *History of the Arabs*. London: Macmillan.
OSTROGORSKY, GEORGE
    1956   *History of the Byzantine state*. Translated by Joan Hussey. Oxford: Blackwell.
TABARI
    1874   *Annals. Chronique de abou-Djafar-Mo'hammed-Ben-Djarir-Ben-Yezid Tabari*. Translated by Hermann Zotenberg. Nogent-Le-Retrou: A. Gouverneur.
THEOPHANES
    1957   Chronicles. In Leopold Breyer, trans., *Bilderstreit und Arabersturm. Byzantinische Geschichtsscheiber*. Vol. 6. Edited by Endre V. Ivanka. Graz: Verlag Styria.
VASILIEV, A. A.
    1952   *History of the Byzantine Empire*. Madison: University of Wisconsin Press.

WEIL, GUSTAV
 1848   *Geschichte der Chalifen.* Mannheim: Wassermann.
 1866   *Geschichte der Islamischen Völker.* Stuttgart: Reiger.

Russia

VERNADSKY, GEORGE
 1959   *Russia at the dawn of the modern age.* Vol. 4. New Haven: Yale University
        Press.
WALSH, WARREN E.
 1958   *Russia and the Soviet Union.* Ann Arbor: University of Michigan Press.

Europe (General)

AMMIANUS MARCELLINUS
 1956   *The Roman history of Ammianus Marcellinus.* Edited and translated by
        John C. Rolfe. London: William Heinemann.
BARNOUW, A. J.
 1944   *The making of modern Holland.* New York: Norton.
BAYNES, NORMAN H.
 1910   Rome and Armenia in the fourth century. *English Historical Review*
        25:625-43.
BLOK, PETER J.
 1938   *Life of Admiral de Ruyter.* Translated by G. J. Renier. London: Benn.
BUFFINGTON, ARTHUR H.
 1929   *The second Hundred Years War, 1689–1815.* New York: Holt.
BURNE, ALFRED HIGGINS
 1956   *The Agincourt war, a military history of the latter part of the Hundred Years
        War from 1369 to 1453.* Fair Lawn, N. J.: Essential Books.
BURY, J. B.
 1897   *A history of the later Roman Empire.* Vol. 2. London: Methuen.
BURY, J. B., ET AL., eds.
 1957   *Cambridge medieval history.* Vol. 1 (Martin Bang, "Expansion of the
        Teutons"; Norman H. Baynes, "The dynasty of Valentinian and
        Theodosius the Great"; M. Manitius, "The Teutonic migrations").
        Vol. 2 (Norman H. Baynes, "The successors of Justinian"; Charles
        Petit-Dutaillis, "Saint Louis"; A. Hamilton Thompson, "Military
        architecture," "The art of war to 1400"). Vol. 7 (A. Colville, "France,
        the Hundred Years' War," "France: Armagnacs and Burgundians";
        B. L. Manning, "England: Edward III and Richard II"). Cambridge:
        University Press.

CADOUX, CECIL JOHN

1947　*Philip of Spain and the Netherlands.* London: Lutterworth.

CASSIUS, DIO COCCEIANUS

1949-　*Dio's Roman history.* Epitome 72, 73. Edited and translated by J. W.
1956　Cahoon. London: William Heinemann.

CHRISTENSEN, ARTHUR

1944　*L'Iran sous les Sassanides.* Copenhagen: Munksgaard.

CHYDOBA, BOHDAN

1952　*Spain and the Empire.* Chicago: University of Chicago Press.

CLOWES, WILLIAM L.

1897　*The royal navy: a history.* Boston: Little, Brown.

COOK, S. A., ET AL., eds.

1952,　*Cambridge ancient history.* Vol. 7 (A. Schulten," Carthaginians in Spain").
1954　Vol. 8 (B. L. Hallward, "Hannibal's invasion of Italy," "The Roman
defensive," "Scipio and victory"; M. Holleaux, "Rome and Macedon:
Philip against the Romans"; B. L. Hallward and M. P. Charlesworth,
"The fall of Carthage"). Vol. 10 (W.W. Tarn and M. P. Charlesworth,
"Triumph of Octavian"; H. Stuart Jones, "The Princeps"; G. H.
Stevenson, "The army and navy"; J.C. Anderson, "The eastern frontier
under Augustus"; F. Oertel, "The economic unification of the Mediterranean region"; F. E. Adcock, "Achievement of Augustus"). Cambridge: University Press.

DIEHL, CHARLES

1957　*Byzantium: greatness and decline.* Translated by Naomi Walford. New
Brunswick: Rutgers University Press.

1960　*Justinien et la civilisation Byzantine au sixième siècle.* New York: Burt
Franklin.

EVAGRIUS

1898　*Ecclesiastical history.* Edited by J. Bidez and L. Parmentier. London:
Methuen.

FULLER, J. F. C.

1955　*Military history.* 3 vols. New York: Funk and Wagnalls.

GEYL, PIETER

1958　*The revolt of the Netherlands* (1555-1609). New York: Barnes and Noble.

GIBBON, EDWARD

1897　*Decline and fall of the Roman Empire.* Edited by J. B. Bury. 7 vols. London:
Methuen.

HARLOW, VINCENT TODD

1952　*The founding of the second British empire, 1763-1793.* London: Longmans.

HARRISON, FREDERICK

1924   *William the silent*. New York: Charles Scribner's Sons.

HERODIAN

1961   *History of the Roman Empire from the death of Marcus Aurelius to the accession of Gordian III*. Book 1. Translated by Edward C. Echols. Berkeley: University of California Press.

HIGGINS, MARTIN J.

1941   International relations at the close of the sixth century. *Catholic Historical Review* 27:279–315.

1939   *The Persian war of the Emperor Maurice*. Washington, D.C.: Catholic University of America.

HISTORIA AUGUSTAE

1922-   Edited and translated by David Magie. London: William Heinemann.
1932

HODGKIN, THOMAS

1885-

1899   *Italy and her invaders*. 8 vols. Oxford: Clarendon Press.

HUME, MARTIN A. S.

1896   *The year after the armada and other historical studies*. London: Fisher Unwin.

1908   *Two English queens and Philip*. London: Methuen.

JOHN OF EPHESUS

1860   *Ecclesiastical history*. Translated by Payne Smith. Oxford: Clarendon.

LANGLOIS, CHARLES VICTOR

1887   *Le règne de Phillippe III le Hardi*. Paris: Hachette.

1901   *Histoire de France 1226–1328*. Paris: Hachette. (Also in *Medieval France*, edited by Arthur A. Tilley, Cambridge: Cambridge University Press, 1922).

LAVISSE, ERNEST

1911   *Histoire de France*. Vol. 7. Paris: Hachette.

LIVIUS, TITUS

1949-   *Livy*. Book 21. Edited and translated by B. O. Foster. London:
1961   William Heinemann.

LOTH, DAVID

1932   *Phillip II of Spain*. London: Routledge.

MALCOLM-SMITH, E.

1937   *British diplomacy in the eighteenth century*. London: Williams and Norgate.

MENANDER

1955   *Byzantinische Geschichte*. Translated by Ernest Doblhofer. Vol. 4. Graz: Verlag Styria.

MENG, JOHN J.
   1929   The Comte de Vergennes. *Records of the American Catholic Historical Society* 40, no. 4.
MERRIMAN, ROGER B.
   1918–
   1934   *The rise of the Spanish empire.* 4 vols. New York: Macmillan.
MOTLEY, JOHN L.
   1929   *The rise of the Dutch republic.* 2 vols. London: George Allen and Unwin.
NUSSBAUM, FREDERICK L.
   1935   *The triumph of science and reason: 1660–1685.* New York: Harper.
OGG, DAVID
   1952   *Europe in the seventeenth century.* London: Black.
OROSIUS, PAULUS
   1964   *Historia contra Paganos (The seven books of history against the pagans).* Translated by Roy J. Deferrari. Washington, D.C.: Catholic University of America Press.
OSTROGORSKY, GEORGE
   1956   *History of the Byzantine state.* Translated by Joan Hussey. Oxford: Blackwell.
PACKARD, LAURENCE BRADFORD
   1929   *The age of Louis XIV.* New York: Holt.
PARKER, H. M. D.
   1963   *A history of the Roman world from A.D. 138 to 337.* Rev. ed. London: Methuen.
PERROY, EDOUARD
   1951   *The Hundred Years War.* London: Eyre and Spottiswoode.
PHOTIUS I, SAINT, PATRIARCH OF CONSTANTINOPLE
   1885   *The ecclesiastical history of Philostorgius, as epitomized by Photius, Patriarch of Constantinople.* Translated by Edward Walford. London: Bohn.
POLYBIUS
   1922- *The histories of Polybius.* Edited and translated by W. R. Paton.
   1927   London: William Heinemann.
POWICKE, SIR MAURICE
   1962   *The Oxford history of England: The thirteenth century.* Oxford: Clarendon Press.
RICHMOND, HERBERT
   1953   The navy as an instrument of policy. Edited by E. A. Hughes. Cambridge: Cambridge University Press.
SOCRATES, SCHOLASTICUS
   1844   *Ecclesiastical history.* Book 4. London: Bagster.

SOZOMENUS, HERMIAS

1846   *Ecclesiastical history*. Books 5, 7. London: Bagster.

SYKES, SIR PERCY

1930   *A history of Persia*. 2 vols. 3d ed. London: Macmillan.

THEOPHYLACTUS, SIMOCATTA

1887   *Historia*. Edited by Carolus De Boor. Leipzig: B. G. Teubner.

THOMPSON, JAMES WESTFALL

1909   *The wars of religion in France, 1559–1576*. New York: Ungar.

TOUT, T.F.

1932   *Edward the first*. London: Macmillan.

TOY, SIDNEY

1939   *Castles, a short history of fortifications from 1600 B.C. to A.D. 1600*. London: Heinemann.

VASILIEV, A. A.

1964   *History of the Byzantine empire*. 2 vols. Madison: University of Wisconsin Press.

VAST, HENRI

1898   *Les grandes traités du règne de Louis XIV*. Paris: Picard.

WARD, A. W., ET AL., eds.

1908- *The Cambridge modern history*. Vol. 5 (George Edmunson, "Administra-
1909   tion of John de Witt and Willliam of Orange"; Richard Lodge,"Austria Poland and Turkey"; Arthur Hassal, "The foreign policy of Louis XIV, 1661-1697"). Vol. 6 (P. E. Roberts, "The English and French in India"). New York: Macmillan.

WATSON, JOHN STEVEN

1960   *The reign of George* III, *1760–1815*. Oxford: Clarendon Press.

WERNHAM, R. B., ED.

1968   *The new Cambridge modern history*. Vol. 3 (J. R. Hale, "Armies, navies and the art of war"; H. G. Koenigsberg, "Western Europe and the power of Spain"). Cambridge: Cambridge University Press.

ZOSIMUS

1794   *Zosimi Historiae*. Lipsiae.

Switzerland

BRAUER-GRAMM, HILDBURG

1957   *Der Landvogt Peter von Hagenbach*. Göttingen: Musterschmidt.

BURY, J. B. ET AL.

1958   *Cambridge medieval history*. Vol. 7 (chapter 7); Vol. 8 (chapter 10). Cambridge: Cambridge University Press.

CHAMPION, PIERRE
  1927   *Louis XI.* Vol. 2. Paris: Librairie Ancienne Honoré Champion.
DE BARANTE, M.
  1854   *Histoire des Ducs de Bourgogne.* Paris: Imprimerie Le Normant.
DE COMMYNE, PHILIPPE
  1925   *Memoires.* Edited by Joseph Calmette. Paris: Librairie Ancienne Honoré
         Champion.
DE LA MARCHE, OLIVIER
  1854   Memoires (1435–1489). In *Nouvelle collection des mémoires relatifs à
         l'histoire de France.* Paris: Didier.
DIERAUER, JOHANNES
  1913 *Geschichte der Schweizerischen Eidgenossenschaft.* Vol. 2. Gotha: F. A. Perthes.
KIRK, JOHN FOSTER
  1864   *History of Charles the Bold.* 3 vols. Philadelphia: Lippincott.
LEWIS,   D. B. WYNDHAM
  1929   *King spider.* New York: Coward-McCann.
MICHELET, J.
  1896   *Louis XI et Charles le Téméraire.* Edited by Arthur R. Ropes. London:
         Clay.
OECHSLI, WILHELM
  1907   *Schweizergeschichte.* Zürich: Verlag der Erziehungsdirektion.
PUTNAM, RUTH
  1908   *Charles the Bold, last Duke of Burgundy.* New York: Putnam.
VON MÜLLER, JOHANNES
  1805- *Die Geschichte der Schweizerischen Eidgenossenschaft.* 5 vols. Leipzig:
  1808   Weldmann.

MAP SOURCES

ANONYMOUS

1957 *Hammond's world atlas and gazetteer.* New York: C. S. Hammond.

DENNOYER-GEPPERT

1954 *European history atlas.* 10th ed. Chicago: Dennoyer-Geppert. Pp. 16-17.

HERMANN, ALBERT

1966 *Historical atlas of China.* Chicago: Aldine. Pp. 22, 43, 55, 56.

HITTI, PHILIP

1960 *History of the Arabs.* 7th ed. London: Macmillan. P. 216.

KIRK, JOHN FOSTER

1864 *History of Charles the Bold.* 3 Vols. Philadelphia: J. P. Lippincott.

MUIR, RAMSEY

1964 *Muir's historical atlas.* New York: Barnes and Noble.

OECHSLI, WILHELM

1907 *Schweizergeschichte.* Zürich: Verlag der Erziehungsdirektion. "Die Alten Orte," "Die Erdgenossenschaft der XIII Orte."

RAND McNALLY

1961 *Historical atlas of the world.* Chicago: Rand McNally. P. 7.

SHEPHERD, WILLIAM

1932 *Atlas of medieval and modern history.* New York: Holt. Pp. 41-43.

STIER, H. E. (Ed.)

1965 *Westermann's Grosser Atlas zur Weltgeschichte.* Braunschweig: Georg Westermann Verlag. Pp. 26, 34, 35, 46, 49.

TOUT, T. F.

1906 *History of England, 1216-1377.* London: Longmans.

VERNADSKY, GEORGE

1959 *Russia at the dawn of the modern age.* Vol. 4. New Haven: Yale University Press. P. 68.

INDEX